D0092718

Lifehacker

The Guide to Working Smarter, Faster, and Better

Third Edition

Adam Pash

Gina Trapani

WILEY

Wiley Publishing, Inc.

Lifehacker: The Guide to Working Smarter, Faster, and Better, Third Edition

Published by
Wiley Publishing, Inc.
10475 Crosspoint Boulevard
Indianapolis, IN 46256
www.wiley.com

ISBN: 978-1-118-01837-8
ISBN: 978-1-118-13343-9 (ebk)
ISBN: 978-1-118-13344-6 (ebk)
ISBN: 978-1-118-13345-3 (ebk)

Manufactured in the United States of America

10 9 8 7 6 5 4 3 2

For general information on our other products and services please contact our Customer Care Department within the United States at (877) 762-2974, outside the United States at (317) 572-3993 or fax (317) 572-4002.

Wiley also publishes its books in a variety of electronic formats. Some content that appears in print may not be available in electronic books.

Library of Congress Control Number: 2011928432

Dedicated to Ellen

Credits

Executive Editor
Carol Long

Project Editor
Victoria Swider

Technical Editor
Gina Trapani

Production Editor
Kathleen Wisor

Copy Editor
Apostrophe Editing Services

Editorial Director
Robyn B. Siesky

Editorial Manager
Mary Beth Wakefield

Freelancer Editorial Manager
Rosemarie Graham

Marketing Manager
Ashley Zurcher

Production Manager
Tim Tate

Vice President and Executive Group Publisher
Richard Swadley

Vice President and Executive Publisher
Barry Pruett

Associate Publisher
Jim Minatel

Project Coordinator, Cover
Katie Crocker

Compositor
Kate Kaminski,
Happenstance Type-O-Rama

Proofreader
Kyle Schlesinger, Word One

Indexer
Robert Swanson

Cover Image
© René Mansi / iStockPhoto

Cover Designer
Ryan Sneed

About the Authors

Adam Pash (http://adampash.com) is a programmer, a writer, and the editor-in-chief of Lifehacker.com. Having written for Lifehacker since 2005, Adam took over the editorial team in 2009. A self-taught software developer, Adam created popular apps such as Texter and MixTape.me. He is a frequent contributor to tech publications, such as *Popular Science* and *PC World*, and is based in Los Angeles, California.

Gina Trapani (http://ginatrapani.org) is the founding editor of Lifehacker .com and led its editorial team from 2005 to 2009. Currently, she leads development on ThinkUp, an open source crowdsourcing platform, which helps policymakers and journalists gain insights from conversations on social networks such as Twitter and Facebook. Gina lives in sunny San Diego, California by way of Brooklyn, New York.

Acknowledgments

I strongly believe in the work we do at Lifehacker, and I am grateful for the opportunity to write a new edition of this book. I spent six years honing the craft of life hacks, but countless others contributed to the book you're holding in your hands.

For starters, I want to thank my wife, Ellen, whose dedication, passion, and talent serve as constant inspiration. Thanks to Lifehacker.com's publisher, Nick Denton, for funding the cadre of writers and geeks dedicated to the ideas that fuel this book. Thanks to my agent, David Fugate, at LaunchBooks, and several folks at Wiley, including Carol Long, Victoria Swider, and San Dee Phillips, for getting these words from my fingers to this page. Untold thanks to my good friend and co-writer Gina Trapani, not only for having founded Lifehacker and bringing me on in its first year, but also for her support, advice, and camaraderie over the years. I'd also like to thank my crew at Lifehacker, especially Kevin Purdy, Whitson Gordon, and Adam Dachis, for all their hard work and creativity. Special thanks to Danny O'Brien for hacking countless lives by coining the term *life hack*, as well as David Allen for his inspirational, oft-quoted work in personal productivity. Also, thanks to my parents, family, and friends.

Last but not least, thanks to the community of readers and commenters at Lifehacker.com. Your emails and comments informed every page of this book.

— Adam Pash

Contents at a Glance

Introduction   xxiii

Chapter 1   Control Your Email   1
Chapter 2   Organize Your Data   39
Chapter 3   Trick Yourself into Getting Done   87
Chapter 4   Clear Your Mind   115
Chapter 5   Firewall Your Attention   147
Chapter 6   Streamline Common Tasks   173
Chapter 7   Automate Repetitive Tasks   215
Chapter 8   Get Your Data to Go   241
Chapter 9   Work Smarter on Your Smart Phone   291
Chapter 10   Master the Web   349
Chapter 11   Hone Your Computer Survival Skills   393
Chapter 12   Manage Multiple Computers   441

Index   467

Contents

Introduction   **xxiii**

Chapter 1   Control Your Email   **1**

Hack 1: Empty Your Inbox (and Keep It Empty)   3

   Why an Empty Inbox?   4

   Set Up the Trusted Trio of Folders   4

   Process Your Messages   6

   Keep It Empty   7

   Your First Time   7

   The Catch   7

Hack 2: Decrease Your Response Time   8

   Process Messages in Batches   8

   The One-Minute Rule   9

   Respond to Task Requests — Before the Task Is Done   9

   Don't Leave It in Your Inbox   10

Hack 3: Craft Effective Messages   10

   Composing a New Message   10

   Replying to a Message   14

Hack 4: Highlight Messages Sent Directly to You   17

   Microsoft Outlook: Color Me Blue   17

   All Other Email Programs: Create a Not-to-Me Filter   18

Hack 5: Use Disposable Email Addresses   19

   Web-Based Public Email Addresses   19

   Multi-Domain Email Addresses   19

Hack 6: Master Message Search   20

   Search Criteria   20

   Saved Search Folders   23

Hack 7: Future-Proof Your Email Address   24
  Bottom Line   25
Hack 8: Consolidate Multiple Email Addresses with Gmail 26
  Receive Messages for Other Addresses in Your Gmail Inbox 26
  Write Messages from Non-Gmail Addresses   28
Hack 9: Script and Automate Repetitive Replies   30
  Make Quick Work of Common Replies   31
Hack 10: Filter Low-Priority Messages   33
  Filter Bacn   34
  Filter CCed Messages   35
  Gmail's Priority Inbox   36
References   38

Chapter 2   Organize Your Data   39
Hack 11: Organize Your Documents Folder   41
  The Big Six   41
  Move Your Home Directory to Another Drive   43
  Beyond the Big Six   44
Hack 12: Instantly Retrieve Files Stored on Your Computer 45
  Searching Your Windows Computer   45
  Searching Your Mac Computer   48
Hack 13: Overhaul Your Filing Cabinet   50
  Give Your Paperwork a Spacious Place to Live   51
  Limit One File Folder per Hanging Folder   51
  Choose a Simple, Logical Naming Scheme   51
  Use a Label Maker   52
  Purge and Archive   52
Hack 14: Instantly Recall Any Number of
  Different Passwords   52
  Don't Use the Same Password for Everything   53
  Remember 100 Different Passwords with One Rule Set   53
Hack 15: Securely Track Your Passwords   54
  One Master Password to Rule All   55
  Find and Use Your Passwords with LastPass   58
Hack 16: Tag Your Bookmarks   59
  Getting Started with Delicious   59
  Add a Bookmark   59
  Tags, Not Folders   60
  Navigating Delicious by URL   61
  Other Delicious Features   61
Hack 17: Organize Your Digital Photos   62
  Import Your Photos into Picasa   62
  Organize and Label Your Collection   63
  Search Your Photos   65
  Other Picasa Features   66

Hack 18: Corral Media Across Folders and Drives 67
Windows 7 Libraries 67
Create and Manage Windows 7 Libraries 68
Hack 19: Create Saved Search Folders 69
Search Folders in Windows 69
Saved Search Folders in Mac OS 71
Hack 20: Create a Password-Protected Disk on Your PC 71
Set Up the Encrypted Volume Location 72
Store and Retrieve Files from the Encrypted Volume 74
Hack 21: Create a Password-Protected Disk on Your Mac 75
Create a New Encrypted Disk Image 75
Access Your Password-Protected Disk 77
Hack 22: Encrypt Your Entire Windows Operating System 77
Set Up Your Encrypted Operating System 77
Hack 23: Set Up 2-Step Verification for Your
Google Account 79
Set Up 2-Step Verification 80
Use 2-Step Verification 82
Hack 24: Design Your Own Planner 84
Why Build Your Own Planner? 85
How to Assemble Your D*I*Y Planner 85
D*I*Y Planner Templates and Sizes 85
References 86

Chapter 3 **Trick Yourself into Getting Done** **87**
Hack 25: Make Your To-Do List Doable 88
You Are the Boss of You 89
How to Order Yourself Around 89
Practice Makes Perfect 93
Hack 26: Set Up a Morning Dash 93
Get One Thing Done First 93
Park on a Downward Slope 94
Hack 27: Map Your Time 95
Your Ideal Time Map 95
Submaps 96
Your Actual Time Map 96
Hack 28: Quick-Log Your Workday 97
Paper 97
Notepad .LOG File (Windows Only) 98
Quick-Log in a Plain-Text File (Windows Only) 99
Set Up Automatic, Rule-Based Time Logging (Windows) 101
Hack 29: Dash Through Tasks with a Timer 102
Do Your First Dash 103
Adjust Your Dash 103
Why Time Constraints Work 104
Timer Software Applications 104

Hack 30: Form New Habits with Jerry Seinfeld's Chain   105
Hack 31: Control Your Workday   107
   Identify and Cut Back on Extra Work   107
   Stop Your Time Sinks   108
   Make Post-Work Appointments   109
   Set Wrap-Up Alerts   109
Hack 32: Turn Tasks into Game Play   109
   Make It to the Next Level   110
   Collaborate, Compete, and Reward   110
   Bribe Yourself   110
   Time Yourself   111
   Apps That Turn Work into Play   111
References   112

Chapter 4   Clear Your Mind   115
Hack 33: Send Reminders to Your Future Self   116
Hack 34: Take Great Notes   120
   Method 1: Symbolize Next Actions   121
   Method 2: Split Your Page into Quadrants   121
   Method 3: Record and Summarize   121
   Print Custom Note Paper   122
Hack 35: Organize Your Life with Remember the Milk   123
   Managing Tasks   124
   Managing Lists and Tags   125
   Setting Task Reminders   126
   Searching Tasks   127
   More RTM Techniques   129
   Recommended RTM Apps and Add-Ons   130
Hack 36: Organize Your Life in Text Files   131
   Why Plain Text?   131
   Using an Editor to Manage Your Text Files   132
   Using the Command Line to Manage Text Files   134
   Introducing todo.sh and todo.txt Touch   134
Hack 37: Set Up a Ubiquitous Note-Taking
Inbox Across Devices   135
   Sync Plain-Text Notes Anywhere with Simplenote   135
   Go Beyond Plain Text with Evernote   138
Hack 38: Off-Load Your Online Reading to a
Distraction-Free Environment   142
   Save Your Reading with Instapaper   142
   Instapaper Tools   144
References   144

Chapter 5   Firewall Your Attention   147
Hack 39: Limit Visits to Time-Wasting Websites   148
   Install and Configure StayFocusd   149

Visiting a Blocked Site   150
Make It Difficult to Disable StayFocusd   150
Hack 40: Permanently Block Time-Wasting Websites   151
The Result   152
Hack 41: Reduce Email Interruptions   153
Shut Down Your Email Program   153
Set Your Email Program to Check for Messages
  Once an Hour   154
Hack 42: Split Your Work Among Multiple Desktops   155
Windows   156
Mac OS X   157
Hack 43: Build a No-Fly Zone   158
Set Yourself Up to Get into the Zone   159
Make Yourself Inaccessible   159
Work at Quieter Times and in Zoned-Off Spaces   160
Hack 44: Set Up Communication Quiet Hours   160
Put Your Communication Break on a Timer with
  Quiet Hours   161
The Nuclear Option: Freedom   162
Hack 45: Clear Your Desktop   162
Windows   163
Mac OS X   164
Hack 46: Make Your House a Usable Home   165
Create a Place for Incoming Stuff   165
Put Items You Need to Remember in Your Path   166
Stow Away Stuff You Don't Use & Put Stuff You Do Use
  Within Easy Reach   166
Strategically Place Items to Make Tasks Easy   166
Make Task-Based Centers   167
Leave Writing Material Everywhere   167
Set Up an Inbox   167
Collaborate with Housemates   167
Hack 47: Sentence Stuff to Death Row   168
Hack 48: Drown Out Distracting Sounds with Pink Noise 169
FM3 Buddha Machine Wall   169
Nature Sounds for Me   170
References   170

Chapter 6   **Streamline Common Tasks**   **173**
Hack 49: Search the Web in Three Keystrokes   174
Use Your Browser's Built-In Search Box   175
Instant Searching: Getting Good with Google Instant   177
Hack 50: Command Your Windows PC from
  the Keyboard   178
Built-In Windows Keyboard Shortcuts   179

Launch Documents and Applications from the Start Menu   180
Quickly Run Programs and Open Files with Launchy   181
Hack 51: Command Your Mac from the Keyboard   182
Built-in Mac OS X Keyboard Shortcuts   183
Basic File and Application Launching with Quicksilver   184
Advanced Quicksilver Actions   185
Hack 52: Reduce Repetitive Typing with Texter
for Windows   187
Set Up Texter Hotstrings   187
More Texter Features   191
Hack 53: Reduce Repetitive Typing with TextExpander
for Mac   192
Configure TextExpander Snippets   192
Advanced TextExpander Usage   195
Hack 54: Automatically Fill in Repetitive Web Forms   196
Create Auto Fill Profiles   197
Automatically Fill Web Forms   199
Hack 55: Batch-Resize Photos   200
Batch Resizing on Windows   200
Batch Resizing on Macs   201
Batch Resizing with Picasa (Windows and Mac)   201
Hack 56: Bypass Free Site Registration with BugMeNot   202
Hack 57: Speed Up Web Pages on a Slow Internet
Connection   204
Configure Your Web Browser for a Slow Connection   204
Block and Disable Bandwidth Hogs   206
Use Tabs to Load Pages While You Work   206
Work Offline Whenever Possible   207
Hack 58: Securely Save Website Passwords   207
Set a Master Password in Firefox   208
Hack 59: Become a Scheduling Black Belt with Google
Calendar   210
Quickly Capture Events   210
Subscribe to Shared Calendars   211
Share a Custom Calendar   211
Book Conference Room B   212
Receive Your Daily Agenda via Email Automatically   212
See This Week's Weather Forecast on Your Calendar   213
Invite Your Friends to Events via GCal   213
Get Your Schedule Details via Text Message   213
Master GCal's Keyboard Shortcuts   214
References   214

Chapter 7   **Automate Repetitive Tasks**   **215**

Hack 60: Set Up an Automated, Bulletproof File
   Back Up Solution   216
     What You Need   217
     Configure Your Backup System   218
     What a CrashPlan+ Account Adds to Your Backup Plan   221
     Restore Files Backed Up with CrashPlan   221
Hack 61: Automatically Back Up Your Files to an
   External Hard Drive (Mac)   223
     Enable Time Machine Backups   223
     Restore Deleted or Overwritten Files   225
     Change Time Machine's Default Backup Interval   226
Hack 62: Automatically Clean Up Your PC   226
     Empty Your Downloads Folder with Belvedere   227
     Empty the Recycle Bin with Belvedere   228
     More Automatic File Processing   228
Hack 63: Automatically Clean Up Your Mac   229
     Empty Your Downloads Folder with Hazel   229
     Take Out the Trash with Hazel   230
     More Automatic File Processing   231
Hack 64: Automatically Reboot and Launch Applications   231
     Automatically Reboot Your Computer   232
     Automatically Launch Software or Documents   233
     Automatically Start a Web-Browsing Session   233
Hack 65: Make Google Search Results Automatically
   Come to You   234
Hack 66: Automatically Download Music, Movies,
   and More   236
     Install and Run wget   236
     Mirror an Entire Website   237
     Resume Partial Downloads on an Intermittent
       Connection   237
     Automatically Download New Music from the Web   238
     Automate wget Downloads on Windows   239
  References   239

Chapter 8   **Get Your Data to Go**   **241**

Hack 67: Access Your Most Important Files
   Anywhere with Dropbox   242
     What Dropbox Does   243
     Share Files with Dropbox   245
     Sync Files and Folders Outside Your Dropbox Folder   246
     Sync Applications and Encrypt Data   247

Hack 68: Manage Your Documents in a Web-Based
Office Suite   247
  Why Move from Desktop Software to Web Applications?   248
  Web Application Alternatives to Desktop Office Software   250
  What You Can Do in an Online Office Suite   251
  Bridge the Gap Between Your Desktop and the Web   253
Hack 69: Carry Your Life on a Flash Drive   255
  Why Use a Flash Drive?   255
  Portable Applications   256
  Useful Data to Store on Your Thumb Drive   258
  Secure Your Drive   258
  Using Your Thumb Drive   260
Hack 70: Create a Virtual Private Network (VPN) with
Hamachi   260
  What is Hamachi VPN?   260
  Set Up Hamachi   261
  What You Can Do Over Hamachi VPN   264
Hack 71: Run a Home Web Server   264
  Step 1: Disable Other Servers or Firewall Software   265
  Step 2: Install Apache HTTP Server   265
  Step 3: Configure Apache to Share Documents   267
  Step 4: Password-Protect Your Website Documents   268
Hack 72: Run Full-Fledged Webapps from Your Home
Computer   270
  Web Applications You Can Run from Your Home
  Computer   271
  Step 1: Install WampServer   272
  Step 2: Place the Webapp Directory on Your Home Server   274
  Step 3: Run Through the Setup   274
Hack 73: Build Your Personal Wikipedia   276
  What You Need   276
  Set Up MediaWiki   276
  Test-Drive Your Wiki   277
  Brief Wikitext Primer   278
Hack 74: Remotely Control Your Home Computer   279
  Step 1: Install the VNC Server   281
  Step 2: Install the VNC Client   282
  More VNC Considerations   283
Hack 75: Give Your Home Computer a Web Address   283
  Step 1: Set Up Your DynDNS Account   284
  Step 2: Set Up Your Computer to Update DynDNS   285
  Step 3: Give Your New Domain a Spin   286
  DynDNS Options   286
Hack 76: Optimize Your Laptop   286
  Extend Your Battery Life   287

Save Your Keyboard and Screen   287
Keep It Cool   288
Set Yourself Up to Work Offline   288
Secure Your Data   289
Carry with Care   289
Back Up   289
Pack Helpful Extras   290
Find a Hotspot   290
References   290

Chapter 9   Work Smarter on Your Smart Phone   291
Hack 77: Speed Up Your Touchscreen Typing   292
Don't Look Before You Leap   292
Punctuation Shortcuts   296
Install an Alternative Keyboard (Android Only)   297
Pick a Keyboard that Suits You (Android Only)   298
Hack 78: Break Down the Barrier Between Your
   Computer and Mobile Phone   299
Computer to iOS   300
Computer to Android   302
Hack 79: Remote Control Your Computer with
   Your Phone   304
Set Up PocketCloud   304
Using PocketCloud   306
Other Recommended Remote Applications   307
Hack 80: Automate Android Functions with Tasker   308
The Anatomy of a Task   308
Example: Silence Your Phone When It's Face Down   309
Hack 81: Set Up One Phone Number to Rule Them All   312
Set Up Google Voice   312
Place Calls and Send Text Messages   314
Add More Phones to Google Voice   314
Set Up Ring Schedules   315
Set Up Custom Call and Voicemail Behavior by Groups   315
Integrate Google Voice with Your Phone   316
Other Benefits of Google Voice   317
Hack 82: Augment Reality with Your Phone   317
Learn About Where You Are   318
Learn About What You See with Google Goggles   319
Get Your Money's Worth   321
Hack 83: Remember Where You've Been Using
   Location Awareness   322
Check In to See Where You've Been   323
Put Your Photos on a Map   325
Use Google Maps to Find Anything   326

Hack 84: Command Your Phone with Your Voice   326
  Use Your Voice to Type Anywhere   327
  Search and Command Your Phone   328
Hack 85: Use Your Camera Phone as a Scanner   330
  Working with CamScanner Scans   332
  Sharing Scanned PDFs   332
Hack 86: Make Your "Dumbphone" Smarter via
  Text Message   333
  Search the Web via Text Message   333
  Access Your Google Calendar via Text Message   335
  Track Your Gas Mileage with Fuelly   336
  Command Twitter "Bots" via Text Message   337
Hack 87: Connect Your Computer to the Internet
  via Mobile Phone by "Tethering"   338
  What You Need   339
  How to Tether   339
Hack 88: Develop Your (Digital) Photographic Memory   341
  Upload Photos to Evernote from Your Camera Phone   342
  Create a Photo Reference Database with Evernote   343
Hack 89: Send and Receive Money on Your Mobile
  Phone with PayPal   344
  PayPal Mobile   344

Chapter 10   Master the Web   **349**
Hack 90: Google Like a Pro   350
  Exact Phrase with Quotations   351
  Include and Exclude Words Using + and –   351
  Search Within a Site   352
  Search Certain Types of Files   352
  Calculations   353
  Synonyms   353
  Combine Criteria and Operators   354
Hack 91: Subscribe to Websites with RSS   355
  How to Subscribe to Website Feeds   355
  Other Popular Feedreaders   357
  Search and Track Dynamic Information with Feeds   358
Hack 92: Quickly Search Within Specific Websites
  from the Address Bar   358
  Download the Bookmark Set   362
  Lifehacker Quick Searches   363
Hack 93: Extend Your Web Browser   364
  How to Install a Firefox Extension   364
  How to Install a Chrome Extension   366
  Recommended Firefox and Chrome Extensions   367

Hack 94: Supercharge Your Firefox Downloads with
DownThemAll!   369
   Download Individual Files with DownThemAll!   369
   Batch-Download Files with Filters   370
   Customize a Filter to Download All the MP3s on
      a Web Page   371
   One-Click Access to dTa Settings   373
Hack 95: Get 10 Useful Bookmarklets   374
Hack 96: Find Reusable Media Online   376
   What's Reusable Media?   376
   Six Reusable-Media Search Engines and Sources   377
Hack 97: Get Your Data on a Map   378
Hack 98: Set Multiple Sites as Your Home Page   380
   Multitab Homepage   380
   Bookmark Sets of Tabs   382
   Open a Set of Tabs   382
Hack 99: Access Unavailable Websites via Google   383
Hack 100: Have a Say in What Google Says About You   384
   But I Already Have a Website   384
   Get Your Domain   385
   Author Your Nameplate   385
   Customize a Nameplate Template   386
   Find a Web Host   387
   Link Up Your Nameplate Site   387
   Get a Nameplate Site Without the Hassle   388
Hack 101: Clear Your Web Browsing Tracks   388
   Go Private or Incognito   389
   Clear Data After a Browsing Session   391
   Go Nuclear   392
Reference   392

Chapter 11   Hone Your Computer Survival Skills   393
Hack 102: Rescue Your PC from Malware   394
   Symptoms   395
   Malware-Removal and -Prevention Tools   395
   How to Clean an Infected System   395
   Web-Browser Hijacking   398
Hack 103: Protect Your PC from Malware   398
   Preventative Malware Protection   399
   Scan a Suspicious File with 30 Antivirus Tools at Once   399
Hack 104: Clean Up Your Startup   400
   Start Menu (Easy)   401
   System Configuration Utility (Medium)   402
   Autoruns (Advanced)   403
   Diagnose and Banish Programs That Are Slowing
      Down Your System   403

Hack 105: Undo System Configuration Changes   405
    Create or Restore a Saved Point with System Restore   406
    When System Restore Takes Snapshots   407
    Limit System Restore's Disk Usage   407
Hack 106: Truly Delete Data from Your Hard Drive   408
    Windows   409
    Mac OS X   410
Hack 107: Compare and Merge Files and Folders
    with WinMerge   411
    Compare and Merge Folders   412
    Diff and Merge Text Files   413
    Compare and Merge Office Documents   413
Hack 108: Firewall Your Windows PC   415
    Does Your Computer Need a Firewall?   415
    ZoneAlarm Software Firewall   416
    Control What Programs Can Connect to the Internet   417
Hack 109: Firewall Your Mac   418
    Choose Your Firewall Setting   419
Hack 110: Speed Up Windows with a Thumb Drive   421
    Enable ReadyBoost for a Flash Drive   421
    Allocate How Much Space ReadyBoost Uses   422
Hack 111: Free Up Hard-Drive Space   423
    Visualize Disk Hogs   423
    Clean Your Entire System with CCleaner   425
Hack 112: Resurrect Deleted Files   425
Hack 113: Hot Image Your PC for Instant Restoration   427
    Create a New System Image   427
    Restore Your System Image   431
Hack 114: Hot Image Your Mac for Instant Restoration   432
    Create a New System Image   433
    Restore Your System Image   434
    Advanced CCC   435
Hack 115: Recover Files from an Unbootable PC   435
    What You Need   436
    Prepare Your KNOPPIX Disk   436
    Set Your Computer to Boot from the DVD Drive   437
    Start KNOPPIX   437
    Rescue Your Data   438
Reference   439

Chapter 12   Manage Multiple Computers   441
Hack 116: Share Windows Files   442
    Share a Folder   442
    Determine Your Computer Name   444
    Access the Shared Folder from Another PC   445

Access the Shared Folder from a Mac   446
Troubleshooting Tips   446
Hack 117: Share Mac Files   447
Share a Folder   447
Access the Shared Folder from Another Mac   449
Access the Shared Folder from a PC   449
Hack 118: Keep Your Web Browser in Sync
Across Computers   450
Enable Your Browser's Default Syncing Tool   451
Beef Up Syncing with Extensions   453
Hack 119: Share a Single Printer Between Computers   454
Share the Printer   455
Connect to the Shared Printer from Windows   456
Connect to the Shared Printer from a Mac   457
Hack 120: Optimize Your Dual Monitors   458
The Basics   458
Get Your Dual-Monitor Wallpaper On   459
Extend Your Taskbar Across Monitors   460
Managing Windows   461
Desktop Pinups and Overlays   462
Hack 121: Control Multiple Computers with a Single
Keyboard and Mouse   462
Set Up the Synergy Server   463
Set Up the Synergy Client   465
Reference   465

Index   **467**

Introduction

"The highest-performing people I know are those who have installed the best tricks in their lives."
—David Allen, productivity expert[1]

Every day, you have dozens of opportunities to get work done faster, smarter, and more efficiently, but you'll find no single, magical productivity secret contained within the pages of this book. Yet we firmly believe that, judiciously applied, the proper combination of shortcuts, tricks, and improvements to your workflow can notably increase the efficiency with which you work, communicate, and accomplish tasks. Small changes, practiced and perfected over time, yield big results.

The goal of this book, the Lifehacker.com website, and the weekly Lifehacker video series is simple: discover, test, and curate shortcuts and tricks for making modern life easier and doing things better. Every year, personal computers, smart phones, email, the Web, and other contemporary technologies play an increasingly significant role in our lives; accordingly, much of this book focuses on using these tools more efficiently. These technologies — intended to improve how we communicate and streamline how we work — often complicate rather than supplement our ability to live and work more productively. This doesn't have to be the case.

We've spent the last six years testing every website, software application, and gadget promising to make your life easier on Lifehacker.com. This book highlights the cream of that crop. These tricks can fast-track you through tedious work, solve common computer problems we all face, and give you access to information anywhere you need it. Whether you're a middle manager at a huge corporation or a freelancer who works at home, a PC or Mac user, someone just comfortable enough to get around your computer or a power user, there's something here for you.

The most precious thing anyone has in this life is time. Spend more time *doing* things and less time fiddling with your computer. This book shows you how.

Computer Manual Meets Productivity Book

This book isn't a computer user manual, and it isn't a productivity system — it's a little bit of each. It isn't an exhaustive guide to all the features of a particular software application or gadget. You won't find seven habits or four steps to becoming a productivity powerhouse. Instead, this book takes established personal-productivity principles and outlines 121 concrete ways to apply those concepts in your everyday work. This is where the rubber hits the road, dear reader: here, you learn how to practice big-picture productivity methods on your computer desktop.

Lifehacker isn't a software or gadget company; we don't champion specific tools or services to promote our own products (although we do write software that we give away for free). We're simply enthusiastic and experienced technologists obsessed with the ways that technology can help get things done. In this book, you can find information you won't get in the user manual: practical applications of the features you should actually care about, and nothing else. Alpha geeks use the tools outlined in this book. Now it's time for you to get in on the good stuff as well.

Pick Your Tricks

Think of this book as a giant buffet of shortcuts. No one person will use all of them. Browse its contents and add to your plate only the ones that can help you. Instead of reading this book from cover to cover, read each chapter introduction, which describes a productivity challenge. The rest of the chapter is a collection of clever tricks — or *hacks* — that can tackle it. The best hacks for your work and life depend on your needs, your skill level, your situation, and your biggest pain points.

For example, do you get too much email and struggle to keep on top of all your incoming messages? Go directly to Chapter 1, "Control Your Email." Have you been procrastinating on checking anything off an impossibly long to-do list? Proceed to Chapter 3, "Trick Yourself into Getting Done." Are constant interruptions and distractions keeping you from getting work done? See Chapter 5, "Firewall Your Attention." Want to shave seconds or minutes off of computer chores you do every day? You want Chapter 6, "Streamline Common Tasks." Eager to put your new smartphone to work and avoid the pitfalls of that tiny touchscreen? Head straight to Chapter 9, "Work Smarter on Your Smart Phone."

To help you choose your best tricks, each hack appears with the skill level of the user to whom it applies, the platform (or operating systems) on which it is performed, and the cost required to accomplish the hack.

Your Skill Level

If you're a power user worried this book will be too basic, or a beginner wondering whether it's too technical, fear not. Each hack in this book has a user skill-level rating — Easy, Medium, or Advanced:

- **Easy:** You are comfortable enough on your computer to get by, but that's it. You know how to browse the folders on your computer's hard drive to attach a document to an email message. You know there are lots of interesting tech tricks out there that you want to know how to do, but you don't know where to start. You want the hacks labeled "Easy."

- **Medium:** You've been using computers for some time now and you're comfortable putting together Excel formulas, downloading music, finding elusive information on Google, or helping your grandpa get his email set up. Maybe you have your own blog, and you set up a wireless Internet connection at home yourself. You should check out the hacks labeled "Medium" and "Easy."

- **Advanced:** You're the family tech-support geek, the one everyone calls when they have a computer problem. You survived a hard drive crash or two; maybe you administer a website. You've delved into the deepest settings on your computer, such as the Windows Registry, or you have experience at the command line — or at least feel confident that you can teach yourself those things easily. Hacks marked "Easy" may be yawners to you, but the "Advanced" and "Medium" hacks can feed your head.

Your Operating System (Matters Less, but Still Matters)

As operating systems converge and the Web matures, desktop operating systems matter less. As application software moves off your desktop, onto the

Web, and into your pockets, it takes only an Internet-connected device with a modern web browser from any OS to get things done (more on that topic in Hack 68). Today, file and network compatibility among Mac, Windows versions, and even Linux is a nonissue. You can do things on your smart phone that were previously relegated to a desktop computer — sometimes even better than you could with a PC. More open-source software is cross-platform and free (such as Mozilla Firefox and Google Chrome, which appear throughout this book). Almost all other software has an equivalent on other operating systems. In the coming years you'll use more computers with more operating systems than you ever did before. (Weren't you just considering switching to a Mac? Or was it Linux?)

Therefore, this book is as operating system-inclusive as possible. Whenever possible, we recommend software that runs on Windows, Mac, and Linux; on mobile platforms, we cover both Apple's iOS and Google's Android operating system. However, the platform listed on many of the hacks is simply "Web," which applies to everyone.

The Cost

You've got enough to spend your money on without dumping hundreds of dollars on software solutions to your problems. More often than not, the hacks in this book won't cost you anything beyond the time it takes to follow the instructions. The free and open source software movement plays a significant role in the Lifehacker ethos, and whenever possible, we opt for free software solutions.

What's New in the Third Edition?

If you need a reminder of how quickly technology transforms the way we live, look back no further than the three years between this and the previous edition of this book, released in March of 2008.

Microsoft launched Windows 7 in the fall of 2009, a considerable and welcome step forward not only for the Windows operating system, but for Windows users. (If you recall, three years ago many Windows users still used Windows XP, having decided that an operating system first released in 2001 was superior to the maligned Windows Vista.) In the summer of 2008, Apple launched their App Store and substantially evolved the iOS operating system, creating new expectations for all smart phones and mobile devices along the way. Google evolved beyond search and productivity webapps, releasing their own web browser, Google Chrome (late summer,

2008) and mobile operating system, Android (fall, 2008). Tablet computers have finally reached mass appeal, starting with the consumer-friendly iPad and expanding to devices powered by Android, BlackBerry, and other mobile operating systems.

This edition reflects these considerable changes. Most significantly, Chapter 9 focuses exclusively on getting more from your smart phone — a now ubiquitous piece of personal technology that was in its nascence when the previous edition was released. You'll also find new and updated hacks in every chapter, employing tools and operating system features that weren't available three years ago. Every OS-specific hack in this book has been updated to work with the most recent versions of Windows and Mac OS X.

What the Heck Is a Lifehacker?

Contrary to the popular misuse of the term to denote a computer criminal, a *hacker* is someone who solves a problem in a clever or little-known way. A *life hack* is a workaround or shortcut that overcomes the everyday difficulties of the modern worker. A *lifehacker* uses clever tech tricks to get work done.

A Brief History of Life Hacks

In 2004, tech journalist Danny O'Brien interviewed several people he called "over-prolific alpha geeks" — skilled and highly productive technologists whose continuous output seemed unaffected by the constant disruptions of modern technology. O'Brien hoped to identify patterns in the way these productive techies managed their work processes. Commonalities did emerge, and the term *life hacks* was born.[2]

These so-called alpha geeks had developed uncommon systems and tricks for getting through their daily drudgery. They used simple, flexible tools such as text files and email. They avoided bloated, complex software. They imposed their own structures on their information and set up mechanisms that filtered and pushed the data they needed in front of their eyes at the right time automatically while keeping the rest at bay.

The life hacks concept resonated with geeks across the Internet, including the one typing these words. A movement was born. In January 2005, Lifehacker.com was born, a daily weblog devoted to life hacks. Six years later, we have the privilege of sharing the best life hacks that came out of that work with you in these pages.

Just remember: on your deathbed, you'll never say, "I wish I'd checked my email more often!" Go forth and start using tech to spend less time working and more time living.

References

1. David Allen, *Getting Things Done* (Penguin Books, 2001), p. 85.
2. "Interview: father of 'life hacks' Danny O'Brien," Lifehacker.com, March 17, 2005 (`http://lifehacker.com/software/interviews/ interview-father-of-life-hacks-danny-obrien-036370.php`).

Control Your Email

Do you wish you received less email? Sure you do. Do you want to live without the convenience of electronic mail? Of course you don't. The greatest double-edged sword in productivity technology, email both empowers and overwhelms its users. But the most successful professionals know how to control their email instead of letting it run their workday.

On one hand, email enables anyone with an Internet-connected device to send information great distances at the press of a button. On the other, you have 1,762 unread messages sitting in your inbox, and you don't know when you'll have time to get through them all. *Ding!* Another one just arrived.

Before email became ubiquitous, to send a letter, a person had to commit the information to paper, stuff and address the envelope, affix postage, and drop it in the mailbox. Days or weeks later, the message arrived on the recipient's desk. Today, email offers the same type of text-based communication, just faster and easier, complete with a cute little envelope icon. But the same ways you deal with arriving postal mail don't work for electronic mail. Incoming messages are incoming messages. But email's effect on workers is vastly different from paper mail for one fundamental reason: volume. The speed, convenience, and low cost of sending email has increased the number of transmissions to levels that turn the postal service green with envy: Reports estimate 294 *billion* emails are sent daily. Approximately 80% of that email is spam, but that still leaves roughly 50 billion legitimate emails every day.

This virtually free and instantaneous message transmission is great for the sender but not for the recipient. The cost and inconvenience of sending postal mail acts as a filter: when that envelope appears in the recipient's mailbox, she can trust that the message is important enough to the sender to warrant the investment.

Electronic mail, however, shifts that burden. With the volume of electronic mail sent each day, the onus is on the recipient — not the sender — to sort through the avalanche of received messages. Email overload is such a common malady in the information age that experts estimate it costs companies billions of dollars a year in worker productivity losses.

Some companies and users resort to extreme tactics to combat email overload:

- In 2004, Stanford professor Lawrence Lessig declared "email bankruptcy" when faced with the thousands of unread messages dating back two years that had accumulated in his inbox. Instead of attempting to open them all — a task he said would have been impossible — he sent an automated apology to his contacts and asked that they resend their unanswered message only if it were still important.[1] A web search for the term "email bankruptcy" shows that several others followed suit, publicly announcing their email bankruptcy on their websites.

- Overwhelmed by the effort that writing lengthy responses requires, designer Mike Davidson instituted a personal policy that any message he writes will be fewer than five sentences. Recipients who wonder about the brevity can get more information about the policy, which he includes in his message signature.[2]

- One cellular company designated a weekly email-free day. Employees refrain from sending or checking email (except from customers) every Friday. Workers report that the freedom from the distraction and interruption once a week helps them accomplish a lot more.[3]

Anyone who's spent hours processing a backlog of email can understand why you'd employ such tactics. It's so easy to let email take the reins of your workday. All you have to do is leave your email software open while you work. Each time it notifies you that a new message has arrived, stop what you're doing, no matter how important it is or how involved you are, and switch to your inbox. Scan the new message. If it's an emergency, deal with it right away. If not, switch back to the task at hand. Try to remember where you were before that message arrived. At the end of the day, wonder how all those read messages accumulated in your inbox, what you're supposed to do about them again, and where the day went.

This is how most people operate. But there is a better way.

You can reduce the amount of time you spend fiddling with email to less than 30 minutes per day. You can empty your inbox and enjoy the feeling that you're completely caught up every workday. You can process your messages in bunches, in between other tasks, when your mind is free and clear. You can hear "Thanks for getting back to me so quickly" from your boss and co-workers more and more often. You can elicit the response you need in shorter exchanges. You can keep your inbox free of a festering pile of unfulfilled obligations. You can become known as responsive — and therefore responsible — engaged, and reliable around the office simply by being on top of your email. Soon, wealth, fame, and fortune will ensue.

You can control your email without declaring bankruptcy or refraining from using it just because it's a certain day of the week. Small changes and better habits practiced every day can get the constant influx of communication working *for* you instead of against you. This chapter provides practical strategies for getting your email under control and keeping it there.

NOTE For updates, links, references, and additional tips and tools regarding the hacks in this book, visit `http://lifehackerbook.com/`. (Append the chapter number — `http://lifehackerbook.com/ch1/`, for example — to go directly to a specific chapter's updates.)

Hack 1: Empty Your Inbox (and Keep It Empty)

Level . . . . **Easy**

Platforms . . . **All**

Cost . . . . **Free**

When you can empty your inbox on a regular basis, you've reached the ultimate level of email control. Emptying the inbox clears away that pile of unidentified pieces of information, keeps it from stacking up higher every day, and frees your mind to worry about more important work.

Why an Empty Inbox?

Your inbox is a temporary holding pen for unprocessed messages. An unprocessed email is one you haven't made a decision about yet. When you get into the habit of deciding what to do with a new message within a day of its arrival, move it out of your inbox.

Some people enjoy keeping their inbox full so that they can glance at a list of most recent messages to see what's going on — what they should be working on, what their group is discussing, the latest funny YouTube video that's making the rounds. But just as you'd never leave a physical paper inbox full of documents whose only commonality is that they're *incoming*, you don't want to leave your email inbox full of messages. An inbox full of read messages does you no favors: You have no way to prioritize what's most important or to access the message contents in their most useful context. For example, a meeting invitation that comes in via email is much more meaningful on your calendar than in your inbox. A website address you want to visit later would do better in your bookmarks than in your email. A project document belongs in its appropriate folder, not in your email program. Everything should have its own place, and the inbox isn't it.

Furthermore, an empty inbox lightens the psychological load of an endless list of messages staring at you every time you check your email. It creates a clear demarcation between what's incoming and what's been resolved or placed into motion.

This hack introduces a simple, three-folder system that keeps your inbox clear and ensures that every message you receive is both findable and actionable without cluttering your inbox.

Set Up the Trusted Trio of Folders

The three folders you need to keep your inbox empty and your messages in process are `Archive`, `Follow Up`, and `Hold`, as shown in Figure 1-1.

NOTE Some email programs — most notably Gmail (`http://gmail.com`) — have a built-in message archive. In that case you don't need to create an `Archive` label or folder. Simply use the program's built-in archived message storage place (which you can get to by clicking All Mail.)

Figure 1-1: Archive, Follow Up, and Hold folders clear your inbox.

The Archive Folder

Most email you receive is stuff you don't need right now but may need to look up later. Archive these messages. The Archive is your long-term email reference library. It's where you place all the messages that contain information you may want to retrieve at some point in the long-term future, including any completed threads, completed requests, memos you've read, questions you've answered, and completed project email. Basically, any email exchange that's closed but that you may want to refer to at some point in the future belongs in the Archive.

The Archive is one single folder, with no subfolders. That's a scary concept to those who enjoy organizing information into specifically named folders. However, you're not a librarian, and you don't have time to waste deciding what message should go in what folder. The archive is completely searchable. You can retrieve any message you place there later using the right search operators. For more on plucking messages out of the Archive (without a complicated folder scheme), see Hack 6, "Master Message Search."

The Follow Up Folder

Messages in your Follow Up folder represent tasks you must complete, whether that's a response that will take more than a minute to write or whether it's another type of action. Each of these messages maps to a task on your to-do list. A message from a long-lost high school friend whom you haven't spoken to in years and a request from the boss to update the quarterly report would both go into the Follow Up folder because you need to follow up with an action. It's not enough to just move this message into the Follow Up folder; make sure you also enter the task onto your to-do list so that you'll actually do it.

The Hold Folder

The Hold folder is a temporary holding pen for important messages you'll need quick access to within the next few days. If you're waiting on someone else to get back to you with crucial information, or you're maintaining a thread about a time-sensitive topic, keep it in the Hold folder.

Examples of messages that would go in Hold are a FedEx confirmation number for a delivery that's on its way, or a message from a co-worker that says, "I'll get back to you Tuesday re: The Big Project."

Review the Hold folder once a week, and clear it out as the messages in it become irrelevant — such as when that FedEx package gets delivered or when your co-worker gets back to you.

Process Your Messages

Now that the three folders are in place, it's time to empty your inbox. Whether you're starting with an overstuffed inbox with months' worth of messages or the two dozen that arrived since you last checked, the method is the same. Beginning with the oldest email in your inbox, open the message and do the following:

- Delete it if you don't need it.

- Respond on the spot to quick questions or requests. Then archive or delete it.

- If it requires action that will take more than one minute to complete, move it to the Follow Up folder and add the task to your to-do list.

- If it's an item you're waiting on or may need within the next few days, move it to Hold. If it's time-sensitive (your co-worker promised you the document by Friday, for instance), add a note on your calendar to check in about the item you're waiting for.

- If it's an informational message you may want to refer to later, move it to the Archive.

Wash, rinse, and repeat for every message in your inbox until it is completely empty.

> **NOTE** This exact folder scheme may not work for everyone, but it's a good start on the road to a simple, well-defined processing system. If you tweak and modify this method, just remember: the fewer folders you have, the easier it is to process each individual message.

Keep It Empty

After you've emptied your inbox, keeping it that way is a matter of repeating the process a few times a day. Schedule regular email sessions, such as once mid-morning, once after lunch, and once in the late afternoon. Train yourself to follow the golden rule:

Never leave a read email in your inbox.

Make a decision about the fate of every message you read the first time you read it — no excuses. Be ruthless about this new practice. File information that incoming messages contain in its right place: dates in your calendar; project documents in their folder; website addresses in your bookmarks. Respond on the spot to messages that need a quick "yes" or "no." Never touch an email in your inbox more than once.

Technologist Mark Hurst wrote, "Consider that an incoming email has the shelf life of Chinese takeout in the refrigerator. It's best to eat it as soon as it arrives; within a day is OK, but after that it starts to get funky."[4]

Your First Time

If you're starting out with an inbox loaded with thousands of messages, emptying it the first time can be an overwhelming task. One way to start with your new good habits *right now* is to move all your existing messages into a separate, special folder (email management expert Merlin Mann calls it the "Email DMZ"[5] — a demilitarized zone).

Resolve to empty your inbox each time you check your email from this moment forward. Then, during each processing session, *after* you empty your inbox, take on a handful of the oldest messages in your "DMZ" folder as well. Slowly but surely, you'll catch up on the backlog *and* hone your new good habits as you go.

The Catch

Just because you have all unresolved messages filed neatly away in Follow Up and Hold doesn't mean you're free and clear. The trick to this system is to consistently review Follow Up folder messages (which should be on your to-do list) and Hold folder messages, and to complete the items stowed away there. To keep from getting lulled into a total sense of completeness, you can mark all the messages in Hold and Follow Up as unread to easily monitor the number of outstanding items.

NOTE Special thanks to Merlin Mann, author of the *Inbox Zero* series (`http://inboxzero.com`) **and "The Inbox Makeover," which appeared in** *Macworld Magazine* **(available at** `http://macworld.com/2005/04/features/tipsinbox/index.php`**) and which greatly influenced the methods outlined in this hack.**

Hack 2: Decrease Your Response Time

Level . . . . **Easy**

Platform . . . . **All**

Cost . . . . **Free**

Responding to your email in a timely manner is one of the best things you can do for your career. But no one emerges from the womb with a natural talent for parrying a constant stream of new messages vying for your attention all day long. Email responsiveness is an acquired skill — the one that just may differentiate you from everyone else in the world who's overwhelmed by an overloaded inbox.

Michael Hyatt, CEO of Thomas Nelson Publishers, agrees. He said, "The truth is, you are building your reputation — your brand — one response at a time. People are shaping their view of you by how you respond to them. If you are slow, they assume you are incompetent and over your head. If you respond quickly, they assume you are competent and on top of your work. Their perception, whether you realize it or not, will determine how fast your career advances and how high you go. You can't afford to be unresponsive. It is a career-killer."[6]

Although it's impossible to instantly respond to the dozens of new email messages you receive every day, you can increase your responsiveness rate without becoming a slave to your inbox. This hack provides strategies for responding to your email in a timely fashion without killing your entire workday.

Process Messages in Batches

Your inbox dictates the ebb and flow of your work if it interrupts you every time a new message arrives. Don't let it.

The explosion of email communication and proliferation of email-enabled smart phones has led many Americans to nonstop inbox monitoring. Seventy-two percent of respondents in a 2010 survey said they checked their email outside regular work hours (That includes in the morning before going to work, vacations, and weekends.) One in five Americans check their work email *from bed*.[7]

The reality is that checking email adds up to a whole lot of time, much of it wasted. The world will not end if an email sits in your inbox for a few hours.

Schedule two or three "meetings" with your inbox each day at predetermined times to process email. If your job requires that you keep your email program running at all times, set it to check for new messages every hour (or two!) instead of every five minutes. (For more on protecting your sanity from the insidiousness of constant email checking, see Hack 41, "Reduce Email Interruptions.")

The One-Minute Rule

When you've begun an email processing session, start at the oldest message you received and work up. Follow the one-minute rule: If a message takes less than one minute to process and respond to, do it on the spot. One minute doesn't sound like a lot of time, but in reality a whole lot can happen in 60 seconds. Dash off quick answers to questions, follow up with questions on requests, and knock down any "Sounds good" and "Let's discuss on the phone; when's a good time?" and "Received the attachment, thanks" type of messages. If you think that a message needs a lengthy, complicated response, consider taking it offline and making a phone call instead.

Most of your new messages will fall under the "can respond in less than a minute" umbrella, so go ahead and answer them.

Respond to Task Requests — Before the Task Is Done

If someone asks you to complete a project or task, it's natural to think, "I don't have time to deal with this right now, so I'll just leave it in my inbox to handle later." There the message atrophies for weeks and a month later, you've never gotten back to the sender, and the task still isn't done. That's the quickest route to Irresponsibleville.

When asked to do something via email, respond right away with the following:

- Questions you may need answered to start
- A request for the task completion deadline
- How busy you are and when you think you can start
- The next time the requester can expect to hear from you regarding the task

An immediate response that says, "I'm booked solid for the next three months. What's your deadline? Drop me a note in September if you're still interested in having me work on this" — which is effectively saying, "No can do" — is much more professional and appreciated than no response at all, or a three-week delay.

Don't Leave It in Your Inbox

Touch a message once in your inbox and commit yourself to taking it to the next step, whether that's dashing off a reply or moving it into your queue for a next step. But whatever you do, don't scan messages in your inbox and just leave them there to scan again later. It's a waste of time to repeat the same action again (and again).

Hack 3: Craft Effective Messages

Level. . . . . . . **Easy**

Platform . . . . **All**

Cost. . . . . **Free**

The old computer-science adage, "Garbage in, garbage out" (GIGO), means that if you give a computer the wrong input, it returns useless output. Humans are much more forgiving than computers, but in many ways GIGO applies to email correspondence as well. The clearer your email messages are, the more likely you'll get the result you want quicker — whether it's a response, a completed task, or an informed recipient.

In an ineffective email message, the sender's expectations aren't clear, the most important information is hard to find, and the body of the message is too long and difficult to read.

You spend at least a couple of hours a day reading and responding to email. How much of that time could be saved if all the messages you sent and received were to the point and free of any unnecessary information?

This hack covers ways to get the most out of email you send with the least amount of time, energy, and work.

Composing a New Message

Keep in mind the following simple strategies for whittling the messages you send down to their most effective state.

Determine Your Purpose

Every email message has a specific purpose. Either you are conveying information or requesting action from the recipient. Before you click that Compose button, know what you expect to get out of the exchange. If you don't know your message's purpose, don't write it.

If you need to flesh out your thoughts by writing, send the email to *yourself*. Then follow up with anything you need to ask or tell others.

Use an Informative Subject Line

First impressions are important in a world in which two dozen different things are already competing for your email recipient's eyeballs and attention. The first thing your correspondent sees is the subject line of your message. Boil that line down to a few words that convey your message's purpose. Think of yourself as a newspaper headline writer, tasked with telling the whole story in just a few words to grab the reader's attention.

Remember that your recipient will use subject lines to scan and sort her inbox, track conversations, prioritize tasks, and absorb information at a glance, so make your subject lines amenable to that.

Here are some examples of bad subject lines:

```
Subject: Hi!
Subject: Just wanted to tell you...
Subject: Can you do me a favor?
Subject: IMPORTANT!!!
```

None of those subject lines gets specific about the content of the message. Yes, this message may be IMPORTANT!!!, but what is it regarding? A "favor" might range from lending the sender your stapler to donating your kidney. One might want to "just tell you" a lot of things, from "I like your tie" to "I hear you're getting fired tomorrow."

Some examples of good subject lines include the following:

```
Subject: Tomorrow's managerial meeting agenda
Subject: Questions about Monday's presentation
Subject: QUESTION: May I quote you in an article?
Subject: FYI: Out of the office Thursday
Subject: REQUEST: Pls comment on the proposed redesign layout
Subject: IMPORTANT: Must fax contract before 3PM today
```

Notice the optional use of prefixes (FYI, REQUEST, IMPORTANT) that convey the message type before addressing the content in the rest of the line. You can even shorten them to Q: for Question, REQ: for Request, and IMPT: for Important.

If your message contains several requests for action or info related to different topics entirely, break it down into separate messages. That can help get each point addressed in specific, relevant conversation threads.

Be Succinct

The purpose of writing an email isn't to hear yourself think; it's to elicit the desired response from the recipient.

The shorter your email, the more likely it is that it will be read and your request filled. No one wants to muddle through a long, wordy missive picking out the questions, task requests, and important points. Respect your recipient's time and expect that your message will be skimmed quickly. Get right to the point and hit Send. Everyone appreciates brevity.

> **NOTE** Lots of email-savvy folks send subject-only messages to convey short bits of information. For example, a blank email with the subject line, `FYI: Out of the office for the rest of the afternoon [EOM]` (where EOM stands for End of Message) says all that it has to. Gmail is even smart enough to understand what EOM means; sending a body-less email with EOM in the subject will skip Gmail's normal "Send this message without body in the text?" prompt.

Put Your Messages on a Diet

If you send messages to people outside your corporate network, where download speeds and email software may differ from your environment, eliminate unnecessary attachments and HTML elements that may weigh down the message. Here are some tips:

- If you attach photos, be sure to rotate them to the correct orientation and resize them. (See Hack 55, "Batch Resize Photos," for a quick way to make your photos better suited for email.)

- Don't assume that everyone has HTML email enabled; many folks (including myself) disable HTML email to avoid marketing trackers and long message downloads.

- Don't assume that your message looks the same way in your recipient's software as it does in yours; all email applications format messages differently.

- In some email software, a long website address that wraps in the message may be unclickable. Use a service such as TinyURL (http://tinyurl.com) or Goo.gl (http://goo.gl/), or Bit.ly (http://bit.ly/) to shorten that address before you send your message.

Facilitate a Complete Response

A few line breaks can go a long way in a message that contains a set of questions, important points, or task requests. Use line breaks and bullet points liberally to make your message easy to read and respond to.

For example, the following message intersperses information with questions in one continuous paragraph:

```
Hi Becky,
Got your message about Tuesday, thanks! What's the conference
room number? Turns out I'm going to drive instead of take the
train. Will I need a parking pass? Also, I have the PowerPoint
presentation on my laptop. Is there a projector available I can
hook it up to, or should I bring my own?
```

It would be a lot easier for Becky to see the bits of the message that require a response if it were formatted this way:

```
Hi Becky,
I'm all set for Tuesday's meeting. A few questions for you:
* What is the conference room number?
* If I drive, how should I get a parking pass?
* Is a projector available that will work with my laptop?
```

The second version clearly delineates what questions the sender needs answered and makes responding in line to the questions much easier for Becky.

Make It Clear Why Everyone Got the Message

Messages that have several recipients in the To: field can spread accountability too thin across a group of people. If everything thinks, "Someone else will take care of it," nothing will get done. As a sender, include multiple recipients on a message only when you absolutely must — and then make it clear in the body of the message why everyone is receiving it, as in the following example:

```
To: Victor Downs, Lorrie Crenshaw, Kyran Deck
Subject: Staff luncheon confirmed for June 18th

We reserved a room for 40 at Lottie's for 1PM on Tuesday, June
18th.

VD: Will the shuttle be available for transportation that day?
Please let Kyran know.
KD: Please send out a staff wide e email invite with directions and
shuttle information by the 4th.
LC: FYI, we'll have to cancel our weekly meeting.
```

Don't Forget the Attachment

It's too easy to dash off a message saying "the file's attached" and then never actually attach the file. The Forgotten Attachment Detector plugin for Microsoft Outlook (free from `www.officelabs.com/projects/ forgottenattachmentdetector/Pages/default.aspx`) notifies you when you try to send a message containing words such as "see attached" or "attachment" in it and no file is attached. Gmail users have it even better — the popular email client notifies you when it thinks you've forgotten an attachment by default.

Replying to a Message

Nothing's worse than sending an email with three questions and getting back the answer to only one. To avoid unnecessary email back-and-forth, answer all the messages that require a response as thoroughly as possible.

Respond to Individual Points Inline

For email that includes lists of questions or response-worthy points, press the Reply button and include your comments inline — that is, interspersed within the original email — to ensure that you address every point. For example, Becky might reply to the earlier message this way:

```
Hi Rich,

Rich Jones wrote:
> * What is the conference room number?
It's room 316 in Building B.

> * If I drive, how should I get a parking pass?
Park in the west lot and give your name at the booth. The guard
will issue you a guest pass there.

> * Is there a projector available that will work with my laptop?
Yes, there is - a member of our tech team will be there to help set
you up.

See you then,
Becky
```

Task Requests

When you receive a request for action, don't delay your response until you're ready to complete the action. Instead, review the request and respond with any questions you need answered before you can get it done right away.

For example, if you receive the following email:

Subject: REQUEST: Please comment on the redesign layout proposal
Let us know what you think about the new font choice and background
color.

you might respond right away:

Subject: Re: REQUEST: Please comment on the redesign layout
proposal

Tamara Smith wrote:
> Let us know what you think about the new font choice and
background color.

Can you send me a link to the new proposal?

Also, when is the deadline for final comments?

Lead by Example

You may be a master at writing effective email, but communication is a
two-way street. Lead by example when you receive poorly written messages.
When you respond, edit an email's unspecific subject line so that further
correspondence on the topic is easily identifiable in your inbox. Break up
someone's run-on message into chunks and respond inline. If the purpose
of the message is unclear to you, respond with the question, "What's my
next step regarding this?" If someone sends you a rambling, 2,000-word
description, reply briefly: "Sounds good." These strategies train others to
not expect long messages from you in real time and to craft better subject
lines and task requests.

Don't Respond in Real Time

Although some folks may live and die by the "Ding! You have new mail!"
of their email client, email was never meant to be instant, real-time communication and shouldn't be used as such. If someone needs to engage
you at this moment in time, he can call. Otherwise, create the expectation
that email to you will not get answered on the spot.

Even if you check your email in real time (and you shouldn't unless you
don't want to get anything else done), don't respond to nonemergency
messages right away, especially from co-workers. It sets an impossible
expectation for the future. Settle on a reasonable maximum response-time
goal; for example, commit to responding to email within 4 to 6 hours on
business days, or within 24 to 48 hours at most.

Get Outside the Inbox

Tone-deafness is the biggest pitfall of textual communication — especially quick, off-the-cuff methods such as email. The sender's facial expression or tone of voice doesn't come inside her email messages, and feelings can be hurt, recipients can be offended, and messages can be taken the wrong way. The American Psychological Association published a study that shows emailers overestimate their ability to convey their tone by about 25 percent when they press the Send button, and overestimate their ability to correctly interpret the tone of messages others send to them as well. [8]

Some issues are too complex or sensitive to be communicated via email. Know when it's appropriate to just pick up the phone and call someone or visit in person to convey a message and answer questions on the spot.

Know When Not to Say a Thing

Even though email correspondence *seems* private, it's not. Copies of every message you've ever sent out were made on servers across the Internet, and business email is saved on your employer's server as well. One study shows that about one-third of large companies in the United States actively monitor their employees' email. [9] This number will only go up as liabilities and privacy issues related to email increase.

Keeping that in mind, never write email when you're upset, emotional, stressed, tired, hungry, drunk, or otherwise impaired. After an email is sent, there's no taking it back, and every email you send is written documentation that can be used in court or to support a case for promotion or firing. Never say something in an email that you wouldn't publish in a company newsletter, say to a newspaper reporter, or announce at a meeting.

If an email upsets you or you're feeling a rant coming on, write it in a text file, save it, and give yourself time to think things over. Later, go back and edit or start over on a more composed note.

> **TIP** If you have a bad habit of dashing off ill-advised emails in the middle of the night that you regret the next morning, try Mail Goggles, one of many features in Gmail Labs (https://mail.google.com/mail/u/0/?shva=1#settings/labs). **Mail Goggles forces you to solve simple math problems before letting you send late night missives. You can schedule it to run during your weak hours, and although you can likely do a little arithmetic no matter what your condition, it may help you wait until morning before you hit Send.**

Hack 4: Highlight Messages Sent Directly to You

Level . . . . **Easy**

Platform . . . . **All**

Cost . . . . **Free**

When you're faced with an inbox full of new, unread email, it's nearly impossible to determine which messages need to be dealt with right away and which can be put off until later. You get CCed on memos and included on large mailing lists, or receive company- or department-wide notifications. When you're pressed for time, those types of messages are all good candidates for later reading. But what about those few messages addressed *only* to you?

Email overload expert Itzy Sabo says, [10]

Such messages are most likely to be more important than the rest of the stuff that fills up my inbox, because:
They have not been sent to a bunch of people, but specifically to me.
They are therefore more likely to relate to my area of responsibility.
They are also more likely to require action.
   If I don't answer, nobody else will.

Microsoft Outlook: Color Me Blue

In Microsoft Outlook 2007, you can make those important to-me-only messages jump out of your inbox with one simple setting: Choose Tools ➪ Organize, and in the Using Colors section, click the Turn On button next to Show Messages Sent Only to Me in Blue, as shown in Figure 1-2.

Figure 1-2: Organize your inbox by highlighting messages addressed only to you.

Unfortunately in Outlook 2010, you have to set up a conditional formatting rule on your own. Following are a list of steps that will get you started.

1. Click the View tab ➪ View Settings ➪ Conditional Formatting.

2. Click Add, name it Messages to Me, and then click Condition.

3. Tick the check box next to "Where I Am," and select The Only Person on the To Line from the drop-down, as shown in Figure 1-3. Click OK.

4. Now click the Font button, and set Outlook to highlight emails sent only to you using whatever formatting you prefer.

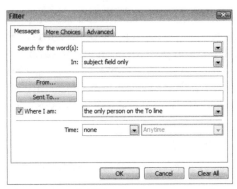

Figure 1-3: Highlight messages sent only to you in Outlook 2010.

Now messages sent only to you will be a different color than the others. During your email processing sessions, you'll do well to deal with the blue messages first. Of course, you can use the color drop-down list to select a different color for your only-to-me emails if you want.

All Other Email Programs: Create a Not-to-Me Filter

Most modern email applications have a rule or filter feature that matches incoming messages against criteria you define and performs some action. Create a not-to-me filter that de-highlights lower priority messages or even moves them to an Inbox–Low Priority folder. See Hack 10, "Filter Low-Priority Messages," for more on using email filters to automatically clean out and prioritize your inbox.

TIP Gmail can indicate messages sent only to your address with the right-angle quotation mark (which looks like a double greater-than sign, or >>) pointing to the message subject. Messages addressed to you and other people get a single greater-than sign (>). Messages without your address in the To: field — such as distribution lists — have no indicator near them. In Gmail's Settings area, turn this on under Personal level indicators.

Hack 5: Use Disposable Email Addresses

Level . . . . **Easy**

Platform . . . . **Web**

Cost. . . . . **Free**

Much of the junk email you receive is from spammers who bought or scraped your email address from a website where you registered for membership. Most registration-based websites require that you use a legitimate email address; often, you have to retrieve an email from that address's inbox to complete registration.

If you hate the idea of giving your email address to any website that asks for it and you want to protect your email address from junk mail and spam, use a disposable email address instead.

Web-Based Public Email Addresses

Several services, such as Mailinator (http://mailinator.com) offer free, public, disposable email addresses. Choose any email name at the mailinator.com domain — such as goaheadspammer@mailinator.com or joe@mailinator .com — and use it to register at a website. Then, visit Mailinator.com to check the public inbox, which doesn't require a password.

CAUTION Remember, anyone can check the joe@mailinator.com inbox, so make sure nothing too personal winds up there!

Dodgit (http://dodgit.com) offers a service similar to Mailinator, with the capability to check all public email accounts at dodgit.com via RSS.

For more on RSS, see Hack 91, "Subscribe to Websites with RSS."

Multi-Domain Email Addresses

If you host your email at your own web domain (see more on that in Hack 7, "Future-Proof Your Email Address," later in this chapter), you have a limitless supply of email names available to you; really, anything followed by @*yourdomain*.com. Each time you sign up for a website, use a unique name that you can block or filter later if you start receiving spam.

For example, if your real email address is adam@example.com, you might register at Amazon.com using the amazon.com@example.com email address, which also comes to you. If Amazon sells your address and you start receiving spam at amazon.com@example.com, you can block further email to that address, and know it was Amazon who sold you out. (This is just an example. In all the years I've been a registered Amazon.com user, I've never received spam at the unique address I use there.)

NOTE For more on how to avoid signing up for a website at all, see Hack 56, "Bypass Free Site Registration with BugMeNot."

Hack 6: Master Message Search

Level. . . . . . . **Easy**

Platforms . . . **All**

Cost. . . . . **Free**

In an earlier hack, you created an archive of closed messages for later reference, and your Archive folder has no subfolders in it. That makes a lot of compulsively organized people who like to have a folder for every sender, project, and day of the week anxious. But in contrast to paper documents, you don't need folders to find where you've stored messages. As long as you know a few key characteristics of the message in question, a well-crafted query can pluck out the email you're looking for immediately — without traversing a six-folder-deep hierarchy.

In the physical world, you can't throw years' worth of letters, cards, and memos into a drawer and then pick out the one Tom sent you about that fabulous rental he got in Key West back in 2007 in seconds. However, that is absolutely possible (and simple with a little know-how) in an email folder containing thousands of messages.

Search Criteria

Most email programs have a built-in message search. Not surprisingly, Google's web-based email product Gmail has the strongest searching capabilities on the market; that said, any decent, modern email client also offers solid searching tools.

Often simple keyword searches are all you need, but you can do even more complex queries with Gmail's advanced search operators. For example, your search for Tom's message might look like Figure 1-4 in Gmail's Search Options area:

Additionally, if you want to search for messages from Tom or Kelly that have the phrase "Key West" or the word "rental," use the OR operator (also signified with the pipe |). As with a Google web search, enclose phrases in quotation marks when you're looking for exact matches. The entire query can go into one search box and looks like this:

```
From:(Tom | Kelly) ("Key West" OR rental)
```

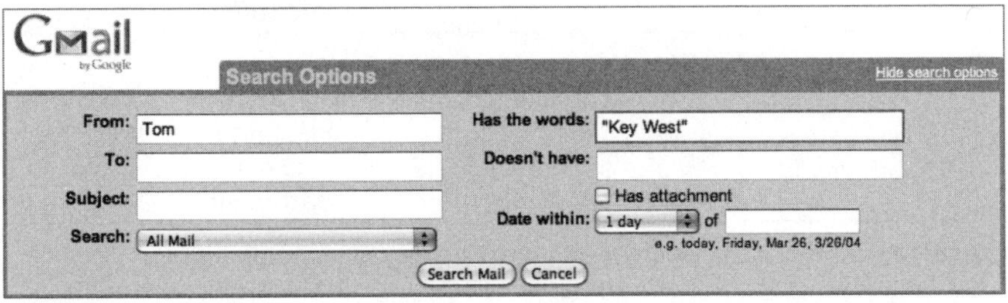

Figure 1-4: Searching for a message from Tom that contains the phrase "Key West."

You can exclude terms as well. For instance, if you want to see all the messages from people except for Joe at a specific company (at the `example.com` domain), you could search for

```
From:(*@example.com AND -joe@example.com)
```

A summary of all Gmail's search operators is available at `http://mail.google.com/support/bin/answer.py?answer=7190`. Here's a sampling of some of the most commonly useful operators:

OPERATOR	DEFINITION	EXAMPLE
`from:`	Specifies the sender.	`from:Amy` Returns messages from Amy.
`to:`	Specifies the recipient.	`to:Jonah` Returns messages addressed to Jonah.
`Subject:`	Searches the subject line.	`subject:lunch` Returns messages with the word *lunch* in the subject line.
OR	Searches for messages with either term A or term B. OR must be in all caps. A pipe (|) works in place of OR.	`from:Jonah OR from:Amy` Returns messages from Jonah or from Amy.

(continued)

(continued)

OPERATOR	DEFINITION	EXAMPLE
`-`	Excludes a term from the search.	`Java -coffee` Returns messages containing the word *Java* but not the word *coffee*.
`has:attachment`	Searches for messages with an attachment.	`from:david has:attachment` Returns messages from David that contain any kind of file attachment.
`filename:`	Searches for an attachment by name or type.	`filename:poem.doc` Returns messages with an attachment named `poem.doc`. `filename:jpg` Returns messages with JPEG photo attachments.
`" "`	Searches for an exact phrase (capitalization isn't considered).	`"Nice job"` Returns messages that contain the phrase *nice job* or *Nice job*. `subject:"dinner and a movie"` Returns messages containing the phrase *dinner and a movie* in the subject.
`( )`	Groups words; used to specify terms that shouldn't be excluded.	`from:amy(dinner OR movie)` Returns messages from Amy that contain either the word *dinner* or the word *movie*. `subject:(dinner movie)` Returns messages in which the subject contains both the word *dinner* and the word *movie*. Note that AND is implied.
`after:`	Search for messages sent after a certain date. (The date must be in yyyy/mm/dd format.)	`after:2010/09/01` Returns messages sent after September 1, 2010.

OPERATOR	DEFINITION	EXAMPLE
`before:`	Search for messages sent before a certain date. (The date must be in yyyy/mm/dd format.)	`before:1997/05/17` Returns messages sent before May 17, 1997. `after:2007/06/01 AND before:2007/07/01` Returns messages sent after June 1, 2007, but before July 1, 2007 (or messages sent in June, 2007).

When you use these operators, a well-crafted query can turn up messages with specific attributes from your `Archive` folder — or entire email archive — in seconds.

Saved Search Folders

Another efficient digital filing technique is to save a search as a folder. No more dragging and dropping or labeling messages by hand; you can create a virtual email folder defined by search criteria.

For example, during the writing of this book, I created a search-based `Book` email folder that contained all the correspondence between my publishing company, Wiley, and me.

To do this in Gmail, you need to enable the Quick Links feature inside Gmail Labs (`https://mail.google.com/mail/u/0/?#settings/labs`).

NOTE Occasionally Google graduates features from its new-feature testing ground, Gmail Labs. If you can't find Quick Links in Labs, there's a good chance it's become a standard feature, meaning you wouldn't need to enable anything to take advantage of the feature.

After you have enabled this feature, you are ready to create your saved search folder:

1. First, execute a search from the Gmail search box.

2. Then, from the left Gmail sidebar, choose Add Quick Link, and provide a name for the saved search. In Figure 1-5, any message whose sender or recipient contained the phrase **wiley.com** or my agent's

email address should be included in the Book folder. The query is defined in Gmail, as shown in Figure 1-5.

3. Finally, the Book saved search appears as a link in the Gmail sidebar; when you click the link, Gmail loads all the messages that match the search.

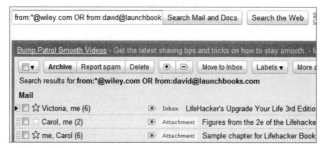

Figure 1-5: The saved search criteria that creates my Book folder.

Microsoft Outlook and Mozilla Thunderbird also offer saved search folders. In Outlook's Mail Folders bar, right-click Search Folders, and choose New Search Folder to create one. In Thunderbird, select File ⇨ New ⇨ Saved Search; then use the Saved Search dialog to name and create your search.

The advantage of saved search folders is that one email can live in any number of saved searches, as long as it fulfills the criteria. Deleting a saved search folder just removes the query — not the messages. Therefore, after this book is completed, I'll delete that folder — but all the messages will remain in their original locations.

Hack 7: Future-Proof Your Email Address

Level . . . . **Easy**

Platform . . . . **All**

Cost . . . . **Free**

Over the years, you've probably employed as many email addresses as pairs of socks, but you don't want to change them as often. Switching your primary email address can be a big inconvenience that leads to missed messages and lost relationships. You give your email address to countless friends, relatives, and web services, and publish it on mailing lists, websites, and documents forever cached in search engine indexes. But if your email address is tied to a former ISP, the company you used to work for, the university you attended, or the embarrassing handle you chose in college, switching to a new address can become a necessity.

Don'ts

- **Don't use your company's or school's email address for personal use.** Someday you will graduate or leave your current company, and you don't want to leave your email messages behind. Certainly your company or school email address is appropriate to use for company and school correspondence, but as your primary individual address, not so much.

- **Don't use the address your ISP gave you.** Remember how nice it was when you upgraded to broadband and RoadRunner gave you that free `name@yourstate.rr.com` email account? Wrong! Someday you will live in another state and use another ISP, and that address won't work anymore. Pass.

Do's

- **Use an address accessible from anywhere.** More and more you use multiple computers at home, at work, and in public places. Make sure you can securely access your email from anywhere, and choose an address that enables you to do so. Many popular web-based email services use more secure SSL logins and have easy-to-use dynamic interfaces (such as Google's Gmail), so use an address at one of them or that works with one of them. You can even use email forwarding to, say, send a copy of every email you send and receive to a web-based account for online searchable archives from anywhere.

- **Choose an easy-to-remember name you won't regret down the road.** Remember when qtGrrl81 was an email handle that made you proud? Well, now that you're a freelancer soliciting business or applying for jobs, you want something more professional. Choose an email address that will be easy to remember and recognize, and one that won't make you cringe when you have to recite it over the phone to your mutual fund company.

Bottom Line

You want an email address that can stick with you for years to come. The most ideal (and most costly) solution is to register a domain name and set up an email address at a provider (such as `yourname@yourname.com`). Your provider goes away and you can move that domain to a new provider, no address change required.

For those who don't want to plunk down the cash for their own domain and email provider, any of the popular, free, web-based mail services are a great option. Gmail and Yahoo! Mail are two free, take-it-with-you web-based email providers.

The problem with relying on a free web-based service for your email is that you lose some control. If Gmail changes its domain, decides to start charging, has server problems, or goes away (all unlikely but possible scenarios), you're affected without much recourse. In a pay-for situation with your own domain name, you can change providers and only you own your data if something goes wrong.

TIP   A service called Google Apps (www.google.com/apps/) enables you to use your custom domain with Google's email service, Gmail, which gives you the best of both worlds. If at some point in the future you want to move away from Gmail, you can simply remap your domain to another service without changing your address.

Hack 8: Consolidate Multiple Email Addresses with Gmail

Level . . . . **Medium**

Platform . . . . **Web**

Cost . . . . **Free**

After reading Hack 7, you've decided to move all your email online to Google's web-based service, Gmail. Great! But what about messages still going to your old email address(es)? Are they destined to be lost in the Internet ether?

Fear not! Gmail is not only an email host; it's also an email client that can fetch mail from any number of external services and consolidate it all in your Gmail inbox. You can avoid telling all your contacts to update your email address again, and you don't miss a single message in your transition to Gmail.

Receive Messages for Other Addresses in Your Gmail Inbox

You have two ways to receive email from other addresses in Gmail: Either use Gmail's Mail Fetcher feature or forward your other addresses' mail to Gmail automatically.

Option 1: Set Up Gmail's POP Mail Fetcher

Most likely, your former email provider offers Post Office Protocol (POP) access for retrieving messages. Gmail's Mail Fetcher feature can retrieve those messages via POP and display them in your inbox alongside messages that come directly to your Gmail address. You can fetch email from up to five other email addresses via POP in Gmail.

To use Gmail's Mail Fetcher, your old email account must offer POP access. Not all free addresses offer POP, but most do. Check the other account's settings or contact customer support to find out whether POP access is available on your non-Gmail account. You need four settings: the POP server address, the port, your username, and a password. Also, if you haven't already, you need to sign up for a free Gmail account at http:// gmail.com.

After you log in to your Gmail account, configure Mail Fetcher to retrieve messages from your old account. Here's how:

1. From the top of any page within Gmail, click Settings.

2. Click Accounts and Import.

3. In the Check Mail Using POP3 section, click Add POP3 Email Account.

4. Enter the full email address of the account you want to access, and click Next Step.

5. Gmail fills in the username, POP server, and port fields when possible, based on the email address, as shown in Figure 1-6. Enter your password.

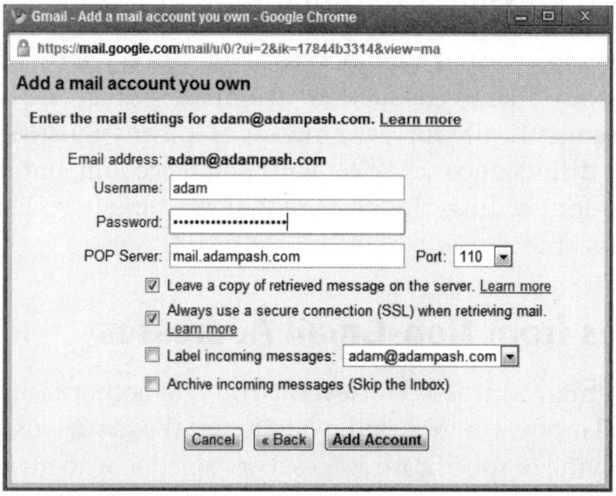

Figure 1-6: Retrieving email via POP for a non-Gmail address.

6. If Gmail is the single place you check mail, deselect the Leave a Copy of Retrieved Message on the Server box. If you want to access the other mail from other software (or if you're just using Gmail as a backup), do select this box. You can also set options to use a secure connection (SSL) to retrieve mail. (Some servers support this; others don't.) And you can choose whether to label or archive incoming messages.

7. After your options are set, click Add Account. Gmail issues an error if your username, password, or other settings are incorrect. When Gmail can fetch messages successfully, it gives you the option to set up a custom From: address. (See the section "Write Messages from Non-Gmail Addresses," later in this chapter, for more on that.)

After you set up Mail Fetcher, Google checks your other account(s) on a regular basis, and new mail appears automatically in your Gmail account.

NOTE Gmail checks for new messages at different rates, depending on previous mail-fetch attempts. You can't customize the default frequency of mail fetches, but Gmail checks accounts more frequently when they receive more email. If your old account's relatively inactive and Gmail's fetching too slowly, you can increase the frequency with which Gmail fetches email from that account by, for example, signing your old address up for an active mailing list or Google Group and then simply filtering those emails out of your new inbox.

Option 2: Forward Messages to Gmail Automatically

If your old address doesn't offer POP access — or you have more than five addresses that you'd like to consolidate in Gmail — you can set your former address to automatically forward messages to Gmail instead. The exact way to do this differs depending on your email account, but if your provider offers auto-forwarding, this feature will most likely be listed in your account options area.

Write Messages from Non-Gmail Addresses

Now that you have email addressed to several different accounts arriving in your single Gmail inbox, you may still want to use those various From: addresses when replying to specific messages. For someone who maintains several different online personas — but accesses them all in Gmail — the option to use various From: addresses when sending mail is crucial. Here's how to set up multiple From: addresses after you log into Gmail:

1. Click Settings along the top of any page, and then select the Accounts and Import tab.

2. Click Send Mail from Another Address in the Send Mail As section.

3. Enter your full name in the Name field, and enter the email address you'd like to send messages from in the Email Address field.

4. Choose to send your mail for this address through either Gmail's servers or through that account's SMTP servers. The former method is easiest and fine for most, but in some clients, such as versions of Microsoft Outlook, messages you send "from" your non-Gmail address will display as From: customaddress@domain.com on behalf of yourusername@gmail.com. To avoid this, you need to send through your other address' servers, which simply require you to supply the proper SMTP server and port along with your username and password.

5. Click Next Step ⇨ and then click Send Verification. Gmail sends a verification message to your other email address to confirm that you'd like to add it to your Gmail account. If you are already receiving this mail in Gmail, it appears in your inbox. Click the link in that message, or enter the confirmation code in the Accounts section of your Gmail account, to complete the process.

You can add several possible From: addresses to your Gmail account, as shown in Figure 1-7.

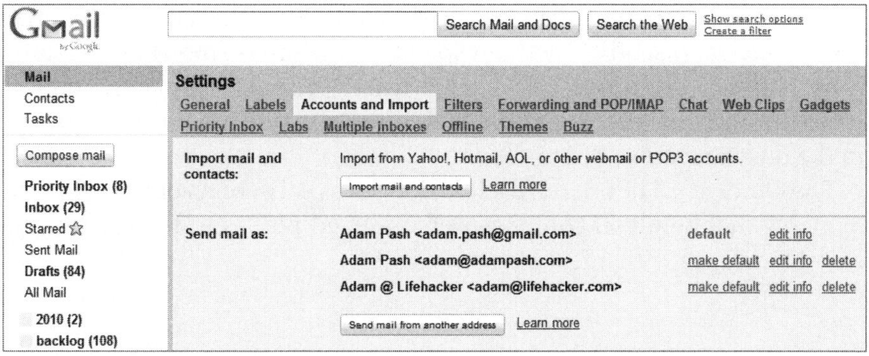

Figure 1-7: List several From: addresses for a given Gmail account.

Set one of your addresses as your default for receiving new messages. You can also set the From: name and a different reply-to address if you'd like (by clicking the Edit Info link).

After you verify that you want to add the address to your account, you can start sending messages using your custom From: address. When you click Compose, you can choose the From: address to use from the drop-down list, as shown in Figure 1-8.

Figure 1-8: Choose the desired From: address from the drop-down list.

Hack 9: Script and Automate Repetitive Replies

Level . . . . **Medium**

Platform . . . . **Windows, Mac OS X, Unix (Thunderbird)**

Cost . . . . **Free**

Is there an echo in your Sent email folder? Do you consistently receive messages that ask the same questions or require the same type of information in response? To knock down repetitive email quickly, build a set of scripted email responses that you can drop into emails quickly, personalize if necessary, and send off without spending the time composing the same information every time. With a set of trusty scripted templates, you can whip through tedious, recurring email like an expert air-traffic controller in the busy airport of your inbox.

The Quicktext Thunderbird extension saves collections of reusable text snippets that help you compose personalized replies to those tiresome email messages with a few keystrokes.

NOTE If Thunderbird isn't your preferred email client, you still have several automated-reply options. Die-hard Gmail users should check out the Canned Responses feature in Gmail Labs, which is similar to (but slightly less powerful than) Quicktext. Or for more on using text substitution to speed up all your repetitive typing, email-related or not, see Hacks 52 and 53, "Reduce Repetitive Typing with Texter for Windows" and "Reduce Repetitive Typing with TextExpander for Mac."

Make Quick Work of Common Replies

In contrast to other text saver utilities, Quicktext is specific to email because it recognizes variables that reference message details — such as the recipient's first or last name, the subject line, or attachment filenames. Quicktext replaces these variables with the right info for speedy yet personalized responses. Easily reply to Lucy Wood's message with a "Dear Ms. Wood" or to Robin Cullen's email with "Hi, Robin" using one keyword or click. No name-typing required.

Here's an example: You have a computer for sale and you post an ad on a message board or in the local newspaper. Within a day, you have an inbox full of messages inquiring about it. You can dash through those messages with Quicktext. Just follow these steps:

1. Download Quicktext from `http://extensions.hesslow.se/ quicktext`. Save the `.xpi` file to your computer.

2. From the Thunderbird Tools menu, choose Add-ons. Click the Install button and browse to the `.xpi` file you saved. Click Install Now. When installation is complete, restart Thunderbird.

3. Click the Write button to start a new email message, and then click Tools ⇨ Quicktext.

4. Click the Add Group button and enter a name for your group — say, **computer sale**.

5. Select your new group; then click Add Template. In the Title input, name this template **lowbid**, and in the text area below the title, enter your snippet (see Step 6). Also set the keyword to **lowbid**, as shown in Figure 1-9.

6. Set the text to the following:

```
Hi [[TO=firstname]],
Thanks for your interest in buying my computer. I've got several
other offers much higher than yours, but I'll let you know if
they fall through. Let me know if you're willing to bid higher.
```

Figure 1-9: Create the lowbid script in Quicktext.

7. Create any more Quicktexts that might apply to computer-inquiry responses. For example, create one called **more info** with the keyword **moreinfo** that reads as follows:

```
Hi [[TO=firstname]],
Thanks for your interest in buying my laptop. It has a 2.4GHz
Intel Core 2 Duo processor with 4GB of RAM and a 128GB hard
drive. Let me know if you need any more information.
```

8. After you set up your scripts, open a message about your for-sale computer. When you press the Reply button, you see a drop-down list of the Quicktext groups you set up. The computer sale and greetings Quicktexts are shown in Figure 1-10.

9. Insert the appropriate reply either by selecting it from the drop-down list or by typing the keyword — `lowbid`, in this example — and pressing the Tab key. Your response, complete with the recipient's first name, is automatically inserted into the message body.

Quicktext can also reference snippets within other snippets. For example, you could set up a group called **greetings** that contains two snippets:

■ **personal**, which is set to

```
Hi [[TO=firstname]],
```

■ **business**, which is set to

```
Dear [[To=firstname]] [[To=lastname]]:
```

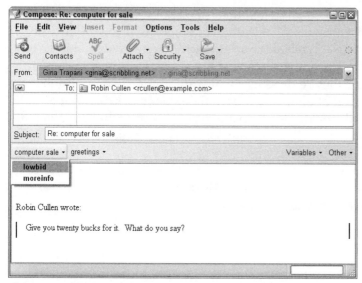

Figure 1-10: Composing a message using a Quicktext script.

Then, in other snippets, you can reference one greeting by using the
`[[TEXT=greetings|personal]]` variable. See the Quicktext homepage
(`http://extensions.hesslow.se/text/3/All+Tags/`) for the full list of
Quicktext variables.

Hack 10: Filter Low-Priority Messages

Level....... **Easy**

Platform.... **All**

Cost........ **Free**

You're head-down at work on that important presentation that's due in two
hours. Ding! An unopened envelope appears in your system tray.

"You have 1 unread message."

Maybe it's your co-worker with game-changing information about the
presentation. Maybe it's your boss asking to see you right away. You switch
and take a look at your inbox. Oh. Aunt Eunice forwarded you a picture
of a kitten in a tutu. Again.

Millions of email messages course over the Internet per second, and a
bunch of them land in your inbox. Your spam filter helps shuttle junk mail
out of sight, but what about messages from CC-happy co-workers, Aunt

Eunice's forwarded emails, Facebook friend notifications, Google Alerts, and mailing-list messages that clutter your inbox with low-priority noise? A group of web users coined the term "bacn" to refer to this "middle class of email" that's "better than spam but not as good as a personal email."[11] In other words, they're messages you want to read eventually, just not right now. Instead of giving your bacn the same priority as your actually important email, put a system in place that clears away the bacn automatically so that you can drill down quickly to what's important.

> **NOTE** Bacn (pronounced "bacon") is an Internet slang term cooked up by a group of web users at PodCamp Pittsburgh 2. It means email that you want to read, but not right away.

Filter Bacn

Set up rules — also called email filters — to make low-priority messages skip your inbox and file themselves away someplace less urgent. An email filter is a list of conditions you define that trigger an action on an incoming email message that matches your filter. Filter actions can be as simple as, "Delete any message from `annoying.person@example.com`" or much more complex, such as, "Any message that doesn't contain any one of my five email addresses in the To: field and does not have the word URGENT in the subject line should be moved to the `Not Important` folder."

The steps for creating a mail filter or rule vary depending on your email client. The following examples use the excellent, free, cross-platform email program Thunderbird, available at `http://mozilla.org/products/thunderbird`.

> **TIP** Apart from Thunderbird, Google's popular email client, Gmail, is particularly adept at filtering incoming messages. Click the Create a Filter link next to Gmail's search box, employ some of the advanced Gmail search tricks you learned in Hack 6, "Master Message Search," and apply the same filters discussed here to your Gmail inbox.

To configure your email filters in Thunderbird, choose Tools ➪ Message Filters and click the New button. Figure 1-11 displays a rule that files Aunt Eunice's forwarded messages and any messages from a mailing list to a folder called `Later`.

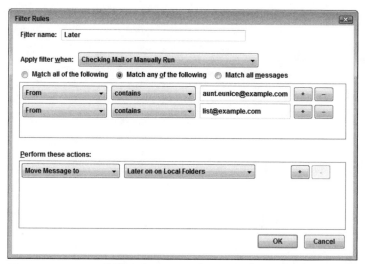

Figure 1-11: A mail filter that moves low-priority incoming messages to a folder called Later in Mozilla Thunderbird.

Filter CCed Messages

One of the most common misuses of email — especially in an office situation — is carbon copying anyone and everyone even tangentially related to the topic of a message. It's safe to assume that messages not directed to you (that is, your email address is not in the To: line) are less urgent and more informative; CCed messages most likely don't require a response or action on your part. On a day when you're firewalling your attention and care about only the most important disruptors, set up a rule that shuttles email you've been CCed on out of your inbox and into a separate folder for searching and browsing later.

To do so, first create a CC folder in your email program. Then set up a rule (filter) to say, "If my email address does not appear in the To: field, file this message" as shown in Figure 1-12.

> **NOTE** Hack 6, "Master Message Search," provides tips for digging up messages based on specific criteria.

When the filter is enabled, all new messages that arrive without your email address in the To: field are automatically filed in the CC folder.

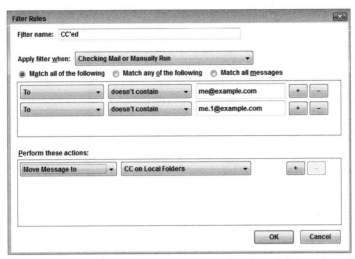

Figure 1-12: An email rule that moves messages not directed to either of two email addresses to a folder called CC.

Gmail's Priority Inbox

If setting up and managing filters for every piece of bacn that makes its way to your inbox sounds like more effort than it's worth, Gmail's Priority Inbox feature may be a better fit for your workflow. Priority Inbox analyzes your email behavior — like which messages you open and reply to — to automatically identify the email that's most important to you. It assigns those messages to your Priority Inbox, which, if Priority Inbox is doing its job, is a bacn-free zone.

To enable Priority Inbox, click the Settings link at the top of any Gmail view, click the Priority Inbox tab, select Show Priority Inbox, and then save your changes. Gmail reloads with Priority Inbox running, and you see a new Priority Inbox link right below your Inbox in Gmail's navigation sidebar. Click it.

By default, Priority Inbox separates your email into three panes, as pictured in Figure 1-13: Important and Unread, Starred, and Everything Else, each signifying just what it sounds like. Important and Unread contains those emails that Gmail believes are a priority to you and which you haven't yet read; Starred contains all messages that you've starred; and Everything Else contains — you guessed it! — everything else.

Figure 1-13: The default Priority Inbox view in Gmail.

TIP The default three inboxes Gmail displays when Priority Inbox is enabled may not be the right fit for you. You can adjust what inbox sections Gmail uses by navigating to Settings ➪ Priority Inbox and adjusting Priority Inbox Sections to better fit your needs.

If you don't feel like Gmail's getting it right — that is, if you see a few less-than-important messages labeled as important, or a few important messages that aren't tagged as important — you can manually add or remove priority to a message. Doing so can also help train Gmail to better identify what's important to you, so the more feedback you give it, the better Priority Inbox will get.

To mark a message as important, simply click the Mark as Important button (it's a yellow label with a plus sign, as shown to the right of the delete button in Figure 1-14) when you're viewing a message or when you've ticked the check box next to a message; to mark a message as unimportant, click the Mark as Not Important button instead.

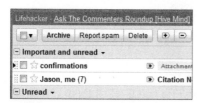

Figure 1-14: The marker with the plus sign indicates an important message.

SHORTCUT

Keyboard junkies, you can promote a message's importance from your keyboard by selecting a message and typing + or =. Mark a message as unimportant by typing -.

References

1. Michael Fitzgerald, "Call It the Dead E-Mail Office," *Wired* (www .wired.com/culture/lifestyle/news/2004/06/63733).

2. Mike Davidson, "A Lo-Fi Solution to Email Overload: Sentenc.es" (www.mikeindustries.com/blog/archive/2007/07/fight-email- overload-with-sentences).

3. "Companies limit email use to boost productivity," *Creston News Advertiser* (http://www.crestonnewsadvertiser.com/articles/ 2007/08/27/news/state_news/8-27ia-exchange-techlimit.txt).

4. Mark Hurst, *Bit Literacy* (Good Experience Press, 2007), 24.

5. Merlin Mann, "Fresh Start: The Email DMZ," *43 Folders* (http://www .43folders.com/2006/01/04/email-dmz/).

6. Michael Hyatt, "What's the Secret to Your Success?," Working Smart weblog (http://michaelhyatt.com/what%e2%80%99s-the-secret- to-your-success.html).

7. "Xobni Survey: 70% of Us Email Outside of Biz Hours; 50% of Americans Email on Vacation," *Xobni Blog*, September 2010 (http://blog.xobni .com/2010/09/02/xobni-survey-70-of-us-email-outside-of-biz- hours-50-of-americans-email-on-vacation/).

8. American Psychological Association (http://apa.org/monitor/ feb06/egos.html).

9. "Companies Read Employee E-Mail," *Wired* (http://wired.com/ news/wireservice/0,71071-0.html?tw=rss.index).

10. Itzy Sabo, "Small Change Makes Big Difference to Email Prioritization: How to Color-code Your Messages," Email Overloaded weblog (http://itzy.wordpress.com/2005/12/27/how-to-color-code- your-messages/).

11. Eric Weiner, "Move Over, Spam: 'Bacn' Is the E-Mail Dish Du Jour," NPR (www.npr.org/templates/story/story .php?storyId=14032271&ft=1&f=1006).

Organize Your Data

Never before have human beings been subjected to the daily onslaught of information as they are in the age of the Internet and email. Bits and pieces of data flow into your digital life constantly. Every day, website addresses, usernames and passwords, appointments, memos, songs, documents, digital images, and videos gather on your computer, vying for your attention and begging the question, "Where do I go?" Chapter 1, "Control Your Email," covered the best strategies for parrying the daily influx of electronic messages. This chapter tackles the best way to organize the data those messages and other information channels contain.

As with email overload, the only way to overcome information overload is to put everything in its place on arrival. But you're not a librarian, and you don't want to spend all your time arranging information in folders all over your hard drive. Although there are infinite ways to organize data into complex, multitiered systems, you're going to take the smart and lazy approach to organization: You'll arrange stuff only as much as is needed to make that data useful to you.

The better organized your personal information library is, the faster you can draw from it and act on it in the future. But better organized does not equal more folders; the fewer buckets your system has, the better.

Following are three key ways in which you need to interact with your data:

- Store it.
- Retrieve it.
- Do something wonderful with it.

When you design your data-organization system, concern yourself with storage and retrieval — that is, make those two actions as simple as possible. Next time you make a purchase online, you're not going to stop and try to remember whether you save receipts in the `shopping` folder, the `receipts` folder, or the `expenditures` folder. You will not ask yourself whether you should save your password in your web browser or add it to the `passwords.doc` file. (Although you might secretly wonder whether either place is secure enough anyway.)

The trick is to set up the most effective digital shelves to stow the different types of information you deal with every day. When you organize those spaces, keep the filing system simple. Create fewer destinations for quick entry. When it comes time for retrieval, you can use advanced search techniques to drill down to what you're looking for.

This chapter shows you how to create systems that make it easy to shuttle incoming bits and pieces into their right places for instant retrieval in the future. You can clear away the amorphous piles of stuff that spring up around you on your physical and digital desktops. Your parking places can have ample space to accommodate every type of item. Your personal "librarians" can fetch what you need when you need it with a quick keyword search. When you receive a new piece of information you may need later — such as a co-worker's change of address or a web page you may use in next month's report — where to place that new bit will be immediately obvious. Moving it into your system will be an automatic act that requires no thought or effort.

Although you may tweak the exact folder schemes and data labels outlined in this chapter for your own purposes, the principles are immutable. While you design your personal system for dealing with information, keep in mind the following:

- Every item has its place.
- Make those places big, general, and as few and simple to identify and remember as possible.
- Do *not* split up those places into complex, multiple subfolder trees that make you stop and think about what should go where or how to navigate to what you need.

- Every item is highly findable and instantly retrievable.

- Purge unneeded information regularly. Archive old items out of sight.

Information streams into your life all day long. You can master the art of immediate, thoughtless filing — the moment a new bit arrives at your digital doorstep. You can build a vast knowledge library each day *and* keep a clear workspace and mind in the process. You're most effective when your data is out of your face but still within reach. The psychological burden of information overload can never weigh you down if you're confident and facile at processing every incoming bit in a flash. This chapter shows you some of the best practices for doing just enough organizing to keep your information accessible without wasting your time.

Whether it's a computer desktop or a physical tabletop, clutter represents procrastination, distraction, and unprocessed information. Let's clear it away.

Hack 11: Organize Your Documents Folder

Level....... **Easy**

Platforms ... **All**

Cost........ **Free**

Every operating system comes with a default location to save user documents. If you've had a computer for any length of time, you know that your computer's My Documents folder can get disorganized quickly. If you frequently find yourself letting files clutter your computer's desktop, or if you spend time rearranging files in a bunch of unmanageable subfolders, it's time for a revamp. You can create a simple set of folders to accommodate every type of file in an accessible way that keeps the files you need to work with right at your fingertips.

The Big Six

Over the years, I've developed a six-folder structure for Documents that I create on every computer I use without fail. This scheme accommodates every file you will accumulate, clears the desktop, smoothly fits in with an automated backup system (see Hack 60, "Set Up an Automated, Bulletproof File Back-Up Solution"), and makes command-line file wrangling a breeze.

In alphabetical order, the six main folders are called bak, docs, docs-archive, junkdrawer, media, and scripts, as shown in Figure 2-1.

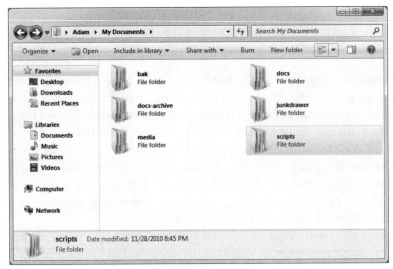

Figure 2-1: The six core folders of a My Documents organization system.

Here's a quick rundown of what each does and what it might contain:

- bak — Short for backup, this is your backup destination of first resort. Your actual data backups should reside on external disks, but bak is where you store, for example, a backup of your main web browser profile, your address book exported to CSV, or a dump of your website's database.

NOTE If you spend a lot of time at the command line, you might prefer the short name bak, but there's no reason you can't name your folder backup — or any name you prefer.

- docs — docs is the Big Kahuna of all six folders. It's the place where all the working files for your current tasks, projects, and clients go. Its contents change frequently, and the folder should be purged often.
  - You can keep subfolders in docs — finance, clients, or creative-writing, for example. The clients folder might have subfolders, too, such as acme and book-in-progress. That gets you three sub-folders into the hierarchy however, and that's as deep as you can go before your file tree gets in the way of your work.
  - docs-archive — Purge your docs folder of closed working files — those for completed projects, former employers, or past tax years, for example — every few weeks. These go into your docs-archive

folder. The archive exists for reference and search, but the separate folder keeps all that extra stuff from cluttering up docs, which is your working task dashboard. The files in docs-archive don't change much, if ever, so you can back them up on a different (less frequent) schedule.

■ junkdrawer — The junkdrawer (or temp or tmp) is a temporary holding pen for files you're working with this moment but don't need to save long term. Your web browser and email program should both save downloaded files and attachments to junkdrawer by default. If you're checking out a video, just testing a script, or need a place to store a software's setup.exe program, place those files into junkdrawer. The junkdrawer files you want to keep should graduate into docs; otherwise, the automated hard-drive janitor (see Hack 62/63, "Automatically Clean Up Your PC/Mac") comes sweeping through and deletes anything older than a couple of weeks from junkdrawer while you sleep.

■ media — Here's where your music, video, and photos folders go. The benefit of having all those space-hogging files under one umbrella parent folder is backup. Chances are, your multimedia backup plan is different than your documents backup because of the sheer amount of disk space required. Drop them all in the media folder, and you can easily exclude them from your backup scheme. Keep in mind that sharing your media with a home web server (see Hack 71, "Run a Home Web Server") works nicely with an all-encompassing media folder, too.

■ scripts — Any executable script or shortcut lives in scripts. This is the place for any batch scripts you use regularly.

Move Your Home Directory to Another Drive

Anyone who's upgraded their computer knows what a pain migrating your existing data to a new machine can be. You may want to move (or redirect) your home directory to a standalone drive to make your data more portable. It's also a particularly handy trick if you dual-boot different operating systems on one machine.

Redirect the Home Directory in Windows 7

The default Windows 7 home directory is located at C:\Users\username\.

Windows 7 makes it easy to completely move — or *redirect* — any folder on your computer. Here's how to redirect your `Documents` folder to a new drive:

1. Open the Start menu and click your username.

2. Right click My Documents; then from the Windows context menu, select Properties.

3. In the My Documents Properties dialog, click the tab labeled Location; then click the Move button.

4. Select the drive or folder you want to move and redirect My Documents to; then click the Select Folder button. Click OK.

5. Windows prompts you to move all the files from the old location to the new location. Click Yes to confirm the move and you're all set.

When redirected, the folder still appears in its original location — for example, C:\Users\username\Documents — but the files are actually stored on your separate drive.

Redirect the Home Directory in Mac OS X

On Macs, the home directory is located at `/Users/username/`.
Moving your home folder to another drive is simple:

1. Open your System Preferences; then click on Accounts.

2. Click the lock on the bottom left of the Accounts window; then enter your password to make changes to your User account.

3. Right-click (or Control-click) the account whose home folder you want to relocate; then click Advanced Options.

4. Click the Choose button next to the Home directory field; then navigate to and select the drive or folder you want to move your Home directory to. Click Open and then OK.

Beyond the Big Six

These may not be the only folders that live in your home directory. For example, a programmer may keep a `code` or `dev` directory as well. Just make sure that any additions don't actually belong within one of the core six. Remember, with simplicity comes effortlessness; the more folders you have, the more easily things get scattered and disorganized — so add to your system sparingly.

Hack 12: Instantly Retrieve Files Stored on Your Computer

Level . . . . **Medium**

Platform . . . . **Windows, Mac OS X**

Cost . . . . **Free**

You can manage documents on your computer in two ways: As an old-fashioned "filer," you can create dozens of folders to organize your data in a complicated structure; or as a new-fangled digital "piler," you can dump data into a single or small set of folders. In your transition from filer to piler, the most important skill you must develop and learn to trust is *search*.

Modern operating systems still use paper as the paradigm for understanding digital documents. Manila folder icons, for example, represent digital folders in all operating systems. Although the metaphor works well enough for new computer users, power users understand that in reality, those so-called folders are just pointers to data on a disk that never actually change location. Digital documents have special characteristics that their paper ancestors do not: your operating system indexes them automatically, making them findable without requiring a human to store them in a big filing cabinet with carefully labeled folders.

When you transition from a paper-based world into a digital document scenario, filing digital documents the way you would paper is natural. But your data is already indexed and searchable without the work of dragging and dropping it into these illusory folders, so it's time to move to the next level: to use and trust that the right search will retrieve the data you need.

Every major operating system offers some sort of file-search feature. Windows 7's and Vista's search feature is significantly improved over Windows XP's, with a built-in search box in every Explorer window and the Start menu. Mac OS X offers Spotlight search, and on the Linux desktop, tools such as Beagle provide users with a single search box to comb through their file system.

Searching Your Windows Computer

With Windows Search, a quick search of your Windows PC is never more than a keystroke away. No matter what you're doing on your computer, pressing the Windows key opens the Start menu with the search field focused and ready to scour your hard drive. Alternatively, the Windows + F keyboard shortcut opens a new Explorer window ready to search.

NOTE If you have an older machine running Windows XP, you can download Windows Search at `www.microsoft.com/downloads/en/details.aspx?FamilyId=55C18CB3-C916-4298-ABA3-5B98904F7CDA`.

Files That Windows Search Indexes

The Windows Search index includes the following:

- Files on your computer, including text, Word, Excel, PowerPoint, PDF, MP3, the contents of ZIP files, and image, audio, and video files
- Email from Outlook, Outlook Express, and Thunderbird
- Media files' metadata; for example, MP3 song files by artist name and title, not just the filename
- Web pages you've viewed using Internet Explorer
- Instant messenger logs

If you want to change the file types and folders that Windows Search indexes, open the Start menu, type `Indexing Options`, and hit Enter to open the Windows Search Indexing Options. (You can also navigate to this through the Control Panel).

From the Indexing Options dialog, you can add or exclude indexed folders by clicking the Modify button. Tick the check box next to folders you'd like to index, or if Windows Search is commonly returning results you don't want, untick the check box next to folders containing those items.

To modify the file types indexed by Windows Search, click the Advanced button to open the Advanced Options dialog; then click the File Types tab. You cannot only add or remove indexed file types, but you can also set whether you want the index to include the contents of that file type or only its properties.

Refine Windows Search

When you start typing into the Windows Search box, your computer searches for indexed items based solely on whether the text you've entered matches text in the document, as shown in Figure 2-2. You can employ advanced search operators to narrow down your results by all sorts of criteria, just like you can on the web (see Hack 90, "Google Like a Pro").

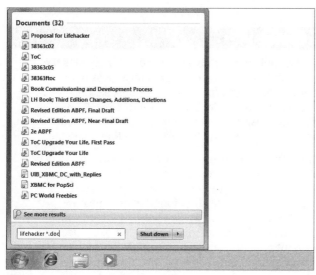

Figure 2-2: Windows Search in action.

Advanced search operators currently include those shown in the following table.

OPERATOR	DESCRIPTION
"..."	Enclose all or part of your query in quotation marks, and your search returns only items that contain that *exact* quoted phrase. For example, the query `"Copyright 2007"` would not return an item containing the phrasing "In 2007, I filed for copyright" because it is not an exact match.
OR	Used to find matches of either word or both. (Note: The word OR must be in all uppercase letters) For example, searching `microsoft OR windows` returns items containing *microsoft*, *windows*, or both.
–	Used directly in front of a word, this symbol causes searches to not return items containing that word. For example, results for the search `bats -baseball` would include all items in the Desktop cache that contain the word *bats*, except for the items that also contain the word *baseball*.
*:	The asterisk wildcard is a placeholder for any text, but in Windows Search, it's mostly handy for narrowing down files based on their extension. For example, a search for `tax *.xls` results in Excel files with the word *tax* in them.

(continued)

(continued)

OPERATOR	DESCRIPTION
`kind:`	Not to be confused with type, this operator restricts the category of files your search returns regardless of its extension. Arguments include `programs`, `docs`, `music`, `email`, and `video`. For example, a search for `dylan kind:music` returns any music files on the computer with the word *dylan* in them, whether it's an MP3, WMA, or other audio file.
`folder:`	Restricts the folder from which your file search results can come. For example, results for the search `basketball folder:C:\Users\username\Documents` include only files found in or beneath the `C:\Users\username\ Documents` folder. You can also search by partial folder paths; for example, if you want to restrict a search to your Movies folder, you could simply type search `folder:movies`.

Email searches can be restricted to matches within email message headers. The available search operators are `Subject:`, `To:`, `From:`, and `CC:`. You can combine any of these operators in a single query; you also can include either or both of the `""` and `-` operators.

See the full list of Windows Search's advanced search operators and the details of how to use them at `www.microsoft.com/windows/products/winfamily/desktopsearch/technicalresources/advquery.mspx`.

Searching Your Mac Computer

In Mac OS X, you can use the built-in Spotlight to search your hard drive from either the menu bar or from within Finder, and both searches are just a keystroke away. You can search with Spotlight from the menu bar at any time by clicking the magnifying glass in the right corner of your desktop or, more quickly, by pressing Command + Space. If Finder's open, just press Command + F to open a new search inside Finder, or open Finder directly to a search from anywhere by pressing Command + Option + Space.

Files That Spotlight Indexes

Spotlight's index includes the following:

- Files on your computer, including text, Word, Excel, PowerPoint, PDF, MP3, the contents of ZIP files, image, audio, and video files
- Email from Mail.app

- Your System Preferences
- Media files' metadata; for example, MP3 song files by artist name and title, not just the filename
- Web pages you've viewed using Safari

For a look at all the file categories Spotlight indexes, open your System Preferences and launch the Spotlight preference pane. From the Search Results tab, you can select or deselect categories Spotlight indexes. (For example, if you have a big music library and you'd prefer to keep those searches inside iTunes, you would untick the Music category.)

You can also adjust the priority Spotlight gives to different categories by dragging and dropping the categories into the order you'd prefer. If you use Spotlight primarily to search for contacts, for example, you might want to move your Contacts to the top of the list. Or if you use it primarily as an application launcher, you'd want Applications at the top.

If you have a folder or folders on your hard drive you'd prefer Spotlight not to index, click the Privacy tab; then click the + button to add folders to the exclude list.

Refine Spotlight Search

As you type your search, Spotlight returns results matching your query based on a number of factors. This is convenient when your search term is relatively unique, but if your search returns too many needles in your file systems haystack, you can use more advanced search operators to narrow down your results, just like you may be familiar with from searching the web (see Hack 90, "Google Like a Pro").

Spotlight's advanced search operators currently include those shown in the following table.

OPERATOR	DESCRIPTION
"..."	Enclose all or part of your query in quotation marks, and your search returns only items that contain that *exact* quoted phrase. For example, the query `"Copyright 2007"` would not return an item containing the phrasing "In 2007, I filed for copyright" because it is not an exact match.
-	Used directly in front of a word, this symbol causes searches to not return items containing that word. For example, results for the search `bats -baseball` would include all items in the Desktop cache that contain the word *bats*, except for the items that also contain the word *baseball*.

(continued)

(continued)

OPERATOR	DESCRIPTION
`name:`	By default Spotlight searches for results based on the name of files *and* their contents. The `name` operator restricts your search to the names of files on your system, ignoring the contents. This operator is also useful as a shortcut for limiting results by file type. For example, a search for `tax type:.xls` results only in filenames containing .xls whose contents include the word *tax*.
`kind:`	This operator restricts the category of files your search returns regardless of its extension. Arguments include `applications`, `documents`, `music`, `email`, and `movies`. For example, a search for `beatles kind:music` returns any music files on a computer with the word *beatles* in them, whether it's an MP3, AAC, or other audio file.

Email searches can be restricted to matches within email message headers. The available search operators are `Subject:`, `To:`, and `From:`. You can combine any of these operators in a single query; you also can include either or both of the `" "` and `-` operators.

Spotlight offers several more search operators not listed here, many of which are easier to use from the Finder Spotlight search rather than the menu bar search. If you want to create laser-specific Spotlight searches, searching from Finder is a better bet. You can limit your searches to specific folders and build iTunes Smart-Playlist-like search queries.

Hack 13: Overhaul Your Filing Cabinet

Level . . . . **Easy**

Platform . . . . **All**

Cost. . . . . **Free**

One of the main clutter culprits in most offices is the To File pile. Often, this heap spontaneously appears right on top of or next to the filing cabinet, which is silly. Instead of adding stuff to the pile, why wouldn't you just file it? The reason is generally an unworkable, messy, overflowing file cabinet.

This hack explains how to revamp your overstuffed, under-labeled file system and turn it into a neat, breezy, and pleasurable place to organize your important paperwork.

Give Your Paperwork a Spacious Place to Live

Face it: That plastic file box or enormous binder held shut with a rubber band just isn't going to cut it. You have personal, financial, insurance, car, client, tax, and medical paperwork to track.

If you've been using an undersized filing cabinet that can't possibly accommodate your stuff — or have no filing cabinet at all — invest in a spacious, well-designed file drawer or cabinet that leaves you room to spare. Lots of room. In fact, *Getting Things Done* author David Allen says that your file drawer should be only three-quarters full: "If you want to get rid of your unconscious resistance to filing, then you must keep the drawers loose enough that you can insert and retrieve files without effort."[1]

If you're out to buy a new filing cabinet, he also advises you not to skimp on quality.

"Nothing is worse than trying to open a heavy file drawer and hearing that awful *screech!* that happens when you wrestle with the roller bearings on one of those $29.95 special-sale cabinets. You really need a file cabinet whose drawer, even when it's three-quarters full, will glide open and click shut with the smoothness and solidity of a door on a German car."

It's true. A tool that's easy and fun to use is a tool you *will* use.

Limit One File Folder per Hanging Folder

As soon as things start to get crowded inside filing-cabinet land, your first instinct is to start putting several manila folders into one hanging folder. Bad idea. Allocate one single manila folder to one single hanging folder. This cleanly separates your folders and makes them easy to ruffle through. (Using hanging folders at all is a matter of preference.)

Keep a supply of both manila folders and hanging folders within reach so that creating a new one is as easy as possible.

Choose a Simple, Logical Naming Scheme

You may be a plain A-to-Z–type person, but there are more ways than one to alphabetize file folders. One great method divides things into categories, such as Car, Client, Taxes, Bank Account; then you preface a folder name with that word. For example, one folder might be Car: Honda Accord and another is Client: Acme, and another Bank Account: ING Direct.

Whatever method you choose, make sure it is obvious and consistent throughout your files to make retrieving paperwork as simple and thoughtless as feasible.

Use a Label Maker

You may be tempted to save money and space and skip getting a label maker. That's understandable. But don't underestimate the value this inexpensive, small tool provides. Neatly labeled folders make a file drawer look sharp, accessible, organized, and professional. Making a new label is a lot more fun and satisfying than scribbling onto a tab with a pen and running out of room, or having to cross something out (or white it out!) and start all over. Printed labels also make your folders legible, and presentable at meetings with clients and co-workers.

The Brother P-Touch Home and Hobby Label Maker (www.amazon.com/ Brother-PT-65-P-touch-Labeler-Screen/dp/B00004VVIX), for example, gets the job done, and it'll set you back about 40 bucks.

Purge and Archive

Over time, it's easy for your filing drawer to get out of control and filled with stuff that doesn't matter anymore or that you simply don't need on hand at all times. In reality, 80 percent of filed paperwork is never referenced again.[2] Purge your paperwork every few months — get rid of the irrelevant stuff, such as user guides you can get on the Web or for gadgets you no longer own, past project research, and former-employer paperwork.

Archive old stuff you don't want to trash but don't need immediate access to by packing it into cardboard file boxes and putting it in storage. Closed bank-account records, old credit reports, and your 1996 taxes are good candidates here.

Hack 14: Instantly Recall Any Number of Different Passwords

Level . . . . **Easy**

Platform . . . . **All**

Cost. . . . . **Free**

Any computer-system administrator will tell you that the easiest and most secure place to store passwords is in your head. However, remembering the dozens of passwords you need to access networks, websites, and computers at work and at home seems like an impossible task — unless you've got the right system.

A good password is easy for you to remember and hard for others to guess. Easy enough for one password, but everywhere you turn you have to come up with another to register for a website or wireless network or to set a PIN. How do you choose new passwords? More important, how do you remember them?

Don't Use the Same Password for Everything

You wouldn't use the same key for your car, home, office, garage, and safety deposit box, so you shouldn't use the same password for all your virtual locks, either. The problem with using the same password for everything you do is that if it's compromised and someone finds it, the rest of your identity is at risk.

If your mutual fund company, for example, has a security breach that exposes usernames and passwords, and you use the same login details there as for your online banking and at Amazon.com, the thieves could compromise not only your mutual fund account but also your bank account and the credit card details stored at Amazon.com. If you give your roommate your wireless-network password and it's the same as your email password, it wouldn't be difficult for your roomie to snoop into your private messages.

The trick is to keep a unique password for each service you use.

Remember 100 Different Passwords with One Rule Set

Remembering a unique password for the dozens of logins you have may sound impossible, but it's not. You don't need to remember 100 passwords if you have one rule set for generating them.

Here's how it works: Create unique passwords by choosing a base password and then applying a single rule that mashes in some form of the service name with it. For example, you could use your base password plus the first three letters of a service name. If your base password were asdf (see how easy that is to type?), for example, then your password for Yahoo! would be ASDFYAH, and your password for eBay would be ASDFEBA.

Another example that incorporates numbers (which some services require in passwords) might involve the same letters to start (say, your initials and a favorite number) plus the first two vowels of a service name. In that case, my password for Amazon would be GMLT10AA and for Lifehacker .com GMLT10IE. (Include obscure middle initials — such as your mother's maiden name or a childhood nickname — that not many people know about for extra security.)

Before you decide on your single password-generation rule, remember that although password requirements differ for each service, a good guideline is a password that's at least eight characters long and includes both letters and numbers. To make a password even more secure — or applicable for services that require special characters — add them around or inside it, such as #GMLT10LIF# or GMLT10#LIF.

One problem with rules-based passwords is that some sites have their own rules that conflict with your own, such as no special characters. In those cases, you have to document or remember the exception to your rule for those services. The next hack explains how you can keep track of passwords that don't follow a single rule.

> **NOTE** A clever password-generator bookmarklet, available at `http://angel.net/~nic/passwd.html`, generates a random password based on a website URL.

CHOOSING YOUR BASE PASSWORD

Following are some options for choosing your base password:Use the first letter of a phrase or song refrain. For example, if you wanted to use the Jackson 5's "I Want You Back," your base password might be IWUB. Remembering the password is a matter of singing the song to yourself.

- Use a pre-established keyboard pattern, such as yui or zxcv. Just look at your keyboard to remember it.

- Use your spouse's initials and your anniversary, such as TFB0602. (This one guarantees that you won't forget an anniversary card, either.)

For extra security, choose an easy-to-remember base, such as your spouse's initials or the word *cat*, and then shift your fingers up one row on the keyboard when you type it. In the case of cat, you get dq5.

Then combine this base with some extra information unique to the service.

Hack 15: Securely Track Your Passwords

Level. . . . . . . **Advanced**

Platform. . . . **All**

Cost. . . . . **Free**

Hack 14 covers how to choose memorable passwords, but what about the passwords you already have? Or passwords that were assigned to you that you can't change? Or passwords for systems with special requirements that your usual password scheme doesn't work for?

Sometimes you just *have* to write down a password to remember it. Don't do it where others can read it, such as on a Post-It note or in an easy-to-read text file or Word document. You can keep a secure and searchable database of those hard-to-remember passwords using the free password management tool LastPass (`http://lastpass.com/`).

One Master Password to Rule All

A LastPass database stores all your passwords in an encrypted state and uses one master password to access that database. LastPass has fields for username, password, URL, and notes associated with each login, and you can create login groups — such as Windows, websites, or Wi-Fi networks — to organize your passwords. LastPass is available in many forms, from web browser extensions to standalone desktop apps; the browser extensions are primarily referred to next because that's where most of your tedious password management takes place.

The web-based LastPass service supports every popular browser and operating system. Best of all, it automatically syncs your passwords between browsers so that you can add your various login credentials once but access them from anywhere you set up LastPass.

LASTPASS SECURITY

If your first instinct is to shudder at the thought of your passwords living on a third-party's servers, I don't blame you. However, LastPass' technology does all the encrypting and decrypting of passwords on your computer, meaning that no one — not even the people working at LastPass — can ever access your passwords. You can read more about LastPass' security and technology at `https://lastpass.com/whylastpass_technology.php`

LastPass is secure and customizable; if you keep it running, it can lock your password database after a certain amount of idle time, requiring you to enter the master password again to access your passwords.

Here's how to set up and store passwords on LastPass:

1. Download LastPass from `https://lastpass.com/misc_download.php` and install. (The LastPass website automatically recommends the version you want to download based on your browser and operating system.)

2. Create a LastPass account by entering your email address and a master password, as shown in Figure 2-3. (Most browsers prompt you to log in or create an account after installation.) Your master password will be the key to all your other passwords, so be sure to choose something secure but memorable. (Hack 14, "Instantly Recall Any Number of Different Passwords" can help here.)

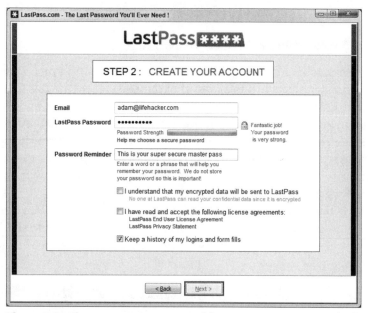

Figure 2-3: Choose a secure password for your master password — it may be the last one you'll need.

3. After you create your account, LastPass checks your browser for saved passwords and form data and offers to import them to your LastPass database. Choose which site information you want LastPass to import.

4. When you complete your initial LastPass setup, you're ready to add passwords to your database. You can manually add items to LastPass by clicking on the LastPass button in your browser and selecting Sites ➪ Add Site, but the easiest way to start is just to use your browser as you normally would. LastPass can detect when you submit login credentials to a website and prompt you to save those credentials to your LastPass database — as shown in Figure 2-4.

5. While you are browsing, if you want LastPass to remember a site, click the Save Site button. From the Save Site dialog, you can option- ally add the site to a group, change the name of the credentials, set

LastPass to automatically fill out your username and password and login when you visit this site, turn off AutoFill, or always require your master password before filling out the credentials. LastPass also displays how secure your password is with an as-you-type quality meter, just below the Password field, shown in Figure 2-5. If you like, it can also automatically generate secure passwords for you.

6. Click Save and your login is entered into the LastPass database. Repeat the process for every login you want to track with LastPass.

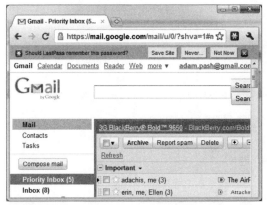

Figure 2-4: LastPass prompts you to save credentials any time you log into a new site.

Figure 2-5: Adding a new password entry into your LastPass vault.

Find and Use Your Passwords with LastPass

Because LastPass is integrated with your browser, it's incredibly smart about filling in your passwords for you whenever you visit a website you saved in your LastPass database. All you need to do is log into LastPass using your email address and master password. After you do that, it can fill in your username and password at any saved site securely and automatically, indicated by the LastPass icons in text inputs, as shown in Figure 2-6. It's a huge timesaver, and all you ever have to remember is the master password.

Figure 2-6: LastPass can fill in passwords and even automatically log you into websites.

Keep in mind, however, that although the capabilities of LastPass this chapter focuses on are browser-based, you're not limited exclusively to saving login information for websites. For example, you can set up a Wi-Fi Networks password group that lists your logins at all the networks you use, including school, home, friends' houses, and coffee shops.

When you're at your friend Mark's house, you can then either browse to the `Wi-Fi Networks` group or simply enter **Mark** in your LastPass Vault's search box to retrieve the `Mark's house` entry. Right-click the entry, select Copy Password, and then drop it into Mark's Wi-Fi login prompt.

You could encrypt a text file with your passwords saved in it, but a text file or Word document doesn't provide the structured password detail entry that a LastPass database does. Because LastPass is a searchable encrypted database, you can use it to store other types of important information, such as software serial numbers, credit card numbers, and PINs. (But remember: although LastPass is very secure, the most secure place on the planet to keep an important piece of information is in your head.)

Hack 16: Tag Your Bookmarks

Level . . . . **Medium**
Platform . . . . **Web**
Cost . . . . **Free**

The Web gets bigger every day, and so does your bookmark list. A social bookmarking service called Delicious (www.delicious.com) stores your bookmarks online and associates keywords (called *tags*) to each bookmark for easy retrieval. Storing your bookmarks online also makes them accessible from every computer you use.

The bare-bones interface of the Delicious service hides the feature-rich, highly hackable nature of this web application. Owned by Yahoo!, Delicious is a fantastic option for any web researcher or power bookmarker who wants to quickly access and organize web content that matters to him. This hack covers just some of the ways to use Delicious to manage your bookmarks, create a personal index of web content, and tap into the community to find even more useful resources on the Web.

Getting Started with Delicious

Register for a free account at www.delicious.com. When you're signed in, your Delicious bookmarks will be available at www.delicious.com/username. A social bookmarking service means, by default, that all your bookmarks are public and viewable by other members of the Delicious community. If you like, you can set bookmarks as private on a case-by-case basis.

Add a Bookmark

The basic way to add a bookmark to Delicious is to use the save link at www.delicious.com/save. But that's also the least efficient way. For faster bookmarking, go to the Delicious browser buttons area at www.delicious.com/help/tools to install a Delicious extension for your browser of choice or drag and drop a Bookmark on Delicious bookmarklet to your browser toolbar. Then, when you browse to a page you want to save, just click the button to add your bookmark.

Tags, Not Folders

Most web browsers organize your bookmarks in folders and subfolders. Arguably the best feature of Delicious is the use of *tags*: labels or keywords that let you view your bookmark list based on single or combined keywords.

For example, to bookmark a web page that describes a foolproof technique for slicing a ripe mango, add it to your Delicious bookmarks and tag it mango, howto, kitchen, fruit, cooking, and summer. One bookmark can have as many tags as you'd like.

If you also bookmarked a page with a great smoothie recipe and you tagged it smoothie, fruit, and recipe, the mango page and the smoothie page would both appear under the fruit tag listing. However, only the mango page would appear under the howto tag. A list of both fruit and summer tags would include only the mango page as well, because the smoothie page was not tagged summer.

To enter a set of tags for a bookmark in Delicious, you simply type a list of words separated by spaces. So, you'd enter **smoothie fruit summer** in the tags field for the smoothie page bookmark. The freeform nature of the tags field makes creating and assigning new tags extremely easy, but it also leaves the door wide open for misspellings and similar tags (such as fruit and fruits). After using Delicious for some time, you'll develop a vocabulary of tags you use often, and Delicious will make suggestions from your tag as you type.

In Figure 2-7, I'm bookmarking a page called Silva Rhetoricae. I've included a description for the bookmark: An exhaustive directory of rhetorical devices from a BYU professor.

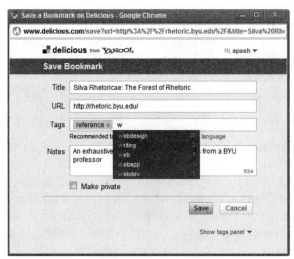

Figure 2-7: Adding tags to a bookmark in Delicious.

As I type the letter w into the tags field, Delicious uses my preestablished tag vocabulary to suggest tags that could match (such as webdesign, writing, web, webapp, and webdev). In this case, I chose writing.

Navigating Delicious by URL

Getting around Delicious is easiest if you use its hackable URL scheme to get what you want. All you need to do is add what you're looking for to the end of the Delicious URL. For example, here's the base URL:

```
http://www.delicious.com/
```

To find bookmarks tagged mango by all delicious users, you simply add tag and mango, like this:

```
http://www.delicious.com/tag/mango
```

To find bookmarks tagged writing by the user ginatrapani, add the username and then the tag:

```
http://www.delicious.com/ginatrapani/writing
```

(Replace ginatrapani/writing with your own username and your tag(s) to quickly find your bookmarks.)

To find bookmarks tagged tech and howto by all Delicious users, combine the tags with + signs:

```
http://www.delicious.com/tag/tech+howto
```

How about bookmarks tagged tutorial, router, and linksys by all Delicious users?

```
http://www.delicious.com/tag/tutorial+router+linksys
```

Find all bookmarked sound files:

```
http://www.delicious.com/tag/system:media:audio
```

Find all bookmarked video files:

```
http://www.delicious.com/tag/system:media:video
```

Find MP3 files tagged mashup:

```
http://www.delicious.com/tag/system:filetype:mp3+mashup
```

Other Delicious Features

You can import your current browser bookmarks into Delicious using its import feature, located at https://secure.delicious.com/settings/

`bookmarks/import`. You can also export your Delicious links at `https://secure.delicious.com/settings/bookmarks/export`.

To keep your Delicious links in sync with your web browser, use the official Delicious extension for your browser of choice, freely available at `www.delicious.com/help/tools`.

Hack 17: Organize Your Digital Photos

Level . . . . **Easy**

Platform . . . . **Windows, Mac OS X**

Cost . . . . **Free**

The ubiquity of digital cameras, camera phones, and cheap storage means that even the most amateur photographers can accumulate hundreds — even thousands — of digital photos on their computers over time. After even just a few months of taking photos, it's easy to wind up with a hard drive cluttered with a bunch of folders filled with images named things like `IMG_8394.jpg`. Pictures don't mean anything unless someone sees them, and no one will see the photos buried on your computer if you can't find what you're looking for.

The problem with digital photos is that your computer doesn't have much information about them. To your computer, a digital picture is just a collection of different-colored dots. Some information is stored inside a photo when it's snapped, such as what your camera settings were and the date and time, but the photo doesn't tell your computer who's in the picture or at what event it was taken. To make your photos searchable (and therefore useful), you have to add metadata such as captions, labels, and ratings to them. Google's free photo organizer for Windows, Mac, and Linux, Picasa (`http://picasa.com`), can help you organize, edit, caption, label, star, and even automatically recognize faces in your digital photos.

Import Your Photos into Picasa

Download Picasa from `http://picasa.com` (free) and install it on your PC. The first time you launch the program, it asks whether it should scan your entire computer, or just specific folders, for photos. Make your choice and Picasa builds its index of all the photos and videos on your computer automatically. When it's complete, you see a list of folders organized by year in the left panel, and you see a grid of images on the right side, as shown in Figure 2-8.

Figure 2-8: Viewing photos in Picasa.

Now you're ready to start organizing and adding meaning to your photos.

Organize and Label Your Collection

Picasa is smart enough that it can actually recognize faces in your digital photos automatically, and with a little help from you, building collections of photos based on who's in them is easy. Combine the People recognition feature with Picasa's Places, Tags, Captions, Albums, and Stars, and you can quickly whip your unorganized jumble of photos into shape.

People

After you imported images from your PC, Picasa scans the photos and identifies those with people in them. The quickest way to start tagging people is to click Unnamed (under People) in the left sidebar, as shown in Figure 2-9. Picasa presents you with faces it has identified in your images and asks you to provide their names.

Figure 2-9: Picasa's People panel helps you identify pictures based on who's in them.

As you do, Picasa learns your friends' faces and automatically suggests matches in future photos. If you also use Gmail, you can log into your Google account with Picasa, and it will match the faces with your contacts, providing as-you-type autocomplete suggestions while you're tagging People. Whenever you tag a new person, Picasa creates an album of photos of that person.

Places

Sometimes you want to know where a photo was taken just as much as you want to know who was in it. To add location to your photos, select the image or images you want to geo-tag; then click the Show/Hide Places Panel button in the bottom right. Search for the location you want to add to the photo, or click the green push pin and drop it on the map to add a Place to the photo.

If your photos were taken using a newer smart phone, there's a good chance that the place it was taken — called geo-location — is already embedded in the file's metadata. If it is, Picasa will recognize this and automatically show its location on the map without you adding anything.

Captions

Double-click an individual photo to focus on it in Picasa. Then click the text labeled Make a Caption! Type in a descriptive phrase using words you'd search for later, such as **Joey in a tuxedo at Mom's wedding**.

Use as many keywords as you think you'll ever use to search for the photo in the future. Avoid nicknames, abbreviations, or otherwise opaque captions — they won't help you later! After you set your caption as previously suggested, a search for *wedding*, *Mom*, *Joey*, or *tuxedo* will turn up that picture.

NOTE The best part of Picasa's caption system is that it actually saves the text *inside* the photo. So if you publish the photo online or decide to stop using Picasa, you don't lose your photo's caption.

Albums

When adding an individual caption to every photo is too monstrous an undertaking, use albums instead. Albums are collections of photos that don't necessarily all exist in the same folder. You can even have one photo live in several albums, which you can't do with folders.

Name your albums something descriptive (such as "Mom's Wedding") and Ctrl+click to select several photos and place them in Picasa's "tray" on the bottom-left side. Then click the Add selected items to an Album button to place those photos into an album.

Stars

After a frenetic photography session or event, one or two special photos often stand out from the rest. Use stars to mark your favorite photos in Picasa. To star (or un-star) a photo, select it in Picasa and click the star button on the bottom panel to toggle the star notation on and off.

Search Your Photos

After you organize your photos into albums with captions, stars, and faces, you can search and sort pictures for easy retrieval. Use Picasa's search box on the top panel to filter your photos down to just what you need. As you type each character, Picasa filters the list of matching photos dynamically, searching on information such as filename, people, caption, album, and folder name.

Click any of the buttons to the left of the search field, shown in Figure 2-10, to filter your search results by Starred photos, photos with faces, movies, and photos that have been geotagged. Using a date slider, you can narrow the list by time period as well.

Figure 2-10: Viewing starred photos in Picasa by date.

Other Picasa Features

Picasa boasts even more useful photo-management features, including these:

- Slideshows to play on your computer or burn to a CD
- Password-protected albums
- Batch moving and renaming photos between folders within Picasa
- Editing tools that can fix red-eye, crop, tune, and otherwise make your pictures look better

- Burning of photo archive DVDs
- Uploading your files to Picasa Web Albums (`http://picasaweb`
  `.com/`) to share your images on the Internet

Hack 18: Corral Media Across Folders and Drives

Level....... **Beginner**

Platform.... **Windows 7**

Cost........ **Free**

It's not always practical to store all your files in your Documents folder. For example, many of us have an extra hard drive (internal or external) on which we store our ever-growing digital media libraries.

Microsoft introduced a new Libraries feature in Windows 7 that enables you to corral folders in different locations (and on different hard drives). Here's how it works.

Windows 7 Libraries

In essence, Windows 7 Libraries are designed to collect files and folders of a common type in one easy-to-access bucket, no matter where those files or folders are located on your hard drive. All folders included in a library are visible within the library, but they're still stored in their original location. (If you delete a library, none of the files or folders in the library will be affected.)

By default, your Windows 7 installation has four libraries: Documents, Music, Pictures, and Videos. If, for example, you store videos you want to watch on-the-go in `C:\Users\username\Videos` on your laptop, but you also store your extensive video collection on an external USB hard drive at `E:\Movies`, you can include both folders in your Video library by navigating to your external hard drive, right-clicking the Movies folder, and selecting Include in library ▷ Videos. The same goes for any library you create, as shown in Figure 2-11.

To remove a folder from a library, navigate to the library; then click the locations link directly below the library title. Use the Library Locations dialog to add or remove folders.

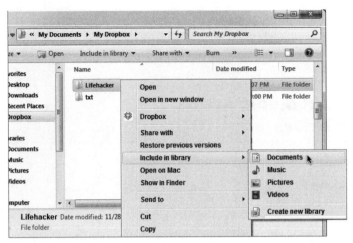

Figure 2-11: Adding a new folder to a library.

Create and Manage Windows 7 Libraries

You can stick with the default libraries if you simply want to use libraries to manage the four default library types, but you can also use libraries for more specific file curation.

One useful aspect of libraries is that they enable you to include files from not just your computer's hard drive, but also folders from external hard drives, or even different computers in your homegroup or on your local network.

Say you wanted to put together a library of photos from your latest family vacation, but some of the photos are on your drive, some are on your significant other's computer, and some are on junior's laptop. Create a new library by right-clicking Libraries in the Explorer sidebar and selecting New ⇨ Library; then give your new library a name — call it Family Vacation.

Add new folders to the Family Vacation library as described above: Right click a folder; then select Include in library ⇨ Family Vacation. It's that simple! Now you can access all your photos in one place, no matter where they are stored.

Hack 19: Create Saved Search Folders

Level . . . . **Easy**

Platform . . . . **Windows (Vista and 7), Mac OS X (10.4+)**

Cost. . . . . **Free**

As you begin to file your documents less and depend on searches more, it makes sense to combine the folder paradigm and search capabilities with saved search folders. A saved search folder is a container for files that match certain criteria. For example, if you have several files in different folders and subfolders on your computer, each with the word *lifehacker* in the title, a search for "all files with the word lifehacker in the title" would list those files. Save that search as a folder, and you get an on-the-fly collection of documents that share the same characteristics in a virtual folder.

The main advantage of saved search folders versus regular old-fashioned folders is that a file can exist in more than one folder at the same time. A Word document named `lifehacker.doc` appears in both the `lifehacker in title` saved search folder and the `All Word documents` saved search folder. This way of organizing your search results allows you to slice and dice your information any way you need it. Saved search folders come in most handy on a temporary basis: while you're working on a certain project, for instance. When you delete a saved search folder, the files inside it aren't deleted; they continue to live on in their respective locations. This hack shows you how to start creating saved search folders in both Windows and Mac OS.

> **NOTE** Windows XP does not feature saved search folders.

Search Folders in Windows

Windows includes a search box on the top-right side of every Explorer window. Run your search by entering criteria (such as the keyword *life-hacker*) there, and Windows returns its file-search results. (By default Windows searches beneath your current folder, but you can expand your search by clicking an alternative root folder at the bottom of the Explorer window, below Search Again In.) When you're satisfied with the results, save the search as a folder by clicking the Save Search button, as shown in Figure 2-12.

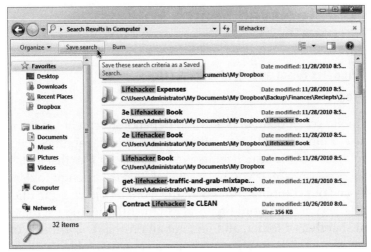

Figure 2-12: Creating a search folder in Windows 7.

The key to creating the most useful search folder is to pinpoint its contents to exactly what you need. The search operators detailed in Hack 12, "Instantly Retrieve Files Stored on Your Computer" work here, and you should use them to narrow down your search even further. For example, searching for Jack -Jill returns documents that include the word Jack but not Jill. A search for Jack OR Jill returns documents that mention Jack, Jill, or both Jack and Jill (Note that OR must be uppercase). A search for "Jack and Jill" (in quotation marks) will do an exact phrase match and return only documents that include the exact words *Jack and Jill*.

After you save your search folder, its icon looks different from a traditional folder, as shown in Figure 2-13

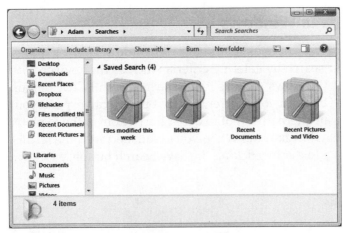

Figure 2-13: Windows 7 saved search folders.

Saved Search Folders in Mac OS

Mac OS X's saved search feature is called Smart Folders (like iTunes' Smart Playlists). To create a Smart Folder, from any Finder window, enter your terms into the search box on the upper-right corner. To add criteria to your search, click the + button. (You can also use the search operators detailed in Hack 12, "Instantly Retrieve Files Stored on Your Computer".) Add as many lines of search criteria as you want, such as the kind of file, the date last modified, the author, and contents, as shown in Figure 2-14.

Figure 2-14: Searching within Finder.

When you're satisfied with your search, click the Save button to save your Smart Folder to a location of your choice. Smart Folders sport a different icon than regular folders; they have a lavender color with a gear image on them.

Hack 20: Create a Password-Protected Disk on Your PC

Level . . . . **Advanced**

Platform . . . . **Windows, Linux**

Cost . . . . **Free**

The next level in organizing your digital stuff is considering privacy and safety. Everyone has some files she wants to protect from intruders or others who have access to her computer. If you use online storage, exchange sensitive information over email, or store data on an easily lost CD or thumb drive, you may want to encrypt that data to keep it from getting into the wrong hands.

When you encrypt data, you use a special algorithm to scramble the bits that make up that file into nonsensical information, which can be restored to its meaningful state only with the right password.

TrueCrypt is a free, open-source encryption application that works on Windows, Mac, and Linux. Given the right credentials, TrueCrypt creates a virtual hard drive that reads and writes encrypted files on-the-fly. This hack explains how to encrypt your private files using TrueCrypt on Windows and Linux.

Set Up the Encrypted Volume Location

Here's how to set up an encrypted virtual disk with TrueCrypt:

1. Download TrueCrypt from `http://truecrypt.org`. Install and launch it.

2. Click the Create Volume button to launch a wizard that prepares the encrypted drive location. Choose Create an Encrypted File Container, click Next, and then select Standard TrueCrypt volume and again click Next.

3. On the Volume Location page, click the Select File button, navigate to the location where you want to store your encrypted files, and type a name for it such as `C:\Users\adam\Documents\4myeyesonly`, as shown in Figure 2-15.

   The name (`4myeyesonly` in this example) isn't the file you want to encrypt; it's the container that will store the files you encrypt. Click Next.

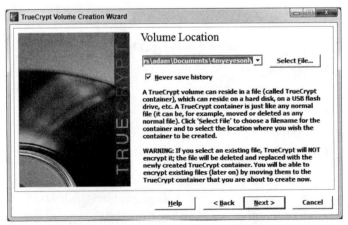

Figure 2-15: Create an encrypted volume with TrueCrypt.

4. Choose your encryption algorithm. The curious can flip through the drop-down list and view info on each option, but you can't go wrong here; the default Advanced Encryption Standard (AES) selection works for most purposes. (Hey, if it works for Top Secret government files,[3] it should work for you.) Click Next.

5. Choose the size of the virtual drive — for example, 100MB, as shown in Figure 2-16.

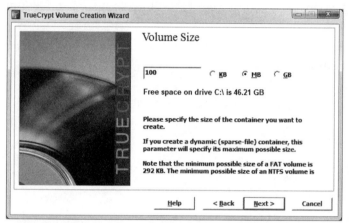

Figure 2-16: Set the size of your encrypted container.

The advantage here is that the file will always look as though it's exactly 100MB, giving no hint as to the actual size of its contents. Click Next.

6. Choose your volume password. TrueCrypt wants something hard to crack, such as 20 characters with letters and numbers mixed together. The whole point here is to keep snoopers at bay, so make your password a non-dictionary word that's difficult to guess. Alternatively, you can use a key-file to lock your volume.

WARNING Keep in mind that if you forget your password or your key-file gets corrupted or lost, the files on your TrueCrypt volume will be inaccessible — forever.

7. Format the volume. This part is fun: TrueCrypt gathers random information from your system — including the location of your mouse pointer — to format the file drive location with random data to make it impossible to read. Click the Format button to go ahead with this operation. (Don't let the word *format* scare you; you're not erasing your hard drive, you're just formatting the drive location file — the 4myeyesonly file in this example — that you just created.)

When the formatting is complete, your encrypted volume location is ready for use.

Store and Retrieve Files from the Encrypted Volume

Your TrueCrypt file can hold your highly sensitive files locked up as tight as a drum. Here's how to get to it:

1. From TrueCrypt, choose Select File, and navigate to the volume file you just created.

2. Select an available drive letter such as x: from the list in TrueCrypt (see Figure 2-17).

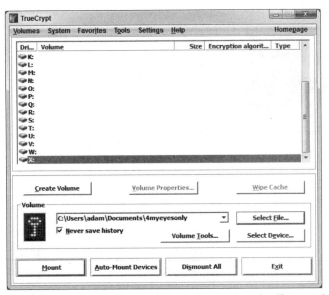

Figure 2-17: To mount a TrueCrypt drive, select the file container and an available drive letter.

3. Click the Mount button and enter your volume password. If you enter the correct password, the virtual drive x: will be mounted.

4. Go to Computer. Listed alongside all the other drives on your computer is a new one: Local Disk X:. Drag and drop all your sensitive data to this drive and work from it as you would any other disk.

5. When you finish working with the data, in TrueCrypt, select the mounted drive (x: in this example) and click the Dismount button. The x: drive will no longer be available; all you have left is the

4myeyesonly file you created, which can be dropped onto a thumb drive, emailed to yourself, burned to CD, or placed on your iPod, totally encrypted.

If someone managed to open this file, its contents would be meaningless, indecipherable nonsense. Only a user with TrueCrypt installed and the password or key-file could mount the drive and access the files on it.

TIP Using TrueCrypt you can secure an entire drive — such as a USB thumb drive. To do so, click Select Device instead of Select File, and choose your thumb drive. You can also install TrueCrypt to the thumb drive.

Hack 21: Create a Password-Protected Disk on Your Mac

Level. . . . . . . **Medium**

Platform . . . . **Mac OS X (10.4 or later)**

Cost. . . . . . . **Free**

If you have files and folders you'd like to keep private and secure on your Mac, you can use Mac OS X's built-in Disk Utility to encrypt a disk image. A disk image is just a file that you can mount like a separate disk and unmount to lock again — like a thumb drive, but without the actual physical drive. Whether you want to password-protect sensitive customer data or your spouse's surprise birthday party plans, an encrypted disk image can lock up any number of files and folders behind a password. This hack covers how to lock and unlock a disk image.

Create a New Encrypted Disk Image

Here's how to create an encrypted disk image:

1. Launch Disk Utility, located in /Applications/Utilities/.

2. From the File menu, choose New ⇨ Blank Disk Image.

3. Enter a name (my-secret-files, for example) for your disk in the Save As dialog. From the Size drop-down list, choose how big you'd like the disk to be. (Make it large enough to accommodate all the data you want to store there.) From the Encryption drop-down list, select 128-Bit AES Encryption (Recommended), as shown in Figure 2-18.

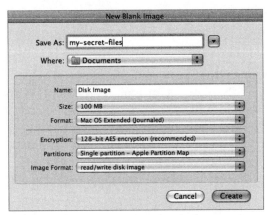

Figure 2-18: Set the name, size, and encryption for your new password-protected disk image.

4. Next, you set a password to access the disk image. Make your password both secure and memorable. (For help choosing a password, click the button with the key icon on it to launch the Password Assistant, which can make suggestions for your password.) By default, your new password will be saved in your Keychain (see Figure 2-19) to make it harder to forget.

Figure 2-19: Set the password needed to mount your new encrypted disk image.

Disk Utility creates and mounts the my-secret-files disk image. After it's created, you see the new disk appear on your Desktop. Move, save, or copy files onto this disk as if it were any other while using your Mac. When you're done adding all your private files to the disk, dismount it as usual (Ctrl+click and choose Eject `my-secret-files`.) Now you can move the `my-secret-files.dmg` file onto any other disk, such as a thumb drive or CD. No one can mount it without the password.

Access Your Password-Protected Disk

To access the files on your encrypted disk image, double-click it, and your Mac will attempt to mount it. If your password is saved in the keychain, the disk will mount and you can save and open files from it as usual. If not, you have to enter your password to mount and decrypt the file for use.

Hack 22: Encrypt Your Entire Windows Operating System

Level . . . . **Advanced**

Platform . . . . **Windows**

Cost . . . . **Free**

Encrypting groups of sensitive files is a good start, but if you have a lot of sensitive material on your PC and don't want to hassle with picking and choosing which belong in your encrypted volume and which don't, you can use TrueCrypt to encrypt your entire system drive so that every file on your computer is encrypted by default.

Set Up Your Encrypted Operating System

Encrypting your entire system drive is similar to creating an encrypted volume. Here's how it works:

1. Download TrueCrypt from `http://truecrypt.org`. Install and launch it.

2. Click the Create Volume button to launch a wizard that prepares the encrypted drive location. Choose Encrypt the System Partition or Entire System Drive; click Next. Select Normal as your type of system encryption and again click Next.

3. On the Area to Encrypt dialog, select Encrypt the Whole Drive unless you've partitioned your drive and want to encrypt only a specific partition (in which case you'd choose Encrypt the Windows System Partition). Click Next.

4. You'll now be prompted to select whether to encrypt the Host Protected Area. The safest answer is No because you'll rarely find sensitive data on a computer's Host Protected Area; if you select Yes and your computer needs access to the Host Protected Area on boot, you may run into problems. I'd recommend choosing No. Click Next.

5. Choose the number of operating systems installed on your computer — single-boot if you're only running one OS, multi-boot if more than one. Click Next.

6. Choose your encryption algorithm. The default AES selection works for most. Click Next.

7. Choose your volume password. TrueCrypt wants something hard to crack, such as 20 characters with letters and numbers mixed together. The whole point here is to keep snoopers at bay, so make your password a non-dictionary word that's difficult to guess. You'll see TrueCrypt collecting random data, as shown in Figure 2-20, which it uses to encrypt your drive. Give it a little help by moving your mouse randomly around the window. Click Next.

Figure 2-20: TrueCrypt generates random data to strengthen your encryption keys.

8. Now TrueCrypt will have generated your encryption keys. Click Next. TrueCrypt will prompt you to create and burn a rescue disk, which enables you to get to your data in the event that something goes wrong with your boot loader or master key at some point down the line. Follow the on-screen instructions, and then verify that the rescue disk was successfully burned. Click Next.

9. You'll now be prompted to securely wipe the unencrypted but deleted files on your computer. The reason: Even after you delete a file on your computer, some recovery methods can still find those files. After your data is encrypted, this isn't a problem — even if someone were able to recover a file you've deleted, the recovered data would still be encrypted. This step enables you to overwrite your currently deleted data before you continue encrypting, in hopes that those recovery methods won't work on your old, unencrypted data. If you're not concerned that someone could recover your unencrypted but deleted files, select None and click Next. If you are, pick your preferred wiping method from the drop-down, and click Next.

10. It's a big deal if something goes wrong when you're encrypting your entire system, so at this point TrueCrypt wants to test that everything's working as expected (and that you can remember your password). Click the Test button, and TrueCrypt restarts your computer and prompts you for the master password you setup earlier. If everything goes according to plan, TrueCrypt launches, noting that the Pretest was completed. Click Encrypt, and TrueCrypt begins the encryption process.

When the encryption is complete, your entire operating system is now encrypted and ready for use.

Hack 23: Set Up 2-Step Verification for Your Google Account

Level . . . . **Medium**

Platform . . . . **All (Web)**

Cost . . . . **Free**

The previous three hacks involved encrypting data on your local hard drive, but as you move to more of a Web-based existence, much of your sensitive data lives in the cloud. And because Google's made such great Web-based productivity applications (in the form of webapps such as Gmail, Google Calendar, and Google Docs), a lot of your sensitive data is inside your Google account. In this hack, you increase the security of your Google account with 2-step verification.

The only thing standing between a hacker and your Google account — and more important, your sensitive information — is your password. Even if you have the strongest password you can possibly randomly generate, if people were to discover that password, they'd have access to all the information in your account.

2-step verification offers a more secure way for Google to verify that you are who you say when you log in to your Google account on a new web browser, through a new application, or on a new mobile device. With 2-step verification, your password isn't enough by itself. As Google puts it:

"2-step verification requires two independent factors for authentication, much like you might see on your banking website: your password, plus a code you only use once."[4]

Those two factors are:

1. Your password (just like always)

2. A single-use verification code that Google sends to your phone in one of three ways:

   ▪ Using the Google Authenticator app available for Android, iPhone, and BlackBerry

   ▪ Via SMS

   ▪ Through a voice call (meaning you could even use a landline if you didn't have a cell phone — the call would read off the code to you)

Both your password and the single-use verification code are required to log in on a new browser. You can then tell Google to remember your login for 30 days.

Set Up 2-Step Verification

If you're convinced that you want the added security, or you at least want to give 2-step verification a try, follow these steps.

1. Log in to your Google account and point your browser to your Google accounts page at www.google.com/accounts/. If you're using Google Apps on a non-Google Domain, (like your personal website) the Admin for your Google Apps account needs to enable 2-step verification for your account.

2. On the right side of the page, under Personal Settings ➪ Security, click the Using 2-Step Verification link. (You can bookmark that link if you like.)

3. Now walk through Google's 2-step verification setup guide, as shown in Figure 2-21. It's quite simple: Just add a new phone that you want to use for your 2-step verification and confirm that it is indeed your phone. If you aren't using an Android, iPhone, or BlackBerry smartphone, verify your phone via SMS. Otherwise, smartphone users should verify their phones using the Google Authenticator app for Android (`https://market.android.com/details?id=com`
`.google.android.apps.authenticator`), iPhone (`http://itunes`
`.apple.com/us/app/google-authenticator/id388497605?mt=8`), or BlackBerry. To verify your phone with these dedicated apps, scan a QR code — the square barcodes that smartphones can read via their built-in cameras.

4. Finally, just follow along with Google's 2-step setup wizard at `www`
`.google.com/accounts/b/0/SmsAuthConfig` for instructions specific to your phone.

Figure 2-21: Google's 2-step verification setup guide walks you through setting up a second device to verify you are who you say.

After you set up your phone, you can also add a backup — a trusted number you can also access if, for example, you lose your phone — so you can still access your account. You can even print off a few backup codes to carry in your wallet or somewhere safe.

Use 2-Step Verification

Now that you've set up 2-step verification, the process for logging into your Google account from a new browser works like this:

1. Visit a Google sign-in page.

2. Enter your username and password, like always.

3. You're now prompted to enter a code, as shown in Figure 2-22, which is tied only to a phone number you provide. You can receive this code on your phone using one of the Google Authenticator apps available for Android, iPhone, and BlackBerry, via SMS or through a voice call (or using one of your printed backup codes if necessary).

4. Enter the code, optionally checking the box to Remember Verification for This Computer for 30 Days, click Verify, and you're in.

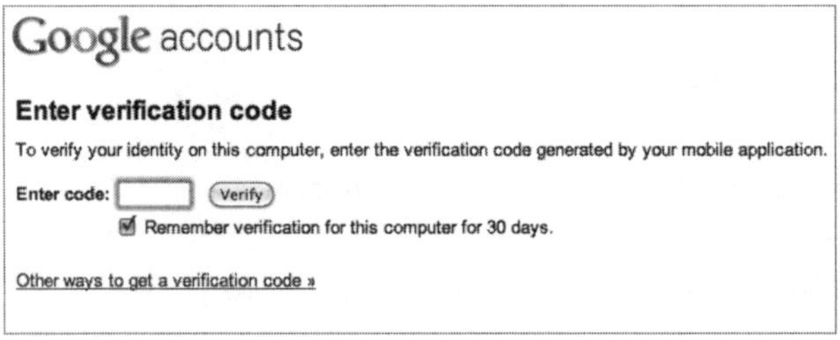

Google accounts

Enter verification code

To verify your identity on this computer, enter the verification code generated by your mobile application.

Enter code: [   ] (Verify)
☑ Remember verification for this computer for 30 days.

Other ways to get a verification code »

Figure 2-22: With 2-step verification enabled, you'll be prompted to verify your identity when you first log into Google from a new browser.

Using 2-step verification is fairly simple, but it does add a bit of hassle to your login. For the most part, the added security is well worth it.

The other change you need to get used to involves logging into your Google account from third-party applications — such as a desktop email client. Because those clients don't support Google's Web-based 2-step verification, you need to create single-use passwords the first time you log in to any new third-party application that needs to access your Google account. You only need to generate the new password for each application once — unless you decide to revoke access to that device. Following is how it works:

Point your browser to the 2-step verification page at www.google.com/accounts/b/0/IssuedAuthSubTokens. (I recommend bookmarking this page, but you can also find the link on your Account settings page under Security ➪ Authorizing applications & Sites.) At the top of this page, you see all the webapps that you've allowed access to your Google account using the preceding verification process; at the bottom of the page, you see the Application-specific passwords section, as shown in Figure 2-23.

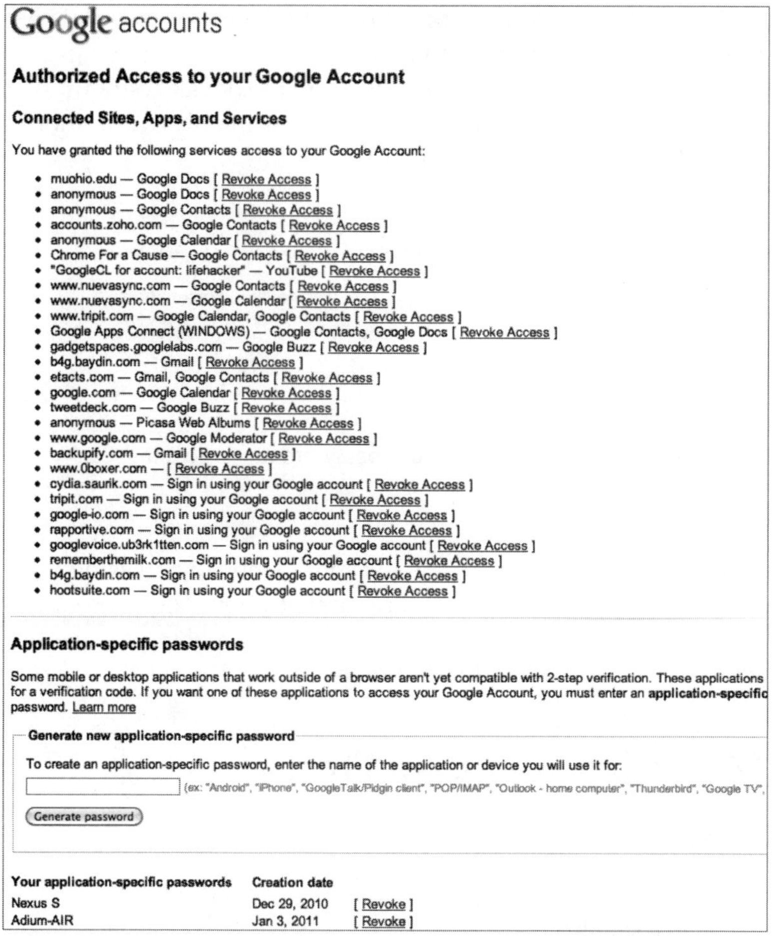

Figure 2-23: Manage websites and applications you've authorized using 2-step verification from one page.

This is where you generate new passwords for devices that can't support the 2-step verification. To do so follow these steps:

1. Type in the name of the device or application that you want to generate a single-use password for.

2. Click Generate password.

3. Google returns a new 16-digit (plus four spaces) password for you to use on that device, as shown in Figure 2-24. After you hide it, you have no way to retrieve it again (a good thing).

Unlike the Web-based 2-step verification process, which resets every 30 days, you have to enter an application-specific password only *once*; it remains active with that single-use password indefinitely. You can, however, revoke any password, device, or application from accessing your Google account at any time — which I've done for the password I generated in Figure 2-24. (Hands off my Google account!) From the device configuration page, you can also clear your phone info and all printable codes, should you lose your phone or misplace a printed code.

Figure 2-24: Google generates a one-time-use password for devices that can't support 2-step verification. [f0224.tif]

As you can see, this process adds a few more steps to accessing your Google account, but it also offers peace of mind that your Google account — and all the personal information within — stays squarely in your control and out of the hands of (the bad kind of) hackers.

Hack 24: Design Your Own Planner

Level . . . . **Easy**

Platform . . . . **All**

Cost . . . . **Office supplies**

There are many good reasons to ditch your expensive, electronic PDA for a paper-based planner system: cost, portability, and maintenance, to name a few. Paper-based planners never run out of battery juice or memory; they never crash or refuse to work the way you expect. Lots of even the most tech-savvy are going retro with paper calendars and to-do lists. This hack explains how to build your own custom paper planner, calendar, and project manager using your computer and your printer.

The D*I*Y Planner system (http://diyplanner.com) is an extensive library of PDF templates from which you can pick and choose. Then, print the pages you need and assemble your planner.

Why Build Your Own Planner?

You can walk into any office-supplies store and choose from a variety of prefab paper planners. But the advantages of a do-it-yourself planner are customization and scalability. Maybe you're thinking about giving up the BlackBerry and you just want to test-drive a paper solution. Maybe you don't want to have to order a new set of custom-print pages from your store-bought planner's manufacturer every time you run out. With a D*I*Y Planner, you can easily add, replace, and reshuffle pages. Refills are a matter of printing a new set of pages.

You can also easily make D*I*Y Planners for your staff that cover custom timelines such as the duration of a particular project. Keep your D*I*Y Planner thin and portable by carrying around only the next couple of weeks' worth of information.

How to Assemble Your D*I*Y Planner

First, decide on the size and type of planner you want to create. The D*I*Y Planner site has templates available to print in several sizes:

- Classic (half pages of 8½×11-inch paper, common in North America)
- Letter size (8½×11-inch paper)
- A4 (the equivalent to letter size in Europe and countries outside North America)
- A5 (half of A4 size)
- Hipster PDA (index cards)

Download the template kit you need from `http://diyplanner.com/templates/official`. Open and print the templates using a PDF reader such as Adobe Acrobat or Foxit (`http://foxitsoftware.com`). Depending on the size you choose, you may have to cut the paper in half (for Classic and A5) and punch holes in it to fit it inside a binder. The Hipster PDA index-card–sized version can be held together with a small binder clip.

D*I*Y Planner Templates and Sizes

The D*I*Y Planner system offers an extensive set of templates, including these:

- Calendar, to-do lists, and note-taking pages
- Stephen Covey's priority matrix

- David Allen's *Getting Things Done* system buckets (such as Next Actions, Waiting, Projects)
- Mind maps
- A photographer release form
- Book notes
- Shopping lists
- Address book
- Contact logs (phone call/email/IM log of contacts)
- Financial ledger
- Meeting agenda
- Goals tracker
- Lined horizontal, lined vertical, and graph paper
- Project outline and notes forms

Print only as many pages of the forms as you need to assemble your custom planner. Later, if you decide to change the planner size you use, or need to add pages for certain kinds of information (such as another address-book page to accommodate contacts whose last names start with *S*, or larger daily calendar pages to write your appointments), simply print the pages and reassemble or add them to your planner.

References

1. David Allen, *Getting Things Done*, (Penguin Books, 2001), p. 100.

2. Calahan, Stephanie L. H. "Statistics." *Calahan Solutions.* (http://www.calahansolutions.net/statistics/)

3. "National Policy on the Use of the Advanced Encryption Standard (AES) to Protect National Security Systems and National Security Information" (http://csrc.nist.gov/groups/ST/toolkit/documents/aes/CNSS15FS.pdf).

4. Nishit Shah, "Advanced sign-in security for your Google account," The Official Gmail Blog (http://gmailblog.blogspot.com/2011/02/advanced-sign-in-security-for-your.html)

CHAPTER 3

Trick Yourself into Getting Done

Just as Mom used to grind up that bitter pill in a bowl of ice cream, you can make working on tough tasks easier to swallow. Checking an item off your to-do list — and the sense of satisfaction and completion that comes with that simple action — is one of the best things that happens during your workday. But there are roadblocks, both environmental and just plain mental, on the way to "done."

Part of the reason you leave the office at night feeling so far behind on work comes from the nature of the modern workplace. Rife with distractions and interruptions, many offices couldn't be less conducive to productivity. Noisy disruptions and drop-by co-workers aside, the reality of information work is that there's always another email to open, another website to visit, another message that makes your smartphone vibrate off the desk. At any moment you have a dozen things you *could* work on, and even that choice is a source of distraction and paralysis. It's easy to spend the day constantly switching gears and reevaluating what's the biggest fire to put out next rather than making progress on important work.

Even when you're alone, with email and phone turned off, procrastination rears its ugly head. Starting in on a tough project feels like an impossible feat; suddenly, rather than spending the afternoon working on the big presentation, you're ripping your CD collection into iTunes. In a culture that says, "You can do anything you want!" your to-do lists fill up with gargantuan tasks that would scare off the most functional person on Earth: "Learn French. Start small business. Buy new house. Go back to school."

The self-sabotage doesn't stop there. A 2005 study[1] shows that people commonly overestimate the amount of time they think they have in the future to get things done, leaving them with overbooked calendars and incomplete commitments. An exaggerated sense of how much time you have — and how much time tasks can take you to complete — can cut off your best efforts at getting things done.

In his excellent book *The War of Art*, writer Steven Pressfield calls the inner force that keeps you from doing your work Resistance with a capital *R*.[2] Pressfield says a true Professional (with a capital *P*) gets her work done no matter how strong Resistance pushes against her. I'd add that the Professional arms herself adequately in the war against Resistance to make victory more likely. In short, she makes the *right* thing to do the *easy* thing to do.

You can organize your tasks and your calendar in a way that speeds you toward the finish line faster, and this chapter shows you how. In contrast to other chapters in this book, the hacks here focus more on adjusting the way you work than on computer tricks. Use these hacks to cross off items on your task list more often and treat yourself to that delicious sense of completion every single day.

Hack 25: Make Your To-Do List Doable

Level . . . . **Easy**

Platform . . . . **All**

Cost . . . . **Free**

There's no better feeling than checking something off your to-do list. Done! Finished! Mission accomplished! Yet it's so easy to let a whole day or week go by without knocking one task off your list. How does that happen? Well, your to-do list can be a tool that guides you through your work, or it can be a big fat pillar of undone time bombs taunting you and your unproductive inadequacy. It all depends on how you write it.

Think of your to-do list as an instruction set your Boss self gives your Assistant self. Like a good computer program, if the instructions are clear, specific, and easily carried out, you're golden. If not, you'll get undesirable results, such as fear, procrastination, and self-loathing. Read on for a closer look at how to write a to-do list that makes getting your stuff done dead-simple.

You Are the Boss of You

At any point during the workday, you are in one of two modes: thinking mode (that's you with the Boss hat on) and action mode (that's you with the Personal Assistant hat on). When a project or task comes up, the steps you need to take start to form in your mind. Now you're in thinking/Boss mode — the guy/gal who gives the orders. Your to-do list is a collection of those orders, which your Assistant personality will later pick up and do.

When you're wearing your Boss hat, it's up to you to write down the instructions in such a way that your Assistant self can just do them without having to think — or stress. Taking the thinking out of the acting is one of the best ways to make your to-do list a cinch to finish off.

How to Order Yourself Around

When it's time to add something to your to-do list, think it through using the following guidelines.

Only Put Items on the List That You're Definitely Doing

Sometimes you think of tasks you're just not ready to do yet. Maybe learning a new language — while it's an eventual goal — just doesn't fit into your life right now. Maybe upgrading the website is low priority because your business is shifting gears in a major way, and any site overhaul will look very different — or maybe won't be needed — in six months.

Instead of letting tasks you're not quite committed to loiter on your to-do list until you're sick of looking at them (and sick of the reminder that you're not quite there yet), move them off to a separate list, a holding area for Someday/Maybe items. You'd tell your assistant to do something only if you absolutely, positively want it done, so only concrete actions you're committed to completing should live on your to-do list.

Break It Down

The quickest route to a task you'll actively avoid working on: Make it a vague monstrosity. Put a nonspecific item such as "Clean out the office" on your to-do list, and I guarantee that's the last thing you'll ever start working on. Actually, "Clean out the office" isn't a to-do at all; it's a *project*. Author of *Getting Things Done* David Allen says projects are not tasks; projects are collections of tasks. That's an important distinction. Internalize it, because your to-do list is not your project list. Don't add multi-action tasks to it, such as "Clean out the office." Break projects down to smaller, easier-to-tackle subtasks, such as "Purge filing cabinet," "Shred old paperwork," and "Box up unneeded books for library drive." Your Assistant self will ask, "What do you want done?" and when Boss you says, "Clean out the office," that won't get you anywhere.

The smaller and more atomic these subtasks are, the more doable they are. Inspirational writer SARK breaks down her tasks into five-minute increments, and calls them "micromovements." She writes, "Micromovements are tiny, tiny little steps you can take toward completions in your life. I'm a recovering procrastinator and I have a short attention span, so I invented micromovements as a method of completing projects in time spans of 5 minutes or less. I always feel like I can handle almost anything for 5 minutes!"[3]

Coming up with those tiny tasks requires thinking up front, when you're putting the task on your list. The following examples contrast vague to-do's (the kind that can throw up roadblocks) next to their doable counterparts.

ROADBLOCK TO-DO'S	DOABLE TO-DO'S
Find a new dentist.	Email Jayne and ask what dentist she goes to.
Replace the broken glass table top.	Measure the table dimensions. Call San Diego Glass at 555-6789 with dimensions.
Learn Italian.	Check U of Whatever's website (whatever.edu) for fall Italian class offerings.
Upgrade website.	Draft a list of five website upgrades.

As you can see, breaking down your tasks into next actions creates more than one task for items that *look* like regular to-do's but turn out to be small projects. For example, replacing the broken glass table top involves measuring the table, calling and ordering a replacement, and possibly going to pick it up, which brings us to the next guideline.

Focus Only on the Next Action

When you have a multi-action task — such as replacing the glass table top — keep only its next sequential action on your to-do list. When the task is complete, refer to your project list (again, separate from to-do's) and add its next action to your to-do list. At any given moment, your to-do list should contain only the next logical action for all your working projects. That's it — just one bite-sized step in each undertaking.

Imagine that you're at your desk, you have a spare 10 minutes before a meeting, and you pull out the preceding roadblock to-do list. Can you find a dentist or learn Italian? No. But you could get an item done from the doable list. You could email a friend about a dentist referral, or check the university website for fall class offerings.

Use Specific, Active Verbs

When you tell yourself to do something, make it an order. An item such as "Acme account checkup" doesn't tell you what has to be done. Make your to-do's specific actions, such as "Phone Rob at Acme re: Q2 sales." Notice I didn't use the word *Contact*; I used *Phone*. Contact could mean phone, email, or IM, but when you take out all the thinking and leave in only action, your verbs will be as specific as possible. Literally imagine instructing a personal assistant on her first day on the job as to what you need done.

Include as Much Information as Possible

When formulating a to-do, the onus is on your Boss self to make it as easy as possible for your Assistant self to get the job done. For example, if you have to make a phone call, include the name or number. Instead of "Donate old furniture," assign yourself "Call Goodwill to schedule pickup, 555-9878." When you're stuck in the doctor's waiting room for 20 minutes with only your cell phone, you can't donate your old furniture, but you sure can make a phone call — if you have the number. Be a good Boss. Arm your Assistant self with all the details she needs to get your work done.

Keep Your List Short

Just as no one wants to look at an email inbox with 2,386 messages in it, no one wants to have an endless to-do list. It's overwhelming and depressing, as though there's no light at the end of the tunnel. Instead, keep your to-do list under 20 items. (This morning, mine's only 17 tasks long, and I call myself a busy person.) Does that sound like too short a list? Remember, your to-do list isn't a dumping ground for project details, or "Someday I'd like to…" items. These are tasks you've committed to completing in the near future, such as the next two weeks. Keep your projects and some-day/maybe items elsewhere. Your to-do list should be short, to-the-point commitments that involve no more deciding as to whether you're actually serious about doing them.

Prioritize Your Tasks

Although your to-do list might have 20 items on it, the reality is that you're going to get only a couple done per day (assuming that you're not writing down things like "get up, shower, make coffee, go to work..." — and you shouldn't be). So make sure the most important tasks are at the very top of your list. How you do this depends on what tool or software you use to track your to-do's, but do make sure you can see at a glance what you need to get done next.

Keep Your List Moving

Although my to-do list is only 20 items or so, it's 20 items that change every day. Every day, two to five tasks get checked off, and two to five tasks get added. Remember, your to-do list is a working document, not some showy testament to organization that quietly gathers dust because you're off doing real work that's not written down anywhere.

Purge and Update Your List Weekly

In addition to sorting by priority, you should sort your list by age. What items have been on your list the longest? Chances are you have mental blockage around the tasks that have been sitting around forever, and they need to be reworded or broken down further. Or perhaps they don't need to get done after all. (Remember! Deleting an item from your to-do list is even *better* than checking it off, because you've saved the time and effort of actually doing it.)

Just as a manager would meet with her staff members once a week, schedule a 20-minute meeting with yourself every Friday or Monday to review your to-do list, project list, and someday/maybe list. Use that time to rewrite any items that aren't broken down as much as they should be, purge irrelevant items, and move next actions from your project list to your to-do list.

This short, weekly ritual can make you feel more on top of your game than ever. It focuses your energy and weeds out any detritus that accumulated over the past week.

Log Your Completed Tasks

As any good assistant does, you want to show the boss exactly how much you accomplished. Make sure you stow your done items somewhere so that you can revel in your own productivity and even refer to past work activities. Your "done" list is a great indicator of whether your to-do list is working. If more than two days go by without a new done item, it's time to revamp your to-do list and get back to best practices.

Practice Makes Perfect

This may seem like a long set of guidelines for something as simple as adding to your to-do list. But 90 percent of the work involved when you're tackling tasks that matter is the planning, and that's true for what may seem to be the most trivial tasks. As with any good habit, practice makes perfect. The more you practice the art of creating effective to-do's, the faster and easier it will come to you, and the more you cross items off your list and leave the office with that delicious sense of completion.

NOTE Many of the concepts in this hack (especially the next action, projects, and someday/maybe lists) come from David Allen's productivity bible, *Getting Things Done*. Also, Merlin Mann's two-part feature on building a smarter to-do list[4] and his follow-up article for Macworld magazine[5] inspired and informed this hack.

Hack 26: Set Up a Morning Dash

Level . . . . **Easy**

Platform . . . . **All**

Cost. . . . . **Free**

You love the sense of satisfaction and accomplishment you feel when you check off an item on your to-do list as done, completed, out the door, in the can. But so many things can keep you from getting to that moment, from unexpected emergencies to long and dragged-out meetings to getting waylaid by a conversation with a co-worker in the hallway.

Although those spontaneous gear shifts are necessary and will inevitably happen, there is one way to ensure that you'll knock at least one task off your list: dedicate the first hour of your day to your most important task — *before* you check your email, listen to your voicemail, or go to any meetings.

Get One Thing Done First

Author of *Never Check Email in the Morning* Julie Morgenstern suggests spending the first hour of your workday email-free. Choose one task — even a small one — and tackle it first thing. Accomplishing something out of the gate sets the tone for the rest of your day and guarantees that no matter how many fires you're tasked with putting out once you've opened your email client, you *still* can say that you got something done. When you're open for business and paying attention to incoming requests, it's too easy to get swept away into the craziness. So get your day started off on the right foot, with just one thing done.

Morgenstern writes, "Change the rhythm of the workday by starting out with your own drumbeat.... When you devote your first hour to concentrated work — a dash — the day starts with *you* in charge of *it* rather than the other way around. It's a bold statement to the world (and yourself) that you can take control, pull away from the frenetic pace, and create the time for quiet work when you need it. In reality, if you don't consciously create the space for the dashes, they won't get done."[6]

To work this hack, you have to set yourself up for your morning dash.

Park on a Downward Slope

The point of this technique is to remove any thought or planning from your first action of the day so that you can get rolling immediately while you're fresh and not distracted by incoming requests. That means you have to choose and gather your materials for the morning dash the evening before.

Near the end of each workday, as you straighten up your desk and get ready to leave the office, decide on the next morning's most important task. Make sure it's small, achievable, and important. That point is critical: to successfully set yourself up for the next morning's dash, you want to choose the smallest and most doable to-do item that still matters.

Keep in mind that much of your work may be dependent on information stored in your email inbox. (I've worked this trick in earnest, only to find that during my dash, I had to open my email to retrieve information, and that bold number of unread messages threatened my focus and concentration.) The key is to set yourself up the night before with *all* the information you need to get your dash completed the next morning. Put all the materials you need to complete the task in a `first thing` folder on your desktop or taskbar.

Write down your small, doable assignment, and place it somewhere you will see it, even if it's a Post-It note on your keyboard. When you arrive the next morning, that's the first thing you're going to do — no matter what.

Hack 27: Map Your Time

Level . . . . **Easy**

Platform . . . . **All (with a spreadsheet or calendaring program)**

Cost . . . . **Free**

The busy person's perennial question is, "Where did the day go?" It's easy to get tossed from one thing to the next like a piece of driftwood caught in the tide of your crazy life. A thousand things compete for your time and attention and tug you here and there, but only you know how you actually want to spend your time. You *can* take control, mindfully structure your days, and deliberately choose the activities — and time limits — that reflect your values and goals.

As with most things, the best way to start keeping your ideal, balanced schedule is to write it down (whether that's on paper or on your computer is up to you). A personal time map helps you align the activities that fill your day with your personal goals more closely.

Your Ideal Time Map

Author of *Time Management from the Inside Out,* Julie Morgenstern, compares the time you have in a day, week, or month to the space in the top of your closet: only a certain amount of stuff can fit in it.[7] Before you start running from one appointment to the next, decide how you want to fill the limited space of your day with a time map. A time map is a simple chart of your waking hours that displays how much time per day you devote to different areas of your life.

For example (and simplicity's sake), say that you decide you want to spend about one-third of your time on work, share one-third of your time with family, and save one-third of your time for yourself. Your time map might look something like Figure 3-1.

Obviously, your ratios will vary and should reflect your life choices. If you're an entrepreneur, for example, work will take up more space. Family time will dominate for parents of young children. An entrepreneurial new parent? Well, you shouldn't expect too much "me" time. When constructing your ideal ratios, be realistic.

Put together your ideal time map using your favorite calendaring software (Microsoft Outlook, iCal, or Google Calendar, for example), or just download the Excel time map template shown in Figure 3-1. It automatically shades in your map and calculates percentages based on focus codes (A, B, C, and D) and is available at http://cache.lifehacker.com/assets/2006/07/timemap.xls.

	Sun	Mon	Tue	Wed	Thu	Fri	Sat
5:00 AM							
6:00 AM							
7:00 AM	A	A	A	A	A	A	A
8:00 AM	A	A	A	A	A	A	A
9:00 AM	C	B	B	B	B	B	C
10:00 AM	C	B	B	B	B	B	C
11:00 AM	C	B	B	B	B	B	C
12:00 PM	C	A	A	A	A	A	C
1:00 PM	C	B	B	B	B	B	C
2:00 PM	C	B	B	B	B	B	C
3:00 PM	C	B	B	B	B	B	C
4:00 PM	C	B	B	B	B	B	C
5:00 PM	C	B	B	B	B	B	C
6:00 PM	C	A	A	A	A	A	C
7:00 PM	C	C	C	C	C	C	C
8:00 PM	C	C	C	C	C	C	C
9:00 PM	A	A	A	A	A	A	C
10:00 PM	A	A	A	A	A	A	C
11:00 PM							
12:00 PM							

		Focus	Code	Hours	%	
		Me	A	36	32%	
		Work	B	40	36%	
		Family	C	36	32%	
			D	0	0%	
				112		

Figure 3-1: A sample time map.

When you're putting together your time map, make sure that you do the following:

- Keep the categories broad and generic, at least for your whole life map. You can do subtime maps (such as a work time map) separately.

- Don't schedule things down to the minute. This is a guide, not an exercise in down-to-the-minute accounting.

- Keep overall ratios in mind, aligned with the things you deem most important in life right now. That is, if career is your top priority, the largest percentage of your map should reflect that.

Now that you've determined how you'd like to place your life's priorities into your days' space, you're halfway to making that a reality.

Submaps

After you create your overall time map, submap sections of it — for example, your time at work. Schedule in blocks of time to process email, attend meetings, and write reports.

Make sure all your job responsibilities are represented — and likewise for your personal and family time.

Your Actual Time Map

Now you're ready to see how your actual schedule lines up with your ideal. Place your time map somewhere in plain view, such as on your desk or the refrigerator. Each day for a couple of weeks, jot down how you spend your time, and then compare your vision to reality. Note how close your actual time map is to your ideal. Adjust the actual; adjust your ideal. Wash, rinse, and repeat.

The more you work with your time map, the more you'll become aware of how that extra hour spent at work — because you were feeling pressured or generous or simply lost track of time — means you'll spend an hour less with your family, doing things that you enjoy, or sleeping.

Most important, when someone asks, "Where did the day go?" you'll have the answer.

Hack 28: Quick-Log Your Workday

Level........**Easy**

Platform....**All**

Cost........**Free**

Keeping tabs on what you actually spend your time doing is not an easy task, but keeping a daily log of your work can help and also provide other benefits.

A daily work log helps you become a better time estimator. By becoming aware of how long things actually take, you can more realistically estimate the length of future assignments and budget your time — and for those who bill by the hour, money — more accurately. A work log enables you to get a real picture of your job responsibilities and how they line up with your ideal time map; it also enables you to look back at a day or week and have a concrete idea of where your time went. It can help you identify time sinks and make strategic decisions about what you can delegate, add, or simply delete from your schedule.

When you start keeping a daily work log, you might be surprised to find out what your workday really consists of.

When keeping a work log, you have several options, from paper to a plain text file to a quick-logger app.

Paper

A plain notebook or standard desk diary with dates on each page is an easy way to jot down what you've accomplished in a day.

For a more specialized work log form, designer Dave Seah created the Emergent Task Timer. This form uses rows of small boxes, each representing

15 minutes of time. You fill out the form as the day progresses, as shown in Figure 3-2.

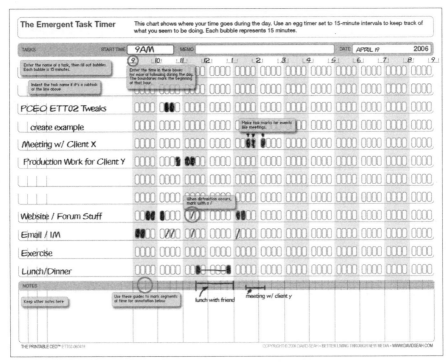

Figure 3-2: Dave Seah's Emergent Task Timer printable PDF form.

Seah's Emergent Task Timer is especially effective for those who work in 15-minute dashes. The Emergent Task Timer is available for download as a PDF file at http://davidseah.com/archives/2006/04/18/the-printable-ceo-iii-emergent-task-timing. (The Printable CEO is a trademark of David Seah.)

Notepad .LOG File (Windows Only)

Alternatively, if you want the searchability and archiving capabilities of a digital work log, a simple text file can get the job done. One of the lesser-known features in Notepad, the Windows simple text editor, is log files: text files that automatically add the current date and time when you update them.

To set up your log file:

1. Open Notepad to create a new file.

2. Enter the word .LOG on the first line. (Use all uppercase letters and don't forget the dot.)

3. Save the file (worklog.txt, for example).

Now any time you open that file in Notepad, the current date and time will be added to it, and the cursor automatically goes to the next line — perfect for logging your current task or keeping any kind of journal.

Quick-Log in a Plain-Text File (Windows Only)

You switch between tasks quickly during your workday, and breaking your concentration to write in a desk diary or double-click a text file may disrupt your flow. However, the process can be streamlined by using a simple script and a keyboard shortcut.

The Quick Logger VB script displays a single input box prompt (see Figure 3-3) where you can enter text such as the description of your current task and append it to your work log.

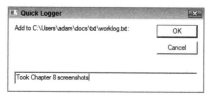

Figure 3-3: The Quick Logger input box.

When you press Enter (or click OK), the text you entered is added to your work log file with the current date and time, as shown in Figure 3-4.

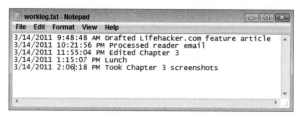

Figure 3-4: A work log generated using the Quick Logger script.

Here's how to set up Quick Logger:

1. Using your favorite text editor, open a new text file and save it as worklog.txt in your documents folder.

2. Enter the following code into a file called `quicklogger.vbs` (or download it from `http://cache.lifehacker.com/software/assets/2006/07/quicklogger.vbs`):

```
'----------------------------------------------------------------
' QuickLogger v.0.1
' Appends the date and a line of text to a file.
' Based on code written by Joshua Fitzgerald, 7/2005.
' Modified by Gina Trapani, 7/2006.
' ----------------------------------------------------------------
Option Explicit

Dim filename
filename = "C:\Users\lifehacker\My Documents\worklog.txt"

Dim text
text = InputBox("Add to "&filename&":", "Quick Logger")
WriteToFile(text)

Sub WriteToFile(text)
 Dim fso
 Dim textFile
 Set fso = CreateObject("Scripting.FileSystemObject")
 Set textFile = fso.OpenTextFile(filename, 8, True)
 textFile.WriteLine Now & " " & text
 textFile.Close
End Sub
```

Save the `.vbs` file to your `documents` (or `scripts`) folder.

3. Edit the line in `quicklogger.vbs` that reads as follows, replacing `C:\Users\lifehacker\My Documents\worklog.txt` with the full path to your work log file.

```
filename = "C:\Users\lifehacker\My Documents\worklog.txt"
```

4. Right-click `quicklogger.vbs` and choose Send To Desktop (Create Shortcut).

5. Right-click the `quicklogger.vbs` shortcut on your Desktop and select Properties. In the Properties panel, set the Shortcut Key to Ctrl+Alt+L by simply typing **L** (Windows fills in Ctrl+Alt for you, as shown in Figure 3-5) and clicking OK.

Now, to append an item to your work log, just press Ctrl+Alt+L, enter your current task in the text box, and press Enter.

Getting into the habit of updating your workday log takes some concentration at first, but with practice, the action becomes second nature. Use your work log to fill out time sheets, analyze your schedule, or explain to the boss what you accomplished that week.

Figure 3-5: Assign a shortcut key to the Quick Logger script.

TIP Add a special notation (such as STAR!) to the best accomplishments listed in your work log. These lines can come in handy when you negotiate your salary, complete your performance review, revise your resume, or interview for your next potential career move.

Set Up Automatic, Rule-Based Time Logging (Windows)

If it turns out that — despite your best efforts — you just don't remember to use your QuickLogger tools, you may want to try out the free application TimeSheet (www.businessrunner.net/timesheet/). With TimeSheet, you can set up rules assigning specific tasks to applications you use on your desktop, and it automatically logs how you spend your time.

You can manually log tasks when you don't have a rule set up that matches your current activity, but the great thing about TimeSheet is that it prompts you to create a new rule when you start working with an application that doesn't currently fit one of your existing rules. For example, the first time you launch Microsoft Word, TimeSheet's Learning Mode prompts you to add a new rule, as shown in Figure 3-6.

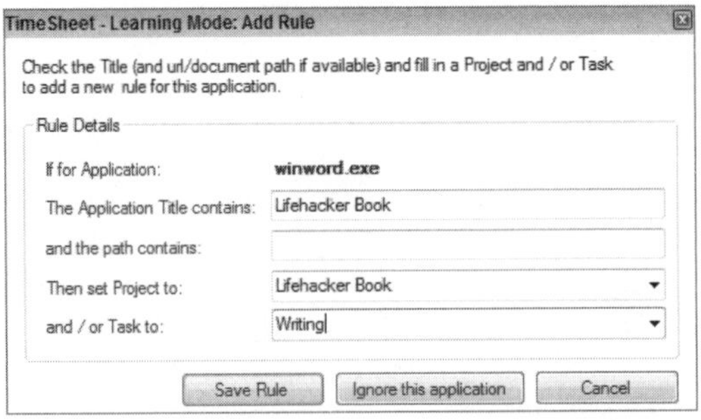

Figure 3-6: TimeSheet makes it easy to create rules that automatically log your workday for you.

In this case, if the application is `winword.exe` and the application title contains the text "Lifehacker Book" (something in the title of all my book-related Word documents), I've set TimeSheet to set the project to "Lifehacker Book" and the task to "Writing".

NOTE For a totally passive option that works on Windows, Mac, and Linux PCs, RescueTime (`www.rescuetime.com`) is a utility that watches what you're doing on your computer, makes pretty accurate guesses about the kind of work you're doing, and organizes that information in a dashboard overview complete with charts and graphs. Just install the desktop tracking utility, run it, and forget about it. You don't even need to regularly check your progress on the site; RescueTime sends a weekly summary email telling you how you're doing.

Hack 29: Dash Through Tasks with a Timer

Level . . . . **Easy**

Platform . . . . **All**

Cost . . . . **Free**

The only way to stop procrastinating is to simply *start* the task you've been putting off. Of course you're thinking: "Thanks a lot, Captain Obvious." We all know that "just do it" *sounds* simple, but in reality, starting on a dreaded to-do can feel impossible. Some tasks are just so big and awful that you can't bring yourself to start in on them because the end seems so far in the future, and the journey there torturous.

The key is to make it as easy as possible to start. Trick yourself into starting by deciding to work on the task for just a handful of minutes and guarantee yourself a break at the end of that time.

For example, commit to work on your task for 10 minutes. Ten minutes! That's one minute for each finger on your two hands. Anyone can work on anything for 10 minutes, and that includes you and that thing you're putting off.

Starting your novel is a daunting task, one most people put off for their entire life. But typing something — anything — for 10 minutes? No problem. This book was written in short bursts of writing regulated by the beep of my favorite kitchen timer. This hack explains how to take timed dashes through your work.

Do Your First Dash

First, get a timer — an egg timer, a digital watch, a cell phone timer, a software timer, the kitchen timer, whatever's available. Pick your biggest, scariest, most put-off task. Choose the next action, set your timer for 10 minutes, start the timer, and begin.

When the timer goes off at the end of the 10 minutes, stop. Get up, walk around, get a drink, and pat yourself on the back for what you've just done: you stopped procrastinating and got *started*.

Then, do it again.

Adjust Your Dash

Ten minutes is a good time period to start running timed dashes. After applying the dash a few times, you'll experience something amazing: when your timer beeps, you'll want to keep working.

As you become more proficient at working the dash, you can adjust the amount of time you set up to work your tasks. Depending on your energy level, available time, and total stress level around a certain task, extend — or shorten — the length of your dash. The goal is to work up to 30-minute or even 60-minute dashes, but everyone has different workplace circumstances and attention spans for bursts of focused activity. Find your comfort zone, set that timer, and go. You'll be amazed at how much you can get done in short, focused bursts.

NOTE Author Francesco Cirillo developed a similar technique in 1992 called the Pomodoro Technique. The idea: Twenty-five minute dashes, followed by five minute breaks. Each dash is called a "pomodoro," and every four pomodoros, you take a longer, 15–20 minute break. [8]

Why Time Constraints Work

What you're actually doing with that timer is creating and committing to a self-imposed deadline, a constraint. Limitations are usually viewed in a negative light, as something that holds you back from achieving goals. In reality, a constraint can be a *help*, not a hindrance. Lots of people work better under pressure because the limitation puts their brains into overdrive and forces them to think quickly and creatively about the best way to spend that little time they have. It makes you race to an imaginary finish line and gets you there more efficiently than if you had all the time in the world.

Game developer and writer Kathy Sierra says that going fast can boost your creativity as well: "One of the best ways to be truly creative — *breakthrough* creative — is to be forced to go fast. Really, really, really fast. From the brain's perspective, it makes sense that extreme speed can unlock creativity. When forced to come up with something under extreme time constraints, we're forced to rely on the more intuitive, subconscious parts of our brain. The time pressure can help suppress the logical/rational/critical parts of your brain. It helps you [equalize] EQ up subconscious creativity (so-called 'right brain') and EQ down conscious thought ('left brain')." [9]

Timer Software Applications

If you have a choice, use a non software-based timer (such as an egg timer, stopwatch, or kitchen timer) for your dash because it's a separate entity that won't get buried in your computer's taskbar or blocked behind another window. A physical timer forces you to look up and reset it by taking your hands off the mouse and keyboard and doing something. It breaks your work trance, gets your eyes off the screen, and encourages you to stand up, stretch, walk around, and not just immediately switch to browsing ESPN.com to check the Yankees score. If you're dashing through intense, computer-based work, a change in mode is important when the timer beeps.

However, if external timers make you feel silly or you don't have one readily available, there are quite a few software-based timers. One of the best I've seen for working dashes on Windows, Mac, or Linux PCs is a free download called Focus Booster (available at www.focusboosterapp.com/; a web-based version is also available at www.focusboosterapp.com/live).

Focus Booster is an interval timer that can set you up for a timed dash plus a timed break for so many times; it's based on the principles of the Pomodoro Technique, so it defaults to a 25-minute dash and 5-minute break, as shown in Figure 3-7, but you can adjust it to fit whatever works best for you. For example, you could do a 10-minute dash plus a 2-minute break (for a total of 12 minutes), 5 times an hour.

Figure 3-7: Interval timer Focus Booster counts down your work dashes and can time your breaks, too.

While Focus Booster is counting down, you can minimize it and forget about it while you work. When it's time to take a break, Focus Booster plays an alarm and then starts timing your break. When your break ends, it plays a different notification.

Hack 30: Form New Habits with Jerry Seinfeld's Chain

Level . . . . **Easy**

Platform . . . . **Web**

Cost. . . . . **Free**

Once upon a time, Jerry Seinfeld gave a young comic advice. He said that to have better jokes, he had to write every day. To help form the habit of writing every day, Seinfeld used a simple system. He told the comedian to get a red felt-tip marker and an extra-large calendar with a whole year on the page to hang on a prominent wall in his home. The comic writes,

> *Seinfeld said that for each day that I do my task of writing, I get to put a big red X over that day on the calendar.*
> *"After a few days you'll have a chain. Just keep at it and the chain will grow longer every day. You'll like seeing that chain, especially when you get a few weeks under your belt. Your only job next is to not break the chain."*
> *"Don't break the chain," he said again for emphasis.*[10]

As anyone does who's achieved success, Seinfeld knows that reaching goals happens by accretion: ordinary everyday effort and small actions that accumulate and grow over time into extraordinary movement, like compounding interest.

You can get your chain started even without a wall calendar and felt-tip marker. At the website Don't Break the Chain (`http://dontbreakthechain .com`), you can create any number of Seinfeldian chains, and check off your newly acquired habit as you practice it, one day at a time. Register for a free account at Don't Break the Chain, and you'll have a new calendar ready for you to start building your chain, as shown in Figure 3-8.

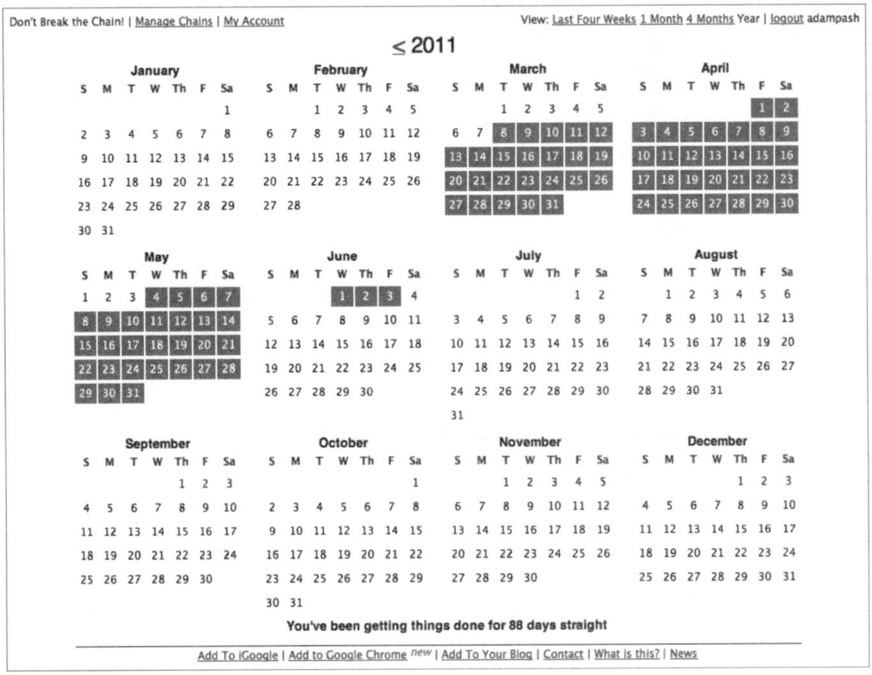

Figure 3-8: Manage your Seinfeldian chain with Don't Break the Chain.

Click the Manage Chains link to name your chain, change the chain's color, or add additional chains. Use the links on the upper-right side to view different time periods, such as the last four weeks (default view), one month, four months, or one year. As Seinfeld said, the more days you mark off, the longer your chain becomes, and the more motivated you'll become to keep it going. After a week or two, switch to the year view and begin coloring in an entire year. Seinfeld said to hang your chain on a prominent wall in your home, so make sure your online version is in a visible place in your digital space. Try making the chain your browser home page or add it to your iGoogle start page. (A widget is available.)

NOTE Benjamin Franklin used a system remarkably similar to Seinfeld's in his quest to form good habits. He marked the days he failed to espouse 13 virtues he laid out for himself on a weekly calendar. Over time, he "had the satisfaction of seeing [the marks] diminish."[11]

Using Seinfeld's method, you can easily form new habits day by day. Just remember: don't break the chain!

NOTE Special thanks to Brad Isaac for contributing the story of his run-in with Seinfeld to Lifehacker.com and this book.

Hack 31: Control Your Workday

Level . . . . **Easy**

Platform . . . . **All**

Cost . . . . **Free**

Getting out of the office on time is tough when there's always another task, project, or walk-by boss request to knock out before you leave. It's easy to lose a day checking email, going to meetings, and putting out fires only to find that at 5 or 6 or 7 p.m., you haven't started something critical.

Getting out of the office is as important to your state of mind — and productivity — as getting in is. But when you're not clear and focused on your highest-priority to-do items, getting out the door on a regular workday with a sense of accomplishment is impossible. Rush hour — that last hour (or two or three) of the workday — becomes your stressful closing window to get to the stuff that, a mere eight hours earlier, you thought you had all day to accomplish.

This hack presents some strategies for reigning in your workday schedule and getting out the door on time with your most important tasks completed.

Identify and Cut Back on Extra Work

It doesn't always feel like it — especially at the beginning of what seems like a long workday — but your time is limited. There are only 24 hours in the day, and you have a seemingly unlimited number of things you could work on. Here's what to do:

Work on the most important tasks first.

Hack 26, "Set up a Morning Dash," covered how to spend the first hour of your day accomplishing the most important task of the day. Beyond that, look for other areas of inefficiency in how you spend your time. Sometimes it's easy to see unnecessary work you can weed out of your day; other times, it's a tougher decision.

For example, say that you're a freelance graphic designer who volunteers your time and expertise on mailing lists and at industry events to network, make contacts, and drum up business. This strategy has worked so well that in recent months; you've acquired a full roster of clients. Now, getting everything done — paying and nonpaying work — is difficult.

Instead of continuing to volunteer as always (whether out of habit or simply to live up to the expectations of others), decide what's more important: delivering your paying clients' projects on time or volunteer work. These decisions are tricky; presumably you've built a reputation among your peers and gotten client work *because* of your volunteer work. You pride yourself on being a leader in your field and enjoy being someone others come to for advice or consultation. However, the days don't get any longer. As your work life's demands increase in one area, others have got to give.

If you have a hard time getting out the door on time or panic at the end of the day because something critical is undone, it's time to reprioritize and reshuffle how you spend your day. Maybe you don't have to meticulously pore over each receipt every month since you got out of debt; instead, just skim the monthly statement and move on. Perhaps no one on staff actually reads that detailed meeting summary you've typed up and emailed out every week for the past year — or maybe it could be shortened to four or five bullet points. People assign themselves duties that can become stale and unnecessary over time. Identify yours and cut them down or out completely.

Figure out what matters most, focus on that, and find ways to cut out anything extraneous. Some things may have to fall by the wayside, but you want to get the most bang for your time buck.

Stop Your Time Sinks

Using Hack 28, "Quick-Log Your Workday," identify the activities that take large amounts of time to complete. Does a particularly chatty client keep you on the phone for 40 minutes? Does your group always get into extended debates over email? Do staff meetings go off the rails and drone on and on and on?

Stop any team of wild horses you're hitched to by deleting, delegating, streamlining, or constraining tasks that take longer than necessary. Be prepared to firmly but politely cut off a call with Chatty Client. Call an impromptu group meeting to discuss whatever debate they're sending long missives about over email. Excuse yourself from meetings — or work with the leader to keep them short and focused on a definite agenda.

Make Post-Work Appointments

If your child has to be picked up at daycare at 5:30, or your buddy's waiting for you at the bowling alley, or you have reservations with your other half for dinner, chances are you will be up and out of your desk chair on time.

Make dates with yourself or friends for the gym, a movie, or simply dinner at home at 6 o'clock sharp to get yourself out the door on time. Carpooling with a co-worker will not only cut off your day at a predetermined time; it'll save you money on gas and tolls, too.

Set Wrap-Up Alerts

At the beginning of the day, decide what time you're going to leave, and set a wrap-up timer. If your spouse is cooking you dinner tonight and you need to be out the door at 6 p.m., set alerts to go off at 5, 5:30, 5:45, and 5:55 p.m. (more, if necessary), saying, "Hey! Time to wrap up and go home!"

Prepare yourself mentally to start closing up shop ahead of time so that you're not surprised when your other half calls at 6:30, wondering where you are. Calendar software — such as Google Calendar, Microsoft Outlook, iCal, or a simple timer (discussed in Hack 29, "Dash Through Tasks With a Timer") — usually supports reminders at specific intervals before a scheduled event. Use them as your early-warning system — "Head home in 30 minutes!"

Hack 32: Turn Tasks into Game Play

Level . . . . **Easy**

Platform . . . . **All**

Cost . . . . **Free**

Marketers get you to do things using game play all the time: frequent-flier miles, those stamped cards at ice cream places that earn you a free cone after you buy eight, and under-the-soda-cap promotions that get you a free song download are all examples. You can use the same technique to psych yourself into getting work done.

Ever wish you could knock down the items on your to-do list with the same gusto you fit blocks together in Tetris or collect gold coins in Super

Mario Bros.? Granted, cleaning out the refrigerator will never be as fun as taking out a sea of grunts in Halo, but if you reframe even the most dreaded task into a game with levels, points, rewards, and a bit of friendly competition, you'll be done before you know it.

Make It to the Next Level

Break your task down into chunks, and track your progress to completion with a level-o-meter. Think of a fundraiser "thermometer" whose red marker rises as more money is raised. In the same manner, you can draw a personal progress bar to track your own road to completion. This technique works especially well for group projects.

Say that you have a 10-page paper due for class. Before you start writing, find a nearby whiteboard or poster board and draw out a progress bar split into 10 sections. Each time you write one page, color in one section of the bar. It's completely mental, but getting to the next level can be a huge motivator.

Collaborate, Compete, and Reward

The best way to knock the *dreaded* out of *dreaded task* is to work alongside someone. To help stay focused, create a friendly competition to help yourselves get through it, with a reward at the end of the work.

For example, my brother and I are both chronically late people. When we once worked in the same office, we'd drive in together, picking one another up on alternate days. We chose a time to be outside for pickup, and any time one of us was late, we marked it down. As we went on, the rules of engagement intensified, with synchronized watches and 60-second grace periods — and whoever accrued five more late marks than the other had to treat for lunch. The end result? We were on time — even early — at the office more than ever. The funny thing is, it became less about the lunch or even getting in on time, and more about the bragging rights and the game of it, enjoyable even at 6:45 in the morning. (Note: this works especially well with a competitive brother.)

Bribe Yourself

Tough tasks can be more fun when there's a reward or reason to enjoy them at the finish. For example, if you save the latest episode of *Mad Men* on your iPod to watch on the treadmill at the gym, you're much more likely to want to get there! If you've promised yourself a smoothie after your presentation's done, or even just a fancy coffee drink after you've finished leading that meeting you prepared for all week, you'll give yourself a much-deserved reward and create a pleasurable light at the end of the tunnel.

Time Yourself

One of the most effective techniques is to knock down big jobs in small, focused, time-based chunks. Set a timer for 60 minutes and dive in, and when the hour is up, stop. Just knowing that the clock is ticking makes you try to get as much as possible done before that timer beeps. This is great for computer-based tasks such as email triage and cleaning out the closet or purging your file cabinet. You can even pick a goal of several items to accomplish in that hour and work to reach it; doing it this way hones your task/time estimation skills as well. See Hack 29, "Dash Through Tasks with a Timer" for more on timed dashes.

Whether you have to do your taxes, clean out the refrigerator, or finally sort through that monstrous pile of clothing that's been collecting in the corner of the bedroom for a month, turning any task into a game can ease the pain and help you psych yourself into knocking it out and checking it off your list as complete.

NOTE This hack was inspired by Amy Jo Kim's "Putting the Fun into Functional" presentation at O'Reilly's Emerging Technology conference in March 2006.

Apps That Turn Work into Play

Making work feel like play isn't always going to be easy — it is still *work*, after all — but if games help motivate you, a few fun tools have been designed specifically to meld work and play into one fun little package.

First, for your on-the-go to-do list, there's Epic Win (www.rexbox.co.uk/epicwin/), an iOS app that combines your to-do list with a role-playing game. Every time you check an item off your list, you gain more experience points and, eventually, level up your Epic Win character.

If household chores are a particularly tough part of your day, or you could use some help motivating individuals in your household, there's Chore Wars (http://www.chorewars.com/), another role-playing game, this time focused around delegating and completing chores in your household.

Finally, if you need some extra help keeping your email inbox empty — like described in Hack 1, "Empty Your Inbox (and Keep It Empty)" — there's 0Boxer (www.0boxer.com/), a game that integrates with your Gmail account and awards you points for every email you archive and reply to, as shown in Figure 3-9. You can even compare your inbox-zero accomplishments with friends who also use 0Boxer.

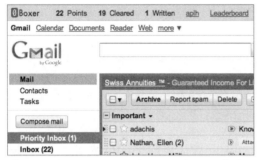

Figure 3-9: 0Boxer awards you points each time you archive, reply to, and otherwise clear out messages from your inbox.

References

1. *Science Daily*, "Why Do We Overcommit? Study Suggests We Think We'll Have More Time In The Future Than We Have Today" (www.sciencedaily.com/releases/2005/02/050211084233.htm).

2. Steven Pressfield, *The War of Art* (Warner Books, 2002).

3. SARK, *The Bodacious Book of Succulence* (Simon & Schuster, 1998), p. 35.

4. Merlin Mann, *43 Folders*, "Building a Smarter To-Do List" (www.43folders.com/2005/09/12/building-a-smarter-to-do-list-part-i/).

5. Merlin Mann, *Macworld*, "How to do a to-do list" (www.macworld.com/2006/07/secrets/augworkingmac/index1.php).

6. Julie Morgenstern, *Never Check Email in the Morning* (Simon & Schuster, 2004), p. 97.

7. Julie Morgenstern, *Time Management from the Inside Out* (Henry Holt, 2004), p. 181.

8. "The Pomodoro Technique," Pomodorotechnique.com (www.pomodorotechnique.com/).

9. Kathy Sierra, "Creating Passionate Users" (http://headrush.typepad.com/creating_passionate_users/2005/12/creativity_on_s.html).

10. Brad Isaac, "Jerry Seinfeld's Productivity Secret," Lifehacker.com (`http://lifehacker.com/software/motivation/jerry-seinfelds-productivity-secret-281626.php`).

11. Benjamin Franklin. (1706–1790). *The Autobiography of Benjamin Franklin.* Available at `http://bartelby.com/1/1/4.html#179`.

Clear Your Mind

Your mind is a powerful computer. But sometimes it works *against* you instead of with you. Your brain makes complex decisions and stores years' worth of information, yet there's one thing it doesn't do well: think of what you need when you need it, and let go of nagging thoughts when you *don't* need them.

When you walk past the dairy section at the grocery store, you don't realize you have only a day's worth of milk left in the fridge at home. When do you remember the milk? When you stand in the kitchen with no milk and a box of cereal in your hand.

Short-term memory is a lot like RAM, the temporary memory on a personal computer. It's where you keep all the things you see and experience, and the thoughts that pop into your head throughout the day: "Gotta call the vet when I get home." "Didn't realize that new Italian place is there; should invite her out to dinner this weekend." "Wonder how much a Spanish class would cost." "Darn, I never emailed Jim back about those forms!"

Productivity expert David Allen says these types of thoughts all represent unfulfilled commitments you've made to yourself — what he calls *open loops* — that distract and overwhelm you, creating stress, anxiety, and a constant sense that there's too much to do: "Your conscious mind, like the computer screen, is a focusing tool, not a storage place. You can think about only two or three things at once. But the incomplete items are still clogging up your short-term-memory space. As with RAM, your short-term memory has a limited capacity; there's only so much 'stuff' you can store in there and still have that part of your brain function at a high level. Most people walk around with their RAM bursting at the seams. They're constantly distracted, their focus disturbed by their own internal mental overload."[1]

Today there are more tools than ever that can help you capture information, organize it, slingshot it back to you at the moment you need it, and access it from any computer or handheld gadget. After you create your "outboard brain,"[2] you'll have a system that you trust to get you what you need when you need it. That way, you can focus all your available brain power on the task you're working on this very moment.

Whether your brain's nagging you to remember that you're due for a dental appointment, or you want to stow away that tidbit you found online for next week's presentation, the only way to deal with all the stuff in your head is to get it off your mind and into a trustworthy system that can help you recall it at the right time and in the right place.

This chapter explores various capture systems that offload distractions, pop-up thoughts, and to-do lists to your computer for easy recall, timely reminders, and, ultimately, a clear head.

Hack 33: Send Reminders to Your Future Self

Level . . . . **Easy**

Platform . . . . **Web**

Cost . . . . **Free**

Every day you have a lot on your mind and a lot to do. As a result, it can be nearly impossible to remember mundane recurring tasks — such as when it's time to change the oil or go to the dentist — or even important yearly events, such as friends' and family members' birthdays.

Most smart phones and calendar software have some kind of reminder feature, but who knows what gadget or type of computer you'll be using next year when Mom's birthday rolls around. What you *do* know is that you'll be checking your email or carrying a cell phone.

There's a simple way to remind yourself of important events and tasks without being tied down to a particular software or device. The free, web-based Google Calendar (http://calendar.google.com) can send an email or text message to you with event and task information on the days and times you specify. You can create a time-based reminder file that emails your future self the data you'll need to know at just the right moment in time.

WEB-BASED CALENDAR AS TICKLER FILE

Productivity expert David Allen advises readers of his book *Getting Things Done* to keep a "tickler file" to track recurring or time-based tasks,[3] such as that bill due on the 9th of each month. Allen's tickler file is a physical, paper accordion file that contains 43 folders: 12 folders (one for each month of the year) plus 31 folders (one for each day of the month). Allen says that every day, you should consult your tickler file and pull any paper reminders of time-based tasks out of it and do them. The first day of each month, you move the 31-day folders into the current month folder.

Although Allen's tickler file concept is incredibly useful (especially for paper reminders), the physical folder implementation is "pull" technology. You (or your staff) must check it every day to see whether a bill or an assignment is due, even on the days when there isn't anything (which is a waste of time on those days). Additionally, it's too easy to forget to check your tickler or not be physically near it on the days you're out of the office.

The calendar-based reminder setup outlined in this hack serves the same purpose as Allen's tickler, except it is "push" technology. Instead of having to check yet another place for tasks, your reminders come to you in your email inbox or on your cell phone, which you're already regularly checking. This method doesn't require that you incorporate a new habit into your day and can also deliver you information "just in time." For example, directions to the office building you're headed toward can arrive on your cell phone exactly half an hour before the meeting.

To get your reminder file started, go to Google Calendar, sign into your Google account, and then follow these steps:

1. Click the Create Event link at the top left of the Calendar.

2. Name your event (Mom's birthday, for example) in the text box that says Click to Add a Title.

3. Enter the date and time of the event. For a birthday or due bill, check the All Day box. For recurring events, such as birthdays or anniversaries, click the Repeat check box and choose the time frame (that is, yearly, monthly, weekly, or daily). Google Calendar is smart

enough to figure out even the strangest recurring event — say the third Saturday of every other month.

4. Enter the reminder message you want to receive about your event in the Description text box. Include all the information you'll need to accomplish the task or manage the event.

5. Adjust the Reminders drop-down menus to set alerts to arrive anywhere from five minutes to four weeks in advance of the event. Choose how to receive the reminder (see Figure 4-1): an email, pop-up dialog, or SMS message. Email notifications are available to any user anytime, but the pop-up dialog appears only when you're logged into Google Calendar on your computer. SMS notifications are only available if you've verified your phone. To do so, navigate to Settings ⇨ Calendar Settings, click the Mobile Setup tab, enter your cell phone number and carrier, and click Send Verification Code. Google will send a verification code via SMS; enter that code, click Finish setup, and you're verified.

6. Click the Save button at the bottom of the page to save your event.

TIP You can also add guests to your repeating event if, for example, you want to remind your significant other of his mother's birthday. Just add an email address to the Add Guests input. If your invitee is also a Google Calendar user, the event will automatically show up on his calendar.

Figure 4-1: Configure your event in Google Calendar.

NOTE Make sure your Google Calendar knows what time zone you're in so that you receive reminders when you expect them. Click Settings ⇨ Calendar Settings on the top right of any Google Calendar page to set your time zone.

That's it; now you're guaranteed to always get a message from yourself before your mother's birthday: "Order flowers for Mom! Her birthday is in two days!"

SHORTCUT

Google's Quick add link, located directly to the right of the Create Event button, enables you to quickly create new events using "plain language" — that is, language you might use if you were telling a personal assistant to add something to your calendar. For more, see Hack 59, "Become a Scheduling Black Belt with Google Calendar."

Repeat these steps for each event or task you want to remind your future self about. Beyond birthdays, due dates, and oil changes, some other ways to use your Google Calendar reminder system include the following:

- **Remember tasks that need to be done far in advance.** You call the fireplace cleaner in February for an appointment, and he tells you to try back in July. Add a summer email reminder that says, "Call Joe Fireplace Cleaner at 555-1212 for an appointment." Notice the inclusion of a phone number: make it as easy as possible for your future self to get the task done.

- **Send yourself info on the go.** On Monday, you make plans to go to the roller derby Friday night with friends. So you add an event to your Google Calendar for 5 p.m. Friday night that sends a text message to your mobile phone: "Gotham Girls roller derby tonight at Skate Key, 4 train to 138th Street. Meet outside at 7:15." Directions and specific time are included — the more info, the better.

- **Interrupt yourself.** You're super involved in a project at work, but you have lunch plans at 1 o'clock across town. So you set up a pop-up reminder to trigger at 12:30 that says, "Lunch at Frank's! Get going or you'll be late!"

- **Don't forget the boring but necessary tasks.** Set up quarterly, monthly, biweekly, or weekly reminders for mundane tasks such as these:
  - Water the plants.
  - Get an appointment for a haircut.
  - Send the rent check.
  - Invoice client.
  - Mail out estimated taxes.

Google Calendar enables almost any recurring time frame for events.

- **Get in on events early.** When you find out that tickets go on sale in two weeks for your favorite band's next show, set up a reminder for the day before to round up the troops and storm Ticketmaster. com; send yourself a reminder to get reservations the day they start accepting them for Restaurant Week; or SMS yourself an hour before an eBay auction is scheduled to end.

- **Create a long-term plan and stick to it.** Say that you commit yourself to a year-long savings plan to sock away $200 a month for that vacation to St. Croix. Send yourself an email each quarter that reads, "Hey, self, you should have $xxx in savings right now. Don't forget how great that Caribbean vacation will be!"

- **Reflect and review.** Each New Year's Day or birthday, write yourself an email describing your successes and failures of the past year, and your hopes for the next. Schedule it to arrive exactly one year later. Sure, this sounds like a lame high school writing assignment, but it's actually a fun way to surprise yourself with insight into where you are and where you've been.

NOTE Remember the Milk (http://rememberthemilk.com) is another excellent personal organizer web application that includes an email or SMS reminder feature. See Hack 35, "Organize Your Life with Remember the Milk," for more on using Remember the Milk to manage all your tasks, not just time-based ones.

Hack 34: Take Great Notes

Level....... **Easy**

Platform.... **Pen and Paper**

Cost........ **Free**

Like it or not, your work life involves meetings — status meetings, conference calls, brainstorming sessions, and at its worst, meetings for the sake of meetings. But a meeting is only as valuable as the action taken after everyone's left the conference room.

Whether you're headed to a business meeting, a university lecture, or a conference session, taking effective notes is a critical skill that moves your projects, your career, and your education forward. This hack covers three practical note-taking methods and how to make your own custom note paper for even better note-taking.

Method 1: Symbolize Next Actions

Using note paper or a simple text file on your laptop, indent each line of your notes from the left margin. Then, use a simple system of symbols to mark off four different information types in the left column space in the margin. The following table describes the most useful symbols:

SYMBOL	DESCRIPTION
[ ] or ❏	A square check box denotes a to-do item.
( ) or o	A circle indicates a task to be assigned to someone else.
*	An asterisk is an important fact.
?	A question mark goes next to items to research or ask about.

After the meeting, a quick vertical scan of the margin area makes it easy to add tasks to your to-do list and calendar, send out requests to others, and check out further research questions.[4]

Method 2: Split Your Page into Quadrants

Another way to visually separate information types is to split your note-taking page into quadrants and record different kinds of information — such as questions, references, to-do lists, and tasks to delegate — into separate areas on the page. Rumor has it that this is how Bill Gates — someone known for taking amazingly detailed meeting notes — gets it done.[5]

Method 3: Record and Summarize

The Cornell note-taking method works best for students or researchers digesting large amounts of information on a daily basis. The purpose of this system is to avoid recopying your notes after the fact; that is, to simply get it right the first time. To use this method, separate the page into different areas, as shown in Figure 4-2.[6]

Use the page sections as follows:

■ **Note-taking area:** Record the lecture, discussion, or meeting as completely as possible using brief sentences in paragraphs. This area will contain the meat of the information to which you will refer later. Capture general ideas, and when the meeting leader or instructor moves on to a new point, skip a few lines and begin a new paragraph.

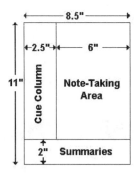

Figure 4-2: A page split into areas for use with the Cornell note-taking method.

- **Cue column:** Jot questions and one-liners that connect main ideas in your notes in the cue column. Later, during a study or review session, cover up the right side of the page and use the left column's cues to help you recall facts.

- **Summary:** After the class or meeting, write a sentence or two at the bottom of the page summarizing the content of your page of notes. Use the summary section to scan your note pages and quickly find topics of discussion.

Print Custom Note Paper

A few free web applications produce custom PDFs of formatted, lined note paper. Print several copies before your next meeting or class and put them in your notes binder.

- **The Notepaper Generator** (http://simson.net/notepaper) Simson. net creates a PDF file of a lined page with a small monthly calendar in the header and an optional summary box in the upper-right corner. Choose your font face and optionally include punch holes as well.

- **The Cornell Method PDF Generator** (http://eleven21.com/ notetaker) prints pages split into the Cornell note paper style with unlined, ruled, or graphed sections. Optionally include your name, the date, and the name of your class, and up to four punch holes for use in a binder. Also, choose the line darkness on a scale from gray to black.

- **Michael Botsko's Notepad Generator** (http://botsko.net/Demos/ notepad_generator; note the capital D in Demos) makes a PDF notes template that includes your name, the page number, date, and project name, plus it splits the page into two sections: one for notes (with lines) and the other for action items with due dates. It also has optional punch holes.

Hack 35: Organize Your Life with Remember the Milk

Level . . . . **Medium**

Platform . . . . **Web**

Cost . . . . **Free**

Even in this advanced age of software, keeping track of your work and personal to-do lists, projects, and due dates isn't easy. Chances are you use a system at the office to track your tasks — such as Microsoft Outlook — and use something else at home — such as a whiteboard on the refrigerator. But the lines between work and life are blurring. You spend more time using different computers and handheld devices while you're on the go. You have work, school, family, home, and side business matters to track. Now it's more important than ever to consolidate your lists into one, always-accessible place. There are dozens of robust, free online organizers out there, but one of the most stable and mature in the bunch is a web application called Remember the Milk (http://rememberthemilk.com).

Because it's a web-based service that you control, you can merge your personal, work, and family lists in a single place with Remember the Milk. Let's take a look at some of Remember the Milk's basic and then more advanced features.

NOTE If you're accustomed to storing your information in desktop software such as Microsoft Outlook, depending entirely on a website like Remember the Milk may seem like a scary prospect. But as dynamic software moves off the desktop and onto the Web, the greatest advantage to users is its accessibility and portability. Using a web application such as Remember the Milk, you can get to your information from any Internet-connected computer with just a web browser. Remember the Milk is also accessible via a number of mobile devices and third-party add-ons, providing better on-the-go access or integration with the tools you already use (such as Outlook). See the Recommended Apps and Add-Ons section at the end of this hack for more favorites.

Managing Tasks

After you register for a free account at Remember the Milk (RTM) and log in, the home page displays the Tasks view, which organizes your tasks into categories — by default: Inbox, Personal, Study, Work, and Sent. RTM automatically includes a starting task in your Personal List Due Today: Try out Remember the Milk. To add a new task to your Personal list, click the Add Task text box (or type the keyboard shortcut "t") and type in a description, as shown in Figure 4-3.

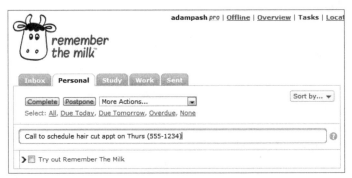

Figure 4-3: Enter a new task by clicking the Add a New Task input on top of your task list.

Press Enter to save the new task in your list. After you create a new task, click the task to view its task box on the right side of the page; it contains editable details about that task. There you can set when it's due, whether it repeats, about how long it will take, where it's located, any associated website addresses, and more. You can even click the Notes tab and add more freehand text information about the task (such as which stylist to request). A simple task such as calling the salon to schedule a haircut appointment probably doesn't need too many more details, but more complex tasks — or tasks you'll share with other users who may need more direction — are good candidates for the notes and URL fields.

If you click the Overview link at the top left of the page, RTM switches to a three-tab view, organizing tasks by when they're due: today, tomorrow, and overdue.

Prioritizing Tasks

You can also prioritize tasks so that more important items show up at the top of the list in a particular color. To do so, select a task and press the 1,

2, or 3 key to assign priority. To remove already assigned priority, press the 4 key.

Completing Tasks

Now that you added a task with details, you officially completed your Try Out Remember the Milk task. To mark it as complete, select the check box next to it, deselect any other tasks, and click the Complete button. It will disappear from your list. It's not gone forever, though. You can always see completed tasks for any list in the List box in the right sidebar. Click the 1 completed link to view the Try Out Remember the Milk task.

Managing Lists and Tags

As you add your to-do's to RTM, you may find that you don't use the lists it has set up for you (Personal, Study, Work). For example, if you're not in school, you probably don't need the Study list. You can delete that list and add other lists that do apply to you. To do so, click the Settings link on the top right of any page in RTM, and then click the Lists tab. Here you can select any list to delete it, archive it, or set it as your default. To add a new list, click the Add List link. The RTM lists you create and manage depend entirely on your life, businesses, and current projects. I've archived a few lists (shown in italics), deleted the Study list, and added Website, and Home Improvement lists to RTM, as shown in Figure 4-4.

Figure 4-4: Enter a new list by clicking Add List, or edit an existing list by selecting it and choosing an action from the drop-down menu.

NOTE The Inbox and Sent lists have lock icons next to them. That's because they're permanent lists that serve a special purpose: to act much the same as email does. The Inbox contains tasks that you emailed or added to RTM without specifying a list, or that other users have sent you. The Sent list contains tasks you sent to other RTM users, such as your co-worker or spouse.

In addition to categorizing your tasks into tabbed lists, you can also slice and dice task lists down further using tags. In the Tasks view, select any task from any list, and in the details box on the right side, click Tags to enter keywords for a task. For example, you may tag the tasks on your Home Improvement list by room, as shown in Figure 4-5.

Figure 4-5: Tag your tasks by specific keywords to subcategorize your to-do lists even further.

After your tasks are tagged, you can easily view the list of home-improvement items for the garage, or for the patio, or for the home office, for example.

WARNING It's easy to waste time organizing your tasks in a rich application such as RTM, which has lots of ways to categorize and input information about something. Remember: the purpose here is to actually get things done, not build a perfectly organized list. Use only the tags, fields, and lists that actually help you and not just satisfy some innate desire to perfect a complex categorization system.

Setting Task Reminders

Remember the Milk can also notify you when tasks are due via a medium of your choice (email, SMS, or instant messenger). For example, when you need to pick up that package before the post office closes at 5 p.m., RTM can send an SMS to your cell phone with a reminder at 4 p.m. To set up task reminders in RTM, click the Settings link on the top right of any RTM page, and then click the Reminders tab. There you can set how far in advance you want task reminders and through what medium(s) you'd like to receive them, as shown in Figure 4-6.

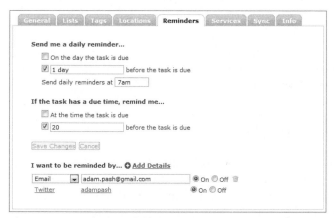

Figure 4-6: Set how and when you want RTM to send you reminders about tasks that have a due date or time.

RTM supports several instant messenger networks for IM reminders, including AIM, Google Talk, ICQ, Yahoo! Messenger, MSN Messenger, Jabber, and Skype. To receive SMS reminders on your cell phone, use the drop-down list to select your cell phone service and add your mobile number.

NOTE Make sure RTM knows what time zone you're in so that you receive reminders when you expect them. In the Settings area, click the General tab, and make sure your time zone is correctly listed there.

Searching Tasks

Quickly search for tasks from RTM's search box, located at the upper-right side of any RTM screen. (You can use the Ctrl+Shift+/ keyboard shortcut to move your cursor into the search box so that you won't have to reach for the mouse.) By default, RTM searches only the main task line of currently undone tasks, not notes and not completed or archived tasks. To extend your search (or narrow it by date or list), click the Show Search Options link, which offers several input fields for tightening your search results, as shown in Figure 4-7.

To collapse the advanced search area, click the Hide Search Options link.

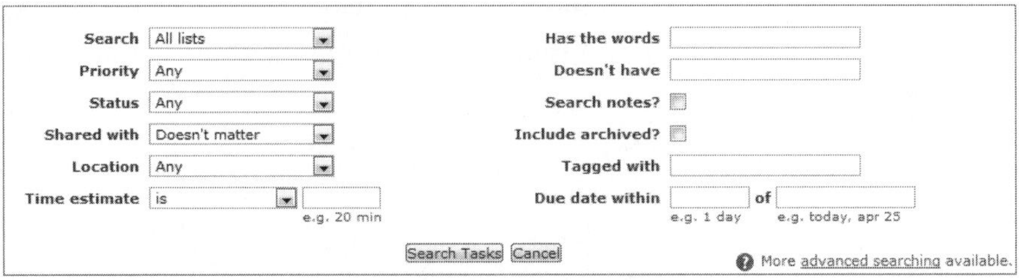

Figure 4-7: Using the search options form, narrow your results by specifying where and how RTM should search your lists.

Advanced Search Operators

You can also do a complex search in RTM from the single search box using advanced operators. For example, to search for the word *salon* in your Personal list, enter **list:personal salon** into the search box. Other useful advanced search operators include the following:

- **priority:** — Specifies the priority of the tasks you're searching. For example, `priority:1` searches the highest-priority tasks and `priority:none` returns all tasks that have no priority assigned.

- **dueWithin:** and **due:** — Specify a date range for due date. For example, `dueWithin:"3 days"` returns tasks due in the next three days. (Enclose any descriptions that involve more than one word in quotation marks to associate the entire phrase with the `dueWithin:` operator.) Similarly, `due: "Oct 10"` shows you all the tasks due on the 10th, and `due:never` displays all tasks with no due date set.

- **timeEstimate:** — Specifies the estimated amount of time a task takes. For example, `timeEstimate: "1 hour"` returns tasks that take an hour to complete; `timeEstimate: "< 1 hour"` returns tasks that take less than an hour.

> **TIP** Get the full list of available advanced search operators at `http://` `rememberthemilk.com/help/answers/search/advanced.rtm`.

Save Searches in Smart Lists

If you do particular searches often, you can save those searches into Smart Lists for one-click access to those results later (saving yourself the effort of typing the search criteria every time). For instance, to save a list of quick tasks — items that take 20 minutes or less to complete — run a search for less-than-20-minute tasks. (Enter `timeEstimate: "< 20 minutes"` into RTM's search box.) On the right side, click the Save tab to make this search a Smart List. There you can name your Smart List — I called my list of less-than-20-minutes-to-complete jobs Quick Tasks — and save it. From there, the Quick Tasks Smart List appears below all lists and shows you a subset of tasks that you can complete in less than 20 minutes each.

For more suggestions of great Smart Lists (such as tasks that have no due date or tasks that have the word *email* in them), see `http://rememberthemilk.com/help/answers/smartlists/whatare.rtm`.

More RTM Techniques

Remember the Milk has several more useful features — read on.

The Weekly Planner

Users who like to work with their to-do list on paper can print the weekly planner view at `http://rememberthemilk.com/printplanner/your.username`. (Substitute `your.username` with your RTM name in the URL.) Available from RTM's default homepage (click the Weekly Planner link), this page gives you a week's worth of tasks with priority and list information and large check boxes ready for you to X off with your pen.

Similarly, for any given list in RTM, use the Print link in the List box on the right side to print all the items on that list.

Add Tasks via Email

RTM users who live out of their email inbox (or have easy access to email on their mobile phone) can easily dash off tasks and send them to RTM via email. In the Settings area, go to the Info tab, and copy to your email application's address book the special, private inbox email address that RTM has assigned to you. From there you can send tasks via email to RTM:

1. Put the special email address in your message's To: field
2. Add the name of the task in your message's subject line
3. Leave the message body empty
4. Send the message, and the task will appear in your RTM Inbox

Advanced email users can even assign priority, tags, and notes using special message-formatting rules. (See `http://rememberthemilk.com/help/answers/sending/emailinbox.rtm` for more info on how to compose your task email messages for RTM.)

Keyboard Shortcuts

Switching between a mouse and keyboard to navigate RTM's web interface can quickly become tiring. To get around faster and more efficiently, teach yourself RTM's extensive set of keyboard shortcuts that enable you to access almost all its features without reaching for the mouse. Print a copy of RTM's keyboard shortcut reference, available at `http://rememberthemilk.com/help/answers/basics/keyboard.rtm`.

View Your RTM Tasks on Your Calendar or Home Page

You don't have to be at the RTM website to see your tasks and due dates. Subscribe to your due tasks in iCal or Google Calendar, or view them on your iGoogle or Netvibes personalized home page. See RTM's Help section for where to find the iGoogle and Netvibes modules and the syndication feeds you can add to iCal or Google Calendar.

Recommended RTM Apps and Add-Ons

The more places you can access and edit your RTM lists, the more useful they'll be, and RTM isn't limited to your web browser. Following are some of the better RTM apps and add-ons for integrating your tasks with other devices and services:

- **MilkSync for Outlook:** Sync your RTM tasks between the website and your Microsoft Outlook tasks. `www.rememberthemilk.com/services/milksync/outlook`

- **RTM for iOS:** Take your RTM tasks with you on your iPhone, iPod touch, and iPad. `www.rememberthemilk.com/services/iphone`

- **RTM for Android:** Use RTM on your Android-powered phone or tablet. `www.rememberthemilk.com/services/android/`

- **RTM for Gmail:** Integrate your RTM tasks directly inside your Gmail account. You can install RTM for Gmail as a free extension for Chrome or Firefox or as an embedded Gmail gadget. `www.rememberthemilk.com/services/gmail`

NOTE Apart from RTM for Gmail, the official RTM apps and add-ons previously listed require a $25 per year RTM Pro account (www.rememberthemilk.com/upgrade). **A pro account gives you access to RTM's mobile apps, Outlook plug-in, and upcoming features.**

For a fuller list of RTM-integrated apps and services, see www.rememberthemilk.com/services.

Hack 36: Organize Your Life in Text Files

Level. . . . . . . **Beginner to Advanced**

Platform . . . . **Windows (Cygwin), Mac OS X, Unix**

Cost. . . . . **Free**

Hack 35, "Organize Your Life with Remember the Milk," describes a rich application that can track your tasks, their priority, category, project, notes, due dates, and more. But all those bells and whistles can be too much of a distraction or learning curve when you just want a quick-and-dirty way to make a list fast, check off items on it, and be done. No matter how many new-fangled personal-organizer applications become available, new computer users and veterans alike still frequently turn to the old standby for tracking to-dos: a file called todo.txt.

A plain-text file is an effective, no-frills way to capture and manage tasks, notes, and other lists. This hack covers some todo.txt best practices and ways to interact with your plain-text files.

Why Plain Text?

Plain text is application- and operating-system agnostic. It's searchable, portable, lightweight, and easily manipulated. It's unstructured. It works when someone else's web server is down or your Outlook .pst file is corrupted. It's free, and because it has been around since the dawn of computing time, it's safe to say that plain text is completely future-proof. There's no exporting and importing and no databases or tags or flags or stars or prioritizing or Insert-Company-Name-Here–induced rules on what you can and can't do with it. It's small enough to fit on even the tiniest USB flash drive or email inbox size limit. It's also dead-simple to use with your favorite text editor.

MORE ON PLAIN TEXT

"Complicated applications crash, or get abandoned by their creators, or just keel over from feature-bloat and become unusable around version 5.0. Power users trust software as far as they have thrown their computers in the past.

One way to think of text files is the grimy residue left over when an application explodes in your face. You put all your data into, say, Palm Desktop, and then one day you lose your Palm or move to a platform that can't read your desktop files. So you export it all into plain text, and try grimly to import it into the next big application. After a while, you just stay with the plain text because it's easier.

Text files have some concrete advantages, too: you can get stuff into them quickly, and you can search them easily. Getting data in and out fast, and in a non-distracting way, is really the most important thing for a filing system. That is its very point."
— Danny O'Brien, Lifehacker Researcher 7

Using an Editor to Manage Your Text Files

The easiest and most common way to interact with your `todo.txt` and other text files is with a simple text editor, most likely the first tool you ever used on a personal computer. Although Windows comes with the Notepad text editor built in (and Mac OS X comes with TextEdit), neither of these has the two main useful features you need. To work with text-file lists effectively, install an editor that can open and edit multiple files at one time and sort the items on your lists. For Windows users, use Notepad++, a free, open-source application available for download at `http://notepad-plus-plus.org`. Mac users: download and install a free copy of TextWrangler, available at `www.barebones.com/products/textwrangler`.

Allocate One Task per Line

For any list-type file such as `todo.txt`, enter exactly one task on a given line. Although at first this may seem to be an unnecessary constraint, there's no limit to how long the line can be, and most text editors wrap it automatically for easy reading. The advantage to the one-item-per-line rule is that you can easily prioritize, sort, and move your items from one file to another.

Sorting Items

Advanced text editors such as TextWrangler and Notepad++ come with the capability to sort the lines of text in a file alphabetically. This lesser-known feature is quite handy for lists such as `todo.txt`: simply mark off task importance using an alphabetical notation that enables you to sort your list to get the high-priority items at the top. Use an uppercase letter surrounded by parentheses at the beginning of your task to enable easy sorting. For example, the following to-do list:

```
Update website news area with latest press release
FedEx status report by 3PM
Call dentist to make appointment for 6 month cleaning
```

could be prioritized this way:

```
(B) Update website news area with latest press release
(A) FedEx status report by 3PM
(C) Call dentist to make appointment for 6-month cleaning
```

Now, with the `todo.txt` file open in your preferred editor, you can sort that list so that the highest-priority item shows at the top. For example, in Notepad++, choose TextFX ➪ Tools ➪ Sort lines case insensitive (at column) — see Figure 4-8) — to reorder the list.

The result places the item prioritized (A) at the top, followed by (B) and then (C). To mark an item as complete, you can either delete it entirely from the file or place an X at the beginning of the line. Then, re-sorting places completed items at the bottom of the file.

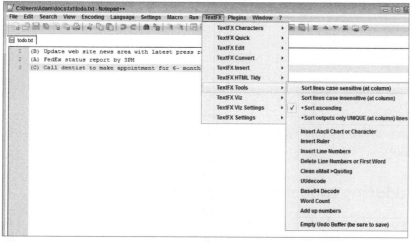

Figure 4-8: Sort lines of text in your list from the Tools menu in Notepad++ for Windows.

Transfer Tasks from One File to Another

If you're following Hack 25's recommendations for keeping your to-do list achievable, you have other lists that contain items that don't belong there, such as `projects.txt` and `somedaymaybe.txt`. As you complete tasks and review your lists, you need to move items among them easily. Using Notepad++ or TextWrangler, you can open all your text files in a single window and cut and paste lines between them to transfer items.

Say, for instance, you're putting the next action for a project onto your working `todo.txt`. Open both files in your editor, which enables you to switch between them by clicking the filename or tab. Cut and paste the appropriate line from `projects.txt` into `todo.txt`, or from `todo.txt` to `somedaymaybe.txt`, and save all your changes.

Using the Command Line to Manage Text Files

Advanced users accustomed to working at the Unix command line know several tools can search, append to, and filter text files. For example, the `grep` command can list all the items in your `todo.txt` that contain the word *email*. Using the Mac OS X Terminal or the Cygwin Unix emulator on Windows, issue the following command (not counting the dollar sign, which represents the prompt):

```
$ grep email todo.txt
```

That prints to the terminal only the lines in `todo.txt` that contain the word *email*. Likewise, you can append a line to the file by using the following command:

```
$ echo "Drop off the dry cleaning" >> todo.txt
```

Similarly, the `sort` command can list your `todo.txt` by priority:

```
$ sort todo.txt
```

Remembering all those commands can be inconvenient, so over the past five years I put together a singular command-line interface to a `todo.txt` file that contains one item per line.[8]

Introducing todo.sh and todo.txt Touch

A freely available bash script called `todo.sh` wraps the aforementioned Unix text commands (and several more) into an interface built specifically for `todo.txt`. Using `todo.sh`, you can automatically sort the contents of your todo.txt by priority, filter lines by keyword, add tasks, prioritize existing tasks using the (A), (B), (C) notation, and more. See http://todotxt.com to download the todo.sh script and get instructions on setting it up on your system.

Whether you use the shortcuts provided by todo.sh, if you follow the todo.txt formatting methodology described in this hack, you can also get your to-do's on-the-go with Todo.txt Touch, an Android application that manages and syncs your to-do's with your desktop todo.txt file via Dropbox. (For more on Dropbox, see Hack 67, "Access Your Most Important Data Anywhere with Dropbox.")

A whole community of users and developers has come together to discuss and devise creative uses for todo.txt and shortcuts. Visit http://todotxt.com and join the mailing list to ask questions, make suggestions, and explore other ways you can put todo.txt to work for you.

Hack 37: Set Up a Ubiquitous Note-Taking Inbox Across Devices

Level....... **Medium**

Platform.... **All**

Cost........ **Free**

Ubiquitous capture — that is, the ability to snag any thought or idea any time and any where it happens to crop up — is a key component to nearly every productivity philosophy. You want to capture those fleeting ideas before they're gone, and you don't want to waste brain power obsessing over remembering them until you can write them down somewhere.

When you have a great idea, want to add something to your "Gifts for E" list, or think of a great opening sentence to that paper you're writing, you want to capture it quickly and painlessly no matter what you're doing. Pen and paper works, but if you're technology-inclined, you want something you can access from your PC, laptop, tablet, or smart phone — and something that can seamlessly sync between all those input devices.

Sync Plain-Text Notes Anywhere with Simplenote

Simplenote (http://simplenoteapp.com) is a web application that does one simple thing extremely well: creating, editing, and managing as many plain text notes as your heart could desire. It has an open API, which means that third-party developers can create (and have created) applications on any platform that sync with Simplenote — making it particularly well suited for ubiquitous capture.

Here's how to get up and running with Simplenote:

1. Visit `http://simplenoteapp.com` and create a new account.

2. Sign into Simplenote's web interface. You'll see a two-paned interface (see Figure 4-9). The left sidebar contains a list of all your notes with a search box on top for searching your notes. The larger pane to the right contains the content of your notes.

3. Create your first note by clicking the plus (+) button next to the search box. Name it **My First Note**. (Titles are determined by the first line of text in a note.) You don't have to do anything special to save your note — Simplenote takes care of all that.

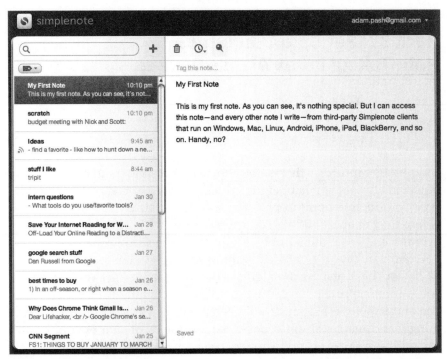

Figure 4-9: Simplenote's default web interface is nice, but you'll probably access your notes more often from a desktop or mobile client.

That's a simple start, but it's not convenient to open a web browser and navigate to Simplenote every time you want to create a new note or add something to an existing note.

Even though Simplenote is a web app, most of the time you won't access your notes using your browser. Instead, use a client that seamlessly syncs notes with the Simplenote API. Simplenote clients run on operating systems ranging from Windows and Mac to iOS and Android (and beyond). Following is a list of native Simplenote clients for popular operating systems:

- **ResophNotes for Windows:** www.resoph.com/ResophNotes/Welcome.html

- **Notational Velocity for Mac:** http://notational.net

- **Simplenote for iOS:** http://simplenoteapp.com/downloads/itunes.html

- **mNote for Android:** http://android.minuo.net/mnote

NOTE Simplenote stores a revision history of your edits, so if you want to see an earlier version of any note, click the Clock button and drag the slider back through previously saved versions of the note, as shown in Figure 4-10.

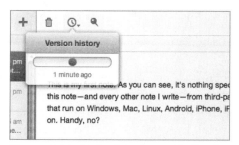

Figure 4-10: Go back in time with Simplenote to see a note's revision history.

You can find a fuller list of third-party downloads from http://simplenoteapp.com/downloads/. What's important is that no matter what device you use to access your notes, anything you write can sync to every other device you've integrated with a Simplenote client.

TIP Like Remember the Milk, described previously, you can tag your notes in Simplenote to quickly sort and access related notes.

For example, say you're at your computer and you remember you need to pick up some toothpaste. You can open your desktop Simplenote client, open your Grocery list, and add **Toothpaste** to the end of it. Later, you're at a friend's house and notice she's stocked up on some delicious in-season clementines. Instead of hoping you'll remember to add **Clementines** to your grocery list when you get home, you can simply pull out your phone, launch your Simplenote client, and add **Clementines** to the same grocery list. It'll sync between Simplenote on the web and your desktop so that you're still looking at the same notes everywhere. When you finally get to the grocery store, you can once again open your phone's Simplenote client and pull up your grocery list.

Go Beyond Plain Text with Evernote

For some people, "notes" extend beyond words they can type into a computer. If you're more of a multimedia note-taker, the plain-text limitations of Simplenote may be too constricting.

Evernote (www.evernote.com) is a ubiquitous capture service that's like a second brain you can dump virtually any information into from nearly any device. Unlike Simplenote, which is limited to plain text notes, Evernote can create rich notes, clip entire web pages, sync camera-phone pictures, and more.

Get to Know Evernote

To start with Evernote, visit www.evernote.com/ and sign up for a new account. You could stick with Evernote's web interface, but it's not as good as the desktop client, so download the desktop version of Evernote for your operating system. While you're at it, install Evernote's Web Clipper to your browser from www.evernote.com/about/download/web_clipper.php.

NOTE Web Clipper is available as an extension for Chrome and Firefox; it installs automatically in Internet Explorer or Safari when you install the desktop client on Windows or Mac, respectively.

After you have everything installed, you're ready to start using Evernote as your universal capture inbox. Here's how it works.

Evernote's three-paned interface (see Figure 4-11) displays your notebooks on the far left pane. Notebooks are like large repositories for similar content. For example, you might create a notebook specifically for home improvement projects, one for your foreign-language study materials, and so on. To create a new notebook, select File ⇨ New Notebook. When you capture a new note, you can choose what notebook to add it to.

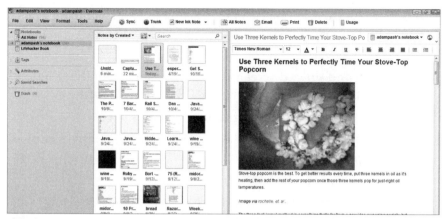

Figure 4-11: Create notebooks and save rich, multimedia notes to your Evernote database.

The middle pane displays a searchable list of content you captured to the active notebook. (Capturing is discussed in the following section.) Click any item in the Notes pane to display the captured text or media in the larger panel to the right.

Capturing Notes with Evernote

To create your first note, launch Evernote on your desktop and click the New Note button. Unlike Simplenote, Evernote enables you to enter rich text, insert images, and attach files (via drag and drop), and incorporate virtually any media you'd like into your notes.

When you save a note, it syncs with your Evernote account online, and to any other computer or mobile device on which you've installed Evernote.

SHORTCUT

To create notes on-the-fly when Evernote's not the active application, simply select any text and images in any application, copy it (Ctrl+C on Windows or Cmd+C on Mac), and then invoke Evernote's universal keyboard shortcut (Win+A in Windows, Cmd+Ctrl+V in OS X) to create a new note from your clipboard.

You aren't limited to clipping text with Evernote. From within the official Evernote applications (for your desktop and mobile device), you can also do the following:

- Capture and upload screenshots to Evernote from the Windows system tray application or the Mac OS X menu bar app.

- Create a new note from your computer's webcam.

- Upload any photo you take with your digital camera or cameraphone.

- Create voice notes from your mobile device.

- Create ink notes that let you sketch out your ideas. (Currently this feature is only available on Windows.)

No matter what form you prefer to take notes in, Evernote can likely handle it. Evernote also excels at capturing information from the web with the help of the Web Clipper browser extension. Here's how to capture a web page to Evernote:

1. Browse to a page on the web you find interesting. It could be a recipe, a great underwater basket-weaving tutorial — whatever. Select the text and images you want to clip.

2. Click the Clip to Evernote button to clip the content to your Evernote database, as shown in Figure 4-12. (If you installed Evernote's Web Clipper, it should be the button that looks like an elephant.)

Figure 4-12: Clip any web content with a click in Evernote, and you'll have access to it forever, in an easy-to-search database.

3. Add tags or any additional notes; then click Done. Evernote saves it to your fully searchable and syncable database, there for you any time you need it.

NOTE Before you get too capture happy, keep in mind that the free version of Evernote limits you to 60 megabytes of uploads per month. If that's not enough for your capturing needs, the $5-per-month premium account offers unlimited uploads.

More Useful Evernote Features

Evernote has more great features: read on!

- **Evernote is completely searchable.** You can search the contents of any note from any device with Evernote. It even scans and analyzes your image for text, so you can search for text *within* images by including pictures from web pages, documents, photos, screenshots, or cameraphone pictures you've uploaded. (For more on taking advantage of Evernote's great character recognition features, see Hack 88, "Develop Your (Digital) Photographic Memory.")

- **Evernote bolsters your pen-and-paper notes.** Because Evernote can recognize text within images — including your handwriting — you can still stick with pen and paper if that's what you prefer in certain situations. After you take your pen-and-paper notes though, consider scanning them or snapping a picture and adding them to Evernote. Now your handwritten notes are also searchable, and they're sitting in the same bucket as all your other notes and bookmarks.

- **Evernote is available for most mobile operating systems.** The more places you can capture notes, the better, so it's handy that Evernote offers official applications for Android, iPhone, iPad, BlackBerry, webOS, and Windows devices. You can find all the official Evernote applications at http://www.evernote.com/about/download/.

- **Evernote supports tagging and advanced search attributes.** Evernote supports tagging like gangbusters, including auto-completion for quick-and-easy tagging. Although the search features of Evernote are robust and useful, you can narrow down your results considerably if you use some tags as a starting point. Tagging is essential to slice and dice through notes and data with Evernote. Similarly, Evernote supports tons of useful search attributes to help you narrow down results. You can filter notes based on when they were created, modified, what kind of media they contain, or the tool you used to capture them (web, mobile, desktop, and so on).

■ **Evernote is an impressive research tool.** Whenever you see information you want to remember, get in the habit of clipping it to Evernote. It's great for building up a personal knowledge database that you can quickly search through any time you need an answer you know you've come across before.

Hack 38: Off-Load Your Online Reading to a Distraction-Free Environment

Level . . . . **Medium**
Platform . . . . **All**
Cost . . . . **Free**

Tabbed browsers are a blessing, but they can also be a curse. Many people pile up tab after tab of unread blog posts, news articles, and Wikipedia entries, creating a de facto to-do list of reading materials and clogging up their browsers.

Hack 25, "Make Your To-Do List Doable," discusses the importance of separating your Someday/Maybe items from your to-do list. You can think of your to-read list in a similar light: Your open browser tabs should contain information you need to access *now*. You start keeping one or two tabs open for those "when I've got time" moments, and the next thing you know, you have 30 tabs open, eating up memory and cluttering up your browser.

Save Your Reading with Instapaper

Free service Instapaper (www.instapaper.com) is "a simple tool to save web pages for reading later." Essentially, when you come across a web page you want to read later, you can save it to Instapaper, which strips the article of ads and other nonessential distractions and makes it accessible for reading later, either on the Instapaper website or from an iOS device — such as an iPhone, iPod touch, or iPad. (The official Instapaper app is only available for iOS; see the Instapaper Tools section for third-party Instapaper clients available for other platforms.)

To set up and start using Instapaper, do the following:

1. Visit www.instapaper.com and create a free account.

2. Navigate to `www.instapaper.com/extras` and drag the Read Later bookmarklet to your browser's bookmark toolbar.

3. Next time you come across one of those web pages you want to read "when you have time," click the Read Later bookmarklet.

4. When you have some free time and want to read that article, open up Instapaper in your browser or on your mobile device to access all your saved articles, ad-free and distraction-free. In the web version of Instapaper, click the Text button next to an article, as shown in Figure 4-13, to view the distraction-free version.

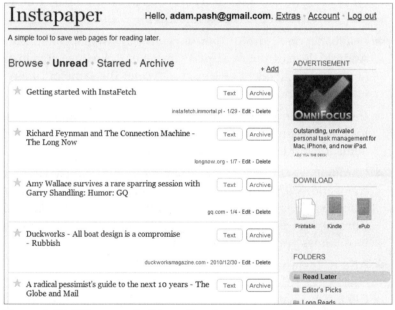

Figure 4-13: When you don't have time to read something on the web, save it to Instapaper instead of cluttering your browser tabs or bookmarks with things you want to read later.

After you read an item, you can archive it, which marks an item as read, so it no longer displays in your Unread inbox. You can visit your archived articles at any time, and you can also star favorites.

NOTE You can also save links or emails (an especially lengthy email or newsletter, for example) to Instapaper using your account's special email address, available on the Extras page at `www.instapaper.com/extras`.

Instapaper Tools

Instapaper is a great tool for distraction-free reading, even if all you ever use is the bookmarklet and the web interface. But Instapaper shines when you start syncing your saved articles for offline reading on mobile devices, or integrating it into your workflow in other ways. Following are a few handy Instapaper tools:

- **Instapaper for iOS:** Perhaps Instapaper's greatest strength is that the official Instapaper iOS app can download and save your read-it-later items offline to your iPhone, iPod touch, or iPad — perfect for reading on the train or when you have a few spare minutes but may not have an Internet connection.

- **Instapaper on Android:** There is no official Instapaper application for Android devices, but third-party Instapaper clients such as InstaFetch (`http://instafetch.immortal.pl`) offer the same offline-reading features to Android users.

- **Instapaper on your Kindle:** You can set up Instapaper to use the Kindle eBook reader's wireless delivery to shuttle your read-it-later items to your eye-friendly eBook reader.

- **Chromapaper extension for Chrome:** As long as you have an Internet connection, you can always access your Instapaper content on the home page from any browser. The Chromapaper extension for Google Chrome (`http://tinyurl.com/4kqxsw6`) adds offline support for those times you don't have a connection.

- **Add to Instapaper from Google Reader:** Instapaper's Read Later bookmarklet also works with the popular newsreader Google Reader. Click Read Later to save any selected Reader item to Instapaper. (For more on Google Reader, see Hack 91, "Subscribe to Websites with RSS.")

References

1. David Allen, *Getting Things Done* (Penguin Books, 2001), 22.
2. Cory Doctorow, "My Blog, My Outboard Brain," O'Reilly Network (`www.oreillynet.com/pub/a/javascript/2002/01/01/cory.html`).
3. David Allen, *Getting Things Done* (Penguin Books, 2001), 173–175.

4. Michael Hyatt, "Recovering the Lost Art of Note-taking." (http://michaelhyatt.com/recovering-the-lost-art-of-note-taking.html).

5. Rob Howard, "Post BillG Review" (http://grokable.com/2003/04/post-billg-review).

6. "Note-Taking and In-Class Skills," San Diego Jewish Academy, (www.writedesignonline.com/human/note-taking.htm).

7. "Interview: Father of 'Life Hacks' Danny O'Brien," Lifehacker.com (http://lifehacker.com/software/interviews/interview-father-of-life-hacks-danny-obrien-036370.php).

8. Gina Trapani, "todo.sh." Lifehacker, April 2006 (http://todotxt.com).

CHAPTER 5

Firewall Your Attention

Your attention is your most endangered resource. The technical props of modern work life — email, instant messaging, cell phones, and constant Internet connectivity — make limitless amounts of information always available at the press of a button. Every minute of every day, advertisements, software notifications, ringing phones, dinging text messages, Facebook notifications, and tweets vie for your attention. But you have a finite number of minutes, hours, and days in your life.

Modern gadgets and software are designed to help you multitask: that's why you can have a dozen windows open on your screen simultaneously, each doing a different job. The problem is that modern computing devices have outpaced humans' capabilities to multitask.

Further, email, cell phones, and instant messenger applications make you reachable and interruptible at any moment in your day. You live in a culture of constant connectivity, and it's easy to get in the habit of responding to those interruptions in kind. But this type of interruption-driven existence can have a devastating effect on your mental focus and your ability to perform. It makes for workers who are distracted, irritated, overwhelmed, and run ragged.

Psychiatrist Edward Hallowell calls the condition Attention Deficit Trait (ADT), a workplace-induced attention deficiency caused by the constant distraction of high-tech devices. He says, "It's sort of like the normal version of attention deficit disorder. But it's a condition induced by modern life, in which you've become so busy attending to so many inputs and outputs that you become increasingly distracted, irritable, impulsive, restless, and, over the long term, underachieving. In other words, it costs you efficiency because you're doing so much or trying to do so much; it's as if you're juggling one more ball than you possibly can."[1]

A University of California at Irvine study showed that businesspeople are interrupted once every 11 minutes on average during the work day.[2] A 2006 *Time* magazine article, which cited the Irvine study, points out that many well-known successful people make a point to shut out these types of interruptions:

> *Some of the world's most creative and productive individuals simply refuse to subject their brains to excess data streams. When a* New York Times *reporter interviewed several winners of MacArthur "genius" grants, a striking number said they kept cell phones and iPods off or away when in transit so that they could use the downtime for thinking. Personal-finance guru Suze Orman, despite an exhausting array of media and entrepreneurial commitments, utterly refuses to check messages, answer her phone, or allow anything else to come between her and whatever she's working on. "I do one thing at a time," she says. "I do it well, and then I move on."[3]*

Orman knows that the key to overcoming ADT is to fully focus on one task at a time. Give yourself the time and space to dig into a problem and reach that state of mind sometimes called *flow*, when you're fully immersed in your task, effortlessly successful, and oblivious to time and external factors.

To get into this zone, block out irrelevant distractions and let in only the information you need to get the job done. Like a computer-system firewall that blocks potential intruders, the techniques presented in this chapter can help you firewall your most precious resource — your attention.

Hack 39: Limit Visits to Time-Wasting Websites

Level........**Advanced**

Platform....**All (Firefox)**

Cost.........**Free**

Picture this: You sit down at your computer to write a report that's due the next day. You fire up a web browser to check the company intranet for a document. For a split second, you glance at your home page. "Wow!" you say. "The Red Sox won in the 17th inning! Let me see what happened…"

Three hours later, no report's been written, and you want to throw yourself out the window.

Sound familiar?

It's too easy to scamper down the rabbit hole of the Web when you have pressing tasks to work on. At one point or another, you've probably burned a few hours clicking around Wikipedia, Amazon, eBay, Flickr, YouTube, Google News, or maybe even Lifehacker when you had a deadline to meet. Surfing efficiently is an exercise in discipline and sometimes outright abstinence is necessary. This hack uses the StayFocusd Chrome extension to blank out certain websites during times you're supposed to be working.

TIP Firefox users looking for a similar tool should try LeechBlock (`https://addons.mozilla.org/en-US/firefox/addon/leechblock`); **you can read more about how to set up LeechBlock at** `http://lifehacker.com/374812`.

Install and Configure StayFocusd

Using the Chrome web browser, download and install the StayFocusd extension from `http://tinyurl.com/ydflsvh`. (For detailed instructions on how to install a browser extension, see Hack 93, "Extend Your Web Browser.")

Now you must determine which sites you burn the most unproductive time on. When you have one offending site in mind, you're ready to go. To set up which sites to block with StayFocusd, simply navigate to an offending site, and then click the StayFocusd button on your Chrome toolbar. A drop-down dialog appears with a link to block this entire site, as shown in Figure 5-1.

Figure 5-1: Set what sites to block by clicking the StayFocusd button on Chrome's toolbar.

StayFocusd allows you ten minutes to browse the sites you add to your blocked list (in total), so by default, you can still indulge a little before you're blocked for good — at least by default. When you visit a site you've added to your blocked list, the StayFocusd button turns red. If you click it, you'll see a timer counting down your allotted browsing time.

You won't always want StayFocusd to play the disapproving watchdog though, so next set the time periods during which StayFocusd should stand between you and these sites. The morning is a good time to slog through the bulk of the day's work, so say you want to allow yourself recreational browsing only after 3 p.m. on weekdays. Follow these steps to do so:

1. Right-click the StayFocusd button and select Options.

2. Click the Active Days link in the sidebar to set the days of the week you want StayFocusd to actively monitor and — if necessary — block you from accessing the sites on your block list. Tick the check boxes next to Monday through Friday.

3. Now click the Active Hours link to adjust the hours during which StayFocusd will restrict your browsing. Set it to the hours you want — for example, say 8 a.m. to 3 p.m. — and click the Set button.

Visiting a Blocked Site

After you save your settings in StayFocusd, whenever you mindlessly hit that time-wasting bookmark after your maximum time allowed per day has run out, you see a message in your browser, as shown in Figure 5-2.

Figure 5-2: The StayFocusd block page.

That's your cue to get back to work and try again later in your allotted time.

Make It Difficult to Disable StayFocusd

Now, a particularly determined procrastinator might say, "If it's a block I can disable, I'll do it." If you find yourself blocked from a time-wasting site that you insist on visiting (and to hell with your deadline), you might think you could go into StayFocusd options and undo the block. However, StayFocusd won't allow you to remove a site from your block list when your time for the day has expired, nor will it allow you to change your allotted time for the day when it's already expired. You also can't turn the extension off for the current day of the week. It even comes with a clever challenge feature that, when enabled (under Options ⇨ Require Challenge), requires you to perform perfectly on a typing test, shown in Figure 5-3, before you can adjust any settings.

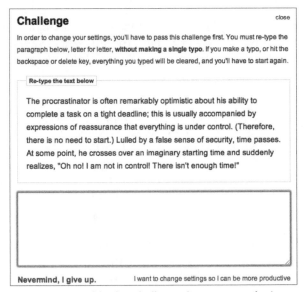

Figure 5-3: Enable the Challenge feature to make it even harder to cheat StayFocusd.

Hack 40: Permanently Block Time-Wasting Websites

Level....... **Advanced**

Platform .... **Windows, Mac OS X**

Cost........ **Free**

Is there a website that's utterly toxic to your mental state or ability to work? Maybe you grind your teeth over your ex's weblog, which details every moment of her happy new life without you. Maybe you've lost hours of your life trolling eBay auctions and you simply can't allow yourself to impulse-buy another autographed Neil Diamond record. Perhaps online backgammon can snatch away hours of your day at the office.

The preceding hack describes how to block time-wasting websites during certain times of the day and week. Alternatively, you can block sites at *all* times, until you explicitly release the restriction. This hack fakes your computer into thinking that those problem sites live on your hard drive — although obviously they don't — and forces a `Server Not Found` error when your fingers impulsively type that tempting, time-sucking URL.

Here's what to do.

Windows

1. Open Notepad or some other text editor (in Windows 7, you need to open your text editor with elevated privileges by right-clicking the editor and clicking Run as Administrator); then open the file named `hosts`, which is located in the following directory: `C:\WINDOWS\SYSTEM32\DRIVERS\ETC`.

2. Add the following on its own line in the `hosts` file:

   ```
   127.0.0.1 ebay.com facebook.com evilex.com
   ```

   Replace the sites listed with the domains that you want to block.

Mac OS X

1. In Finder, choose Go ➪ Go to Folder.

2. In the Go to Folder dialog, type **/etc/**.

3. From the `/etc/` folder window, locate the `hosts` file and Cmd+click it. From the context menu, choose Get Info. In the Ownership & Permissions area, set `You Can` to `Read & Write`.

4. Now open the `hosts` file in a text editor.

5. Add the following on its own line in the `hosts` file:

   ```
   127.0.0.1 ebay.com facebook.com evilex.com
   ```

   Replace the sites listed with the domains that you want to block.

The Result

After you complete the steps for your operating system, save the `hosts` file and quit your editor.

Now when you visit one of your blocked sites, you get a Server Not Found error. (If you're running a web server at home, as detailed in Hack 71, "Run a Home Web Server," your own server's files appear.)

The advantage of this method over Hack 39, "Limit Visits to Time-Wasting Websites" is that the sites are blocked from every browser, not just Chrome (StayFocusd) or Firefox (LeechBlock), on that computer. The downside is that when you decide it's an okay time to browse eBay, you have to manually comment out the following line in the `hosts` file by adding a **#** to the beginning of the line, like this:

```
#127.0.0.1 metafilter.com flickr.com
```

That's a deliberately huge inconvenience — one that can help keep your wandering clicker in line when you're under a deadline.

Hack 41: Reduce Email Interruptions

Level . . . . **Easy**

Platform . . . . **All**

Cost. . . . . **Free**

In contrast to phone calls, SMS, and instant messenger, email was never intended for real-time communication. However, most people treat it as if it were. You most likely work with your email program open all day long, letting it check for new messages every five minutes or less and notify you of unread incoming email on the spot.

It's so difficult to ignore that little unopened envelope, isn't it? Maybe those new messages contain juicy gossip, or photos of the baby, or heaping praise from the boss. Maybe they contain details of an emergency that has to be dealt with right this second. Most likely, they contain an unimportant Facebook notification or misspelled details of how to buy "cheap V1@gr@," but nevertheless, the impulse to look at them is powerful. Unread email is just another shot of the information drug your hungry mind craves. It cries out to you, "Open me! Open me!"

However, when you need to focus, do yourself a favor: actively control when you check your email. Two strategies can help.

Shut Down Your Email Program

The simplest (but perhaps least practical) way to stop letting your inbox run your day is to quit your email software. Make your default work mode email-free. Open your inbox only at designated processing times. Commit to just two or three times during a workday — say, first thing in the morning, just after lunch, and an hour before you leave — to check for and process unread messages. This means responding, filing, and taking any action those messages warrant on the spot. If two or three email checks per day just isn't realistic, you can check more often; the most important thing is that you schedule your email check-ins rather than stay on constant alert for the Pavlovian "DING" of your inbox.

NOTE Hack 2, "Decrease Your Response Time," provides strategies for processing email to avoid a pileup of read-but-not-processed messages.

Set Your Email Program to Check for Messages Once an Hour

Your work situation may demand that your email program be open all the time — say, if you work in Outlook using its calendar and tasks lists. You can still reduce the constant interruption of the new mail notification: set your mail client to check for new messages once an hour.

By default, Microsoft Outlook checks for unread email every five minutes. That means — with spam, cc-happy co-workers, mailing lists, and bored friends at work — you potentially can be interrupted 12 times an hour, or 108 times during a nine-hour workday, by new emails. Change this setting to every 60 minutes to reduce the number of interruptions from 108 to 9 times a day.

The method for changing that setting varies, depending on your email program. If you use Microsoft Outlook, choose Tools ➪ Options. In the Mail Setup tab, click the Send/Receive button to change the frequency setting, as shown in Figure 5-4.

The amount of time you choose to let pass before checking for new messages is up to you, but even once an hour can be excessive. If you're truly ready to toss the email monkey off your back, try processing email two or three times a day, at times you determine.

NOTE If you're used to getting push email notifications on your cell phone the minute a new email hits your inbox, slowing down email notifications may seem extremely difficult. Your goal is to cut back on those constant interruptions. Find your phone's email settings and, like you've done with your desktop client, change the settings to check your email once an hour or less.

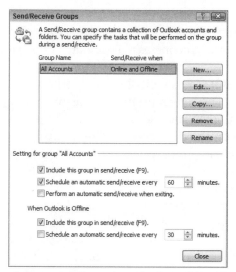

Figure 5-4: Microsoft Outlook Send/Receive options.

Hack 42: Split Your Work Among Multiple Desktops

Level . . . . **Easy**

Platform . . . . **Windows, Mac OS X**

Cost. . . . . **Free**

The more space you have to lay out your materials, the easier it is to get a job done. Imagine a cook in a kitchen with restricted counter space. She has to remove the first ingredient from the refrigerator, put it on the counter, chop, measure, and add it to the recipe. To use more ingredients, she has to return the first to the refrigerator to make room for the second, and so on. But what if she had a larger countertop that could accommodate all the ingredients at one time? The chef could spend less time switching between ingredients and more time cooking.

The same concept applies to the amount of screen real estate you have on your computer monitor. Modern operating systems make multitasking with overlapping windows on one screen possible, but that requires some amount of task switching and window resizing to get to what you need.

A second or even third monitor, however, gives you more space to work. A 2006 survey by Jon Peddie Research, cited in a *New York Times* article,[4] showed that multimonitor computer setups can increase a computer worker's productivity by 20 to 30 percent.

Microsoft Corporation founder Bill Gates splits his work onto three screens that make up one desktop: "The screen on the left has my list of emails. On the center screen is usually the specific email I'm reading and responding to. And my browser is on the right screen. This setup gives me the ability to glance and see what new has come in while I'm working on something, and to bring up a link that's related to an email and look at it while the email is still in front of me."[5]

More recently, technologist Clay Johnson argued that today's larger and pixel-dense monitors enable us to reap the benefits of multimonitor setups of yesteryear without collecting a desk full of monitors. Johnson says that for most people, the optimal monitor setup provides about 2,500 x 1,400 pixels.[6] Whether your pixel landscape matches up to or surpasses that screen space, using essentially extra virtual desktops you can switch to at any time to separate your work into distinct workspaces helps you focus on one task at a time. (Hack 120, "Optimize Your Dual Monitors," has tips for putting more than one physical screen to best use.)

For example, use one desktop for the task at hand; the second for your task resource documents, calendar, or to-do list; the third for web access; and the last for email. Here's how to set it up.

Windows

Virtual desktop manager Dexpot is free for personal use; download it from `www.dexpot.de/` and install.

Dexpot can create and manage up to 20 virtual desktops (although you'll never need that many) and customize them extensively. Give each of your desktops a name, background image, screensaver, and other characteristics using Dexpot. Right-click the Dexpot icon in your system tray, and select Configure Desktops to do just that, as shown in Figure 5-5.

For instance, I created three desktops, named Email and Messaging, Writing, and Browsing. Using Dexpot's Desktop Rules feature, you can even create automatic actions based on what you do on a desktop — for example, if you launch your web browser on a desktop other than Browsing, Dexpot can automatically move it there.

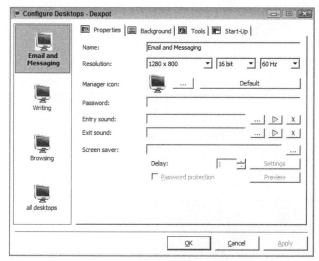

Figure 5-5: Configure your virtual desktops with Dexpot.

Mac OS X

The latest version of Mac OS X comes with a virtual desktops feature, Spaces, built right in. To enable Spaces, from System Preferences choose the Exposé & Spaces pane. From the Spaces tab, select the Enable Spaces check box. (Optionally, also select Show Spaces in Menu Bar to add a Spaces button to the menu bar.)

By default, you get four virtual desktops, or Spaces. Use the + and – buttons next to Rows and Columns to add or delete Spaces. You can have as many as sixteen Spaces and as few as two. To bind certain applications to certain Spaces, use the Application Assignments list. (This comes in handy if you always want to keep iTunes, for instance, in Space 2.) You can also set a certain application to show up on every Space, meaning it will be visible regardless of which Space you're in.

The most useful way to interact with Spaces is using the keyboard shortcuts, which you can also customize in Spaces' System Preferences pane, as shown in Figure 5-6. In System Preferences ⇨ Exposé & Spaces, choose how many Spaces you want, which applications should be associated with what Spaces, and your Spaces keyboard shortcuts.

By default, you can use the F8 key to invoke a birds-eye view — or complete grid — of your Spaces. Using the mouse, you can drag and drop application windows from one of your Spaces to another one here. You can also switch between Spaces using keyboard shortcuts; by default, Control+any arrow key scrolls through Spaces, and Control+any number key transports you directly to a specific Space.

More information on using Spaces is available at: `www.apple.com/macosx/ what-is-macosx/apps-and-utilities.html#spaces`.

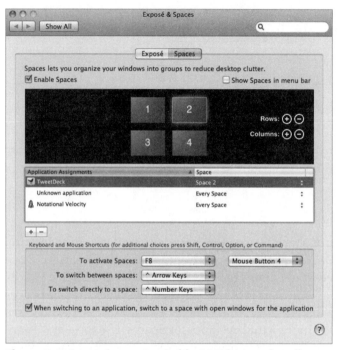

Figure 5-6: Spaces is a customizable OS X feature that allows you to separate applications across virtual desktops.

Hack 43: Build a No-Fly Zone

Level . . . . **Easy**

Platform . . . . **All**

Cost. . . . . **Free**

Many modern office spaces have open layouts to "promote interaction between departments" — which effectively means they're set up to distract you all day long. Low-wall cubes, side-by-side desks, required use of an instant messenger (IM) — all make for a workday that's interruption-driven instead of task-driven. Office seating arrangements that mix up personnel can place employees who do involved mental work such as programming or number-crunching next to loud salespeople chatting up clients all day on the phone.

For people who don't have their own office with a door they can close, getting actual work done at the office can be a serious challenge. Co-workers drop by, IM windows pop up, you're dragged off to meetings or hijacked to deal with the latest department crisis; these are all time-suckers that can leave you worn out at 6 p.m., wondering where the day went.

When you're a cog in a larger workplace machine, changing your office's culture might not be possible. But for your own sanity and productivity, do what you can to protect yourself from extraneous interruptions at the office.

Set Yourself Up to Get into the Zone

It takes 15 minutes of uninterrupted time to get into "the zone," that wonderfully productive place where you lose all sense of time and space and get a job done. Protect yourself from interruptions before you start on an involved mental task to give yourself that 15-minute runway.

Forward your office phone to voicemail and silence your cell phone. Shut down instant messenger. If it must be on, set your status to "Busy" or "Here but working, chat later." Shut down your email client. If you're waiting for a crucial message, set your email program to receive messages quietly (with no audio or visual alerts) and forward any must-get-through email to your phone.

Shut down every application running on your computer that doesn't have to do with the task at hand. If you don't need the Web to complete your task, disconnect your machine from the network. I know it's extreme, but I'm serious. If you're a programmer, download language documentation locally before you start to avoid the temptation of the web browser.

Make Yourself Inaccessible

If your office uses Outlook or a shared calendar, schedule an appointment with yourself that shows you as busy when you're working on your task to avoid meeting requests during that time. (This is especially useful for recurring tasks such as writing weekly status reports.)

Signal to your co-workers in whatever ways are possible that you shouldn't be interrupted unless absolutely necessary. If it's acceptable at your workplace, put on headphones — noise-canceling headphones are best — and listen to music to block out sound. (A former co-worker of mine once confessed that he put on headphones without anything playing on them just so that people wouldn't randomly interrupt him.)

NOTE See Hack 48, "Drown Out Distracting Sounds with Pink Noise," for more on masking office noise.

If interruption by your manager or co-workers is a big problem, work out a way that you can signal that you're available to chat or that you're super-involved at the moment at your desk. Make an agreement with others that when the "Do Not Disturb" sign is up, they won't stop by asking if you want to get coffee or what you thought of last night's episode of *Mad Men*.

Work at Quieter Times and in Zoned-Off Spaces

If all else fails, find times and space at your office where it's easier to get work done. Come in a little earlier or stay later or move your lunch break to the opposite time of your co-workers. A couple of programmers who worked at a frenetic office used to schedule a two-hour meeting together in a conference room a couple of times a week, where they'd go with their laptops to code in peace and quiet. A complete change of scenery can help boost your productivity and keep you from the ringing phone and chatty cube mate.

Hack 44: Set Up Communication Quiet Hours

Level . . . . **Medium**

Platform . . . . **Windows and Mac OS X**

Cost. . . . . **Free to $10**

What follows is a common scenario (real or imagined) that keeps some of us from turning off those flow-disrupting communication tools: You shut down your IM and email applications, and you successfully made it into "the zone." It's going so well that you actually do lose all sense of time, and you've completely forgotten to re-open your communication channels. As a result, you missed an important email that you needed to respond to, no one could get in touch with you over IM, and you weren't able to respond to that workplace "crisis" in a timely manner.

For most, this scenario is more imagined than real — a result of the conditioning that has trained you to respond to that digital "DING!" as soon as you hear it. Real or not, you can benefit from setting up some sort of "quiet hours" — times when you can completely go off the grid for a set period of time. Here's how to block out your computer distractions but ensure you'll remember to get back online when necessary.

Put Your Communication Break on a Timer with Quiet Hours

To address this scenario, I developed a free application called Quiet Hours[7] that enables you to shut down your biggest desktop distractions for a user-determined period of time with the reassurance that it will relaunch them after your communication-free time has ended. Here's how it works:

1. Download Quiet Hours from `http://lifehacker.com/5747234` and follow the installation instructions. Launch Quiet Hours.

2. Drag and drop applications you want to turn off for a set period to the Quiet Hours window, shown in Figure 5-7. For example, you may want to include IM, your newsreader, email, Skype, or any other application that commonly pops up distracting notifications.

3. Set the amount of time you'd like to go off the radar; then click Start.

4. When your distraction-free time is almost at an end, Quiet Hours asks if you're ready to launch your apps. Let the countdown finish to go back on the grid; click "Give me 10 more minutes" to extend your distraction-free time another 10 minutes.

Figure 5-7: Drag applications you want to relaunch after a set period of time to Quiet Hours.

The Nuclear Option: Freedom

If your computer distractions have more to do with the never-ending river of diversions that flow through your Internet connection than with specific applications — that is, if you get your best work done when you have absolutely no Internet connection — then a tool like Quiet Hours may not be enough. You may be better off disconnecting altogether.

For some people, that's easy to do. You simply unplug your Ethernet cable or turn off your laptop's Wi-Fi antenna. Those methods are simple and effective, but they're also easy to cheat; just reconnect the Ethernet cable or switch your wireless antenna back on, and you're back online.

If you need a little help in the self-control department, Freedom (`http://macfreedom.com`) is a $10 utility (a free trial is available) for Windows and Mac that blocks your whole computer from using the Internet for any set period of time, up to eight hours.

Used by notable writers such as Dave Eggers,[8] Nora Ephron,[9] and Seth Godin,[10] Freedom doesn't enable you to simply click a button to reconnect. When you start a Freedom session, you have to either wait for your session to expire or completely reboot your computer to regain access to the Internet. As the Freedom download page explains, "The hassle of rebooting means you're less likely to cheat, and you'll enjoy enhanced productivity."

Hack 45: Clear Your Desktop

Level . . . . **Easy**

Platform . . . . **Windows, Mac OS X**

Cost . . . . **Free**

It's amazing how fast your computer's desktop can fill up with shortcuts and files and turn into a virtual candy store of colorful icons beckoning your mouse pointer: "Click me! Click me!" It's tempting to leave documents on your desktop because you'll know they'll be in sight at all times. But at what cost?

A cluttered virtual desktop is as bad as a cluttered physical desktop. It's visually distracting and makes it easy to get derailed from the task at hand. ("Hey, lemme peek at that hilarious LOLcat just one more time!") Clear your virtual desktop by removing all the icons you don't need. Here's how.

Windows

On Windows, most modern software puts a shortcut to itself on your computer desktop by default when you install it. Your web browser and email program might save files they download directly to your desktop. To maintain a completely clear desktop with absolutely nothing taking up space, you can disable desktop icons entirely by following these steps.

1. Drag and drop all the files you've saved on your desktop into the My Documents folder. (See Hack 11, "Organize Your Documents Folder," for ways to get your My Documents folder under control.)

2. Delete all the shortcuts to software applications on your desktop that already exist in Windows' Start menu.

3. To disable desktop items entirely, right-click the desktop, and from the View submenu, untick Show Desktop Icons.

4. In the latest version of Windows, you can pin any program to the Taskbar via drag and drop for quick launching without having to navigate the Start menu. As for all your other programs? Fear not: They're still quickly accessible through a Start menu search, or safely tucked away in the Programs Files folder.

5. For easy access to your oft-used folders, pin specific folders to the Windows Explorer jump list in your Taskbar, again via drag and drop. After pinning a folder, right-clicking the Explorer icon pulls up your pinned folders, as shown in Figure 5-8.

Figure 5-8: Pin oft-used folders to Explorer in your Windows task bar.

Mac OS X

Mac applications are a lot less likely to add shortcuts to your desktop; however, it is still easy to save downloaded files to your Mac's desktop. Here's how to clear up things and still make all your favorite applications and documents accessible.

1. Drag and drop all the files on your desktop to your documents folder in Finder.

2. Delete any shortcuts left on your desktop.

3. Drag and drop your frequently launched programs to the Dock (to the left of the trash bin).

4. For easy access to your Documents and Applications folders, drag and drop them to the Dock as well. When clicked, the folders reveal the contents in a vertical menu, grid, or fan of items, as shown in Figure 5-9. You can change the default by right-clicking your folder and selecting Fan, List, or Grid from the context menu.

Make it a habit to file away programs and documents in folders rather than on your desktop to maintain a clutter-free virtual work environment.

Figure 5-9: Place the Applications folder on the Dock as a menu to access all your software.

Hack 46: Make Your House a Usable Home

Level....... **Easy**

Platform.... **All**

Cost........ **Free**

Ever been on the way out the door and you can't find your keys? Dashing around the house tearing through every nook and cranny in a stressed-out frenzy isn't the best way to start the day, but we've all been there.

It's so easy to sabotage yourself every day without even realizing it. The moment you put your keys in the pocket of the jacket you tossed over the kitchen chair, you didn't think, "I'm going to make it really difficult for myself tomorrow morning when I have to leave for that big interview." Yet there are so many small ways in which you can unconsciously make life harder on yourself. Personal sabotage — whether it's in the form of convincing yourself you'll magically remember to pick up milk at the store or thoughtlessly surfing the Web when you have a looming deadline — is a reversible habit with a little thought and planning.

In the same way a basketball teammate serves up the perfect pass for an alley-oop slam dunk, you can be your own teammate and set yourself up for success in life and work.

Take a look at your living space with a focus on usability. Your home should be a tool that helps you get things done, a space that's a pleasure to be in, and a launch pad for daily tasks and life goals. Whether you want to relax after work, phone a family member, or keep track of a dry-cleaning receipt, there are lots of simple ways to create a living space that makes getting things done a breeze.

Create a Place for Incoming Stuff

Every day you walk into the house with your hands full of mail, pockets full of change, and a cell phone that needs recharging. Instead of dumping that pile of bills onto the coffee table, scattering a mess of pennies and dimes on your dresser, and tossing the phone onto a table, create useful places to drop off stuff without having to think: a change jar that goes to Coinstar every few months, an indoor mailbox for you and your housemates, and a phone-charging center with an easily accessible plug. After a long day at work, you don't want to have to think about where to put stuff when you walk in the door. So make it a no-brainer.

Put Items You Need to Remember in Your Path

Make it hard to forget where you put your keys, your cell phone, that check you're supposed to mail, or the dry-cleaning receipt. Section off a space near the door where you can easily pick up items on your way out. Hang a key rack. Place a snail-mail outbox nearby for letters and bills that need to be dropped at the post office. If the door of your apartment is metal, try keeping a few magnets stuck to it to hold receipts, mail, and notes you'll be sure to see on your way out the door.

Stow Away Stuff You Don't Use & Put Stuff You Do Use Within Easy Reach

Surround yourself with the things you use and either get rid of the things you don't or stow them away. For example, if you've ripped all your audio CDs to MP3 and listen to them only in that format, why line your living room walls with CDs that never get touched? Box up your CDs and store them up on a high shelf in the closet to make room for the things in the living room that you do use (or better yet, rip them to MP3 and sell them). In the kitchen, if you rarely make waffles but you're on a grilled-cheese kick, put the waffle-maker on the top shelf and leave the Foreman grill at eye level.

Strategically Place Items to Make Tasks Easy

Having all the things you need to complete a task on hand is half the battle. One of my favorite household life hacks is the sheet-folding trick: fold the flat and fitted sheets into a set and place them *inside* one pillowcase, along with any other pillowcases for those sheets. The convenient packaging precludes the need to rummage through the linen closet matching up sheet sets when the time comes to make the bed.

There are lots of ways to make tasks easier with strategic placement: Make recycling easy by placing the bin in the area where the most paper or glass is generated — say, the home office or kitchen. Keep your cell phone on your nightstand, and use it as your alarm clock and weather notifier in case of rain or snow — not only will you know the time and temperature, but you won't waste time looking for your cell in the morning!

Make Task-Based Centers

Place all the items you need to complete a task in an area sectioned off for that activity — such as a computer-repair center, a bill-paying center, or a gift-wrapping center. Keep ink and paper next to the printer; folders and tabs on the filing cabinet; and stamps, envelopes, and address stickers in a mail center. Incorporate the defragging process — placing related items next to one another — into your regular cleaning routine.

Leave Writing Material Everywhere

Keep pens and pads all over the house: by the phone, on the kitchen counter, on the night table, and in the bathroom. You never know when a thought that needs to be recorded will strike. An idea, a forgotten to-do, the solution to a problem you're having at work, a dream you want to remember, an image or drawing, or a phone number should all be jotted down without effort. Easily available capture tools keep nagging thoughts from cluttering your mind.

NOTE If you prefer taking digital notes to the analog pen-and-paper route, see Hack 37, "Set Up a Ubiquitous Note-Taking Inbox Across Devices" for more on how you can achieve the same goal with a digital spin.

Set Up an Inbox

Make a place to put real-life items that come streaming into your day so that you can process them at times *you* determine instead of letting them interrupt you. Snail mail, receipts, business cards, random paperwork, notes you've scribbled to yourself should all be shuttled directly into your inbox for later sorting and processing. A plastic or metal office inbox does just fine; any kind of box or even designated desk space would work. You get bonus points if you can get your housemate or partner to get an inbox, too — that way, you can leave things for him or her to see without having piles of stuff gathering around the house.

Collaborate with Housemates

Simple tools can make sharing household tasks easy. Place a magnetic dirty/clean flippy sign on the dishwasher so that everyone knows when it has to be emptied and when it can be loaded. Stick a magnetic whiteboard to the fridge with an ongoing shopping list. Use it to leave notes or to-do lists, too, such as "Call plumber about the toilet! 555-3456." A magnetic whiteboard calendar is also a handy way to keep track of household schedules, especially for busy families.

> **TIP** GroceryIQ (`http://www.groceryiq.com`) **is a website and application for Android and iOS that creates shopping lists by using your phone's camera to scan bar codes. (You can add items manually when bar codes aren't available). Pull out your phone and launch GroceryIQ next time your running errands for a sorted-by-aisle grocery list that can make grocery shopping a breeze.**

Hack 47: Sentence Stuff to Death Row

Level . . . . **Easy**

Platform . . . . **All**

Cost . . . . **Free**

Endless streams of information compete for your attention. RSS feeds, mailing lists, and news sites are all great ways to keep up with what's going on in the world and within your industry. However, because putting your ear to yet another new information channel is so easy, it's equally easy to find yourself swimming in a sea of unread items that pile up while you focus on other things. Prune your information channels down to the ones most worth your time to keep up a solid attention firewall. One technique for doing so, coined by blogger Michael Hyatt, involves sentencing certain information streams to a virtual "death row."

Maybe it's the mailing list you once enjoyed but that has become more boring than informative. Maybe it's that weblog that seemed so fun and original six months ago that's slowly lost your interest. Whether you're decluttering your home or your digital space, sometimes it's hard to know what you can safely toss and what to hang onto. A simple method for choosing what goes and what stays is to make a folder called `death row` on your hard drive, in your email program, or in your RSS reader — or all three. Place any feeds, lists, or files you're not sure are useful to you anymore in there.

Give yourself six weeks. (Create a reminder in your calendar using the methods described in Hack 33: "Send Reminders to Your Future Self.") If within that time, you never looked up something in that feed, or list, or used one of those files, out it goes. If you did use an item, reinstate it into your regular rotation.

Hack 48: Drown Out Distracting Sounds with Pink Noise

Level . . . . **Easy**

Platform . . . . **Mac OS X, Windows**

Cost . . . . **Free**

If your co-worker's conversation down the hall is distracting you, or your downstairs neighbor's television is blaring up through your floor, block out the sound with neutralizing noise. The right concoction of nature sounds, white noise, or calm music can mask distracting ambient sounds such as passing car subwoofers or neighborhood industrial noise.

FM3 Buddha Machine Wall

The FM3 Buddha Machine Wall, shown in Figure 5-10, is a web-based tool (`http://aux.zendesk.com/wall`) that neutralizes office noise with a variety of configurable ambient loops. Created by online customer support service Zendesk, the FM3 Buddha Machine Wall seems a bit inscrutable at first glance, but start clicking speakers and buttons, and you can create a distraction-killing loop of your own in no time.

Figure 5-10: Mix and match neutralizing sounds to block out distracting noise.

NOTE If you fall in love with the FM3 Buddha Machine Wall, you can download the app for on-the-go distraction blocking on your iOS device for $0.99 at `http://itunes.apple.com/app/buddha-machine/id294730223`.

Nature Sounds for Me

Some people prefer the soothing sounds of nature to electronic ambience. Nature Sounds for Me (`http://naturesoundsfor.me`) enables you to mix and match Mother Nature's ambient tracks, including weather sounds (such as rain or thunder), animal sounds (such as birds or crickets), and other relaxing or chatter-drowning ambient sounds (such as static, wind chimes, or a heartbeat) to create a mix perfect for your needs. You can export the resulting mix to a .WAV file and sync it to your smartphone or digital music player for on-the-go ambient mixes.

References

1. Alorie Gilbert, "Why Can't You Pay Attention Anymore?" CNET News.com (`http://news.com.com/Why+cant+you+pay+attention+anymore/2008-1022_3-5637632.html`).

2. Jerry Useem, "Making Your Work Work For You," *CNN Money*, March 2006 (`http://money.cnn.com/magazines/fortune/fortune_archive/2006/03/20/8371789/index.htm`).

3. Claudia Wallis and Sonja Steptoe, "Help! I've Lost My Focus," *Time* magazine, Jan 10, 2006 (`http://time.com/time/archive/preview/0,10987,1147199,00.html`).

4. Ivan Berger, "The Virtues of a Second Screen," *The New York Times*, April 20, 2006 (`http://nytimes.com/2006/04/20/technology/20basics.html`).

5. Bill Gates, "How I Work: Bill Gates," *Fortune* Magazine, Mar 30, 2006 (`http://money.cnn.com/2006/03/30/news/newsmakers/gates_howiwork_fortune`).

6. Clay Johnson, "Is the Multiple-Monitor Productivity Boost a Myth?" *Info Vegan*, Aug 18, 2010 (`http://infovegan.com/2010/08/18/manage-pixels-not-monitors`).

7. Adam Pash, "Quiet Hours." Lifehacker, April 2011 (`http://lifehacker.com/5747234`).

8. Rachel Cooke, "Hurrah, I've finally slipped through the net," *Guardian*, Apr 11, 2010 (www.guardian.co.uk/commentisfree/2010/apr/11/internet-google).

9. Edward Lewin, "On Location with Nora Ephron," *The New York Times*, Nov 24, 2010 (www.nytimes.com/2010/11/28/magazine/28FOB-domains-t.html).

10. Seth Godin, "Lost in a digital world," *Seth's Blog*, Jan 10, 2011 (http://sethgodin.typepad.com/seths_blog/2011/01/lost-in-a-digital-world.html).

Streamline Common Tasks

You can get your work done faster with the right shortcuts — for the price of *learning* those shortcuts, that is. Shortcuts get you where you want to go faster, but they're not obvious, and it takes practice to incorporate them into your habits. The difference between taking main roads across town and taking the back roads is that the main roads are easier but take longer. If you drive across town every day, however, it's worth your time to learn the back-road shortcut.

The same principle applies to your work processes. No doubt you perform dozens of repetitive actions every day, such as typing **www.google.com** into your browser's address bar; clicking the Start button and navigating to the Programs menu; or typing **Let me know if you have any questions** at the end of an email. These are opportunities for shortcuts that can add up to large savings over time. Every movement, every task, every action is a candidate for optimization and streamlining.

Imagine that working a few new shortcuts into your day saves two seconds on each of four tasks you perform twenty times a day. That amounts to about two and a half minutes of saved time a day, which adds up to 667 minutes or more than 11 hours a year (taking into account weekends and two weeks of vacation). All told, you can save more than an entire workday every year just by learning how to search Google or sign an email by taking the back roads.

NOTE More realistically, you're simply teaching yourself to do things more quickly and efficiently. When you tackle a task that requires common steps, there's little friction between you and the task, and you can breeze through steps that would otherwise make the task feel considerably more tedious.

The key is learning the shortcuts that can benefit you most. Identify the activities you perform most often, learn the shortcuts, and then train yourself to use them every time.

A WORD ABOUT KEYBOARD SHORTCUTS

One of the most common ways to streamline a computing task is to learn the keyboard command for an action. Moving your hand off your keyboard, placing it on the mouse, moving the mouse pointer over a button or menu, and clicking is inherently a time- and effort-intensive motion. Most modern software comes with keyboard shortcuts that can achieve the same end in half the time.

Many of the hacks in this chapter discuss keyboard shortcuts for useful applications such as Google search or Windows. These shortcuts may seem arcane and overly complicated. You may ask, "Why press Ctrl+Shift+M when I can just click the button?" As with the back roads, keyboard shortcuts take practice to learn but save you travel time on trips you take often.

The hacks in this chapter cover how to streamline common computer processes so that you can spend less time moving the mouse or tapping the keyboard and more time getting things done.

Hack 49: Search the Web in Three Keystrokes

Level . . . . **Easy**

Platform . . . . **All (Firefox and Chrome)**

Cost . . . . **Free**

If you're online at work, chances are you search for information on the Web several times a day. There are dozens of ways to do a web search from your desktop, but the most common method takes the longest:

1. With your web browser open, select the entire URL of the current page in the address bar.

2. Replace it by typing **www.google.com**.

3. Press Enter.

4. Type your search term — say, **lifehacker** — into Google's search box.

5. Click the Google Search button or press Enter.

You'd probably follow these same steps for lots of other web searches, too, at sites like Amazon, Wikipedia, or Twitter.
There are much faster ways.

Use Your Browser's Built-In Search Box

The free, open-source web browser Firefox (`http://mozilla.org/products/firefox`) comes equipped with a Google web search box built into its interface, in the upper-right corner, as shown in Figure 6-1.

Figure 6-1: The Mozilla Firefox web browser comes with a search box built in to the right of the address bar.

Another favorite free and open source web browser is Google Chrome (`www.google.com/chrome/`), which also has a Google search box built in, but instead of separating the address bar and the search box, Chrome combines them into one omnibox into which you can enter both URLs and search queries.
Both browsers run on all platforms, and you can learn how to speed up searches in both next.

In Firefox

You can execute a web search from the Firefox search box without ever taking your hands off the keyboard; just use the key combination Ctrl+K (Cmd+K on Macs). Here's how to Google Lifehacker using this shortcut:

1. With the Firefox web browser open, press Ctrl+K.

2. Type **lifehacker**.

3. Press Enter.

Firefox magically transports you to the search results page for Lifehacker without ever visiting the Google home page. This method cuts your search down to three keystrokes plus your typed search terms — and no mouse movement.

This dedicated search box doesn't work just for Google. Firefox comes preloaded with Yahoo!, Amazon, eBay, Answers.com, Wikipedia, and Creative Commons searches as well. Visit Firefox Add-ons at `https://addons.mozilla.org/search-engines.php` to install other useful engines such as the Wikipedia, Internet Movie Database (IMDb), the Merriam-Webster dictionary, `Weather.com`, and `Ask.com`. See Hack 93, "Extend Your Web Browser" for more on browser add ons.

To switch search engines, use Ctrl+_ or Ctrl+_. For example, to search for Lifehacker on Amazon do the following:

1. Press Ctrl+K to move the cursor to the search box.

2. Press Ctrl+_ twice to switch to Amazon.

3. Type **lifehacker** and press Enter.

TIP   To open your search results in a new tab from the Firefox search box or Chrome omnibox, press Alt+Enter (instead of just Enter) after entering your search term.

In Chrome

To execute a search for Lifehacker from Chrome without making the long and wasteful trip to your mouse, use this shortcut:

1. With Google Chrome open, press Ctrl+L to move the cursor to the address bar.

2. Type **lifehacker**.

3. Press Enter.

Unlike Firefox, Chrome doesn't offer a quick shortcut for changing the default search engine with which the omnibox executes your searches. It does, however, create search shortcuts for other sites in a clever way, discussed next.

NOTE   If you'd rather not use Google as your default search engine in Chrome, you can change the default by clicking the Wrench button, navigating to Preferences, and selecting an alternative default in the Search drop-down menu.

Most application launcher programs such as Quicksilver for Mac (http://quicksilver.blacktree.com) and Launchy for Windows (www.launchy.net) also support quick web search queries. See Hack 50, "Command Your Windows PC from the Keyboard," and Hack 51, "Command Your Mac from the Keyboard," in this chapter for more on those.

SHORTCUT

If you regularly search using more than one search engine, the preceding search techniques are nice, but you can do better. To polish your quick-searching skills, learn to use keyword searches detailed in Hack 92, "Quickly Search Within Specific Websites from the Address Bar."

Instant Searching: Getting Good with Google Instant

Now that you can search the Web without taking your hands off the keyboard, you can extend your keyboard mastery to Google's page of search results. Google Instant shows you search results from Google as you type, but you can also autocomplete your query, move up and down the list of links, and open the ones you're interested in without clicking.

Here's how keyboard shortcuts work in Google Instant:

1. Visit http://google.com/ and start typing your query. Google Instant shows search results related to your query as you type — before you press Enter or click Search; it also attempts to predict your query.

2. To accept Google's autocomplete text prediction while you're typing, just press Tab. For example, if you type **lifeh**, Google Instant suggests Lifehacker. If you press Tab, it autocompletes that text, so you don't need to finish typing it out. You can then continue typing — and continue accepting suggestions — in the same way to quickly fill out your query.

3. You can then navigate the autocomplete results using your up and down keys. The results below will automatically update to reflect the results for the currently highlighted query.

4. Now, if you arrow through the autocomplete options and you see a top result you like, pressing the right arrow key performs an I'm Feeling Lucky search — which, essentially, opens the top search result for the query you're already looking at.

That's just what you can do from the search box. After you execute a query by pressing Enter or clicking the Search button, you can navigate the results with the up and down arrow keys, preview any result by pressing the right arrow (shown in Figure 6-2), or open a selected result by pressing Enter. (Shift+Enter opens the result in a new tab or window.)

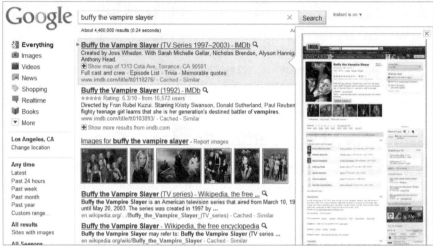

Figure 6-2: Google Instant's keyboard shortcuts enable you to preview and move up and down the list of search-result links using your arrow keys.

Hack 50: Command Your Windows PC from the Keyboard

Level....... **Medium**

Platform .... **Windows**

Cost........ **Free**

The graphical user interface revolutionized personal computing because it made using a computer so much more visual. However, using the mouse is one of the most inefficient ways to drive a computer. Think about it: you must move your hand from the keyboard to the mouse pad, drag the pointer across the screen until it's over a button or icon, and then double-click to open a document or launch an application.

You can save an enormous amount of time by using keyboard shortcuts to navigate your computer's operating system and programs. This hack describes how to bypass the mouse and launch programs and documents on your Windows PC without ever taking your hands off the keyboard.

Built-In Windows Keyboard Shortcuts

Microsoft Windows has several built-in keyboard shortcuts that can reduce the number of times you reach for the mouse during your workday. Here are some of the essential — and classic — shortcuts for navigating Windows:

SHORTCUT	RESULT
Alt+Tab or Win+Tab	Cycle through open programs (release keys when you see the screen you want).
Windows+D	Show the desktop.
Windows+L	Lock your workstation.
Windows+R	Show the Run box.
Windows	Open the Start menu.
Ctrl+Esc	Open the Start menu.

The following are indispensable editing shortcuts:

SHORTCUT	RESULT
Ctrl+S	Save the current document.
Ctrl+C	Copy selected text to clipboard.
Ctrl+X	Cut selected text or object and place on the clipboard.
Ctrl+V	Paste the contents of the clipboard into the current document.
Ctrl+Z	Undo the last action you performed.
Ctrl+Y	Redo the last action you undid.
Ctrl+B	Bold the selected text.
Ctrl+I	Italicize the selected text.
Ctrl+U	Underline the selected text.

If you're a long-time Windows user, many of the shortcuts above may be old hat by now. In Windows 7, Microsoft added a slew of great new shortcuts you may not know:

SHORTCUT	RESULT
Win+Home	Clear all but the active window.
Win+Space	All windows become transparent so you can see through to the desktop.
Win+_	Maximize the active window.
Shift+Win+_	Maximize the active window vertically.
Win+_	Minimize the window/Restore the window if it's maximized.
Win+_ or Win+_	Dock the window to each side of the monitor.
Shift+Win+_ or Shift+Win+_	Move the window to the monitor on the left or right.
Ctrl+I	Italicize the selected text.
Ctrl+U	Underline the selected text.

You might use some of these shortcuts all the time and some none of the time. To find the key combinations most useful for your workflow, look over the complete list of Windows 7 keyboard shortcuts at http://windows.microsoft.com/en-US/windows7/Keyboard-shortcuts.

Launch Documents and Applications from the Start Menu

One of the most powerful and easiest-to-remember keyboard shortcuts in Windows is simple: with your cursor in the search box, one tap on the Windows key summons the Start menu. From there you can begin typing the name of any program, bookmark, or document — such as **Picasa** or **novel** — and Windows automatically suggests matches in the menu, as shown in Figure 6-3.

Use your up and down arrow keys to traverse the list of search results. Press Enter when you've selected the one you'd like to launch, such as the Picasa photo manager software.

Figure 6-3: Tap the Windows key once and type to search for any application, file, bookmark, and more.

Quickly Run Programs and Open Files with Launchy

Windows' Start Menu Search is powerful and convenient if all you want is to search for and launch files and applications, but a free program called Launchy gives you similar functionality and more.

According to its developer, Launchy is "designed to help you forget about your Start menu, the icons on your desktop, and even your file manager," and it does. After you get into the habit of using Launchy, mousing through Start menu subfolders or clicking through Explorer window after Explorer window will seem like a quaint activity of the past. To get started, follow these steps:

1. Download Launchy from `http://launchy.net` and install it.

2. When you have Launchy installed and running, press Alt+Spacebar to invoke its plain-Jane black input field.

3. Type the name of any document, program, or bookmark, and Launchy suggests a list of search matches. Use the arrow keys to move up and down the list.

4. Open the one you need with a tap on the Enter key. Figure 6-4 displays Launchy in action, finding a Google Chrome shortcut after I've typed only `chr`.

Figure 6-4: Invoke Launchy with its default key combination, Alt+Spacebar, and begin typing the name of any program, file, or bookmark on your system.

To configure the directories Launchy indexes and tweak other application behavior, right-click the Launchy prompt and choose Preferences.

So far, Launchy may sound a lot like Windows' built-in search, but Launchy isn't just an application or file launcher. You can also use it to run a Google search, navigate your file system without Explorer, and interface with web applications such as Remember the Milk (`http://rememberthemilk.com`) and Google Calendar (`http://calendar.google.com`). For more advanced uses of Launchy, see `http://lifehacker.com/284127/`.

Hack 51: Command Your Mac from the Keyboard

Level........**Medium**

Platform....**Mac OS X**

Cost........**Free**

The mouse is a convenient tool for visually interacting with your computer, and it's the tool most users turn to when it's time to navigate to another application, launch an application, or perform other common tasks. While you certainly *can* rely on your mouse to interact with your computer, moving your hand to the mouse every time you need to perform a common action is rarely the quickest or most efficient way to get things done on your Mac.

With the right keyboard shortcuts in your arsenal, your keyboard is a significantly better tool for commanding your Mac. Save considerable time by using keyboard shortcuts to navigate your computer's operating system and programs. This hack explains how to ditch the mouse and how to launch applications and documents on your Mac without ever taking your hands off the keyboard.

Built-in Mac OS X Keyboard Shortcuts

Mac OS X is full of convenient keyboard shortcuts for performing common actions more quickly without needless pointing and clicking. Here are some of your Mac's most essential shortcuts:

SHORTCUT	RESULT
Cmd+Tab	Cycle through open programs (release keys when you see the screen you want).
Cmd+`	Cycle through windows within the current application.
Shift+Cmd+Q	Log out of your Mac.
Cmd+Q	Quit the active application.
Cmd+Space	Open the Spotlight search box.

Note that Mac keyboards also have built-in keys that activate special OS X functionality. For example, on current Mac keyboards, the Exposé button shares a place with the F3 key. Pressing it will activate Exposé and give you an overview of you open windows.

When you're working with text, the following are your must-know editing shortcuts:

SHORTCUT	RESULT
Cmd+S	Save the current document.
Cmd+C	Copy selected text to clipboard.
Cmd+X	Cut selected text or object and place on the clipboard.
Cmd+V	Paste the contents of the clipboard into the current document.

(continued)

(continued)

SHORTCUT	RESULT
Cmd+Z	Undo the last action you performed.
Cmd+Shift+Z	Redo the last action you undid.
Cmd+B	Bold the selected text.
Cmd+I	Italicize the selected text.
Cmd+U	Underline the selected text.

The keyboard shortcuts that most fit your workflow will vary depending on the kind of work you do most often on your Mac. For a fuller list of Mac OS X keyboard shortcuts, see http://support.apple.com/kb/HT1343.

TIP If you commonly mouse through an application's menu items to access a command that isn't available through a keyboard shortcut, OS X has a tool built into the Keyboard and Mouse preference pane that enables you to create a keyboard shortcut for any action, detailed at http://lifehacker.com/343328.

Basic File and Application Launching with Quicksilver

Skip time-wasting point-and-click mouse movement on your Mac using free software Quicksilver, a keyboard interface to an astonishing variety of computing actions. At its most basic level of functionality, Quicksilver launches applications and opens documents, much the same as Launchy for Windows, as outlined in the previous hack.

Here's how to start using Quicksilver as a keyboard launcher:

1. Download and install the latest version of Quicksilver from http://qsapp.com/. As of this writing, beta 58 is the most recent version available.

2. To invoke the Quicksilver commander, press Option+Spacebar (Quicksilver's default key combination). Begin to type the name of the application or document you'd like to open; for example, type **Wor**. Quicksilver suggests Microsoft Word as a match (or whatever files and programs you have installed that contain "Wor" in the title) and displays a drop-down list of other possible matches on the right, as shown in Figure 6-5.

3. Press Enter to open Microsoft Word, or press the down arrow key to choose another option. Quicksilver adapts its suggestions to your most-used applications and documents, so the next time you invoke Quicksilver with Option+Spacebar and type **Wor**, it will suggest the item you previously launched at the top of the list.

Figure 6-5: Quicksilver launcher matches programs that contain "Wor" in the title.

SHORTCUT

For even faster navigation of Quicksilver search results, invoke Quicksilver, press Cmd+, (comma) to open Quicksilver's preferences, and click the Command item in the left sidebar. Choose Select Next Result from the Spacebar behavior drop-down menu; this enables you to navigate results without moving your hand from the home row to the up and down keys. Pressing the spacebar moves you down one result, and pressing Shift+spacebar moves you up one result.

Advanced Quicksilver Actions

In its most basic usage (just described), Quicksilver uses a two-paned interface that enables you to select a subject in the first pane — the file, application, or other subject — and an action (Open) in the second pane. But Quicksilver offers a wide variety of actions beyond Open that can take additional information in a third pane. Advanced three-pane Quicksilver actions come in the form of subject-action-object.

For example, you can select a file called chapter4.doc in the first pane, select Move To as the action in the second, and tab to the third pane to choose the book folder. This three-paned action (see Figure 6-6) moves the file to that folder.

Figure 6-6: Quicksilver's three-paned subject-action-object function can perform custom actions, such as moving a file to a destination folder.

Other actions that Quicksilver can perform on your Mac include the following:

- **Manipulate an iTunes music library.** Start playing an album, song, or playlist; browse your library by genre, artist, or album; or rate songs as they're playing on-the-fly without switching out of your current working application.

- **Email a document to a contact.** Select a document and choose Email To (Compose) as the action; select a contact in your address book as the recipient, without opening your email software (see Figure 6-7).

- **Append text to a file.** Invoke Quicksilver and press the period key (.) to start free-form entering text. In the Action panel, choose Append To and in the third panel, choose a text file, such as todo.txt or shoppinglist.txt, to add a line to the file without a text editor.

- **Look up a word in the dictionary.** Type a word to look up in the first panel and choose Dictionary as your action to get the definition.

Figure 6-7: Quicksilver plugins, such as the Apple Mail plugin, enable you to do more with Quicksilver — such as dash off an email to Mom.

NOTE Several of the actions listed here may require additional Quicksilver plugins to work as described. Browse the Plug-ins tab of the Quicksilver preferences to find and enable advanced actions you'd like to perform with Quicksilver.

Quicksilver is not just a keyboard launcher; with the right plugins, it can do almost anything on your Mac via the keyboard that you do with your mouse. It would take an entire book just to describe all the things Quicksilver can do on your Mac. If this hack makes you want to learn more, view Quicksilver tutorials and video demonstrations at http://lifehackerbook.com/ch6.

Hack 52: Reduce Repetitive Typing with Texter for Windows

Level . . . . **Medium**

Platform . . . . **Windows**

Cost. . . . . **Free**

If you spend your day at a keyboard, chances are, you type particular phrases — such as "Thanks for contacting us" — several times throughout the day. Maybe you've acquired a maddening habit of typing *teh* instead of *the* when your fingers are flying over the keys. Perhaps you enter the current date into documents all the time, or you tend to use Internet acronyms such as "imo" to stand for "in my opinion."

These are all situations in which text substitution can save you time. You can define short abbreviations for phrases you use often or misspellings you're prone to, and automatically expand those abbreviations to their full, intended form. This hack explains how to do that using the free Windows application Texter.

Set Up Texter Hotstrings

To start using Texter, follow these steps:

1. Download Texter from http://lifehacker.com/238306/ and install it to your computer. (Texter is a portable application, so you can either use the installer or just download Texter.exe and put it in any folder on your desktop.)

2. Double-click `Texter.exe` to run the program for the first time.

3. A green icon with the letters "LH" on it appear in your Windows system tray; right-click it and choose Manage Hotstrings to start configuring abbreviations that will do your typing for you.

Adding Hotstrings

The next step is to create a new hotstring. To do so, follow these instructions:

1. Click the + sign. In the Hotstring field, enter your abbreviation — **btw**, for example. In the text area, type your hotstring's full replacement: **by the way**. Choose the key that triggers the replacement (Enter, Tab, or Space) or select the Instant check box (see Figure 6-8) to make the replacement happen automatically.

Figure 6-8: Adding a new hotstring – btw – that expands to "by the way" as soon as it's typed.

2. Click OK to save your new hotstring, which appears in Texter's management dialog along with the rest of the hotstrings you set up, as shown in Figure 6-9.

3. After you save a hotstring, when Texter is enabled and running, type that hotstring and press the trigger key (not required for instant replacements), and Texter expands it to your replacement. For example, the next time you type **btw**, Texter deletes btw and replaces it with *by the way*, producing ten characters for the effort of typing three.

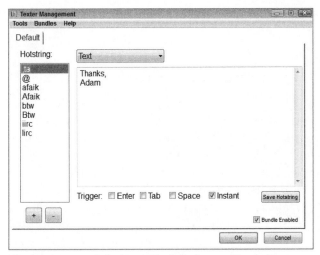

Figure 6-9: Managing Texter's default set of hotstrings.

Choosing the Right Hotstring Trigger

Different trigger keys work better for different types of replacements. For example, if you'd like the word *address* to expand to your street address, you need to assign a specific trigger key — one that you wouldn't normally press after typing *address,* such as Tab — to the hotstring. Sometimes you'll type the word *address* and want it to remain *address* and not automatically expand, so the Instant replacement setting (or even Space or Enter trigger key) wouldn't work as well there.

For common typos, however, you want to use the Instant option as your trigger. For example, if you often type *teh* when you mean *the,* you want Texter to automatically correct you without your having to press a specific trigger key.

Configuring Bundles

You can find many uses for text expansion, including the following:

■ Email form letters or signatures. (See Hack 9, "Script and Automate Repetitive Replies," about scripting repetitive email responses.)

■ Common misspellings (for example *teh* or *htis*).

- Common phrases (for example *as far as I know* or *Thanks for contacting us*).

- Document templates.

- Personal data (for example name, address, phone number, or email address).

Using Texter you can divide your hotstrings into "bundles," or groups. For example, to create a Texter bundle for common misspellings, from the Bundles menu choose Add and name your bundle a single word (such as **Typos**). The Typos bundle appears in its own tab in the Texter management dialog, where you can add hotstrings for *teh* and *htis* that automatically become *the* and *this*. To create another bundle for common phrases, choose Bundles ➪ Add and name it **Acronyms**. There you can set up hotstrings such as *btw*, which expands to *by the way*, and *afaik*, for *as far as I know*. Bundles are just a way to organize and separate your Texter hotstrings by category or purpose (see Figure 6-10).

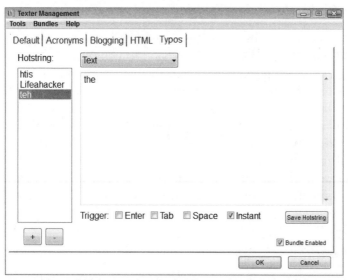

Figure 6-10: Managing multiple bundles of Texter hotstrings.

You can also export and import Texter bundles for easy sharing among colleagues.

More Texter Features

More ways to get the most out of Texter include the following:

- **Automatically start Texter when your computer does.** To make sure Texter starts working when you do, from the Tools menu, choose Preferences, and on the General tab, select Run Texter at Startup. Texter launches automatically with Windows.

- **Print a cheat sheet.** Setting up three dozen hotstrings is one thing, but training your typing fingers to use them is another. From Texter's Tools menu, choose Preferences, and on the Print tab, click Create Printable Texter Cheatsheet to make a paper reference that you can pin to your bulletin board while you learn your Texter hotstrings and triggers.

- **Store and run Texter from a thumb drive.** Texter is a completely self-contained program that can live and run from an external USB thumb drive. If you use different computers throughout the day, just plug in the drive where Texter and its data are stored, launch it, and access all your hotstrings.

- **Sync your Texter hotstrings between computers.** You can also take advantage of Texter's portable nature to sync Texter between computers using the file-syncing utility Dropbox. Simply create a new folder called **Texter** in your Dropbox folder, copy Texter to it, and run it from there. All your Texter hotstrings automatically sync with any computer on which you install Dropbox. (For more on Dropbox, see Hack 67, "Access Your Most Important Files Anywhere with Dropbox".)

- **Create a new hotstring or manage hotstrings using keyboard shortcuts.** By default you can summon the New Hotstring dialog box by pressing Ctrl+Shift+H whenever Texter runs. Likewise, you can launch the Manage Hotstrings dialog box using Ctrl+Shift+M.

- **Revel in how much time Texter has saved you.** After you've come to depend on Texter to do your typing for you, check out how many hours of time it has saved you. In the Preferences dialog box (get to it from the Tools menu), check the Stats tab to see how many replacements Texter has made for you and how many characters and hours of time saved that translates into.

For more advanced Texter usage (including cursor placement and clipboard insertion), check out the Texter documentation at http://lifehacker .com/238306/.

Hack 53: Reduce Repetitive Typing with TextExpander for Mac

Level . . . . **Medium**

Platform . . . . **Mac OS X**

Cost **$34.95**

In the same vein as Hack 51, "Command Your Mac from the Keyboard," Mac users can save thousands of keystrokes daily using the text-substitution application TextExpander. Everyone has phrases, information, or misspellings they type every day. With the TextExpander typing utility, you can automatically replace abbreviations such as *imo* with the phrase *in my opinion* or end email messages with two characters — say, *bt*, which magically turn into *Best, Tom*. Here's how.

Configure TextExpander Snippets

Start using TextExpander Snippets by following these instructions:

1. Download TextExpander (available at `http://smilesoftware.com/TextExpander/`) and install it on your Mac. An individual license costs $34.95, but you can try TextExpander for free.

2. In System Preferences, launch the TextExpander pane, which is listed under Other. Here you can set up a set of text *snippets*, or abbreviations, that TextExpander replaces with text you define.

Adding New Snippets

To create a new expanding snippet, perform the following:

1. Click the plus sign on the bottom left of the TextExpander panel and choose New Snippet (or simply press Cmd+N).

2. On the right side of the panel, enter the expanded content — **by the way**, in this example — and at the bottom of the panel, in the Abbreviation field, type the snippet **btw**, as shown in Figure 6-11.

Your expanded content can be formatted as text and pictures (such as your company logo or red, bold, warning text) and plain text. To insert a picture or color, or to size, bold, italicize, or otherwise format your text, select Formatted Text ⇨ Pictures in the Content drop-down list.

Figure 6-11: Create a new snippet, *btw*, that TextExpander replaces with *by the way*.

Set the Text Expansion Delimiter

By default, your TextExpander snippets are replaced as soon as you type them. However, if you use real words as your snippets, you may not always want them to expand. For example, if you use *email* to expand to your email address, you can never type just the word *email*.

To avoid this conflict, set TextExpander to use a delimiter key that triggers replacements instead of having them happen as you type.

1. In the Expansion tab of the TextExpander, click the Set Delimiters button to specify which keys should trigger your replacement (the Tab key, for instance).

2. Then, from the Expand abbreviations drop-down list, choose At delimiter (abandon delimiter), as shown in Figure 6-12.

NOTE Choosing At delimiter (keep delimiter) can preserve the delimiter character after your replacement, such as a Tab, carriage return, or space. This means that if you type your snippet plus your delimiter key, TextExpander replaces the snippet and keeps the delimiter after it. Otherwise, TextExpander replaces the snippet and removes the delimiter character.

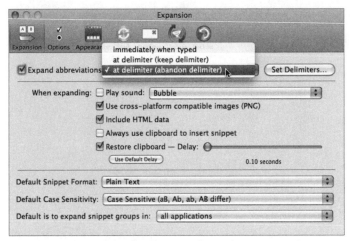

Figure 6-12: Set TextExpander to make replacements when you press the specified delimiter key.

You can see more options in the Preferences area, such as limiting expansions to certain applications and making your snippets case-sensitive, case-insensitive, or case-adaptive based on how you type the snippet (that is, **Btw** expands to **By the way** and **btw** expands to **by the way**).

Managing Snippet Groups

TextExpander can organize your snippets into folders by purpose, application specifics, or any other category. For example, you may keep a Common Misspellings group that automatically corrects typos for you, an Email Form Letters group that works only in your email software, or a Bookmarks group that fills in long web addresses in your web browser. Figure 6-13 shows some example categories.

SmileOnMyMac, the company that makes TextExpander, offers useful prefab TextExpander groups you can import: the AutoCorrect snippet file (about 100 common typos and their corrections); the TidBITS AutoCorrect Dictionary (more than 2,400 misspellings and their corrections); and the HTML Code Snippet file (for bloggers or website editors). They are all free and easily installable by selecting File ➪ Add Predefined Group.

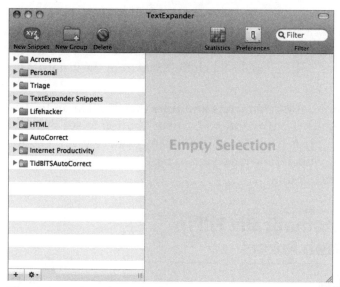

Figure 6-13: Organize your TextExpander snippets into groups.

Advanced TextExpander Usage

Following are some more things you can do with TextExpander:

- **Program cursor movement.** Set your cursor's position within the replacement after it has been expanded using the special % | variable in your snippet content. Alternatively, program particular cursor movements (such as two characters to the left or three characters to the right). Use the Cursor item on the drop-down list to the left of the Label input field to insert cursor-movement variables.

- **Add variables that insert date, time, and Clipboard contents into your snippet.** From the drop-down list on the left of the Label input field, choose to insert special dynamic variables such as the current time, date, day of week, month, year, or contents of the Clipboard inside a snippet.

- **Synchronize your snippets.** If you use the file-syncing tool Dropbox or subscribe to Apple's MobileMe, you can sync snippets between Macs by enabling syncing in the Sync tab of the TextExpander Preferences.

- **Access your snippets in iOS.** TextExpander is also available as an application on Apple mobile devices running iOS. At the time of this writing, that includes the iPhone, iPod touch, and iPad. You can download TextExpander touch for $5.00 from the iTunes App Store.

- **View the number of characters and time that TextExpander has saved you.** Click TextExpander's Statistics button to see the total number of snippets it expanded, how many characters it typed for you, and how much time it saved you based on a typing speed of 400 characters per minute.

Hack 54: Automatically Fill in Repetitive Web Forms

Level . . . . **Medium**

Platform . . . . **All Platforms**

Cost . . . . **Free**

As a citizen of the web, you frequently enter repetitive information about yourself into forms. Every time you sign up for a new website with your email address or username, enter in your shipping address, or type in your credit card information for purchases, you waste precious time typing out the same information. Manually typing this information every time is also error prone, which is why sites often ask you, for example, to retype your email address — which takes even more of your time.

You could use text expansion tools to speed up this process, as discussed in Hacks 52, "Reduce Repetitive Typing with Texter for Windows," and 53, "Reduce Repetitive Typing with TextExpander for Mac," but you still have to tab through the form to fill out each field, and with sensitive data — such as your credit card number — those utilities' plain-text storage won't cut the security mustard.

This hack details how to automatically and securely fill in repetitive web forms with the free browser plug-in LastPass (http://lastpass.com/).

NOTE For more on how to use LastPass to securely track and fill in your website logins, see Hack 15, "Securely Track Your Passwords."

LastPass stores the information you give to it in an encrypted state and uses one master password to access that database. (Read more about LastPass' security at https://lastpass.com/whylastpass_technology.php.)

It's most commonly used as a password manager, but it's also great at filling in repetitive forms. LastPass is available on all platforms, from web browser extensions to standalone desktop apps. You can download and install LastPass for your platform and browser of choice at `https://lastpass.com/misc_download.php`.

Create Auto Fill Profiles

Before LastPass can start filling in your repetitive form data, you need to create a new profile. If this is your first time installing LastPass, the Setup Wizard should prompt you to create a form profile. If you've already installed LastPass, click the LastPass button in your browser toolbar and select Fill Forms ⇨ Add Profile. LastPass opens an Add Form Fill profile dialog, as shown in Figure 6-14.

Figure 6-14: Enter your repetitive form data into LastPass and let it fill it in for you next time.

Enter profile information in each field you want LastPass to automatically fill in. LastPass can autofill basic information, such as your name, preferred username, gender, and birthday, along with your address, contact information, credit card, and bank account, along with any custom fields that aren't available by default. You can leave any field empty if you prefer LastPass not automatically fill in that information — say, for example, you'd rather not keep your Social Security number in LastPass. The extension automatically fills in only the information you give it.

It's one more form to fill, I know, but when you finish filling it out, you may never have to repetitively type out that info on a website again. When you finish, click Save Form Fill profile.

LASTPASS SECURITY

Passwords are one thing, but credit card and Social Security numbers are among some of the most sensitive data you have. Hack 15 explains how to use LastPass to manage your passwords, but it's natural that storing other financial and personal information might make you a little uncomfortable. Ultimately you have to decide for yourself if you feel secure putting that information in LastPass' hands, but as a reminder: the LastPass tools do all the encrypting and decrypting of your private information on your computer, meaning that no one — not even the people working at LastPass or anyone monitoring your internet connection — can access your passwords without your master password. You can read more about LastPass security and technology at https:// lastpass.com/whylastpass_technology.php.

LastPass also allows you to create as many profiles as you like. Say you use one email address and username when you want to associate an account with your real-life information and another that's for more disposable accounts that you don't want associated with your real-life persona.

For example, say you test a new website; here you may want to use disposable information that doesn't point back to the real-world you — call that profile "The Fake Me." Then if you fill out shipping information for something you order online, you'd want to use real information; create a profile called "The Real Me" with real data for those purposes.

NOTE In case you have more credit cards than personas, LastPass enables you to create autofill profiles individually for credit cards. Click the LastPass button ⇨ Fill Forms ⇨ Add Credit Card.

You likely use one profile more often than your others, so to set your default profile:

1. Click LastPass ⇨ Preferences

2. In the General tab, choose your preferred default in the Form Fill drop-down, as shown in Figure 6-15.

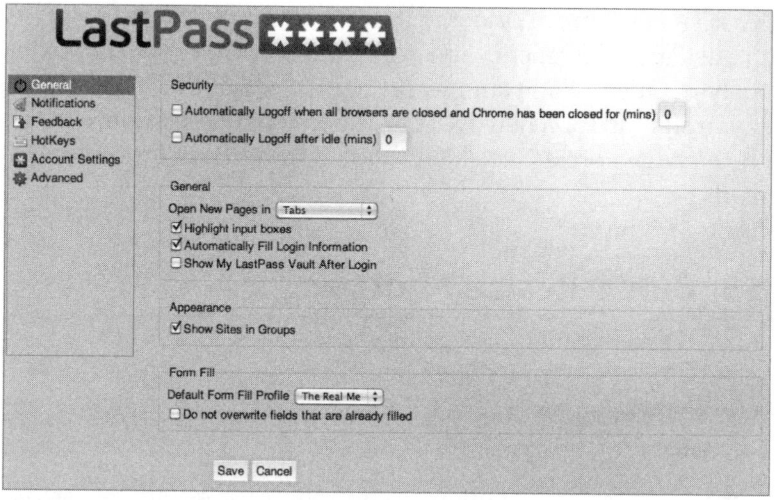

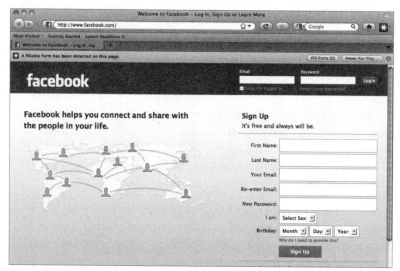

Figure 6-15: Choose a default profile for quick access to your most-used form data.

Automatically Fill Web Forms

Next time you visit a website asking for form information, LastPass notifies you that it's identified a form on the page and offers to fill in the form for you, as shown in Figure 6-16. What once may have taken you a minute or so of tabbing through fields and typing out tedious information now only takes a couple of clicks of your mouse.

Figure 6-16: When you navigate to a page that contains personal form information, LastPass offers to fill the form for you.

Add a custom keyboard shortcut to the autofill process in the HotKeys tab of your LastPass Preferences. (You need to set a default form fill profile, as previously detailed.) For example, set your shortcut to Ctrl+Alt+1, so whenever you sign up for a new website, fill out credit card information, or ship a new gadget, press Ctrl+Alt+1, and all the tedious form filling is taken care of.

Hack 55: Batch-Resize Photos

Level . . . . **Easy**

Platform . . . . **Windows**

Cost. . . . . **Free**

Everyone likes emailing digital photos, but no one likes receiving pictures that are so huge they take forever to download and require you to scroll left and right and up and down to see the entire image. Luckily, with just two clicks or a simple drag and drop, you can easily resize a large group of photos that you downloaded from your digital camera.

Batch Resizing on Windows

Image Resizer is a free utility that plugs into Windows Explorer. Following explains how to easily resize a batch of pictures using this tool:

1. Download and install Image Resizer from the right side of the page at http://imageresizer.codeplex.com/.

2. Browse to any folder where you store your digital photos, select the photos you want to resize, right-click, and choose Resize Pictures from the context menu to open the Image Resizer dialog box. Click the Advanced button to see all the options, as shown in Figure 6-17.

3. From there, choose one of the Image Resizer suggested dimensions, or enter your custom width and height. Be sure to select the Make Pictures Smaller but Not Larger option if you don't want to size up — and you won't, because making digital photos larger degrades quality. Click OK.

By default, Image Resizer creates copies of the files and adds the chosen size to the filename. For example, if your original photo filename was Jeremy001.jpg and you resized it using the Small setting, the new version will be named Jeremy001 (Small).jpg.

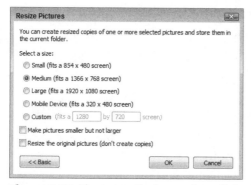

Figure 6-17: The Image Resizer options dialog box.

Batch Resizing on Macs

ThumbsUp is a free application that resizes images you drag and drop onto the app. Following explains how to easily resize a batch of pictures using this tool:

1. Download ThumbsUp from the Freeware Applications and Services section at www.devon-technologies.com/download/. After you install it to your Applications folder, drag it into your Dock for easy access.

2. The only time you need to run ThumbsUp by itself is to set your resizing preferences — which you need to do only whenever you want to adjust the output sizes or file format. So launch ThumbsUp to open its Preferences dialog, set your preferred resizing dimensions, and then exit the application.

3. Now, to batch resize photos using the settings you just created, simply drag and drop your images onto ThumbsUp in your Dock. ThumbsUp resizes the images, saves the new versions to the same folder as the originals, and exits.

By default, ThumbsUp creates a copy of your image with the text "_thumb" appended to the filename (you can change this to anything you prefer); if you dropped an image named Vacation001.jpg onto ThumbsUp, you get a resized file called Vacation001_thumb.jpg.

Batch Resizing with Picasa (Windows and Mac)

Alternatively, if you're looking for a complete photo manager that can do more extensive photo processing, including batch resizing, red-eye reduction, photo rating, keyword assigning, search, and lots of fun effects, then Picasa is the program for you.

1. Download and install a copy of Google's free Picasa (http://picasa.google.com/).

2. After Picasa indexes all your photos, select the ones you want to resize so that they appear in the Picture Tray on the bottom left.

3. Then click the Export button on the lower right. Here you can copy the photos at a new size to another folder on your hard drive for emailing, publishing online, or burning to CD.

If you plan to email the photos, you can cut out the Export step and just send the photos, automatically resized, via email. To adjust the default size for sending pictures, open the Picasa Preferences, click the E-mail tab, and set your preferred size. See Hack 17, "Organize Your Digital Photos" for more on managing your photo collection with Picasa.

Hack 56: Bypass Free Site Registration with BugMeNot

Level . . . . **Easy**

Platforms . . . **All**

Cost. . . . . **Free**

Many websites require you to register on them for free and to sign in with a username and password to view their contents. An active surfer can easily accumulate dozens of logins for various sites across the Web. But what about when you don't want to go through the whole rigmarole of registering for a website — you simply want inside?

The website BugMeNot (http://bugmenot.com) maintains a public database of shared usernames and passwords for free websites. If you come across a site that prompts you to log in to view its content, bypass the registration process by heading to BugMeNot to search for an already created username and password. Not all BugMeNot logins will work, but you can see the percentage success rate for a particular login and report whether it worked for you as well. If you can't find a BugMeNot login that works, create one and share it with the BugMeNot community.

Following are three ways to use BugMeNot:

- Enter the address of the site you want to log into on `http://bugmenot.com` to get a list of possible logins. Copy and paste the login you choose to the input fields on the website you are trying to view.

- Drag the BugMeNot bookmarklet from the BugMeNot homepage to your web browser's bookmarks toolbar. (For a more detailed explanation of bookmarklets, see Hack 95, "Get 10 Useful Bookmarklets.") When you come to a site you'd like to log into, click the bookmarklet and get login detail suggestions in a pop-up window. Copy and paste the suggested login to the input fields on the website you are trying to view.

- Download and install the BugMeNot browser extension, available at `https://addons.mozilla.org/en-US/firefox/addon/bugmenot/` for Firefox users or `https://chrome.google.com/extensions/detail/lackfehpdclhclidcbbfcemcpolgdgnb` for Google Chrome users. Next time you're presented with a username-and-password prompt in Firefox, right-click inside the username text box and choose Login with BugMeNot. In Chrome, click the BugMeNot icon in the address bar (or press Ctrl+I) to automatically fill in the login credentials using a username and password from BugMeNot. Notice that the login field, as shown in Figure 6-18, displays the success rate for those credentials, and you can click the drop-down menu to try a different username and password combination. See Hack 93, "Extend Your Web Browser," for more on how to install a browser extension.

Figure 6-18: The BugMeNot extension for Chrome automatically fills login information and enables you to select different logins from a drop-down menu.

NOTE BugMeNot does not work on websites that require a paid subscription to view, and some sites block BugMeNot. The most popular BugMeNot sites that usually do work include *The New York Times* (`http://nytimes.com`), *The Washington Post* (`http://washingtonpost.com`), and IMDb (`http://imdb.com`), the Internet Movie Database.

Hack 57: Speed Up Web Pages on a Slow Internet Connection

Level . . . . **Easy**

Platform . . . . **All**

Cost . . . . **Free**

It may feel as though centuries have passed since the last time you heard the unmistakable mating call of your computer's modem dialing into an ISP. But even in today's broadband-saturated world, you can't always find a speedy Internet connection — while traveling, for example, or when your high-speed connection isn't available.

When you surf the Web on a slow connection, it can seem as though grass grows faster than the download progress meter on your web browser moves. Still, it's not difficult to optimize your browsing setup for the fastest way to log on, get what you need done, and get off. This hack covers some strategies for squeezing the most productivity out of a limited flow of bytes over a slow Internet connection, be it via an analog dial-up line or a tethered cell phone data connection. (See Hack 87, "Connect Your Computer to the Internet via Mobile Phone by 'Tethering'," for more on dialing into the Internet from your mobile phone on the go.)

Configure Your Web Browser for a Slow Connection

Chances are, your web browser's setup assumes that your Internet connection is fast and ever present. A couple of small changes for your slow-connection session can make a big difference:

- Increase the size of your browser's cache so that you re-download the same web page elements less often. The default cache size in Firefox, for example, is 50MB. Your hard drive probably has plenty of free space, so consider increasing this number to 100MB or more. To do so in Firefox, choose Tools ➪ Options ➪ Advanced and from the Network tab, set the number in the Cache section, as shown in Figure 6-19.

- If you want real speed and your inner aesthete won't be too offended, under Content, deselect Load Images Automatically. This, of course, takes away the pretty pictures on web pages, but it significantly speeds up page load on a slow connection. You can also specify sites that should be exceptions to the no-images rule using the — you guessed it — Exceptions button, as shown in Figure 6-20. To disable images in Google Chrome, click the Wrench button, select Preferences, click Under the Hood in the left sidebar; then click the Content Settings button and select Do Not Show Any Images. Like Firefox, you can set exceptions.

Figure 6-19: Increase the size of the cache to decrease the number of repeated downloads.

Figure 6-20: Set Firefox to not download images to speed up page load.

TIP Advanced users can employ their browser's Profile feature to set up slow-connection preferences separately from their default profile, and switch to it as necessary. See more on how to manage profiles in Firefox at `http://mozilla.org/support/firefox/profile`; Chrome users on Windows looking for easy profile switching should check out Google Chrome Backup `www.parhelia-tools.com/products/gcb/googlechrome.aspx`.

Block and Disable Bandwidth Hogs

Five minutes on a slow connection and you begin to resent every unnecessary pixel, advertisement, and Flash movie on the Web. Install an ad blocker to both save bandwidth and avoid losing minutes of your life when some web page suggests you shoot the turkey and win an iPad in one of its banner ads.

- Firefox users, try Adblock Plus (`https://addons.mozilla.org/en-US/firefox/addon/adblock-plus/`) or FlashBlock (`https://addons.mozilla.org/en-US/firefox/addon/flashblock/`)
- Chrome users, try AdBlock (`http://tinyurl.com/yddouf2`) or FlashBlock (`http://tinyurl.com/ye5srym`).

Speaking of bandwidth hogs, if your BitTorrent client is running, or your podcast-downloading software (such as iTunes) is set to automatically download new episodes when you connect to the Internet, you'll qualify for Social Security before you can view your browser's home page. Be sure to disable or quit any bandwidth hogs you don't need when you're on a slow connection.

Use Tabs to Load Pages While You Work

The real beauty of tabbed browsing shows its efficient self in the face of a slow Internet connection. When searching the Web for information or clicking links from your newsreader, click your mouse scroll wheel or Control/Command+click to open each link in a new tab. That way, you can read one page while others load in background tabs.

If your time on the slow connection is limited (maybe you paid for an hour of Internet time at the airport), log on, open a bunch of pages in multiple tabs, disconnect, and read offline.

Speaking of offline....

Work Offline Whenever Possible

Yes, always-online web applications are popular these days, but you're not always online. The capability to work offline makes a huge difference in productivity when you're dependent on a slow connection. Following is a quick list of offline work examples that can help you get things done when all you have is a slow connection:

- Use a desktop RSS reader and download all unread articles for offline reading. (See Hack 91, "Subscribe to Websites with RSS," for more on using RSS.)

- Save web pages to your hard drive for reading later. (Chapter 10, "Master the Web," provides many hacks for improving your web experience.)

- Web mail users, install a desktop email client such as Mozilla Thunderbird (www.mozillamessaging.com/) and download your messages for offline reading and responding.

A slow connection to the Internet can be an exercise in utter frustration, but tweaking your tools to fit the task can make it a lot more bearable.

Hack 58: Securely Save Website Passwords

Level . . . . **Easy**
Platform . . . . **Firefox**
Cost . . . . **Free**

One of the most convenient features in Firefox is its capability to save the passwords you use to log on to websites — such as your web mail and online banking — so that you don't have to type them in every time. Those saved passwords automatically fill in as asterisks in the Password field, but did you know how easy it is to see what they are? In Firefox, choose Tools ⇨ Options. In the Security tab, under Passwords, click the Show Passwords button. Then click the Show Passwords button in the dialog box — and there they are, all your high-security passwords in plain text and full sight.

Now consider how easy it would be for your Firefox-loving housemate to log onto your Gmail, or the computer-sharing temp at the office to get into your checking account, or for a laptop thief to log into your PayPal account. Not such a great feature anymore, eh? But fear not! You don't have to go back to retyping your passwords every time you visit a login-only site.

This hack describes how to secure your saved passwords in Firefox without requiring you give up the convenience of those auto-filled login details.

Set a Master Password in Firefox

The master password is a single password that locks the rest of your saved passwords away from prying eyes. It's a password you have to enter once a session — each time you restart Firefox.

To set your master password in Firefox, choose Tools ⇨ Options and, on the Security tab, under Passwords, select the Use a Master Password check box to set the master password (see Figure 6-21).

Figure 6-21: Set your master password in the Firefox Options dialog box.

> **NOTE** Google Chrome doesn't include a master password feature at the time of this writing. To add more security to your passwords in Chrome — and to take your password security to the next level in Firefox and virtually any other browser — see Hack 15, "Securely Track Your Passwords."

When you set your master password, Firefox has a neat Password Quality Meter that displays how difficult your password is to crack. Try different combinations of words, numbers, and symbols to get this secure-o-meter as high as possible. For example the password `lifehacker` scored low on the quality meter, but `l1f3h4ck3r` registered about 90 percent (see Figure 6-22), making it fairly hard to crack.

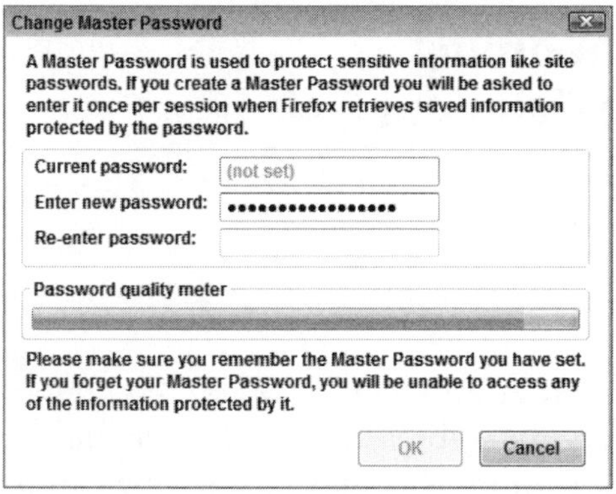

Figure 6-22: The master password quality level.

Now, the trick is to pick something you will always remember, because if you forget your master password, you cannot access any of your saved passwords. That would be bad. (Hack 14, "Instantly Recall Any Number of Different Passwords," offers help in creating great passwords you won't forget.)

After you set your master password, close Firefox. When you re-open and go to a page where you've saved a password — such as Yahoo! Mail — you get a security prompt, as shown in Figure 6-23.

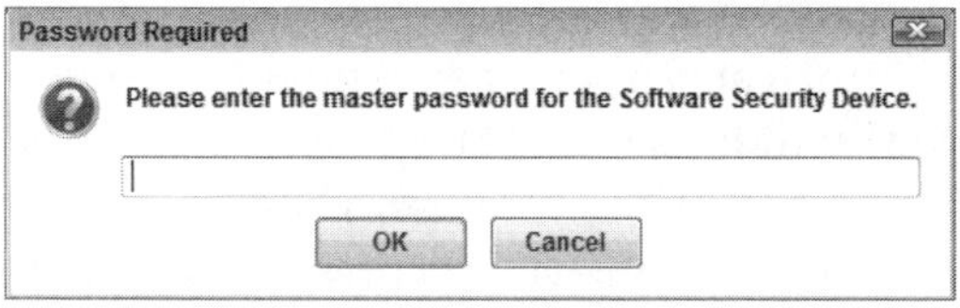

Figure 6-23: The master password prompt.

Enter your master password, click OK, and your Yahoo! Mail login details fill in automatically.

The master password prompt is a bit of an inconvenience but much less so than entering a password every time you visit login-only sites. It buys you the expediency of saved passwords with the security of having to be authorized to access them.

NOTE The Firefox Master Password is difficult — but not impossible — to crack. If there are passwords to websites you absolutely don't want stored on your computer, when you enter them and Firefox asks whether it should save them, just click No.

Hack 59: Become a Scheduling Black Belt with Google Calendar

Level . . . . **Easy**

Platform . . . . **Web**

Cost . . . . **Free**

In Hack 33, "Send Reminders to Your Future Self," you learned how to schedule events and reminders using the web-based Google Calendar, or GCal. GCal has many more useful features that make it a strong candidate for your central work and life calendar application. This hack covers more advanced uses for GCal, such as adding and getting events from anywhere, subscribing to multiple calendars, sharing calendars, booking inanimate objects such as a conference room, and inviting multiple people to events.

Quickly Capture Events

When Google Calendar is loaded in your web browser, you can press the Q key to summon a single field to enter an event. Forget typing in seventeen fields for all the event details; GCal understands natural language such as "tomorrow at 1 p.m.," as shown in Figure 6-24.

For example, you could write "Lunch at Nathan's next Thursday at noon for an hour" and Google Calendar will parse your language and create a new event for that day and time, with "Lunch at Nathan's" as your event title and one hour as the event length. You can even set an event as recurring by adding something like "on the first Tuesday of every month" or "yearly" to the Quick add text.

Currently the only downside to using Quick add is that you can't set reminders; instead, it uses your default *email* reminder which you can set by clicking Settings ➪ Calendar settings ➪ Calendars ➪ Notifications and then setting your preferred defaults in the Event reminders section. For more details on using the Quick add feature, visit www.google.com/support/calendar/bin/answer.py?hl=en&answer=36604.

Figure 6-24: Use the Quick Add feature to add events to your Google Calendar by pressing the Q key and typing in event details in a natural language.

SHORTCUT

You can access that handy Quick Add feature no matter what you're doing using Launchy (Windows) or Quicksilver (Mac) application launchers described in Hacks 50 and 51. Launchy users, download the Google Calendar plugin from www.davidkarlsson.info/launchy/gcal.zip, unzip the file, and move the unzipped plugins folder to C:\Program Files (x86)\Launchy (Click Yes when you're prompted to Confirm Folder Replace). Restart Launchy, and enable the GCal plugin by opening the Launchy preferences, clicking Plugins, and adding your Google account information. In Quicksilver, open the Preferences, navigate to the Plug-ins tab, and find and enable the Google Calendar module.

Subscribe to Shared Calendars

When's Passover this year? What day of the week does Cinco de Mayo land on? Browse GCal's list of shared public calendars to add sets of dates, from the phases of the moon to religious and regional holidays. Click the Add link on the bottom left side of the GCal sidebar, and then click the Browse Interesting Calendars link to pick and choose from a list of shared calendars.

Share a Custom Calendar

You can also create and share your own calendars such as your softball team's game schedule with co-workers and friends, or a work-related calendar with your personal GCal. For example, my Lifehacker Editor Vacations calendar is accessible to my personal GCal account.

Google Calendar can also display any calendar available in the iCal file format, like your favorite baseball team's schedule, most likely available on the Web. Website iCal Share (http://icalshare.com/) is a growing, user-submitted repository of television, sports, and entertainment iCal calendars, accessible from your Google Calendar.

Book Conference Room B

GCal can even help you schedule the use of inanimate objects, such as the office projector or meeting space. Using GCal's auto-accept invitations feature, any invitation to the Conference Room B calendar that doesn't conflict with another meeting can automatically be entered. From Google's Help section, here's how to set up a calendar to manage conference room bookings:[1]

1. Create a secondary calendar named Conference Room B.

2. In the calendar list on the left, click the down-arrow button next to Conference Room B, select Calendar Settings, and then select the Calendar Details tab.

3. Enable the auto-accept invitations feature by selecting Auto-Accept Invitations That Do Not Conflict.

4. Click Save.

5. Click the down-arrow next to the calendar you created and select Share This Calendar.

6. Enter the email addresses of the users to whom you want to grant access to your resource.

7. Select the desired shared permission level (must be See All Event Details or higher).

Receive Your Daily Agenda via Email Automatically

If you live out of your inbox and not from a calendar, you'll love GCal's daily agenda email feature. Get a simple list of the day's events emailed to you at 5 a.m. daily automatically. (Find the magic check box to turn that on by clicking the drop-down arrow next to a calendar in the GCal sidebar, then clicking Calendar Settings and the Notifications tab.)

See This Week's Weather Forecast on Your Calendar

Wondering how to dress for the cookout this weekend? See how the weather might affect this week's upcoming events by turning on the forecast right inside GCal. To do so, in General Settings, enter your location and select whether you want to see the temperature in Celsius or Fahrenheit. Figure 6-25 shows the result: a small weather-forecast icon on each day right inside your calendar. Hover your mouse pointer over the icon to get the forecasted high and low temperature; click it for the four-day forecast.

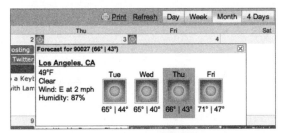

Figure 6-25: With the Google Calendar embedded weather forecast enabled, a small icon appears on each day of the upcoming week in your calendar.

Invite Your Friends to Events via GCal

Anyone else over Evite? Google Calendar doesn't have that festive Evite feel, but it doesn't have the overbearing ads or busy design, either. GCal can send and manage event invitations, and the recipients can leave comments on an event as well.

Get Your Schedule Details via Text Message

Thumb-happy text-messaging fans will put GCal's SMS access to good use. Text the word **next** to short code GVENT (48368) from your GCal-verified cell phone to get the next event on your schedule. **Day** will get your day's agenda, and **nday** will send back tomorrow's events. You can also SMS new event details (such as **Pumpkin picking Oct 25 at 3 p.m.**) to GVENT to add them to your calendar.

Master GCal's Keyboard Shortcuts

The fastest way to become a black belt with most apps is to navigate them right from your keyboard. As with Gmail, GCal comes with a hefty set of keyboard shortcuts, detailed in Google's Help documents.[2] Here's a quick summary:

SHORTCUT KEY	DEFINITION
C	Create event
/	Search
P	Previous date range
N	Next date range
T	Jump to Today
D	Day view
X	Customized view
W	Week view
M	Month view
A	Agenda view
Q	Quick Add
Esc	Back to calendar

References

1. Google Help Center, "Share & Manage Calendars," available at (www.google.com/support/calendar/bin/answer.py?answer=44105&topic=8605).

2. Google Help Center, "Calendar Basics," available at (www.google.com/support/calendar/bin/answer.py?answer=37034&topic=8556).

CHAPTER 7

Automate Repetitive Tasks

Thirty years ago, we thought that by the 21st century we'd all have personal robots doing our laundry, cooking meals, and cleaning our houses — like the Jetsons' robot maid, Rosie. Although that scenario hasn't become reality yet, your personal computer *can* perform certain menial tasks, automatically and unsupervised, on a schedule you set. Your PC isn't as advanced or charming as Rosie, but it can clean up after itself and take the work out of repetitive computing jobs.

Computers are built to relieve us of dull work, not create more work. Refrigerators switch on and off to maintain a certain temperature. Your paycheck gets deposited directly into your account so you don't have to visit the bank. Streetlights snap on at dusk so that humans don't have to canvass the neighborhood flipping switches. And you can automate personal computing tasks to run in the background automatically.

If you examine your work processes over time, you'll notice that certain activities come up repeatedly, whether it's filing certain email messages into the same folders, starting up those same three programs first thing in the morning, deleting old files you don't need, or downloading new songs from your favorite bands' websites. The first step is to identify those repetitive actions. The next step is to program your computer to perform them so that you don't have to do them by hand again.

RESISTANCE TO AUTOMATION AND THE ATTRACTION OF BUSYWORK

The type of work ripe for automation is busywork: well-defined tasks that happen the same way every time and require virtually no thinking. Although it may be boring, ironically, busywork's appeal is its simplicity. You can get it done with little mental effort, by just going through the motions, and get that rewarding feeling of accomplishment. With busywork, there's little chance of failure and there's a high degree of familiarity. But keeping busy with tasks that you could delegate to your computer (or another person) also keeps you away from the larger projects, decisions, and mental work only *you* can do. Next time you find yourself doing that same tedious job again by hand, ask yourself whether it's the best use of your time.

Chances are, you already have a few scheduled processes running on your computer. Certain types of software, such as virus and spyware scanners, come with prescheduled runtimes built in. But few users configure their own automatic processes and schedule them, and that's a shame. Granted, the initial time investment of automating a job can seem high, but in the long run, the payback more than makes up for it.

Almost every hack in this book involves automating life and work tasks in one way or another. This chapter covers automatic actions that take the work out of using a computer itself, such as backing up your files, opening programs, or searching the Web for the same terms more than once. All these are tasks your computer can do all by itself while you're asleep or at lunch or in a meeting. Save yourself from the doldrums of tedious computer work with the following hacks that automate important — but boring — tasks so that you can concentrate on more appealing work.

Hack 60: Set Up an Automated, Bulletproof File Back Up Solution

Level . . . . **Medium**

Platform . . . . **Windows, Mac, and Linux**

Cost . . . . **$75 and up (for external hard drive); as low as $1.50/month (for CrashPlan+)**

More and more, the fragments of your life exist as particles on a disk mounted inside your computer. The photos from your one-year-old niece's birthday, the interview you did with great-grandpa Gus, your working manuscript of the Great American Novel, the first email messages you exchanged with your spouse — not to mention crucial professional data — all exist as bits of information on storage devices susceptible to temperature changes, power surges, fire, theft, static, and just plain wear and tear.

Hard drives fail. It's a fact of computing life. It's not a matter of *whether* your computer's disk will stop working; it's a matter of *when*. The question is how much it will disrupt your life — and it won't, if you have a backup copy.

Backing up your data is the dullest but most indispensable thing you do on your computer. But who remembers to do it? You don't have to.

In this hack, you automate backups for your computer, both on-site, to an external hard drive, *and* off-site, to the Internet. This system can even email you if something goes wrong, so it's the ultimate set-it-and-forget-it situation. After you get this up and running, you'll never have to worry about losing data again.

LOCAL BACKUP VERSUS ONLINE BACKUP – WHY YOU SHOULD HAVE BOTH

Local external drive backups are great for quick recovery when you've accidentally deleted a file, or if your computer's internal hard drive crashes. But what if your house burns down or gets burglarized – including your backup drive? Hurricane Katrina victims can tell you that no matter how diligently you back up your computer to a local hard drive, you will still lose your photos, documents, and other important files if you don't keep a copy off-site, preferably out of state. Some users keep an extra hard drive with a copy of their important files at the office or at their mother's house in case of theft or fire. But that requires manually transporting your hard drive back and forth on a regular basis, and you want to set it and forget it.

What You Need

- A Windows, Mac, or Linux PC.

- **CrashPlan.** Available as a free download from `http://b5.crashplan` `.com/consumer/download.html`.

- **An external hard drive for local backup.** Purchase an external hard drive that connects via USB. When deciding capacity, go for 10 times the amount of data you want to back up. For example, if the size of your `My Documents` folder is 10GB, then look to purchase a 100GB hard drive. (If a drive the size you need isn't available, calculate the size of your home directory without space-hogging subdirectories, such as My Music, My Videos, and My Pictures. You have the option to reduce the number of copies you keep of those large files to save space.)

■ **A CrashPlan+ account for off-site backups.** In addition to local backups, CrashPlan can also back up your files off-site to their servers (which they call CrashPlan Central). As of this writing, unlimited backup at CrashPlan costs $5 per month per computer, or $10 per month for a household of two to ten computers (if you pay for a year in advance). You can compare your CrashPlan options at http://b5.crashplan.com/consumer/crashplan-plus.html. You don't have to pay for CrashPlan+, but I'd strongly recommend doing so for your offsite backups.

Configure Your Backup System

The first time you install the CrashPlan software, you also need to register for an account. (You have to register whether you're going to pay for off-site back up with CrashPlan+.)

Choose the Files and Folders You Want to Back Up

After you registered, the software scans your system, suggests which directories it should back up, and lets you know how much space those files will use in the Files section of CrashPlan's Backup window. If you don't want to go with CrashPlan's suggestions, you can manually choose which files and folders it backs up. To do so, click the Change button (see Figure 7-1).

Figure 7-1: Click the Change button to choose which folders CrashPlan should back up.

Choose Your Backup Destinations

You have four Destination options to which you can back up your files, all of which are accessible through the Destinations tab in the CrashPlan desktop application. You can back up your files to any combination of the following destinations:

- **Friends:** Back up to a friend's computer over the Internet
- **Computers:** Back up to another computer on your home network
- **Folders:** Use CrashPlan to back up files to an external hard drive
- **Online:** Back up to CrashPlan's servers

CrashPlan is completely free to use with every destination but Online, which requires a paid CrashPlan+ account. To achieve both on-site and off-site backups, you should strongly consider backing up to a local drive and to CrashPlan's servers with a paid CrashPlan+ account.

> **TIP** If you don't want to pay for your off-site backups, CrashPlan has a clever trick up its sleeve: It enables you to back up to a friend's computer across the Internet. Your friend needs CrashPlan installed and hard drive space to accommodate you, but it's a handy option if you're not backing up a lot of files.

Choosing your backup destinations is simple:

1. Click the Destinations tab.
2. Click the type of destination you want to set up (as shown in Figure 7-2).
3. Point CrashPlan to the appropriate hard drive, folder, computer, or CrashPlan+ account you're setting up.

Set Your Preferences

CrashPlan's Settings also contain preferences for your automatic backup schedule. By default, CrashPlan backs up files every 15 minutes, so you're always backed up (you can change it as often as every 1 minute), but if you'd prefer to schedule your backups less often — for example, when you're away from your computer or not using the Internet — you can adjust the settings by following these steps:

1. Click the Backup tab.
2. Select Between Specified Times from the Backup Will Run drop-down menu.

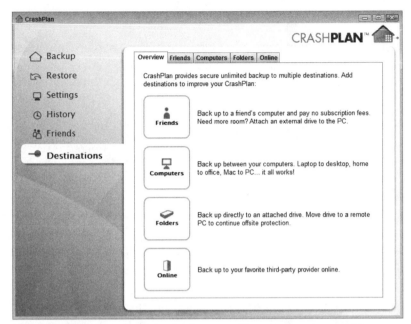

Figure 7-2: You can choose to backup your files to one or more of four destinations.

3. Set your preferred backup times. From the Settings panel, you can also adjust how it should notify you and how much bandwidth and computer power it should use to get its job done.

4. After you configure CrashPlan's Settings the way you want, click the Save button.

NOTE If you're on a Mac, you may prefer to use OS X's built-in Time Machine for local backup. CrashPlan is still an excellent option for off-site back up, but it's hard to beat Time Machine for local file redundancy.

Start Your Backup

After you configure CrashPlan to your liking:

1. Click the Backup tab.

2. Click the Start Backup button.

3. Click the Start button to the left of the progress bar. (It looks like a Play button.)

Your first backup can take a long time depending on how much data you back up and, if you back up off-site, how fast your Internet connection is. On a laptop, CrashPlan estimates it will take days to complete a backup to CrashPlan's servers. For a local backup, it'll take just a few hours.

CrashPlan does differential — or incremental — backups; that is, it backs up only portions of your files that have changed since the last time they were backed up, so while your initial backup may take a long time, subsequent backups will take significantly less time, so don't let the first backup discourage you.

What a CrashPlan+ Account Adds to Your Backup Plan

The main benefit of a paid CrashPlan account is that it's a reliable, off-site storage option. If someone stole both your laptop and your external drive, for example, you could still recover all your backed up files from CrashPlan's servers.

CrashPlan's backup process encrypts the files on your computer using either an encryption key it chooses or your own private key. CrashPlan uses stronger encryption algorithms with its paid accounts than it's free account (though both are encrypted), so you don't have to worry about anyone intercepting your files when they're transferred over the Internet.

If you delete a file on your computer, CrashPlan marks it as deleted but holds onto a copy on its side forever unless you tell it not to. That way, you can recover a deleted file no matter how much time has passed.

Restore Files Backed Up with CrashPlan

After you complete at least one backup with CrashPlan, you can restore files copied to its servers or to your other backup destinations in one of three ways:

- Open the CrashPlan software on your computer, click the Restore tab, select the backup destination you want to restore from, and pick and choose the files you want to copy back to your system from your backups. Click the Restore button. (see Figure 7-3).

- On the CrashPlan website, from the My Account page, click on Computers, and then click the Restore button next to the computer you want to restore files on. You can browse your backup, tick the check box next to files you want to restore, and then click Restore.

▪ If you're not using the computer with the CrashPlan software installed, you can download the restored files as a ZIP archive. This feature is only available for paid CrashPlan accounts.

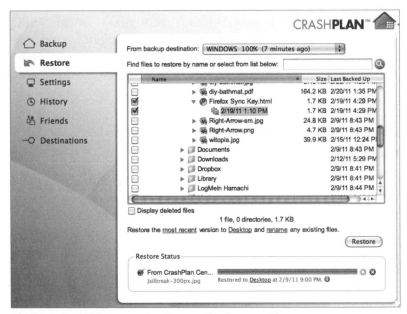

Figure 7-3: Navigate your backups and select any file you want to restore.

For a detailed guide to all the ins and outs of CrashPlan, see the official CrashPlan documentation at http://support.crashplan.com/doku.php/how_to.

NOTE CrashPlan is an automated backup solution, and even though it can back up files between your computers, it does so in an encrypted format, which means you can't browse those files on the destination computer. To add backup-style synchronization and redundancy to your important files in addition to anywhere-access, see Hack 67, "Access Your Most Important Files Anywhere with Dropbox."

CRASHPLAN ALTERNATIVES

Since the dawn of computing, businesses have been concerned about data backup. But now, as consumers generate more data, there's a new market for individual online backup, and you have several good choices of service. If CrashPlan isn't for you, consider BackBlaze (http://backblaze.com/), **Carbonite** (http://carbonite.com/), **or Mozy** (http://mozy.com/).

Hack 61: Automatically Back Up Your Files to an External Hard Drive (Mac)

Level . . . . **Easy**

Platform . . . . **Mac OS X**

Cost . . . . **$75 and up (for external hard drive)**

Data-conscious users can back up their files off-site using a service like CrashPlan, detailed in Hack 60, "Set Up an Automated, Bulletproof File Back Up Solution." Instead of using CrashPlan for local backups, however, Mac users have an even better on-site backup solution: All recent versions of Mac OS X ship with a comprehensive local backup application called Time Machine that requires only two steps to set up. Here's how to turn on Time Machine and use it to restore deleted files on your computer.

Enable Time Machine Backups

All you need to start backing up your Mac with Time Machine is an external hard drive. The larger the drive capacity, the more backups Time Machine can store on it, so purchase the largest drive that you can afford for best results. The price of hard drives is always falling, but you shouldn't have to spend much more than $100 to $150 for an external drive that will work for you.

When you plug in your external hard drive to your Mac for the first time, OS X asks whether you want to use that drive for Time Machine backups. Simply click Use as Backup Disk (see Figure 7-4) to turn on Time Machine.

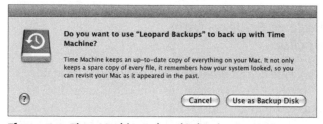

Figure 7-4: Time Machine asks whether it can use your external disk for backups when you plug it into your Mac.

Time Machine's first backup takes a long time because it copies all your Mac's files to the external drive. Every backup after that happens on its own, without your intervention and it copies only files that have changed, so it completes quicker. The only way you'll know Time Machine is working is by the sound of your hard drive.

What Time Machine Does

In short, Time Machine performs automatic, incremental backups of your Mac over time. *Incremental* means that it copies only files that have changed since the previous backup, instead of making a whole, full new copy. (Therefore, incremental backups save disk space.) As long as your external drive is connected and Time Machine is enabled, it will save hourly backups of your Mac's files automatically and keep a backup of the last 24 hours, and daily backups for the past month and weekly backups older than a month. The only files that might not get backed up with Time Machine are files you create and delete inside the space of an hour.

If you put your Mac to sleep or shut down in the midst of a Time Machine backup, when you wake or restart it, it automatically resumes where it was when it left off. If your external drive isn't connected to your Mac, Time Machine backups won't happen again until the drive is present, and then it copies all the files that changed since the last backup.

When your external hard drive is full, Time Machine alerts you and deletes the oldest backup that it has stored (presumably, if you have a spacious drive, a weekly backup older than a month ago.) Time Machine's backups aren't stored in any special format, either; you can browse to your external drive in Finder, where you can see a folder named Backups .backupdb. That folder contains dated subfolders of Time Machine's backups, with all the files available to copy, view, or otherwise manipulate like any other file on your Mac.

Switch Disks or Exclude Folders- from Time Machine's Backup

The beauty of Time Machine is that it has so few user options that need to be configured. However, there are two settings you can change in System Preferences' Time Machine panel. Using the Options button (shown in Figure 7-5), you can opt to exclude certain folders from Time Machine's backup process (such as space-hogging video files that you back up or store elsewhere, or photos you automatically upload online anyway). You can also change the disk Time Machine uses to store backups by clicking the Change Disk button (also shown in Figure 7-5).

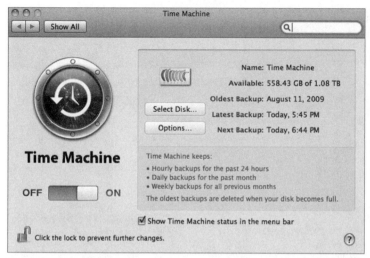

Figure 7-5: Exclude directories from Time Machine's backups using the Options dialog box, or change the disk Time Machine uses in the Time Machine area of System Preferences.

Restore Deleted or Overwritten Files

When Time Machine is on and backing up your Mac, you'll likely not give it another thought until you've accidentally deleted or overwritten an important file. To restore a past or deleted file, start Time Machine, which displays the backups it has stored of your Mac in a dramatic line of Finder windows that extend back in space. Use the timeline on the right side of the screen to fly back and forth between Time Machine backups of a folder. When you find the files you need in a past backup, select them and click the Restore button on the lower-right side of the screen, as shown in Figure 7-6.

Time Machine saves snapshots of your Mac only to a local external drive, which means that if that drive breaks or if it's lost or stolen, you lose all your backups. Although using Time Machine only is better than nothing, to ensure that your important data is backed up in case of a natural disaster or theft, consider backing up to an online storage service over the Internet. See Hack 60, "Set Up an Automated, Bulletproof File Back Up Solution," for more on setting that up.

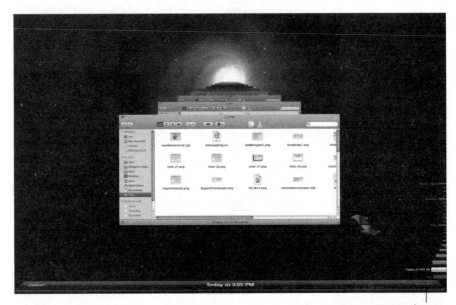

Restore button

Figure 7-6: Fly back in time and find the past version of a file; then click the Restore button to copy it back to your Mac.

Change Time Machine's Default Backup Interval

For some users, Time Machine's hourly backups cause system slowdowns while running, and for others hourly backups may simply seem like overkill. TimeMachineEditor (http://timesoftware.free.fr/timemachineeditor/) is a free application that allows you to change Time Machine's default backup interval to whatever fits your needs.

Use the app's basic Interval schedule to adjust how many hours Time Machine should wait between backups, or select the Calendar Intervals option from the drop-down menu to set more precise intervals by day, week, or month.

Hack 62: Automatically Clean Up Your PC

Level.......**Advanced**

Platform....**Windows**

Cost........**Free**

During the course of a workday, you save all sorts of disposable files on your computer: video, images, and songs meant for a single viewing or hearing; PDF files you have to print; and software installers and Zip files you extract and do whatever you need with the contents. The end result is a lot of digital detritus clogging your hard drive for no good reason. But you don't want to clean up after yourself every time you work with a set of files you don't need to keep.

Few people are disorganized because it's their preference. But organization takes time, and however little time it may be, it's generally easier to do nothing than to take a few seconds to file something away in the appropriate folder.

In this hack, you set up a virtual butler I created, called Belvedere[1] that sweeps through your hard drive regularly and deletes any file or performs other actions on files that meet criteria you define — for example files that have been sitting around for more than x days, like old garbage starting to stink. This program constantly recovers space on your hard drive and moves files around so your hard drive remains organized and clean. Download Belvedere from `http://lifehacker.com/#!341950/`.

Empty Your Downloads Folder with Belvedere

After you install and launch Belvedere, you'll notice a new icon running in your system tray. Right-click the Belvedere icon and click Manage to create a new rule. Click the + button below the Folders section (bottom left) to add a new watched folder, like your Downloads folder, to Belvedere. After you add a folder, select it; then click the + button below the Rules pane to create a new action for that folder based on a set of criteria.

The Create a rule dialog enables you to create your criteria and then define an action for any file that matches your rule — much like an email filter. For your Downloads folder, for example, you may want to create a rule that can move any file to your Recycle Bin that's been sitting untouched in your Downloads folder for the past 14 days, like you see in Figure 7-7. Next simply select the Enabled check box to start using it.

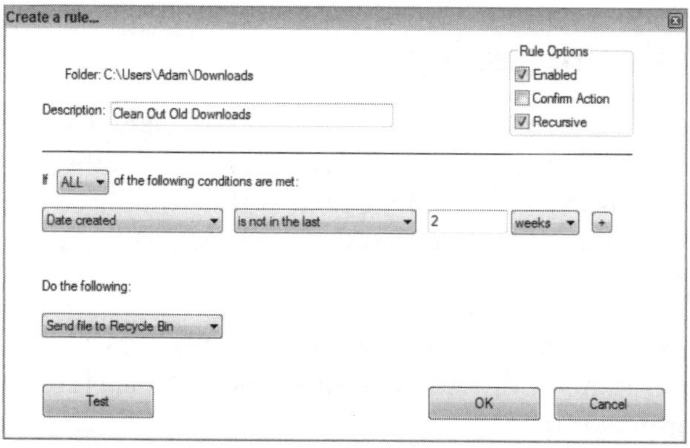

Figure 7-7: Automatically clean out old files from your Downloads folder.

WARNING Automation can be convenient, but make sure your Belvedere rules are doing what you expect before you turn them on so that you don't end up recycling files you want to keep. Click the Test button to verify what files match a rule before you set the rule into action.

Empty the Recycle Bin with Belvedere

If your Recycle Bin is bursting with trash simply because you don't remember to regularly empty it, you can let Belvedere worry about it for you. Launch Belvedere, click the Recycle Bin tab, and tick Allow Belvedere to manage my Recycle Bin, as shown in Figure 7-8. Tell it how often to empty your Recycle Bin; then click Save Preferences.

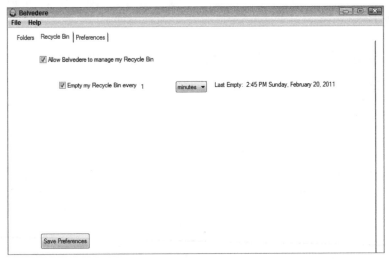

Figure 7-8: Set Belvedere to regularly clean out your Recycle Bin.

More Automatic File Processing

Most people use Belvedere to keep their desktops and Downloads folders clean, but Belvedere can do much more than delete files. Try out the different conditions and actions available in its Create a Rule dialog to get a better idea of how you might use it to automate common actions. With Belvedere, you can do the following:

- Automatically move media files, such as MP3s, to your iTunes library. (Specifically, to the Automatically Add to iTunes folder, which iTunes regularly scans for new music.)

- Move images, documents, and other ephemera from your messy Desktop into neat, organized folders.

- Launch files that meet specific conditions. For example, you could watch a folder for a TORRENT file and automatically start downloading files via BitTorrent.

Hack 63: Automatically Clean Up Your Mac

Level . . . . **Medium**

Platform . . . . **Mac OS X**

Cost. **$21.95**

Just as in the physical world, it's easy to let digital clutter accumulate on your Mac. Chances are, your Downloads folder contains no-longer-relevant files, or your desktop is covered in documents, images, and songs you finished with last week. Hack 62, "Automatically Clean Up Your PC," features a Windows program that cleans and organizes your PC based on a set of rules. That program is based on Hazel, an automated, rules-based file manager for Mac. That means Hazel does essentially the same thing for Mac users as Belvedere does for PC users. Download a 14-day free trial of Hazel, available at http://www.noodlesoft.com/hazel.php. (A license costs $21.95.) Here's how Hazel can keep your Mac's hard drive free of files you don't need anymore.

Empty Your Downloads Folder with Hazel

After you install Hazel, go to its pane in System Preferences. (It will be listed under the Other heading.) To add a new folder rule, click the + button under the Folder list (bottom-left pane) and choose a folder, such as Downloads, to add it to the list. Select it and then, to create a new rules-based action, click the + button under the Rules box (bottom-right pane). Here you can set up automatic actions based on file criteria, as shown in Figure 7-9.

Think of Hazel's rules as email filters: They work according to simple if-then logic. The rule pictured in Figure 7-9 says that if a file in the Downloads folder were added (that is, downloaded and saved there) more than four weeks ago, Hazel should delete it. When Hazel is running, it will automatically recover space in your Downloads folder occupied by files you saved there more than four weeks ago.

You can use similar rules on any folders you set up as temporary workspaces to keep them clean and tidy.

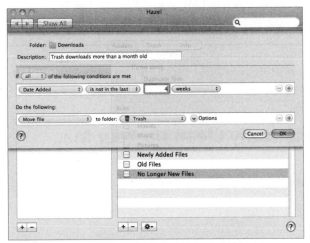

Figure 7-9: Set up a Hazel rule to delete files in the `Downloads` folder that haven't been opened in more than a month.

Take Out the Trash with Hazel

Hazel can also automatically manage your Mac's Trash bin, so you don't have to empty it by hand, or worry that the files there are taking up too much space on your hard drive. In Hazel's System Preferences pane, go to the Trash tab. There you can set Hazel to automatically delete files that have been sitting in the Trash for more than a certain amount of time, or set it to keep the total size of the Trash under a certain file size, as shown in Figure 7-10.

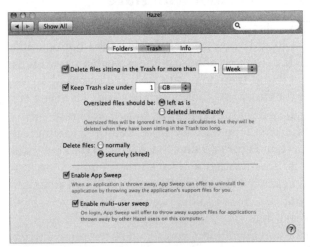

Figure 7-10: Set up Hazel to automatically keep your Trash bin under control.

Also in the Trash tab, you can enable Hazel's App Sweep feature, which monitors the applications installed on your Mac and the related settings and files it adds to your system. When you delete a program, Hazel prompts you to delete any related files that application would otherwise leave behind.

More Automatic File Processing

Hazel can do much more than just delete old files. Experiment with its rich criteria options and possible actions to see what's useful for you. To see some examples, choose Load Sample Rules from the drop-down list beneath the Rules area. With Hazel, you can do the following:

- Automatically move media files such as MP3s, videos, or photos to your iTunes library or iPhoto library. (This works well with Hack 66, "Automatically Download Music, Movies, and More.")
- Automatically sort images into subfolders named by date.
- Label or add a keyword to any file based on any rule ("added in the last hour," for example).

Hack 64: Automatically Reboot and Launch Applications

Level . . . . **Easy**

Platform . . . . **Windows**

Cost . . . . **Free**

Windows PC users know that every once in a while, your computer can slow down or run into problems that are magically resolved when you restart. A PC that's on continuously 24 hours a day — especially when it's hard at work at night running the automated tasks outlined in this chapter — can benefit from a regular reboot to clear out memory and end any hanging software processes. Furthermore, chances are, you start your workday with a set number of software applications, such as Microsoft Outlook and your morning-paper web sites.

In this hack, you schedule an early morning reboot and launch the software you need to get to work before you even sit down at your desk.

Automatically Reboot Your Computer

It's the middle of the night. Your computer has backed itself up, defragged the hard drives, and fetched you new music from all over the Web. Now it's time to begin the new day with a fresh start.

1. Choose Start, type **task scheduler**, and press Enter.

2. In the Task Scheduler window, click Create Task.

3. Name the new job Reboot; then click the Triggers tab.

4. Click New; then set the task schedule to Daily, one hour before you usually sit down at your computer.

5. On the Action tab, click New and enter the following in the Program/ script input, as shown in Figure 7-11.

```
C:\WINDOWS\system32\shutdown.exe -r -t 01
```

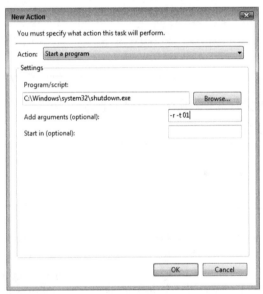

Figure 7-11: The Reboot scheduled task.

Notice that the arguments `-r  -t  01` are pasted separately in the Add Arguments box.

You don't want your PC to reboot if it's in the middle of something else, so on the Conditions tab, select the Start the Task Only If The Computer Is Idle For option, and enter a time frame, such as 10 minutes. If your Windows login has a password, you have to enter it to authorize Windows to run the task with your username's system rights.

If the Reboot job doesn't run because the computer is busy at that time, it shouldn't try again after you start working, so make sure the Wait for Idle For option is set to 1 hour.

Automatically Launch Software or Documents

Schedule the applications you normally launch by hand to start on their own before you sit down at your computer in the morning as well. Enter the path to any software program in a newly scheduled task's Run text box. For example, provided that it has been installed in the default location, Microsoft Outlook 2010 installs in Windows 7 with the following command:

```
"C:\Program Files (x86)\Microsoft Office\Office14\OUTLOOK.EXE"
```

Additionally, you can launch specific documents rather than just programs. For instance, if you absolutely must start the day editing Chapter 7 of your book, create a task that is simply the path of the document:

```
"D:/data/lifehacker/docs/lifehacker-book/chapter7.doc"
```

Doing so opens the chapter7.doc file in Microsoft Word automatically. Or schedule a playlist to launch and begin playing first thing in the morning for a custom alarm clock.

NOTE Set the most important thing you have to work on the next morning automatically. Hack 26, "Set Up a Morning Dash," explains how to make the first hour of the day the most productive.

If you schedule your Reboot task an hour before you arrive at work, have the auto software launch job run about 15 minutes after that. That way, your computer will restart and then launch your morning programs so that you can just walk in with your coffee in hand and start to work. (However, if you have a password set up on your PC — always a good idea security-wise — programs can't start automatically after reboot until you log in by hand.)

Automatically Start a Web-Browsing Session

If you spend time browsing the Web at work, chances are, you have a set of pages that you visit to start the day, like your morning paper. Your computer can easily fetch your favorite web pages before you reach your desk so that your morning reads are waiting for you.

Set up a task to open your web browser the same way you did with Outlook. Then add all the pages you'd like to load automatically, separated by a space, to the Run line. The resulting command for a Firefox web browser would look something like this:

```
"C:\Program Files (x86)\Mozilla Firefox\firefox.exe" lifehacker.com
nytimes.com gmail.com
```

The same command for Google Chrome users would look like this:

```
"C:\Users\lifehacker\appdata\local\Google\Chrome\Application\
chrome.exe" lifehacker.com nytimes.com gmail.com
```

NOTE The free Firefox web browser is available for download at http://www.mozilla.com/en-US/firefox/. **Google Chrome is available at** http://www.google.com/chrome/.

In this example, when you arrive at your computer, a browser window will be open with all your morning sites preloaded.

Hack 65: Make Google Search Results Automatically Come to You

Level . . . . **Beginner**

Platform . . . . **Web**

Cost . . . . **Free**

Keeping up with any news published online about a certain topic used to mean searching the Web for it every so often, or checking various online news sites. But not any more. Google offers free email alerts or delivers items via an RSS feed when certain search terms appear on web pages, as they are published.

For example, say you want to know whenever the product your company makes is mentioned online — in the news, on blogs, or on any web page out there. Instead of searching the Web for your product's name every week, let Google Alerts do that for you. To set up an alert, go to http://google.com/alerts. You can create an alert without a Google account, but if you have one, you should log in so that you can manage your alerts later. Next, enter your search term, the type of alert you want to receive, and the email frequency, as shown in Figure 7-12. To see what kind of results will match your query, click the Preview Results link.

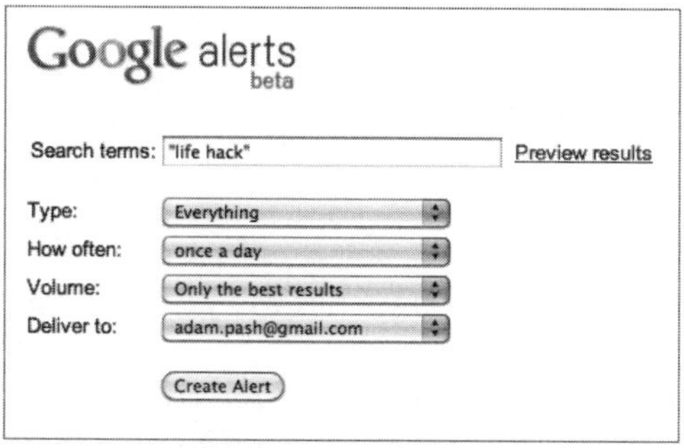

Figure 7-12: Enter your search term, type of alert, and email frequency in Google Alerts.

TIP If you prefer Google delivers alerts via RSS rather than email, select Feed from the Deliver to drop-down. For more, see Hack 91, "Subscribe to Websites with RSS."

Your Google Alert will let you know when your term appears in news pages, blogs, general web search results, discussion forums, video results, real-time results (which include status updates from Twitter), or all the above. After you create your alert, click the Preview results link to inspect the kind of content the email you receive will contain. Watch out: If you enter popular search terms, you will get inundated with frequent or long messages, so make your searches as specific as possible. To avoid receiving too much email, use the Once a Day or Once a Week frequency setting, instead of As-It-Happens (which is better suited for time-sensitive temporary news alerts).

TIP Narrow your alert results by using advanced search operators such as AND, OR, and enclosing phrases in quotation marks. See Hack 90, "Google Like a Pro," for more on pinpointing results you want with the right search term.

By default, your Google Alerts will be sent to your Gmail account, but you can use Gmail's filters to forward them to any email address you'd like (such as your company email address). Just create a filter that forwards all messages from googlealerts-noreply@google.com to your desired destination address.

Hack 66: Automatically Download Music, Movies, and More

Level....... **Advanced**

Platform .... **All**

Cost........ **Free**

Your web browser does a good job of fetching web documents and displaying them, but there are times when you need an extra-strength program to get those tougher download jobs done.

A versatile, old-school Unix program called wget is a handy tool that makes downloading tasks configurable. Whether you want to mirror an entire website, automatically download music or movies from a set of favorite weblogs, or transfer huge files painlessly on a slow or intermittent network connection, the wget program — the noninteractive network retriever — is for you.

Install and Run wget

Download the Mac or Windows version of wget from `http://lifehackerbook` `.com/links/wget`. After downloading, extract the files to `C:\wget` in Windows or `/Applications/wget` on the Mac.

To run `wget`, launch a command line (the Mac Terminal or Windows Command Prompt). At the command-line prompt, switch to the directory where `wget` is installed by typing:

```
cd c:\wget\
```

on Windows or

```
cd /Applications/wget/
```

on the Mac. Then type the `wget` command you want from the examples described in the upcoming sections, and press Enter.

The format of `wget` commands is as follows:

```
wget [option]... [URL]...
```

URL is the address of the file(s) you want `wget` to download. The magic in this little tool is the long menu of options available that make some highly customized and scriptable downloading tasks possible. This hack covers some examples of what you can do with `wget` and a few dashes and letters in the `[option]` part of the command.

NOTE For the full take on all the `wget` program's secret options sauce, type `wget--help` at the command line or check out the complete `wget` manual online, available at `http://gnu.org/software/wget/manual`.

Mirror an Entire Website

Say you want to back up your blog or create a local copy of an entire directory of a website for archiving or reading later. The following command saves all the pages that exist at the `example.com` website in a folder named `example.com` on your computer:

```
wget -m http://example.com
```

The `-m` switch in the command stands for "mirror this site."

To retrieve all the pages on a site and the pages to which that site links, use the following command:

```
wget -H -r --level=1 -k -p http://example.com
```

In plain English, this translates into Download all the pages (`-r`, recursive) on `http://example.com` plus one level (`--level=1`) into any other sites it links to (`-H`, span hosts) and convert the links in the downloaded version to point to the other sites' downloaded version (`-k`). Also, get all the components, such as images, that make up each page (`-p`).

WARNING Those with small hard drives, beware! This command downloads a *lot* of data from large sites with several links (such as blogs). Don't try to back up the Web, because you'll run out of disk space!

Resume Partial Downloads on an Intermittent Connection

Say you're using the wireless connection at the airport, and it's time to board the plane — with just a minute left on that download you started half an hour ago. When you make it back home and reconnect to the network, you can use the `-c` (continue) option to direct wget to resume a partial download where it left off.

For example, you want to download the 151MB installer file for free office-suite software OpenOffice.org (`http://openoffice.org`). Use the following `wget` command:

```
wget http://download.services.openoffice.org/files/stable/3.3.0/
OOo_3.3.0_Win_x86_install-wJRE_en-US.exe
```

Mid-download, you get the boarding call and have to close your laptop and get on the plane. When you reopen it back home, you can add a -c to your wget command and resume fetching the partially downloaded file, like this:

```
wget -c http://download.services.openoffice.org/files/stable/3.3.0/
OOo_3.3.0_Win_x86_install-wJRE_en-US.exe
```

This feature also comes in handy when you share bandwidth with others or need to pause a download while you work on another bandwidth-intensive task. For instance, if that movie download is affecting the quality of your Internet phone call, stop the download and after you've hung up the phone, resume the download using the wget -c switch.

WARNING Most — but not all — servers on the Internet support resuming partial downloads. The -c switch should work with all FTP servers, and with HTTP servers that support the Range header.

NOTE If the URL of the file you're downloading contains ampersand (&) characters, be sure to enclose the URL in quotation marks in the command, like this:

```
wget -c "http://example.com/?p1=y&p2=n"
```

Automatically Download New Music from the Web

These days, tons of directories, aggregators, filters, and weblogs point to interesting types of media. You can use wget to create a text-file list of your favorite sites that, say, link to MP3 music files, and schedule it to automatically download any newly added MP3s from those sites each day to your computer.[2]

Here's how:

1. Create a text file called mp3_sites.txt and list URLs of your favorite sources of music online (such as http://del.icio.us/tag/system:filetype:mp3 or http://stereogum.com), one per line.

2. Use the following wget command to go out and fetch those MP3s:

   ```
   wget -r -l1 -H -t1 -nd -N -np -A.mp3 -erobots=off -i mp3_sites.
   txt
   ```

   That wget recipe recursively (-r) downloads only MP3 files (-A.mp3) linked from the sites (-H) one level out (-l1) listed in mp3_sites.txt (-i mp3_sites.txt) that are newer (-N) than any you've already downloaded. There are a few other specifications in there — such as to not create a new directory for every music file (-nd), to ignore robots.txt (-erobots=off), and to not crawl up to the parent directory of a link (-np).

When this command is scheduled with the list of sites you specify, you get an ever-refreshed folder of new music files that wget fetches for you. With a good set of trusted sources, you'll never have to go looking for new music again — wget can do all the work for you.

TIP Use this technique to download all your favorite bookmarks for offline usage as well. If you keep your bookmarks online in Delicious, use wget to download the contents of your favorite pages to your hard drive. Then, using Google Desktop Search, you can search the contents of your bookmarks even when you're offline.

Automate wget Downloads on Windows

To schedule a wget download task to run at a certain time, open a new document in a plain-text editor such as Notepad. Type the wget command you want to schedule, and save the file with a .bat extension, such as getnewmusic.bat.

In Windows Task Scheduler, browse to getnewmusic.bat in the Programs section, and set the schedule as usual.

NOTE See Hack 64, "Automatically Reboot and Launch Applications," for more details on setting up a recurring job in Windows Task Scheduler.

References

1. Pash, Adam, "Belvedere" (http://lifehacker.com/#!341950/)
2. Jeffrey Veen, "MP3 Blogs and wget" (http://veen.com/jeff/archives/000573.html).

CHAPTER 8

Get Your Data to Go

To get things done today, you need the right information at your finger-tips, no matter where you are. You will travel, relocate, switch jobs, use more computers, and generate larger quantities of data in your lifetime than any previous generation has. Your ability (or inability) to access that information on the go can make the difference between success and failure in work and life.

Every day, you create a digital trail that details your life. Your Sent mail folder describes your professional and personal relationships. Your digital photo and video archive documents family vacations, graduations, births, and the car accident you got into last year. You have your college papers, your résumé, and professional documents created at your last three jobs stowed away on your hard drive.

Years ago, you may have stored all the data you needed on a 1.44MB floppy disk. Now, in the age of MP3 players, ubiquitous broadband, personal camcorders, and digital cameras, you create and collect dozens of gigabytes of data per year. Modern smartphones have converged the creation and consumption of nearly every type of digital media into one device; as of this writing, one high-quality photo taken with a cameraphone is nearly 3MB.

You have three main ways to retrieve this data when you're not sitting at the computer on which it lives:

- **Store it "in the cloud" using web applications (webapps).** Hack 67, "Access Your Most Important Files Anywhere with Dropbox," and Hack 68, "Manage Your Documents in a Web-Based Office Suite," cover ways to use web applications to store your data online, and even revise and collaborate on documents using only a browser.

- **Take your software and files with you on a portable device.** With the right software installed on your USB thumb drive, you may not need to take your laptop everywhere. Hack 69, "Carry Your Life on a Flash Drive," describes how to run your favorite portable applications directly from a flash drive.

- **Turn your home computer into a personal server and connect to it from anywhere.** If your home computer is your central digital nervous system and you have always-on broadband Internet access at home, you can get to your files from anywhere — across town or an ocean. Hack 70, "Create a Virtual Private Network (VPN) with Hamachi," details how to create a personal virtual private network to access your home computer from anywhere securely. Hacks 71, "Run a Home Web Server," and 74, "Remotely Control Your Home Computer," walk you through creating a home web server to browse and download files and to control your home computer's desktop remotely over the Internet.

Your data is your life. Secure, easy access to it — no matter where you are — is a must. Whether it's taking it with you on a keychain, storing it up in the cloud, or connecting to your home server from anywhere, this chapter's hacks cover several ways to get your data on the go.

Hack 67: Access Your Most Important Files Anywhere with Dropbox

Level....... **Beginner**

Platform.... **All**

Cost........ **Free**

Between workplace computers, laptops, desktops, and smartphones, you no longer live in a one-computer world. For most people, it's not uncommon to work from at least two different computers during the course of a day. But when you jump from one computer to another, you still need access to the latest version of your most important files — whether it's an important PowerPoint file for a big presentation at work, a new website you're working on in your spare time, your `todo.txt` file, or the next chapter of your novel.

Carrying those important documents on a USB thumb drive used to be the most painless way to ensure you didn't end up with multiple versions of a document spread across different computers, but a clever application called Dropbox (`www.dropbox.com`) makes it easier than ever to access your most important files anywhere, without creating duplicates or lugging around an external USB drive.

What Dropbox Does

Dropbox is a web service and free application (for Windows, Mac, and Linux) that instantaneously backs up and synchronizes files over the Internet to any computer on which you install the Dropbox client. When you first create an account and run the application on a computer, it generates a Dropbox folder on your hard drive (`C:\Users\adam\My Dropbox` on Windows; `~/Dropbox` on Mac).

The Dropbox application runs in the background, constantly monitoring the Dropbox folder. Any file you place inside your Dropbox folder automatically synchronizes over the Internet to Dropbox's servers and to any other computer on which you installed Dropbox. Each time you add a new file or change a file, Dropbox backs up and synchronizes the file — again, to Dropbox's servers *and* to every computer you installed the application to, often in a matter of seconds. You can see Dropbox working by glancing at your system tray (Windows) or menu bar (Mac OS X). When everything's synced, you see the Dropbox icon with a green check mark; when Dropbox is in the process of syncing files, you see the blue syncing arrows, as shown in Figure 8-1.

Dropbox also saves a file revision history, so if you accidentally saved a file but wanted to revert to an old version, or just wanted to recover a file you accidentally deleted, Dropbox can recover any previous version. Just right-click any file in your Dropbox folder and select Dropbox ➪ View Previous Versions, as shown in Figure 8-2.

NOTE Dropbox's free account gives you a healthy 2GB worth of storage for syncing your files, which is plenty for simple document syncing. If you need more space, Dropbox currently has two upgrade plans: $10 a month to increase your storage to 50GB, or $20 a month for 100GB of Dropbox storage.

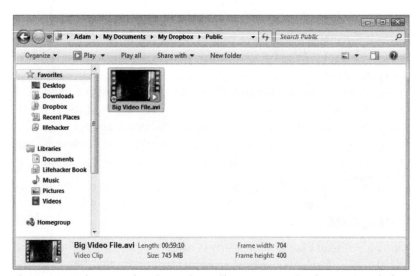

Figure 8-1: When Dropbox is syncing a file, you see a circular sync symbol on the bottom-left corner of the file icon.

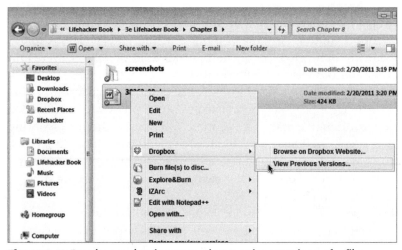

Figure 8-2: Dropbox makes it easy to view previous versions of a file.

Now, no matter which of your computers you use, you have one folder that contains the most recent version of all your most important files. While writing this book, for example, Dropbox kept every chapter synced between computers. This made it possible to write a new section at home on a desktop computer, save it, and then grab a laptop, head to a coffee shop, and still access the latest version of the chapter. It's not necessary to save the file to a flash drive or email it; as long as there is an Internet connection, all the important files remain up to date.

If you're at a computer where you can't or don't want to install Dropbox, you can still access files in your Dropbox folder by logging into your Dropbox account and clicking the Files tab, as shown in Figure 8-3. This web interface contains the same folder structure you see in your Dropbox folder on your desktop, and from the web interface, you can upload new files, download files, create new folders, and more.

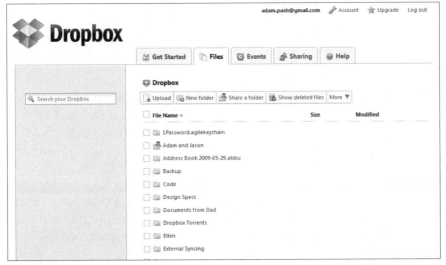

Figure 8-3: Dropbox's web interface gives you access to your synced files from any computer with a browser and Internet connection.

Share Files with Dropbox

In addition to seamlessly syncing files between your computers, you can also share files with Dropbox in two ways:

■ **Place a file in your Public folder.** When you install Dropbox, it automatically creates a folder inside the Dropbox folder called `Public`. You can share files in this folder with people by simply sending them a public link to the file, which you can get by right-clicking the file in Explorer (Windows) or Finder (Mac) and selecting Dropbox ➪ Copy Public Link, as shown in Figure 8-4.

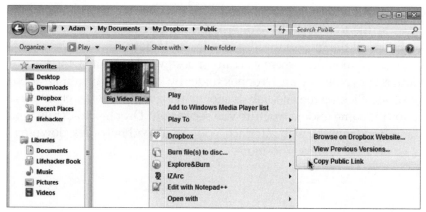

Figure 8-4: Share any file in your Public folder by sharing its public link.

■ **Use shared folders.** You can also turn any folder inside your Dropbox folder to a shared folder. Shared folders work exactly like any other Dropbox folder except they're collaborative, so if you add a file to that folder or save changes to a file inside that folder, those changes are synced to your collaborators, as well. Likewise, if someone else you're sharing the folder with adds or changes a file, those changes automatically push to your computer. To share a folder, right-click any folder inside your Dropbox folder and select Dropbox ⇨ Share This Folder. The Dropbox website opens, and you can enter the email addresses of everyone with whom you want to share that folder.

Sync Files and Folders Outside Your Dropbox Folder

Dropbox works well because of its simplicity: It's one folder on your computer that's constantly synced. However, you may run into an occasion where you'd prefer to sync folders located *outside* your Dropbox folder.

As of this writing, Dropbox doesn't have this option built in, but third-party developers have created simple utilities that do enable you to sync folders stored outside of Dropbox. On Windows, the utility is called Dropbox Folder Sync (http://wiki.dropbox.com/DropboxAddons/ DropboxFolderSync). On Mac OS X, it's called MacDropAny (http://wiki .dropbox.com/DropboxAddons/MacDropAny).

> **TIP** If you want to move a folder to Dropbox from your Windows User folder — like your Documents folder — you don't need to use Dropbox Folder Sync. Just right-click your Documents folder, select Properties, and then click the Location tab. Change the file path to your Dropbox folder, and click the Move button.

When installed, the Windows-only Dropbox Folder Sync adds a Sync with a Dropbox item to your right-click context menu, so syncing an item outside your Dropbox folder involves right-clicking that folder in Explorer and selecting Sync with Dropbox.

> **NOTE** Both Dropbox Folder Sync and MacDropAny work in the same basic way: They move the original folder to your Dropbox folder and then create a symbolic link in its place. The symbolic link points to the folder that the utility just moved to Dropbox, but the folder appears and works as though it still lives in its original location.

To sync a file or folder outside your Dropbox folder with the Mac-only MacDropAny, simply run the app, choose the folder you want to sync, choose where you want the folder to be located inside Dropbox, and then give it a name.

Sync Applications and Encrypt Data

Hack 69, "Carry Your Life on a Flash Drive," details how to carry portable applications with you on a flash drive so that you're not only accessing the same data, but also using exactly the same applications and settings from any computer. That hack also details how to create a secure, encrypted folder you can carry anywhere. Both tips also work with Dropbox, giving you more clever ways to keep your applications and data accessible and secure whether you're using your home or work computer.

> **NOTE** Dropbox is also available as a mobile application for Android, iOS, and BlackBerry. You can find the right app for your smartphone at www.dropbox.com/anywhere.

Hack 68: Manage Your Documents in a Web-Based Office Suite

Level . . . . **Beginner**
Platform . . . . **Web**
Cost. . . . . **Free**

A profound shift in modern computing is afoot: a move from desktop software to the Web. Mature web browsers, always-on broadband Internet connections, and an increase in mobile users has spurred a new breed of websites that aren't just static pages — they're hosted software applications (web applications, or webapps) that you access from your browser.

Typing a memo, calculating charts in a spreadsheet, or designing a slideshow presentation once required specialized and expensive software, such as WordPerfect or Microsoft PowerPoint, that you'd install on your computer. Today, a new crop of completely web-based office applications can create and manage those types of files, and you need only a web browser to use them. Several hacks in this book encourage you to move from desktop software to web applications — such as controlling your email with Gmail or managing your schedule in Google Calendar. You can do the same with your word processor documents, spreadsheets, and slideshows. This hack covers how (and why).

Why Move from Desktop Software to Web Applications?

All you need to start using an online office suite is a computer with a web browser connected to the Internet and a free account at the service you choose (such as Google Docs at `http://docs.google.com` or Zoho at `http://zoho.com`). There are several advantages to abandoning your expensive desktop office suite in favor of web applications:

- No special software is required to create, revise, open, and save a new spreadsheet or slideshow, which eliminates the need to purchase or install Microsoft Office.

- You can access online office suites from any computer with a web browser and Internet connection, regardless of operating system or location.

- The most recent revision of your document is always available in one place, eliminating the need to copy your documents to a disk to take them with you or to back them up.

- Advancing web technologies enable webapps to do things previously relegated to desktop applications. For example, in Google Docs you can drag and drop files from your computer directly into a docu-ment, just as you would in Microsoft Word, provided that you use a modern browser.

- You can easily collaborate on documents stored in a single place with several other people, whose edits will be saved in that one place. You don't need to send emails with document attachments for others to revise and risk having to deal with multiple, confusing versions.

For example, when my writers are working on feature articles for Lifehacker .com, the editing process used to be tedious: Someone would finish a draft, email it to me, then I'd edit it and email it back. Now, instead of that inefficient back-and-forth, we collaborate on the document with Google Docs, and any number of us can edit the document simultaneously without worrying about editing over each other or creating conflicting revisions. Figure 8-5 shows one such document.

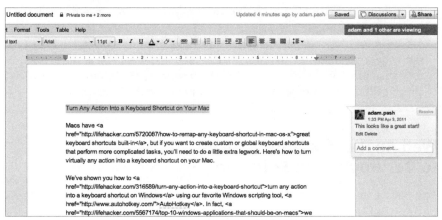

Figure 8-5: View a collaborative document in Google Docs.

Working with web-based office applications probably sounds like a mobile, multicomputer user's nirvana, right? But there are some downsides; here's a look of some of them:

- The full-featured version of Microsoft Word, for instance, has many more features than any online word processor does. You'll be surprised at how many features online office suites do support, though: advanced formatting, spreadsheet formulas, and What You See Is What You Get (WYSIWYG) layouts. But you couldn't do a mail merge, for example, from a web-based word processor.

- Your data is stored on someone else's server. The advantage is that it will still be there if your computer crashes, but some users might be concerned about privacy and security, especially if your documents contain confidential information.

- You must be connected to the Internet to access your documents (for now, that is — see the sidebar for more information). But if you're on a cross-country flight and want to edit a document stored online, unless you exported it to your local desktop first and have the right desktop software installed to open it, you can't access it.

WORKING OFFLINE WITH WEB APPLICATIONS

Web-based applications like Zoho Office Suite, Gmail, and Google Calendar are all online, so they require a constant Internet connection to use them, right? Not necessarily. New web technologies — specifically, database features available in HTML5, the next revision of the HTML specification — enable browsers to store data offline, and modern browsers are already starting to take advantage of some of those advancements. As of this writing, built-in offline capabilities aren't available for webapps like Google Docs, but it's only a matter of time. Previously, a browser add-on called Google Gears (http://gears.google.com) introduced offline access to webapps that took advantage of it, but Gears isn't currently being maintained by Google. Instead, most webapps are focusing on native browser solutions, such as the upcoming HTML5 features. In short, offline access to web application data is on the horizon.

Web Application Alternatives to Desktop Office Software

You have several options for managing and storing your office documents online. Two major players — Google Docs and Zoho — offer suites of multiple applications such as word processors, spreadsheets, and presentation apps (the online answer to Microsoft PowerPoint). In 2010, Microsoft launched its own web-based companion to Microsoft Office called Office Web Apps on SkyDrive. Other companies specialize in a single type of office application. Following is a partial list of web applications you may use the next time you want to create a certain type of office document.

DESKTOP	WEBAPP ALTERNATIVE
WORD PROCESSOR	
Microsoft Word WordPerfect	Zoho Writer (http://writer.zoho.com)
	Google Docs (http://docs.google.com)
	Office Web Apps (http://office.live.com)
	ThinkFree (http://thinkfree.com)

DESKTOP	WEBAPP ALTERNATIVE
SPREADSHEET	
Microsoft Excel Lotus 1-2-3	Zoho Sheet (http://sheet.zoho.com)
	Google Docs (http://docs.google.com)
	Office Web Apps (http://office.live.com)
PRESENTATION	
Microsoft PowerPoint Keynote	Zoho Show (http://show.zoho.com)
	Google Docs (http://docs.google.com)
	Office Web Apps (http://office.live.com)
	280 Slides (http://280slides.com)
	SlideRocket (www.sliderocket.com)

NOTE Google Docs and Zoho both offer similar office suites with only a subtle difference. Google Docs is aimed at consumers, whereas Zoho is intended for business users. Both are free for individual use. Although many users may opt for Google Docs because of familiarity with the Google brand, overall, Zoho's suite includes more features within its applications.

What You Can Do in an Online Office Suite

Web-based document editors have several features that complement but also separate them from desktop software. Most office webapps enable you to do the following:

- **Import and export files for use on the desktop.** What if you use Zoho Writer but your co-worker uses Microsoft Word? Not a problem. You can draft your document in Writer and click the Export button to download a Word document (.doc file), OpenOffice.org document (.sxw file), PDF, text, HTML, or rich-text document that can be edited on the desktop as usual. Likewise, if you have an existing Word document, for example, you can import it into a web-based office app for viewing or editing. Figure 8-6 shows this chapter's Word document as it appears uploaded to Google Docs. Microsoft's Office Web Apps offers even tighter integration for Windows users with a browser that supports ActiveX, enabling you to open your web document directly in its desktop counterpart with the click of a button.

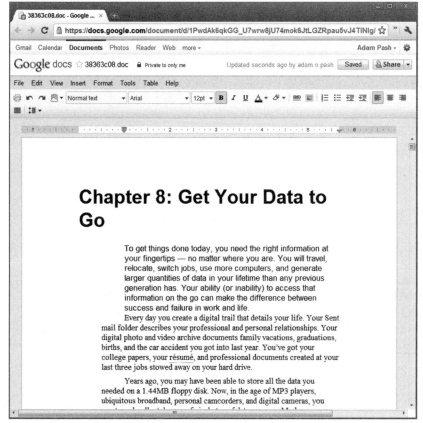

Figure 8-6: Upload existing Microsoft Word documents to an online word processor such as Google Docs to back it up, share, or edit it from any web browser.

- **Collaborate or share with specific people.** For any given document, you can email co-workers, friends, or family members and give them view-only or edit rights to the document in progress, which enables you to easily collaborate without clunky email attachments. Several online apps (such as Zoho Writer and Google Docs) enable users to chat in-document while editing and viewing it.

■ **Publish your document.** Make your document viewable by anyone who visits its URL, or embed documents you create onto your weblog or company intranet page. Rather than send emails around with a document attached, you simply include the link to the published document to share it with others, as shown in Figure 8-7.

Figure 8-7: Share your document by emailing a URL instead of a file attachment.

Bridge the Gap Between Your Desktop and the Web

If you're still not ready to ditch the advanced features of Microsoft Office for web-based alternatives, you can enjoy some of the niceties of the cloud while continuing to use the desktop Office suite. Here are three options:

■ As of this writing, the latest version of Microsoft Office includes integration with Office Web Apps. When you edit a document on your desktop, select File ➪ Save & Send ➪ Save to Web to save the document to Windows Live SkyDrive, Microsoft's online file storage tool, as shown in Figure 8-8. When saved to SkyDrive, you can edit a document on your desktop with Office or on the Web using Office Web Apps, and the changes remain synced between the two.

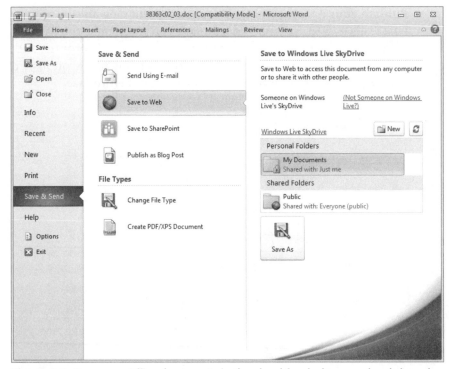

Figure 8-8: Save your Office documents in the cloud for desktop- and web-based access with SkyDrive.

- Google Cloud Connect is a Microsoft Office add-on developed by Google that synchronizes your Office documents with Google Docs. The tool is currently in beta, but you can sign up to use it at `http://bit.ly/hU5tdJ`.

- If accessing your files from any computer is the main attraction for moving your documents to the cloud, you can use a file-syncing service such as Dropbox (`www.dropbox.com`) to ensure you're always working on the same version of a file no matter which computer you use. For more details, see Hack 67, "Access Your Most Important Files Anywhere with Dropbox."

NOTE You may have noticed that Microsoft's set of tools are a little confusing — if only because of their strange naming conventions. Think of it like this: Microsoft Office runs on your desktop, and Office Web Apps runs in your browser. Windows Live SkyDrive is the glue that connects the two. If you can get around the long names, the integration between the desktop and cloud is worth a try.

Hack 69: Carry Your Life on a Flash Drive

Level . . . . **Medium**

Platform . . . . **Windows (with a flash drive)**

Cost. . . . . **Free**

Portable hard drives such as USB flash drives get cheaper, smaller in size, and larger in capacity by the day. Instead of lugging around your laptop or emailing yourself files, store your favorite software applications and important data on a thumb (flash) drive about the size of a car key. Then plug it into any computer for quick and easy access on the go.

This hack covers popular portable applications and some practical uses for these small drives.

Why Use a Flash Drive?

Consider a few scenarios in which a USB drive loaded with your favorite applications and important documents might come in handy:

- You work on a set of files on several different computers (such as at the office and at home, on the laptop and the desktop) and you want easy access to them from one place.

- Your IT department doesn't give you administrative rights to install your favorite software on your office computer.

- You'd like to back up your files and store them offsite, such as home files at the office or work files at home. (You can store USB drives in a safety deposit box or mail one to Mom in Florida every few months, too.)

- You don't want to download and install your favorite application at every computer you use.

- You want to avoid using your in-laws' hijacked web browser to download virus scanners and spyware cleaners; instead, you want to take the tools you need to fix their computer along on your flash drive.

NOTE Earlier in this chapter, Hack 67, "Access Your Most Important Files Anywhere with Dropbox," shows you how to use the file-syncing service Dropbox to sync files between computers and the cloud. You can also store and run your portable applications from your Dropbox folder. The main difference between using Dropbox and using your thumb drive: Dropbox requires an Internet connection to stay in sync.

Portable Applications

When you install software on your computer, the setup program makes changes to the Windows Registry and stores special files (called DLLs) throughout your PC's file system so that the program can run. Portable apps — software programs meant to run from a single hard drive — don't require any changes to the operating system. They are self-contained and stand alone on one drive. Portable applications meant for use on flash drives are often stripped down to the bare essentials to take up the least amount of disk space possible, but it is still important to keep in mind that size does matter when purchasing a flash drive. The more space you have, the more programs and information you can store.

Some popular portable software applications include the following:

- **Web browser:** Portable Firefox, 77MB installed. Includes all Firefox profile information such as bookmarks and extensions.

  http://portableapps.com/apps/internet/firefox_portable

- **Web browser:** Portable Chrome, 76MB installed. Includes Chrome profile information such as bookmarks and extensions.

  http://portableapps.com/apps/internet/google_chrome_portable

- **Office suite:** Portable OpenOffice.org, 230MB installed. Spreadsheet, word processor, and presentation software.

  http://portableapps.com/apps/office/openoffice_portable

- **Email:** Portable Thunderbird, 34MB installed. Email, address book, and mail filters.

  http://portableapps.com/apps/internet/thunderbird_portable

- **Instant messenger:** Portable Pidgin, about 51MB installed. Multiprotocol instant-messaging client works with AIM, Google Talk, Yahoo! Messenger, MSN Messenger, and more.

  http://portableapps.com/apps/internet/pidgin_portable

- **Virus scanner:** Portable ClamWin, about 35MB installed (with definitions). Open source Windows virus scanner.

  `http://portableapps.com/apps/utilities/clamwin_portable`

- **Remote login:** RealVNC Free Edition Viewer (standalone version), 266KB installed. Log in to your remote VNC (virtual network computing) server with the RealVNC viewer. (See Hack 74, "Remotely Control Your Home Computer," for more information on using the VNC.)

  `www.realvnc.com/products/free/4.1/winvncviewer.html`

What kind of space are we talking about? Those seven portable programs total slightly over 503MB, or about 25 percent of a 2GB flash drive, which leaves plenty of space for work files.

For a constantly updated directory of software fit for toting around on a thumb drive, keep an eye on John Haller's website, Portable Apps (`http://portableapps.com`).

The Portable Apps site also offers an entire suite of software packages for your flash drive in a single download. The suite includes a web browser, email client, web editor, office suite, word processor, calendar/scheduler, instant-messaging client, and FTP client, ready to save to your flash drive and use. Two flavors are available for download: Standard and Light (smaller file size). Download it for free at `http://portableapps.com/suite`. The Standard version, unzipped and installed, takes up 400MB; the Light, a mere 150 MB.

Several other software applications discussed in other hacks in this book are small enough to fit on a thumb drive or offer a portable version:

- **LastPass password manager:** See Hack 15, "Securely Track Your Passwords," for more on using LastPass.

- **TrueCrypt data encryption utility:** See Hack 20, "Create a Password-Protected Disk on Your PC," for more on making your files inaccessible in case your thumb drive is lost or stolen.

- **Texter text replacement:** See Hack 52, "Reduce Repetitive Typing with Texter for Windows," for more details on creating custom abbreviation replacement and common misspelling correction programs with the free, portable-drive-friendly Windows program called Texter.

Useful Data to Store on Your Thumb Drive

Software is worthless without data. Store your important files on your flash drive for access on any computer. That includes your:

- To-do list
- Address book
- Passwords: Be sure to encrypt this file for security! (See the following section, "Secure Your Drive," for more information.)
- Multimedia: Photos, music, and video (depending on the size of your drive)
- Office documents
- `ReturnIfLost.txt` file with your contact information
- Website bookmarks

Secure Your Drive

Flash drives are tiny and convenient, but they're also easily lost, damaged, stolen, and transported. More and more cases of stolen laptops and hard drives have spelled disaster for companies and individuals who handle sensitive customer data or private company documents.

Here are a few strategies for securing the data on your thumb drive:

Lock Sensitive Text Files

Free software LockNote, available at `http://locknote.steganos.com`, is a standalone text-file encryption program.

1. Save the `LockNote.exe` file to your thumb drive. Launch it and enter any textual information you'd like to secure — passwords, addresses, phone numbers, account numbers, and so on.

2. Close the document and LockNote prompts you for a password and scrambles the file so that anyone without the password can't open it.

The `LockNote.exe` file weighs in at about 402KB — about 0.39 MB — and is worth the space if you deal with sensitive, confidential material.

Encrypt Your Data

If you have different types of existing files, you can create a password-protected ZIP archive of them.

1. Using free software 7-Zip, available at `http://7zip.org`, add the files you want to save on your flash drive to a new ZIP archive, and set a password to open them, as shown in Figure 8-9.

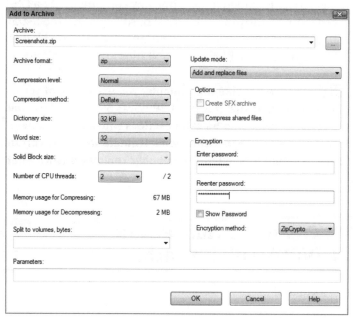

Figure 8-9: Set a password on the zipped files for security.

2. Make sure you change the Archive Format from `7z` to `zip` so that Windows can extract the file without 7-Zip.

3. Finally, move the resulting archive (`.zip` file) to your thumb drive.

You can browse the file and folder names within a password-protected ZIP file, but the individual files cannot be extracted nor the contents viewed without entering the password. A stronger, alternative encryption method employs the free software TrueCrypt (`http://truecrypt.org/downloads.php`). For detailed instructions on how to encrypt an entire thumb drive — or just a particular folder or set of files with TrueCrypt — see Hack 20, "Create a Password-Protected Disk on Your PC."

Make Your Drive Returnable

Place an "If found, please return" text file with contact information on your flash drive to increase the chances that it'll be returned in case of loss. But don't encrypt this file — it should be readable by anyone!

Using Your Thumb Drive

When your flash drive is loaded, plug it into any computer with a USB drive and access it the same as any other internal hard drive. All the usual Mac/PC compatibility issues apply (for example, an .exe file won't launch on a Mac), but Office documents, PDFs, and text files are cross-platform.

> ▇▇▇▇ **WARNING** If you're not sure the computer you use is free of spyware and viruses, assume that it is not. USB drives are the perfect way to spread computer nasties, so be extra cautious with a promiscuous thumb drive. For this reason, network administrators sometimes disable the capability to mount a thumb drive on public computers (such as at libraries).

Hack 70: Create a Virtual Private Network (VPN) with Hamachi

Level....... **Advanced**

Platform.... **All**

Cost........ **Free**

You can perform actions between computers on your local network that you can't from out on the Internet, such as listen to a shared iTunes library or access files in shared folders. But using the free, virtual private network (VPN) application Hamachi (https://secure.logmein.com/products/hamachi2), you can securely access your computer from anywhere on the Internet as if you were home on your local network.

This hack uses LogMeIn Hamachi to create a VPN between a PC and a Mac and to listen to a shared iTunes library over the Internet.

What is Hamachi VPN?

The free Hamachi desktop application gives you a secure, zero-configuration LAN over the Internet. Any application that works over a local network can be used with Hamachi over the Internet, such as Windows file sharing, iTunes, Remote Desktop, FTP, VNC, and gaming. All Hamachi's connections are secure, encrypted, authenticated, and peer-to-peer. Although Hamachi acts as a mediator between your computers and creates the tunnel for its communication, Hamachi's servers don't listen in on or log your activity.

You might use Hamachi in the following situations:

- You're on the road with your laptop and want secure access to your PC's files.

- Your office or dorm-room computer is behind a restrictive firewall that doesn't allow you to reach it from the Internet.

- You want to add encryption to insecure network protocols such as VNC.

- You want to set up a shared folder of files for friends and family to access.

Sound useful? Read on to start.

Set Up Hamachi

The following sections lead you through downloading and installing Hamachi's VPN and setting up your Hamachi network.

Download and Install Hamachi

Download the right version of Hamachi for your operating system from `https://secure.logmein.com/products/hamachi2/download.aspx`. For the most part, the Windows installation is a regular wizard — just click Next to step through it.

NOTE Hamachi is free for personal, noncommercial use on up to 16 computers. Although available for Windows, Mac, and Linux, this hack focuses on the Windows setup specifically. The Mac application is nearly identical, but the Linux version is currently available as a command-line only tool.

During installation, Hamachi attempts to install a virtual network adapter. If you have Windows Firewall enabled (or any firewall, for that matter), the firewall program may ask whether you want to allow traffic to and from the Hamachi client. You do. Click the Unblock button to allow Hamachi traffic through your firewall.

Create Your Hamachi Network

When Hamachi is installed, launch the application and click the blue power button. It prompts you to create a new network or join an existing network. Click Create New Network, and give your network a name (for instance, `lifehacker-home`) and a password (if you'd like), as shown in Figure 8-10. Click the Create button.

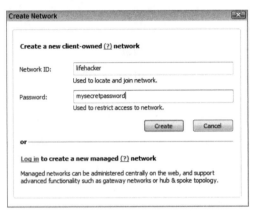

Figure 8-10: Set your new VPN's name and the password. Any computers that join your network must enter these.

Now your computer will be a member of the new network and get its own Hamachi IP address (in addition to its regular IP address). It will also have a nickname that can identify it on your network.

Invite Others to Join Your Hamachi Network

Right away, you can tell your friends or co-workers your Hamachi network's name and password so that they, too, can join it with the Hamachi client installed on their computers. Alternatively, you can join your own network from another computer (such as your PC at the office). For example, I've connected my Mac (nicknamed `Air`) to the `lifehacker-home` network, and the Hamachi client on my PC displays my Mac online, as shown in Figure 8-11.

Figure 8-11: The Hamachi client displays which computers in your network are online.

You can also administer your Hamachi network from its web interface when you're not running the Hamachi client itself, but you need to have created the network from the web interface. Log into the LogMeIn website at https://secure.logmein.com and click the Network link in the left sidebar to view a list of networks you own (see Figure 8-12). From the web interface, you can create or delete networks, add clients, accept requests to join your network, and even evict computers to which you want to deny access. Click a network name to see all the computers on that network.

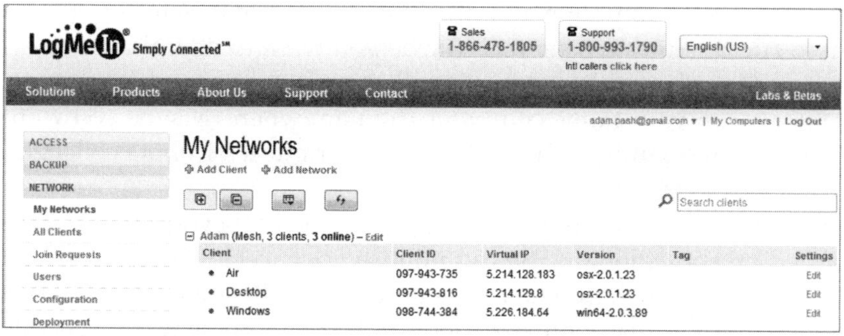

Figure 8-12: View the list of computers connected to your Hamachi network from the control panel at secure.logmein.com.

Now you're ready to put your private network to good use.

What You Can Do Over Hamachi VPN

Anything you can do over a local network — your home wireless network, for example — you can do over the Internet between two computers on a Hamachi VPN. Share files, printers, or stream your iTunes library from your home Mac to your office PC. Browse shared Windows folders, access your home media server over FTP, remotely control your computer over VNC, or access a private home web server over Hamachi VPN, which adds an extra layer of security and privacy. See Hacks 71, "Run a Home Web Server" and 74, "Remotely Control Your Home Computer" in this chapter, and couple those techniques with Hamachi to encrypt and restrict access to your home computer.

Hack 71: Run a Home Web Server

Level . . . . **Advanced**

Platform . . . . **Windows**

Cost. . . . . **Free**

A web server is software that continuously runs on a computer and enables other computers to download documents from it. Any web page you view has traveled over a network connection from the site's hosting web server to the browser on your computer. Web servers are usually loud, scary, headless machines in cold, windowless rooms, but with this hack, you can run one under your desk at home.

Setting up a home web server enables anyone (with the right password) to connect to your computer and download files from it. Why would you want to run a home web server? Maybe you want to download files — perhaps some of your digital music collection so you can play a song at the office — on your home computer from anywhere. Maybe you want your friends and family to have access to your music or photo collection from anywhere, too.

There are tons of uses for your personal web server beyond a password-protected jukebox though: You can publish your weblog at home, host a personal wiki, and share video files and photos. Basically, any file you want to publish as read-only is a good candidate. A home web server has the advantage over special server/client software because it requires only a web browser to connect to it.

WARNING Running a server on your home computer is a risky under-taking. Before you start, ensure that your computer has all the latest patches and security updates (visit `http://windowsupdate.microsoft.com` to make sure) and perform a thorough spyware and virus scan. This hack is for advanced users who feel comfortable editing textual configuration files and exposing port 80 on their home computers to the Internet. You should be running a strong firewall with explicit user-set rules.

Here's what you need to start:

- A Windows PC
- An always-on broadband (DSL or cable) Internet connection

Step 1: Disable Other Servers or Firewall Software

Disable and stop any firewall or server software you may have running, including Windows Firewall, Skype, Trillian, or any other instant-messaging applications. This is extremely important, and if you don't do it, you can cause the server installation and startup to fail miserably. These programs and services can be started and used again as usual when you're done setting up the web server.

Step 2: Install Apache HTTP Server

Download the Apache HTTP server, available at `http://httpd.apache.org/download.cgi` and complete the following:

1. Use the link under Best Available Version next to Win32 Binary (no mod_ssl) (MSI Installer). If the Windows binary is not available on the home page, click the Other Files link, and go to the `binaries` folder, and from the `win32` folder, download the most recent `.msi` file. As of this writing, that file is `apache_2.2.17-win32-x86-no_ssl.msi`.

2. Double-click the downloaded file to start the Installation Wizard. Accept the license agreement.

3. When you reach the screen prompting for server information, enter your own email address and **homeip.net** as the network domain information, as shown in Figure 8-13.

NOTE It doesn't matter what domain you put as the server name. I chose `homeip.net` because it's descriptive and is one of the DynDNS home domains. See Hack 75, "Give Your Home Computer a Web Address," for more information on DynDNS.

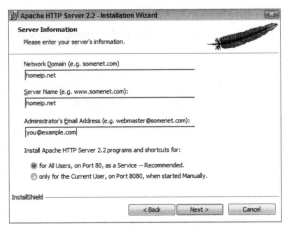

Figure 8-13: Set the web server options.

Complete the Installation

The installation process is almost complete. To finish:

1. Set the server to run on port 80 for all users. If Windows Firewall (or any other firewall you may be running) asks what it should do about the server running on port 80, choose to unblock or allow Apache to run on it.

2. Choose the Typical installation type, and use the default location for the Apache files, which is `C:\Program Files (x86)\Apache Software Foundation\Apache 2.x\`.

3. When the installation is complete, open your web browser and go to `http://localhost/`. If the page you see reads something along the lines of "If you can see this, it means that the installation of the Apache web server software on this system was successful" — or more simply, a page that declares "It works!" — you're golden.

Common Problem

A common installation error with Apache reads, "Only one usage of each socket address (`protocol/network address/port`) is normally permitted: `make_sock`: could not bind to address `0.0.0.0:80` no listening sockets available, shutting down. Unable to open logs." This means that some other server program (such as Skype) is interfering with Apache. To figure out what program it is, open a command prompt and type: **netstat -a -o**

Find the PID (Process ID) of the program running on your local machine on port 80 (or http). Then open the Windows Task Manager (Ctrl+Alt+Delete). Choose View ➪ Select Columns and select PID. Match the PID to the running process to find out which server program is running; then stop that program. Now retry the Apache installation.

Step 3: Configure Apache to Share Documents

To make your music collection available via your new web server, browse to the folder that contains Apache's configuration files, located at `c:\Program Files\Apache Software Foundation\Apache 2.x\conf\`. Make a copy of the main configuration file, `httpd.conf`, before you make any changes — just in case. Save the copy as `httpd.backup.conf` in that same directory.

Because of security restrictions in the latest version of Windows, you need to run your text editor with elevated permissions to save changes to `httpd.conf`, so right-click your text editor — for example, `Notepad.exe` — and select Run as administrator before opening the file. When you run as administrator, open the `C:\Program Files (x86)\Apache Software Foundation\Apache 2.x\conf\httpd.conf` file. The contents of this file look long and scary, but most of the defaults work just fine. You just have to change a few settings.

1. First, comment out the line that starts with `DocumentRoot` by adding a **#** at the beginning of the line and add another with your directory, like this:

   ```
   # DocumentRoot "C:/Program Files (x86)/Apache Software
   Foundation/Apache2.2/htdocs"
   DocumentRoot "C:/Users/username/ /Music"
   ```

   where `C:/Users/username/ Music/` corresponds to the location of your music files.

   NOTE Although Windows directory structure normally uses back-slashes, Apache's default `httpd.conf` uses forward slashes, so that's what is used in this hack.

2. Then, comment out the line that starts with `<Directory "C:/Program` and add another line with your directory, like this:

   ```
   #<Directory "C:/Program Files/Apache Group/Apache2/htdocs">
   <Directory "C:/Users/username/Music">
   ```

3. Last, about 20 lines later, there's a line that reads

```
AllowOverride None
```

Change it to

```
AllowOverride All
```

When you finish, save `httpd.conf`. Then click the Apache icon in your taskbar and choose Restart. If Apache restarts successfully, you edited the file correctly. Visit `http://localhost/` in your web browser. This time, you should see a listing of your music files.

> **NOTE** If Apache doesn't start correctly, it's because it can't read the `httpd.conf` file, which means you probably had a typo in your changes. Check your changes carefully, save, and restart Apache to try again. If necessary, copy `httpd.backup.conf` to `httpd.conf` to start all over again.

Step 4: Password-Protect Your Website Documents

You don't want just anyone to download your music. Your bandwidth and files are private and precious, so you want to lock things down. You can use a VPN to restrict access to your home web server; see Hack 70, "Create a Virtual Private Network (VPN) with Hamachi," for more information on how to do that. If you don't want to make everyone who accesses your web server have to run special VPN software, you can create a simple browser password prompt instead. Here's how:

1. Open a command prompt. (Choose Start ➪ Run, type **cmd**, and press Enter.) Change to the Apache bin directory by typing:

```
cd "C:\Program Files (x86)\Apache Software Foundation\Apache
2.x\bin"
```

where `Apache 2.x` matches the version you installed (Apache 2.2, for example).

2. Create a password file by typing:

```
htpasswd -c "C:\Users\username\My Documents\; i
web-server-pass-file" penny
```

Replace the path with wherever your password file should be located (which can be any folder *except* the web server's document root that you set up previously). Replace `penny` with your preferred username.

3. When prompted, enter the password you want. After you do that, a password file will be created.

Now, follow these steps to apply that login to your music directory:

1. Open a new file in a plain-text editor such as Notepad. Enter the following text into it:

```
AuthType Basic
AuthName "This is a private area, please log in"

AuthUserFile "C:\Users\username\Documents\; i
web-server-pass-file"
AuthGroupFile /dev/null

<Limit GET POST PUT>
require valid-user
</Limit>
```

Make sure you replace `C:\Users\username\Documents\web-server-pass-file` in the text with the path to the password file you created.

2. Name the file `.htaccess` and save this new file in the web server's document root you set earlier (in this example, `C:\Users\username\Music`). Don't forget the dot in the beginning, before `htaccess`. In other words, you are saving the file as `C:\Documents and Settings\penelope\My Documents\My Music\.htaccess`.

NOTE If you use Notepad to create your `.htaccess` file, put quotation marks around the filename — `".htaccess"` — when you save the file so that Notepad doesn't automatically put a `.txt` extension on the file. (If the file has a `.txt` file extension, your password won't work!) Alternatively, choose All Files from the Save As Type drop-down list before you save the file.

3. Point your web browser to `http://localhost/`. You are prompted to log in as shown in Figure 8-14.

4. Enter the username and password you set up in your password file, and you're in.

Congratulations! You have a home web server running.

If you are not behind a firewall, you can access your web server from other computers by typing your computer's IP address into a web browser's address bar. (If you're not sure what your IP is, visit WhatIsMyIP at `http://whatismyip.com` to find out.) If your IP is 12.34.567.890 for example, type **http://12.34.567.890** into a browser's address bar.

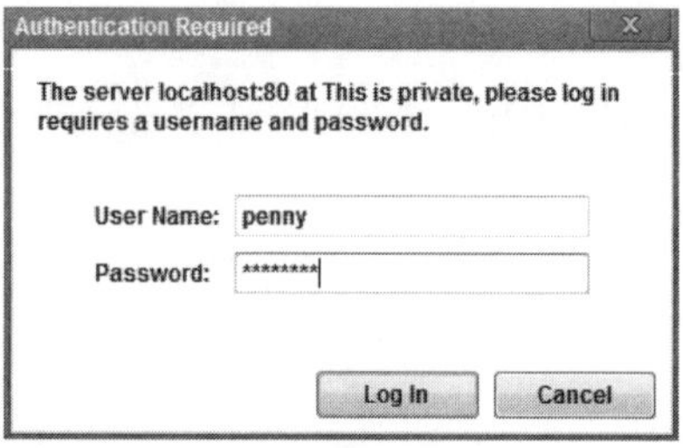

Figure 8-14: Localhost prompts you for a user name and password.

NOTE Depending on your Internet service provider, your computer's IP address may change, but there's an easy way to set up a memorable name that doesn't change. See Hack 75, "Give Your Home Computer a Web Address," for more information.

If you are behind a firewall (such as through a wireless router), you need to open port 80 on the firewall and forward it to your computer. Consult your router's manual, on how to do this. In the meantime, enjoy accessing the files on your home computer from anywhere via your home web server!

Hack 72: Run Full-Fledged Webapps from Your Home Computer

Level . . . . **Advanced**

Platform . . . . **Windows**

Cost. . . . . **Free**

In the previous hack, you set up a home web server capable of serving files — like your MP3 collection — to any computer over the Internet. It's a handy trick for accessing files away from home, but your home web server can also run full-fledged webapps — like your own blog or online photo gallery.

In addition to a web server, most webapps require a software stack that includes a database server (for storing data in your webapps) and a programming or scripting language (for generating dynamic pages and communicating with the database). This hack looks at some free webapps you can run on your home server and details how to set up a server stack on Windows using the free WampServer software (www.wampserver.com/en).

NOTE Mac users interested in a simple-to-set-up PHP/MySQL/Apache server stack should check out Wamp-like OS X alternative, MAMP, available for free at `www.mamp.info/en/`. The following instructions focus on Windows and WampServer, but the same basic rules apply to Macs and MAMP.

Web Applications You Can Run from Your Home Computer

You may be surprised with all feature-rich web applications you can download and easily set up on your home computer. The following options are free and open source:

- **WordPress:** A popular blogging platform.

  `http://wordpress.org`

- **Gallery:** A photo gallery webapp.

  `http://gallery.menalto.com`

- **MediaWiki:** A collaborative wiki tool — the same one that powers Wikipedia.

  `www.mediawiki.org`

- **dotProject:** A project management webapp.

  `www.dotproject.net`

- **WebCalendar:** A web-based calendar application.

  `www.k5n.us/webcalendar.php`

- **phpBB:** A popular web forum platform.

  `www.phpbb.com`

The installation process for each webapp varies slightly, but it generally looks like this:

1. Install and configure WampServer.

WARNING Running a server on your personal computer can be a security risk. Make sure you are behind a firewall that prevents unauthorized access to your server. See Hack 108, "Firewall Your Windows PC," for more information.

2. Download the webapp source and move it to a folder in your web server's document root.

3. Open your browser to the root folder of the webapp, and run through the Installation Wizard.

That's the quick version. Now let's walk through it in a little more detail, using the popular weblog platform WordPress as an example.

NOTE Some installations are more complex than others. The next hack, "Build Your Personal Wikipedia," covers a more detailed installation of MediaWiki, where you learn the basics of writing a wiki.

What You Need

- **A Windows computer**, not already running Apache web server
- **WampServer software**, the all-in-one PHP/MySQL/Apache installation for Windows, available as a free download at www.wampserver.com/en
- **WordPress**, available as a free download at http://wordpress.org

Step 1: Install WampServer

1. Download WampServer and install it in the C:\wamp\ directory. (If you want to install it elsewhere, make sure the folder you choose has no spaces or special characters in its name.) Check the Autostart option and the default DocumentRoot folder. Windows Firewall may ask whether it should block the web server; if so, click the Unblock option. When the installation completes, visit http://localhost/ in your web browser to see the front page of your new web server (see Figure 8-15).

2. You're already behind or running a firewall (right?), but just to be on the safe side, assign a password to your new database server. (It's good to be healthily paranoid where security's concerned.) From the home page of your WampServer installation (http://localhost), go to the Tools section, and click the phpMyAdmin link.

3. Then, click the Privileges link. Select all users except root, and click Go beneath Remove Selected Users.

4. From the Privileges page, click the Add a New User link to create a new database user. You could use the default root user for all your database work, but for security reasons, it's best to create a new user. Enter a user name (I'm calling my user lifehacker), password, and set the Host to local. Click the Check All link in the Global Privileges section, then click the Go button.

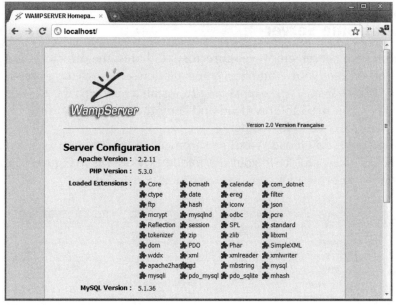

Figure 8-15: The WampServer front page.

5. Click the Privileges link, then click the Edit button next to the `root` user and change the password to something you'll remember and save. If you refresh phpMyAdmin or try to navigate to any other page, you'll get an Access Denied error. That's because phpMyAdmin no longer has access to your database because it doesn't have your new `root` password.

6. To remedy this, open the `C:\wamp\apps\phpmyadmin\config.inc.php` file in a text editor such as Notepad, or better, Notepad++ (`http://notepad-plus-plus.org`). Change the line that reads:

   ```
   $cfg['Servers'][$i]['password'] = '';
   ```
   to:

   ```
   $cfg['Servers'][$i]['password'] = 'yournewpassword';
   ```
   where `yournewpassword` is the password you just set up in phpMyAdmin. Refresh the phpMyAdmin interface in your web browser, and you can view your database information. (If you have trouble, you may need to restart your browser or clear you cookies first.)

7. Finally, you may need to create a database for the webapp you're installing. So for a WordPress installation, for example, click Databases, enter **wordpress** in the Create new database input, and then click Create.

Step 2: Place the Webapp Directory on Your Home Server

By default, your server's root web directory — that is, the directory that contains all the files your WampServer installation serves when you navigate to a URL — lives in `C:\wamp\www\`. To install a new webapp to your home server, you need to download and copy the folder containing the webapp's source code to that folder.

So for example, download WordPress from `http://wordpress.org` and unzip the `wordpress` folder to your `www` folder, as shown as in Figure 8-16. Then point your browser to `http://localhost/wordpress`.

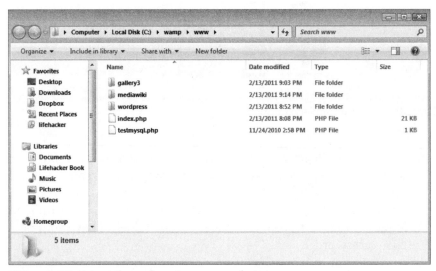

Figure 8-16: Extract the webapp's source code to `C:\wamp\www\`.

Step 3: Run Through the Setup

You'll see a message prompting you to create WordPress's configuration file, called `wp-config.php`. From there, follow these steps to complete set up:

1. Click the Create a Configuration File button, and walk through the Database Configuration Wizard.

2. When you're prompted for the database name, enter `wordpress` (or whatever you called the database you previously created). Likewise, use the MySQL username and password you created in step 4 of the WampServer setup, as shown in Figure 8-17.

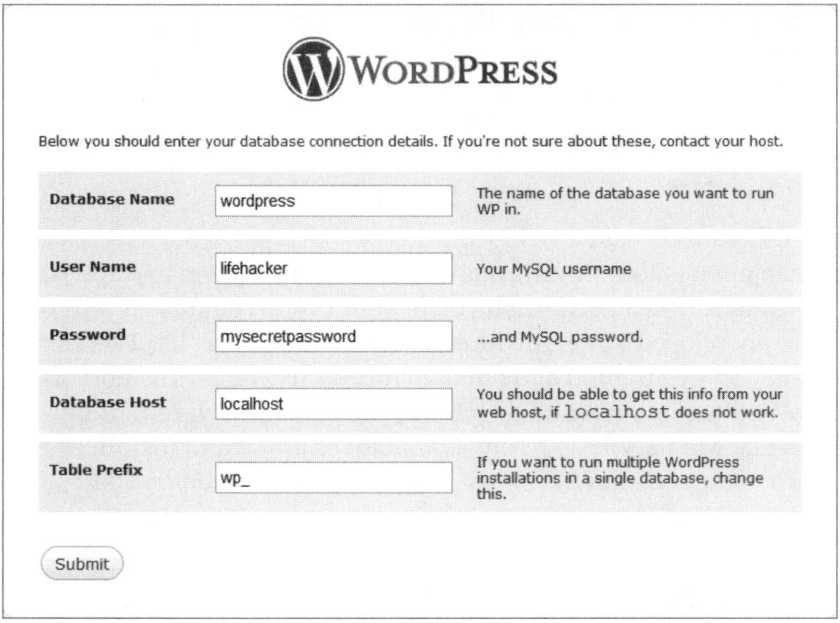

WORDPRESS

Below you should enter your database connection details. If you're not sure about these, contact your host.

Database Name	wordpress	The name of the database you want to run WP in.
User Name	lifehacker	Your MySQL username
Password	mysecretpassword	...and MySQL password.
Database Host	localhost	You should be able to get this info from your web host, if localhost does not work.
Table Prefix	wp_	If you want to run multiple WordPress installations in a single database, change this.

(Submit)

Figure 8-17: Enter your database username and password to configure your WordPress installation.

3. If everything goes as planned, you're now ready to install WordPress. Click the install link, or point your browser to `http://localhost/wordpress/wp-admin/install.php`.

4. From there, simply follow along with the Installation Wizard, entering the name of your site, your WordPress username and password (neither of which need to match your MySQL credentials), and your email address.

When you complete the setup, your WordPress blog should be up and running at `http://localhost/wordpress`.

NOTE Not every open source webapp installs in exactly the same way as WordPress, but the same basic rules apply. The application needs access to your MySQL server and a database in which to store its data. In some instances you may be required to manually edit configuration files in a text editor — like in Hack 73, "Build Your Personal Wikipedia" — but now that you have your first home-installed webapp under your belt, you have a good idea where to start. And remember — README files are your friend!

Hack 73: Build Your Personal Wikipedia

Level........**Advanced**

Platform....**Windows**

Cost.........**Free**

The collaboratively edited Wikipedia (`http://en.wikipedia.org`) is a vast, searchable repository of information, constantly written and rewritten by its readers. Do you ever wish you or your group could have your own editable encyclopedia of brain dumps and documentation like Wikipedia? You can! Clear your mind and build your collective offline memory using MediaWiki (`http://mediawiki.org`), the same software that powers Wikipedia. MediaWiki is freely available for anyone to install. In this hack, you set up MediaWiki on your Windows PC and add and edit pages to your new, local *personalpedia*.

What You Need

- **A Windows computer**, not already running Apache web server.
- **WampServer software**, the all-in-one PHP/MySQL/Apache installation for Windows, available as a free download at `www.wampserver.com/en`. See Hack 72, "Run Full-Fledged Webapps from Your Home Computer," to learn how to set up WampServer.
- **MediaWiki**, available as a free download at `http://mediawiki.org`.

Set Up MediaWiki

Setting up MediaWiki involves configuring the WampServer web and database servers, which you did in the previous hack, and configuring the MediaWiki source files, which are covered here.

WARNING Running a server on your personal computer can be a security risk. Make sure you are behind a firewall that prevents unauthorized access to your server. See Hack 108, "Firewall Your Windows PC," for more information.

1. Download MediaWiki and extract the MediaWiki file package using a utility such as the free 7-Zip (`http://7-zip.org`), which handles both .zip and .tar archive file formats. Rename the resulting folder (probably called `mediawiki-1.16.0`, although your version may

differ) to a folder called `mywikipedia` and move the entire directory to `C:\wamp\www\mywikipedia`.

2. Access your new MediaWiki installation in your web browser at `http://localhost/mywikipedia`. Click the Set Up The Wiki link. The next screen is where you enter all MediaWiki's configuration options.

3. This will seem like a long, complicated questionnaire, but it really isn't. Accept all the default values, *except* you must set a wiki name, a WikiSysOp password, and your database password. As with WampServer in the pervious hack, you should use a non-root user for your database; the one you created when you set up WampServer will work. MediaWiki creates your database for you, so you don't need to do anything in `phpMyAdmin` at this point.

4. When you finish configuring your wiki, click the Install MediaWiki! button and let MediaWiki work its magic. If all goes well, you get a message at the bottom of the screen that reads, "Installation successful! Move the `config/LocalSettings.php` file into the parent directory and then follow *this link* to your wiki." To do that, cut and paste the `C:\wamp\www\mywikipedia\config\LocalSettings.php` file to `C:\wamp\www\mywikipedia\LocalSettings.php`.

   Then click the link to visit your new wiki installation, located at `http://localhost/mywikipedia`. Welcome to your new wiki!

5. You might notice that the default logo in the upper-left corner isn't personal. To set it to something you like, crop and resize an image of your choice to 135 x 135 pixels and save it as `C:\wamp\www\mywikipedia\skins\common\images\mywikilogo.jpg`. Then, open the `c:\wamp\www\mywikipedia\LocalSettings.php` file and add a line that reads:

   ```
   $wgLogo = "/mywikipedia/skins/common/images/mywikilogo.jpg";
   ```

   Refresh the wiki front page to see your new logo.

Test-Drive Your Wiki

Now you have a new, clean, customized local installation of MediaWiki all ready to use however you want. Wikipedia is strong evidence that the best application of a wiki is group collaboration. However, wikis also come in handy for individual use to track lists, notes, links, images, or anything else you want to search or reference over time.

Wikis are especially good for writing projects because they keep every page's revision history and enable easy adding and editing of pages. The editorial team at Lifehacker.com uses a MediaWiki installation to collaborate on site ideas and drafts. You can also use a wiki to keep personal notes on programming techniques, to track software serial numbers, and to save quotes you like, and other relevant links and articles.

NOTE View a video demonstration of using MediaWiki to draft a novel manuscript at `http://lifehacker.com/163707`.

To begin editing a page in your new wiki, simply click the Edit link at the top of a page, as shown in Figure 8-18.

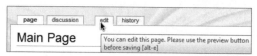

| page | discussion | edit | history |

Main Page   You can edit this page. Please use the preview button before saving [alt-e]

Figure 8-18: Click the link to edit your MediaWiki wiki.

Edit mode displays a page's text inside a text area. You see some square brackets and other markup around the text, too. This is the special formatting markup called Wikitext that lays out MediaWiki pages.

Brief Wikitext Primer

Using Wikitext, you can bold and italicize text, link text, add headers and sub-headers, and link to other pages inside your wiki. The following are some common Wikitext markup usages:

- Denote a page's section header with two equal signs prefixed and suffixed around the section name, like so:

  ```
  == Section Header Name ==
  ```

- A subsection uses three equal signs:

  ```
  === Subsection Name ===
  ```

- Two square brackets link to a page inside your wiki — a page called Favorite Quotes, for example — would be achieved like this:

  ```
  [[Favorite Quotes]]
  ```

- Create a link to an external web page with square brackets containing first the URL followed by the text of the link, like this:

  ```
  [http://lifehacker.com Lifehacker]
  ```

- External links off of the MediaWiki site are followed by a little arrow, as shown in Figure 8-19.

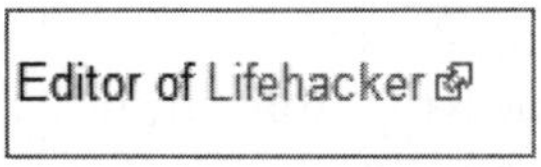

Editor of Lifehacker ᵭ

Figure 8-19: MediaWiki link
to another website.

MediaWiki's User's Guide offers a full reference for MediaWiki
markup at `http://meta.wikimedia.org/wiki/MediaWiki_User%27s_`
`Guide:_Editing_overview`.

NOTE Later in this book, you can find hacks that explain how to assign
a domain name to your home web server and how to access a home
server behind a router/firewall, so you can access your personal wiki
from anywhere.

Hack 74: Remotely Control
Your Home Computer

Level . . . . **Advanced**

Platform . . . . **Windows, Mac OS X**

Cost . . . . **Free**

Ever been at a friend's house and wanted to show off a photo you left
saved on your home computer? Want to check from the office that your
daughter's doing homework and not instant messaging with friends at
home? Need to grab a file on your home hard drive when you're miles
away? With a relatively old protocol called VNC and some free software,
you can remotely control your home computer from anywhere.

In this hack, you set up a VNC server on your home computer, which
can enable you to connect to your desktop and drive it from any Internet-
connected computer.

WARNING As mentioned earlier, running a server and opening a port
on your home computer to the Internet is a risky undertaking. Make sure
your computer has all the latest security patches, has been checked for
spyware and viruses, and that you're using strong passwords. The VNC
protocol is not inherently secure. This hack assumes that you're comfortable with basic networking concepts. In case this fine print has scared
you off, LogMeIn (`http://logmein.com`) is a web-based application that
also provides remote desktop control, which may be a better option for
some folks. VNC is preferable because it's free, it doesn't require third-
party intervention, and it works across operating systems.

The VNC protocol remotely controls another computer over a network. Think of it as a window into your home computer's desktop from any other computer (see Figure 8-20).

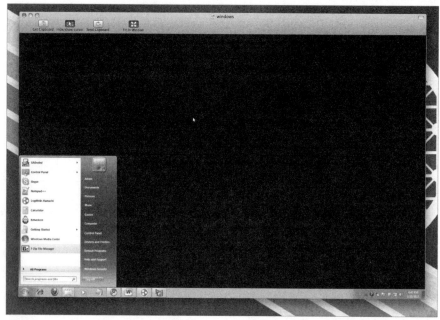

Figure 8-20: An open VNC connection to a Windows PC from a Mac.

Your keystrokes and mouse clicks travel over the network and happen on the remote computer — your home computer — in real time; anyone at the remote computer can watch the action as it happens.

Here are a few things you can do with a VNC server running at home:

- Start downloading a large file, such as a movie, in the morning so that it's there when you get home in the evening.

- Search your home computer's IM logs, address book, or file system for important information from the office.

- Help Mom figure out why Microsoft Word doesn't start without having to go to her house (even though Mom would like to see you more often).

- Control a headless (monitor-less) machine such as a media center or file server in another room in the house from the laptop on the couch.

VNC requires two components for a successful connection: the server on your home computer and the viewer on the remote computer. Ready to set them up?

Step 1: Install the VNC Server

There are several free VNC servers for Windows and Mac, so pick the section that you need.

Windows

TightVNC (http://tightvnc.com) is a free Windows VNC server and client software package. TightVNC is a nice choice because it enables file transfers and high compression levels for slow connections. Download TightVNC from http://tightvnc.com/download.php and run the installation on your home computer. Start the server and set a password for incoming connections.

If you're running a firewall, it may prompt you about whether to allow the VNC server to run: allow it.

TightVNC can be set to run as a Windows service, which means your Windows usernames and passwords can be used to authenticate on the VNC server connection. If you choose this option, be sure all your Windows passwords are set and strong, and that any password-less guest accounts are disabled.

Mac

Mac OS 10.5 and above users have a VNC server built into their computer already, but Apple calls it Screen Sharing. To turn on the server in OS X, in System Preferences, go to the Sharing pane and select Screen Sharing, as shown in Figure 8-21. You can also limit which users can remotely control your Mac and set a screen-sharing password by clicking the Computer Settings button.

NOTE If you plan to remotely control your Mac from a Windows VNC client, be sure to click the Computer Settings button and set a password for VNC viewers. Otherwise, you will run into a security error on non-Mac viewers.

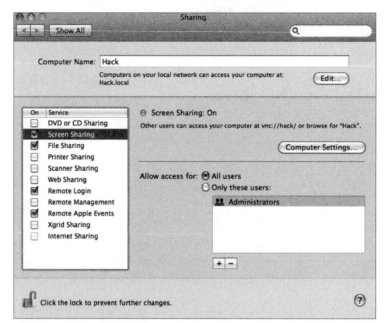

Figure 8-21: Turn on Mac OS's built-in VNC server in System Preferences' Sharing pane.

About the Server

If your VNC server is connected directly to the Internet, it is now listening for Internet requests on port 5900, VNC's default port (which is also configurable). Visit WhatIsMyIP (http://whatismyip.com) from your home computer to determine its IP address, and write it down.

If your home computer is behind a home network router with a firewall, remote computers cannot connect. You must open a port on your router's firewall and forward requests to your computer. Consult your router's manual for more information on how to do that, or check out the website Port Forward at http://portforward.com for port forwarding instructions listed by device.

Step 2: Install the VNC Client

On the remote Windows computer, also download and install TightVNC (http://tightvnc.com), but this time, start the viewer instead of the server. If you're on a Mac, download the free Chicken of the VNC (http://sourceforge .net/projects/cotvnc) Mac viewer to connect to your home PC. Enter your home computer's IP address and password to connect.

NOTE Alternatively, you can enter your home computer's domain name. Then, when connecting using the VNC viewer, you can enter a URL like `pennyscomputer.dyndns.org` **instead of an IP address.**

When connected, you're virtually sitting at your home desktop from anywhere in the world.

More VNC Considerations

A few extra VNC tips to consider:

- VNC is not a secure protocol — connection information is sent over the network "in the clear," which means someone listening on the network can see your transmissions. Also, you may not make the connection if the server computer is behind a firewall you don't control (such as at the office). If you set up VNC to work across a virtual private network, however, the connection will be encrypted and can bypass any restrictive firewalls. See Hack 70, "Create a Virtual Private Network (VPN) with Hamachi," for how to set up Hamachi.

- For slower network connections, set the compression to Best. The window image quality will be lower, but the connection response will be snappier.

- Bring a VNC viewer with you on a USB memory stick, like RealVNC Free Edition Viewer (`www.realvnc.com/products/free/4.1/winvncviewer.html`), so that you don't have to download and install it on every computer you want to use to connect to your server.

- Avoid having to install a server on Mom's computer; email her the 166K self-extracting SingleClick UltraVNC server, available at `www.uvnc.com/addons/singleclick.html`, for your next tech-support phone session.

Hack 75: Give Your Home Computer a Web Address

Level . . . . **Advanced**
Platform . . . . **All**
Cost . . . . **Free**

Accessing your home computer from the Internet is a lot easier if a memorable, permanent web address such as `yourname.com` points to it.

Depending on how your Internet service provider works, your home computer's IP address may change over time, which means you need to keep track of the current one to reach your home computer. To avoid that, you can get a permanent web address that is made up of words (not numbers, as the IP address is) and automatically resolves to a dynamic IP. This way, addressing your home computer is much simpler.

Why would you want to assign a domain name to your home web server? Maybe you want to start a blog that you're going to host at home instead of buying a web-hosting plan and you want the URL to be unforgettable. Maybe you want to set up a personal home page at `yourname.com` for business purposes or so that folks can easily find your website. Or maybe your home computer's IP address changes and you don't want to have to worry about keeping track to access your server.

> **NOTE** This tutorial assumes that you already have a web or VNC server running at home. If you don't, check out the preceding hacks for setting up one.

A dynamic DNS service, such as DynDNS (`http://dyndns.com`), is a constantly updated database of IP addresses and domain names. For free, you can get one of the available DynDNS domain names plus a custom subdomain (such as `lifehacker.getmyip.net`); or for a small fee, you can register your own domain (such as `joesmith.com`) and set it to resolve to your home-computer web server with DynDNS.

> **WARNING** Some corporate and university networks and ISPs don't allow computers outside the network to access computers with internal IP addresses. To test whether your home computer's IP address is accessible from the outside, visit **Network Tools** (`http://network-tools.com`) **from your home computer and choose the Ping option. If the ping is successful (meaning it doesn't time out), your computer is accessible from the outside.**

Step 1: Set Up Your DynDNS Account

Let's get started setting up your account.

1. From your home computer, register for a free account at DynDNS (`http://dyndns.com`). Agree to the site's terms and use a legitimate email address to complete registration. (Sometimes, DynDNS may send an email asking you to confirm that you want to continue maintaining your computer's IP record, so to continue your service, make sure you use an address you check regularly.)

2. Log into your new account. Go to the My Services area and next to Host Services, click Add Hostname. Enter a custom subdomain (such as your name) and choose from a list of domains. The result can be anything from `lifehacker.dyndns.org` to `john.is-a-geek.com`. DynDNS automatically detects your current IP address, so just click the Your Current Location link to automatically fill it in. In Figure 8-22, I've typed in the custom subdomain "lifehacker" and chosen `dyndns.org` from the drop-down list.

3. Click Add to Cart and then Proceed to Checkout. (Don't worry — despite how that sounds, the dynamic DNS service doesn't cost anything.)

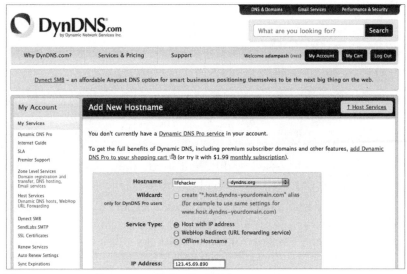

Figure 8-22: Configure your dynamic DNS host.

Step 2: Set Up Your Computer to Update DynDNS

Now that your computer is registered with DynDNS, each time its IP address changes, it lets DynDNS know. You can have this updating done either with free updater client software or through your router.

If your computer is connected directly to the Internet, download the DynDNS updater client for Mac, Windows, or Linux, available at `https://dyndns.com/support/clients`. Install and enter your DynDNS information so that your computer can send its current IP address to the DynDNS database when it changes.

If you are behind a router, you're in luck: Most modern routers support dynamic DNS services. Consult your router's manual to find out how to set the dynamic DNS service provider (in this case, DynDNS.com), the hostname (whatever you chose at DynDNS.com), and your DynDNS.com username and password.

Step 3: Give Your New Domain a Spin

Enter your new, full domain name (in this example, http://lifehacker .homeip.net) in your web browser's address bar, and your home web server's home page should appear. From here you can publicize or bookmark your server's new domain name no matter how often your IP address changes.

DynDNS Options

DynDNS has a couple of options to consider.

- **Enable wildcard:** Enables you to set up sub-subdomains. For example, blog.johnsmith.mine.nu can resolve to a weblog, whereas jukebox. johnsmith.mine.nu can resolve to a music directory. Virtual hosts must be configured for your Apache web server to display the right site when addressed by different subdomains. Get more information on setting up virtual hosts at http://lifehacker.com/147913.

- **Custom domain name:** Upgrade your account to use a custom domain name like yourname.com. Assign a domain name you've purchased to your home server for about 25 bucks a year (DynDNS's fee) plus the cost of the domain registration. See more info on Custom DNS at https://dyndns.com/services/dns/custom.

Hack 76: Optimize Your Laptop

Level . . . . **Easy**
Platforms . . . **All**
Cost . . . . **Free**

You just bought a shiny new laptop to use on your commute to the office, on business trips and vacations, and at the coffee shop down the street. You'll be more productive than ever, right?

More folks than ever are hitting the pavement with a notebook computer under one arm, but any road warrior can tell you that life with a laptop isn't always easy. This hack provides some hints and tips for extending the life of your laptop and easing the pain of the never-ending outlet and hotspot hunt.

Extend Your Battery Life

Laptop productivity on the cold, cruel, and often electrical outlet-less road depends entirely on how much juice your battery has left. Following are a few ways to increase the life of your laptop battery when there's no outlet in sight:

- **Dim the display.** The screen draws the most power from your laptop's battery. Dim it to the lowest setting you can stand to preserve battery life.

- **Turn off unnecessary processes.** If you don't need them, disable Wi-Fi and Bluetooth detection, spyware and virus scanning, unnecessary graphic effects (like Windows' Aero Glass), and desktop search file indexing while you're on battery power only. Eject any CD, DVD, or other unneeded disk to prevent your computer from spinning or scanning it for no reason.

- **Enable the power-saver profile.** Use the Microsoft Windows Power Saver Option (in Control Panel ⇨ Hardware and Sound ⇨ Power Options) and Mac OS X Energy Saver (in System Preferences), both of which set your computer to use resources as sparingly as possible when battery life is most important.

- **Recalibrate your battery's fuel gauge.** Do a deliberate full discharge of your laptop's lithium-ion battery every 30 charges or so; then recharge to calibrate the battery-life gauge. If it isn't recalibrated, the gauge can read inaccurately and cut off your laptop's operation prematurely because it thinks the battery is depleted when it's not.

- **Let Aerofoil automatically tweak your settings.** Free Windows application AeroFoil (http://silentdevelopment.blogspot.com/2010/05/aerofoil-151-released.html) automatically changes your Windows power saving settings, turns off Aero Glass, and tweaks other power-hungry settings when you run on battery power.

Save Your Keyboard and Screen

There are crumbs at the coffee shop, sand at the beach house, and right now your fingers are covered in chip grease. Use a protective cover on your keyboard to prevent stray crumbs from getting into the cracks. It will do double duty by also protecting your laptop's screen from scratches caused by the keys when the top is closed. The iSkin (`http://iskin.com`) is a thin, rubbery cover that fits Apple laptops and stays on while you type.

Alternatively, you can cut a piece of rubberized shelf liner to fit inside your laptop when you close — sort of like the bologna in a sandwich. Some people also use a thin piece of cloth cut to fit the keyboard.

If your laptop keyboard is already a hideout for crumbs and pet hair, purchase a can of compressed air to blow out any debris stuck between the keys.

Keep It Cool

After an hour or so of usage, a laptop computer can burn one's unprotected thighs and wrists. The Apple User Guide for the new MacBook Pro model states, "Do not place your MacBook Pro on your lap or other body surface for extended periods of time. Prolonged body contact can cause discomfort and potentially a burn.[1] "

If laptop heat is a problem, get material that doesn't conduct heat well between your skin and your computer, such as a lap desk or your laptop sleeve. Long-sleeved shirts with big cuffs help on wrists when the top of your keyboard gets hot to the touch, too.

Additionally, overheating is one of the most common reasons for laptop hardware failure. Be aware of how hot your machine gets.

Set Yourself Up to Work Offline

You have 10 hours to kill on that transatlantic flight without Internet access. Or your favorite coffee shop's wireless network is down. It's not always easy to get online with your laptop, so be prepared to work offline as much as possible.

For example, don't depend entirely on web-based email on your laptop. The Mozilla Thunderbird email client (`www.mozillamessaging.com`) is must-have software that enables you to download your email locally and work with it offline. Thunderbird also has excellent SMTP server management, so you can quickly switch which server you send your mail through when you *do* get online. Need to use the secure SMTP server at the office for work mail? No problem. You can set up multiple SMTP servers and associate them with different email accounts using Thunderbird.

Secure Your Data

While you're out and about on open wireless networks, make sure you have a secure firewall installed on your laptop and that its settings are extremely restrictive. (See Hack 108, "Firewall Your Windows PC," for more on running a software firewall.)

Also, turn off folder sharing and any local servers you have running (such as a web, FTP, or VNC server) to keep others from peeking in on your data. Make sure your laptop's logins have strong passwords assigned.

Lastly, consider encrypting the data on your disk in case of theft; you can use a utility such as Mac OS X's FileVault to do so.

NOTE Hack 20, "Create a Password-Protected Disk on Your PC," and Hack 106, "Truly Delete Data from Your Hard Drive," provide practical methods for making your documents inaccessible to laptop thieves and snoops.

Carry with Care

Your laptop spends a lot of time swinging over your shoulder, banging around on your back, bumping into the guy next to you on the subway, and sliding around on your car's back seat. Wrapping it up in that spare Linux T-shirt and shoving it into your messenger bag full of gadgets probably isn't a good idea, either. Make sure your laptop is snug as a bug in a rug. Invest in a padded sleeve or bag made to carry laptops that'll protect it if your bag falls over or is accidentally kicked.

Back Up

Portable computers deal with a lot more wear and tear than desktops, which increases the risk of hard-drive failure. Make sure you back up the data on your laptop regularly, and often. Create a docking station at home where you can plug in to recharge the battery and hook up an external drive to back up your data.

NOTE If you have a tough time remembering to plug in your external drive, Hack 60, "Set Up an Automated, Bulletproof File Back Up Solution," details how to automate local and off-site backups over your home network and over the Internet using CrashPlan.

Pack Helpful Extras

If you have a CD-R or DVD-R drive in your laptop, keep a few spare blanks or a USB drive for easy backup on the road. A two-prong-to-three-prong electrical-plug adaptor, an extra battery (charged), an Ethernet cable or phone cord, and an extra mouse might all be helpful additions to your portable arsenal.

Find a Hotspot

A few websites and desktop software applications can help you find wireless hotspots while you're online and off, including the following:

- **JiWire** (http://jiwire.com/search-hotspot-locations.htm). Results include both pay-for and free hotspots all over the country. JiWire also offers a downloadable Wi-Fi directory that's accessible when you're offline and looking for a hotspot, available for iPhone (www.jiwire.com/iphone) and Android (www.jiwire.com/android).

- **NetStumbler** (Windows only, available as a free download at www.netstumbler.com/downloads). View all the wireless networks within range of your computer and find out whether they require a password and how strong the signal is. The main advantage to using NetStumbler instead of the Windows built-in wireless network listing is that NetStumbler displays wireless signals that do not broadcast their name. (These signals are *not* included in the Windows default list.)

- **iStumbler** (Mac only, available as a free download at http://istumbler.net). As does NetStumbler for Windows, iStumbler lists all the wireless networks in range (broadcasting their SSID or not), as well as Bluetooth devices and Bonjour networks.

References

1. "MacBook Pro: Care, Use, and Safety Information." Apple (www.apple.com/support/macbookpro/care).

CHAPTER 9

Work Smarter on Your Smart Phone

Not long ago, most of us had one computer, maybe a bulky laptop that we'd lug around when we wanted to get things done on the go. If you needed Internet access, you'd go looking for a coffee shop in hopes of finding a serviceable Wi-Fi connection. Today, you carry a full-fledged computer-plus-phone in your pocket, with always-on access to the Web, email, social networking, and so on.

Your smartphone is a double-edged sword. On one hand, it's great knowing that wherever you are, you can access your email, look up movie show-times, find a coffee shop, or finish reading that article you bookmarked. On the other, you're working with a cramped screen, typing clumsily on a software keyboard, and stumbling to shuttle information back and forth between your computer and smartphone. It's a great gadget for staying connected, but as an emerging technology, it's also rife with productivity pitfalls.

Every day you become more reliant on this vital new tool in your productivity toolkit. This chapter's hacks include tips, tools, and methods for getting things done faster and better on your smartphone. Some cover tips and shortcuts for typing and navigating faster (Hack 77, "Speed Up Your Touchscreen Typing"); others help you automate common or repetitive tasks (Hack 80, "Automate Android Functions with Tasker"). Learn how to break down the barrier between your smartphone and desktop with Hack 78, "Break Down the Barrier Between Your Computer and Mobile Phone," and when you can't, learn how to remote control other devices from your smartphone in Hack 79, "Remote Control Your Computer with Your Phone." Although this chapter focuses primarily on Google's Android and Apple's iOS operating systems, you also learn to get more from any phone, no matter what its level of "smartness" (Hack 86, "Make Your 'Dumbphone' Smarter via Text Message").

Your smartphone may allow you to carry your life in your pocket, but it's also one more piece of technology you can use more effectively. This chapter will teach you how.

Hack 77: Speed Up Your Touchscreen Typing

Level . . . . **Easy**

Platform . . . . **iOS and Android**

Cost. . . . . **Free**

The software keyboard on mobile touchscreen operating systems is both a blessing and a curse: If your smartphone doesn't include a hardware keyboard, your phone has considerably more screen real estate and less bulk; but if you don't know how to best use that software keyboard, touchscreen, and the few buttons on your device, you can waste precious time hunting and pecking at your screen.

On the flip side, you can save a lot of time typing on and navigating through iOS or Android if you know the right tricks and shortcuts. This hack describes how to type on your smartphone faster and more efficiently.

NOTE Many of the tips in this chapter apply to both Apple's iOS operating system (which includes the iPhone, iPod touch, and iPad) and Google's Android operating system (which encompasses a broad range of smartphones and tablets). The following text notes when a tip is specific to one operating system or another.

Don't Look Before You Leap

You may have mastered touch typing on your desktop keyboard, but typing on the smartphone software keyboard can make you feel like you've reverted to the classic, time-wasting hunt-and-peck method you abandoned years ago. If your touchscreen typing style involves examining the keyboard and pecking out one character at a time with your index finger, backspacing, and correcting every typo as you go, you have plenty of room for improvement. Your parents may have taught you to look before you leap, but that time-tested axiom doesn't apply to your touchscreens.

That's because both Android and iOS include smart autocorrect features, so when you type a misspelled word — something off-the-mark, such as **tuoicsl** — the phone can recognize that you probably meant to type **typical** and displays its guess in a drop-down (on iOS, shown in Figure 9-1) or as one of many possible suggestions on Android's default keyboard (shown in Figure 9-2). Your phone can automatically correct your misspelling as soon as you tap the spacebar. It does this by analyzing possible words you may have wanted to spell using letters in the vicinity of the letters you typed. If what you type isn't in the keyboard's dictionary, your device assumes you wanted one of those other dictionary words and automatically suggests — and corrects — using what it sees as the most likely option.

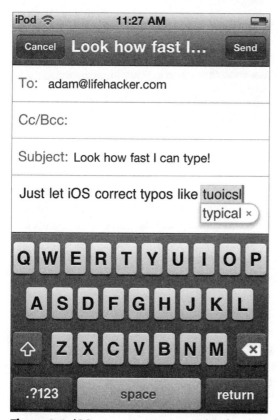

Figure 9-1: iOS can autocorrect egregiously misspelled words.

Figure 9-2: Android's stock keyboard can also autocorrect misspelled words.

In most instances, you can also ignore punctuation and let the device do the heavy lifting for you. For example, rather than pressing the **Shift+I** everytime you want to use the first-person pronoun, just type a lowercase i and press **Space**. Both keyboards automatically replace i with I.

These smartphones can also predict what you're going to type based on words in their dictionary and offer to autocomplete your word as soon as it has a suggestion. Because I type Lifehacker a lot, when I type lifeha, the iPhone can predict that I'm on my way to typing out Lifehacker, suggest the word in the drop-down (shown in Figure 9-3), and complete the word with the press of the spacebar. Similarly, the stock Android keyboard can predict what you're typing and suggest several possible options. Either way, rather than typing out all seven letters, you can just type a few, press Space, and move on.

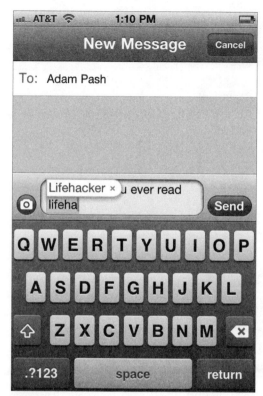

Figure 9-3: Touchscreen operating keyboards predict what you're going to type to save you time.

NOTE The Android keyboard predicts multiple options, whereas iOS predicts only one at a time. You can choose any Android prediction by tapping your preferred option. Otherwise, Android replaces what you type with the option listed in **bold** when you press Space.

If the keyboard automatically replaces a word that you didn't want it to replace, press the **Backspace** key. iOS displays a bubble (shown in Figure 9-4) with what you originally typed; tap it to revert to that word. On Android, after hitting **Backspace**, you can tap the word you originally typed or choose one of the other suggestions.

Knowing this, try typing using two thumbs and peck away as quickly as possible, aiming for the general vicinity of the letters you need. Rather than worrying about whether a word is spelled correctly as you type, put your faith in autocorrect; and then revise words as you go. You'll likely notice a significant uptick in your typing speed, with little if any increase in mistakes.

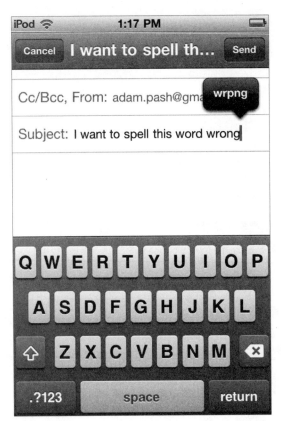

Figure 9-4: Put your cursor next to an unwanted autocorrect and tap the bubble to revert to the word you originally typed.

Punctuation Shortcuts

You can also speed up the amount of time it takes to punctuate the words you're typing with shortcuts. Here are a few of the best:

- **Double-tap the spacebar:** This shortcut couldn't be simpler. When you reach the end of a sentence, double-tap on the spacebar. Both iOS and Android automatically insert a period at the end of your sentence and capitalize the first letter of the next word you type.

- **Ignore apostrophes:** Adding an apostrophe to contractions can disrupt your typing. Just ignore them; your keyboard is smart enough to know that `isnt` should be `isn't` and automatically adds the apostrophe for you.

- **Drag-and-release:** This shortcut is a little more complicated but handy when you want to quickly insert punctuation other than the period. Press-and-hold on the keyboard's number/punctuation button (labeled ?123), drag your finger to the character you want to insert from the number/punctuation screen, and then release (just tap these two buttons on Android). iOS inserts that character and then reverts back to the main QWERTY keyboard; Android inserts that character and switches back to the main keyboard when you press Space.

TIP Hack 53, "Reduce Repetitive Typing with TextExpander for Mac," explains how to automatically expand short snippets of text to longer, commonly typed chunks of text — such as your home address. The text-expansion application TextExpander (Mac) is also available for iOS devices; if you do a lot of repetitive typing on the go, it's worth setting up TextExpander on your iPhone, iPod touch, or iPad. It's a slightly different process than detailed in Hack 53, but most of the same rules apply. The only catch: because of limitations in the iOS operating system, TextExpander works only with applications that specifically support it.

Install an Alternative Keyboard (Android Only)

In contrast to the iPhone, smartphones that run Google's Android operating system aren't limited to using the software keyboard that their phone shipped with. Instead, you can install and switch to a third-party keyboard from the Android Market that fits your typing style.

Here's how to switch the keyboard on your Android phone:

1. Open the Android Market, either on your phone or in your browser at https://market.android.com.

2. Search for a keyboard to install. (See the following list of popular Android keyboards from which to choose.)

3. The set-up process varies by keyboard, but your best bet to enable a new keyboard works like this:

    1. Launch the keyboard after you finish downloading and installing it — often you have to open the downloaded keyboard to finish the installation process.

    2. Open Settings ⇨ Locale and Text, and make sure your keyboard is enabled under Text Settings. (Some keyboards require enabling; others do not.)

    3. Now tap Select Input Method and choose the keyboard you want to use, as shown in Figure 9-5.

Figure 9-5: Android enables you to switch to your preferred keyboard at any time.

Next time you tap in a text input, notice that your device uses the keyboard you last chose here.

TIP You can quickly switch between keyboards you already installed by tapping and holding inside any text input and selecting Input Method to open the same Select Input Method dialog shown in Figure 9-5.

Pick a Keyboard that Suits You (Android Only)

The Android Market is filled with alternative keyboards, but the following are a few recommendations:

- **Android's Default Keyboard (free):** The stock keyboard that ships with Android works as described in the beginning of this chapter. It's a great keyboard in its own right and perfectly adequate for many users.

- **SwiftKey ($1.99):** Analyzes your current and future text messages to learn how you write and automatically predict new words before you even begin typing them (`https://market.android.com/details?id=com.touchtype.swiftkey`). A free trial is available for 30 days.

- **SlideIt ($6.29):** Slide your finger between letters of the word you want to spell without removing your fingertip from the screen; SlideIt recognizes the gesture and translate it into a word (`https://market.android.com/details?id=com.dasur.slideit`).

- **Swype:** Like SlideIt, Swype is a gesture-based keyboard. Slide (or *swype*) your finger from one key to the next without lifting off the screen, and Swype turns it into a word. As of this writing, Swype is in beta and available only as a stock feature on specific devices.

If you prefer holding the phone with one hand while pecking with your index finger, you'll get the most mileage from gesture-based keyboards such as Swype and SlideIt. If you prefer the two-thumbed typing approach, keyboards such as SwiftKey or the default Android keyboard are a better fit.

NOTE Android users can also take some of the hassle out of typing by using the operating system's built-in voice-to-text transcription, detailed in Hack 84, "Command Your Phone with Your Voice."

Hack 78: Break Down the Barrier Between Your Computer and Mobile Phone

Level. . . . . . . **Easy**

Platform . . . . **iOS/Android**

Cost. . . . . **Free**

Your smartphone and your desktop computer share a lot of duties, but each device has its strengths and weaknesses. You may prefer to look up directions from the comfort of your desktop because you can type in an address more quickly on your full-size keyboard, but ultimately you want the directions shuttled over to your phone so that you can use them on the go. You could send an email to yourself containing the link to the directions and then open it from your phone, but that's not streamlined and can create a lot of clutter in your inbox.

This hack covers tricks and tools that break down the barriers between your desktop and your smartphone, making it easier to shuttle bits and pieces of information back and forth between the two so that you can work from whichever device is more convenient.

NOTE The most common sharing scenario involves sending links and text from your desktop browser to your phone, so the following sections walk through setting up one-click sharing tools on iOS and Android devices.

Computer to iOS

The free service Site to Phone (www.sitetophone.com) sends links and text from your desktop or laptop to your phone with the click of a button. Here's how to set it up:

1. Open www.sitetophone.com/create.php in your computer's web browser. Site to Phone can create a unique ID and generate a URL for that ID — such as http://sitetophone.com/848054-3693 — as shown in Figure 9-6.

2. Without closing the page on your desktop's browser, open that URL in your phone's browser, bookmark it, and add it to your phone's home screen so that you can easily access it later. To do this on iOS, tap the More button (the icon of an arrow coming out of a box) and tap Add to Home Screen.

3. Click the Complete Setup link on your phone.

NOTE This section focuses on iOS, but Site to Phone is compatible with every mobile operating system, including BlackBerry, webOS, and Windows Phone 7. The service also supports Android devices, but Android users have an even better tool, called Chrome to Phone, detailed in the following section.

At this point, your desktop browser verifies that you finished setting up your phone and redirects you to the homepage, where you see a Quick Send text box into which you can paste any text or link. Test out your new setup:

1. From your desktop, paste a link into the Quick Send text box, and click Send to Phone.

2. Next, on your phone, launch Site to Phone from the home screen with the bookmark you just created. Your mobile browser automatically redirects to the link you shared.

⬆ Site to Phone

| Home | Login | **Create** | Addons |

Create a Site to Phone ID

You're almost done!

The ID that has been generated for you is 848054-3693 (if you want to you can set an email and password later).

Please visit the web address shown below **on your phone** to complete the registration.

Web address

http://sitetophone.com/848054-3693

Status

○ Waiting for phone to connect to the web address

Figure 9-6: Site to Phone creates a unique ID for sharing links and text.

Site to Phone isn't limited to links; you can paste and share any text using the tool. When doing so, instead of redirecting to another site, Site to Phone displays the nonlink text in your browser, ready to be copied and pasted wherever you need it.

You may find that navigating to the Site to Phone website every time you want to share text or a link with your phone is tedious, so you can streamline the process by installing the Site to Phone bookmarklet, the Chrome extension, or the Internet Explorer add-on from `http://sitetophone` `.com/addons.php`.

The best option — the Chrome extension — adds a Site to Phone button to Chrome's toolbar and a Send to Phone option to your browser's right-click context menu. This extension will share both URLs and Text.

- To share the URL of a page you're currently viewing, click the Send to Phone button.

- To share text on a page, highlight the text you want to share, right-click, and select Send text to phone, as shown in Figure 9-7.

Figure 9-7: Share highlighted text from your right-click menu.

Computer to Android

Chrome to Phone is a Chrome extension and Android app that shares links and text between Google's desktop web browser, Chrome, and the Android operating system. It works similarly to Site to Phone but features tighter integration with Android, so it can automatically load links in your browser or copy text to your clipboard. Here's how to set it up:

1. Using the Google Chrome web browser on your desktop, install the Chrome to Phone extension from http://tinyurl.com/2wnjloy. The extension adds a Chrome to Phone button in your toolbar. Click it; then click the Sign In link and log in using your Google account.

2. On your Android phone, download and install the Chrome to Phone app from https://market.android.com/details?id=com.google .android.apps.chrometophone.

3. When installed, launch Chrome to Phone on your Android device; select the Google account you want to associate with it (this should be the same account you used when you logged into Chrome to Phone from your desktop); and set your Link Action preference to Automatically launch links, as shown in Figure 9-8.

4. Now, to shuttle a page you're looking at from your desktop to your Android phone, click the Chrome to Phone button on the Chrome toolbar. In a few seconds, the page automatically opens on your Android device. If you want to send text instead of a link, select any text on a page and, again, click the Chrome to Phone button. Instead of automatically launching the page with your Android device's browser, Chrome to Phone copies the selected text to your device's clipboard — as shown in the notification in Figure 9-9.

NOTE If Firefox is your browser of choice, the FoxToPhone extension for Firefox (https://addons.mozilla.org/en-US/firefox/addon/ foxtophone-aka-sendtophone) integrates with the Chrome to Phone app on Android devices.

The Chrome to Phone desktop extension also adds an item to Chrome's right-click context menu, so you can, for example, right-click an image on any web page and select Chrome to Phone to open that image directly on your phone.

Figure 9-8: Chrome to Phone can automatically launch links or copy text to your clipboard.

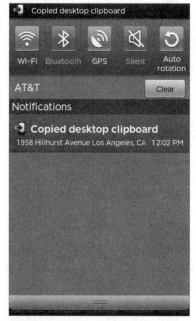

Figure 9-9: Select text and click the Chrome to Phone button from your desktop to view the same text on your Android device.

TIP   Open Chrome to Phone on Android at any time to browse your link-sharing history for today, the last seven days, last month, or older.

NOTE   For a better method of sharing reading material between devices, see Hack 38, "Off-Load Your Online Reading to a Distraction-Free Environment"; for more seamless note-taking tools, Hack 37, "Set Up a Ubiquitous Note-Taking Inbox Across Devices" sets you up with a better experience moving between your computer and your phone.

Hack 79: Remote Control Your Computer with Your Phone

Level . . . . **Advanced**

Platform . . . . **iOS and Android**

Cost . . . . **Free**

In Hack 74, "Remotely Control Your Home Computer," you set up a VNC server on your home computer so that you could control it from anywhere as though you were sitting down in front of it. VNC is a great tool when you need access to your computer from another one, but when you don't have your laptop or an Internet connection handy, you can still access your home computer from the always-connected smartphone in your pocket.

In this hack, you learn how to access and remotely control a computer running a VNC server using a free VNC client app called PocketCloud (www.wyse.com/products/software/pocketcloud/).

NOTE   This hack assumes that you set up a VNC server on your computer, as detailed in Hack 74. If you haven't, you need to do so before proceeding. You'll also get more mileage from this hack if you give your home computer a dedicated Web address and open port 5900 (the default VNC port) on your firewall.

Set Up PocketCloud

PocketCloud is available for both Android and iOS devices, so download the client that suits your smartphone from either the Android Market or iTunes App Store. The app is available as both a free and paid app. The most important difference between the two is that the free app is limited to saving one connection. The PocketCloud Pro ($15) is ad-free, can save multiple connections, and includes a few other advanced features.

After you install PocketCloud to your device, you're ready to set it up. You can proceed in one of two ways:

- Download the companion application for Windows or Mac, available at http://tinyurl.com/31b6q21, associate it with a Google account, and use it to walk through an Auto Discovery process.

- Manually set up your VNC connection using the information you already gathered when you set up your VNC server.

Some may prefer the first option, but it can be more complicated, so the following example uses the second option. Here's how that works.

NOTE The screenshots depict the iOS version of PocketCloud, but the two are virtually identical, so the same steps apply to both.

1. Launch PocketCloud and, if prompted, choose to Skip Auto Discovery.

2. Click the + button in the top-right corner of the app to manually add a new connection, and when prompted, choose Remote Shadowing (VNC).

NOTE PocketCloud supports Microsoft's Remote Desktop Protocol (RDP), but VNC is often preferable because it's free and works across all operating systems, and because RDP isn't included in all versions of Windows. However, the setup process won't vary much if you prefer RDP. For more VNC considerations, see Hack 74, "Remotely Control Your Home Computer."

3. Give the computer you connect to a Nickname. In Figure 9-10, I've named mine simply My Desktop.

4. Enter the IP address or URL of your VNC server. If you assigned a domain name to your computer (as detailed in Hack 75, "Give Your Home Computer a Web Address") so you can remote control your computer from anywhere, you can enter that here. If not, enter your computer's local IP address — which looks something like 192.168.X.X.

5. Enter the password you set up for your VNC server. Unless you changed the port for some reason, the default of 5900 should work.

6. Finally, select your operating system, then tap the Save button.

Figure 9-10: Enter a nickname, URL, and password to set up your VNC connection.

Now tap your newly created connection on the My Computers screen. When PocketCloud connects, you'll be able to control your computer's desktop from your phone.

Using PocketCloud

Things work a little differently when remote controlling your computer from a small touchscreen. Here are a few pointers to start:

- **Navigating on a small screen:** Your smartphone doesn't have the same pixel space as your desktop, so to read text and interact with the screen you control, you need to zoom in and out. The iOS version of PocketCloud supports pinch-to-zoom, so just pinch your fingers in and out to zoom in and out on the screen; on Android, click the zoom in and out buttons. Tap and drag anywhere on the screen to move the viewport to a new area when you're zoomed in.

- **Clicking on items:** You can send mouse clicks to the desktop you control by either tapping the screen where you want to click or by enabling the Touch Pointer tool. (On iOS, tap the icon that looks like a mouse pointer; on Android, open the menu and tap Touch Pointer.) This overlays a mouse pointer on your screen that you can drag over anything you want to click. Tap the center of the radial overlay to send a left mouse click. When you drag the Touch Pointer, the radial menu also gives you other options, as shown in Figure 9-11, to right-click, scroll the page, or access other menu options.

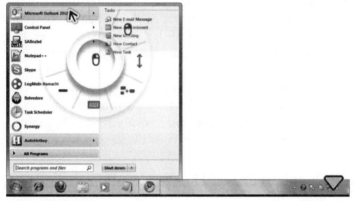

Figure 9-11: Tap the screen to send mouse clicks or use the Touch Pointer.

- **Typing:** Tap the keyboard button to open the keyboard, type, or send keystrokes and key combinations to your remote PC. The operating system-specific keyboards provide you with common special key combinations or function keys, so you can type nearly anything you normally type on a traditional keyboard.

It may not be exactly the same as sitting in front of the computer with a keyboard and a mouse, but to access your home computer from any-where your phone has a data connection can be a lifesaver under the right circumstances.

Other Recommended Remote Applications

Aside from remote controlling the desktops of other computers, your phone can also act as a universal remote with the flexibility to play music anywhere in your home, control your home theater, and more. You can find several other remote control solutions at Lifehacker.com for iOS (http://lifehacker .com/5709968) and Android (http://lifehacker.com/5709967).

Hack 80: Automate Android Functions with Tasker

Level . . . . **Advanced**

Platform . . . . **Android**

Cost . . . . **About $6**

Although mobile phones introduce many new conveniences to your life, they also afford ample opportunities in which to embarrass yourself: Forgetting to silence it before a movie, meeting, or class is one of the most common ways to do so. Even if your phone doesn't ring, you scold your forgetful self and add it to the list of things you have to remember to do repeatedly and, undoubtedly, forget about at your own peril.

Wouldn't it be nice, though, if your phone were smart enough to silence itself when you walked into your favorite movie theater? Or if it were aware that when you're driving, it should read your text messages aloud so you're not tempted to do something irresponsible? Or, more simply, what if it could automatically launch your music app when you plug in your headphones?

The Android application Tasker (`https://market.android.com/details?id=net.dinglisch.android.taskerm`) is capable of doing all these things, and a great deal more, by enabling you to set up specific actions for your phone to take based on various contexts you define. In the spirit of Chapter 7, "Automate Repetitive Tasks," this hack explains how to use Tasker to automate common or repetitive tasks on your Android phone.

The Anatomy of a Task

Each automated workflow you set up in Tasker is called a *Profile*. Profiles consist of two parts: a *Context* and an *Action*. The Context defines when a Profile should run; the Action defines what should happen when the Profile runs.

Some common Contexts include the following:

- An application you launched (for example when Google Maps is launched)
- Your phone's orientation (for example face up, face down)
- You phone's location

- The time of day
- Your battery level

Some common Actions you could take include the following:

- Enabling a service (for example GPS, Bluetooth, and Wi-Fi)
- Adjusting the phone's volume or silencing the phone
- Launching an application
- Displaying a system notification
- Playing or stopping music

You can combine more than one Context in a profile — for example, a Profile that runs when your phone is plugged in after midnight. Likewise, a Profile can perform more than one action.

Thinking up Tasker Profiles that solve problems or automate repetitive actions is a matter of considering what you commonly do on your phone and then digging through Tasker's Context and Action menus to see how you might build a Profile to help.

Example: Silence Your Phone When It's Face Down

To build your first profile, consider the example at the beginning of this hack: You're sitting in a meeting and realize you forgot to silence your phone. It's sitting on the table in front of you, and it could ring at any moment! What to do?

With Tasker, you can create a Profile that automatically silences your phone when it's laying face down. Rather than picking up your phone to press the silence button, you can just turn it over and let Tasker take care of the rest. To be extra cautious, you could even tell Tasker to turn off Wi-Fi as well — or go into Airplane mode — to ensure you don't receive any embarrassing interruptions. Here's how to set that up:

1. Launch Tasker, tap the New button, and give your new Profile a name — something like Noise Killer.

2. Tasker prompts you to add your first Context. In this case, you want the Profile to trigger when your phone's orientation is face down, so tap State ➪ Orientation, and then select Face Down from the Orientation drop-down menu, as shown in Figure 9-12. Tap Done.

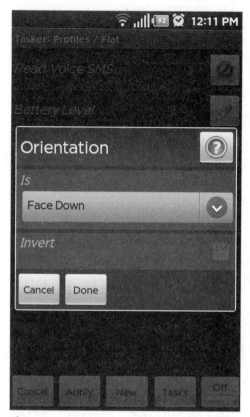

Figure 9-12: Set your Context to trigger when your phone is laying face down.

3. Tasker will not prompt you to choose a Task to perform when your Context is met. Tap New Task, tap OK to skip giving it a name (you only need to give Actions a name if you want to reuse the action in another Profile), and then tap the + button.

4. In this example, you want to set your phone to Silent Mode, so tap Audio ➪ Silent Mode. Select On from the drop-down menu (you want this action to turn on Silent Mode), and then tap Done.

That's all there is to it — you created your first Tasker Profile. To test it, make sure the Profile has a green check mark next to it in the Profiles list (shown in Figure 9-13) and that Tasker is turned On in the bottom-right corner of the screen; then tap Apply. Tasker exits, but you see an Ongoing notification from Tasker in your Notification bar. This means it's active and watching for Contexts that match your Profile.

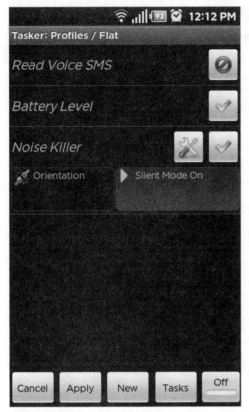

Figure 9-13: Enable, disable, and edit your existing Tasker Profiles.

Now, when you turn your phone face down, Tasker mutes your audio, and you won't embarrass yourself in front of your boss with your obnoxious ringtone or text message notification. When you flip your phone right-side up, Tasker returns your phone's volume to its previous state. Since the Tasker profile only activates when you lay your phone face down, it won't inadvertently mute your phone while it's upright in your pocket or bag.

NOTE This hack exposes the tip of the Tasker iceberg; it can also save your battery, set your phone to read text messages aloud while you're driving, and more. See other Tasker suggestions at http://lifehacker .com/5601133.

Hack 81: Set Up One Phone Number to Rule Them All

Level . . . . **Easy**

Platform . . . . **All**

Cost . . . . **Free**

There's little question that cell phones have improved the ability to "reach out and touch someone" from anywhere, at any time, but they've also added one more inbox you have to monitor, manage, and control; one more number to hand out to people; one more place you can miss calls; and one more place you have to check for messages.

For example, you may currently be juggling a personal cell phone, a landline, and a work phone. If Dad wants to get a hold of you, he may try all three before he gets you, leave messages at two, and give up by the third — which may be the only one you actually check for messages.

Google's free telephone application, Google Voice (www.google.com/voice), rings all your phones from one number, provides free, unlimited text messaging, and consolidates all your phone-related communication (such as phone calls, text messages, and voicemail) to one centralized hub. This hack explains how to set up and make the most of Google Voice on your phones.

> **NOTE** Although Google Voice's marquee feature is its ability to ring multiple phones with one number, it has plenty of useful features for single-line users, detailed next.

Set Up Google Voice

Starting with a Google Voice account is a simple four-step process:

1. First, visit http://voice.google.com and create an account or log into your existing Google account. Then, Google Voice will prompt you to choose your new number, as shown in Figure 9-14. To do so, enter your preferred area code, or enter your city or ZIP code to let Google choose an area code for you based on your location. You can also enter a preferred word, phrase, or number that you'd like Google to try matching. (There's no guarantee you'll get what you want, but it doesn't hurt to try!) Click Search Available Numbers, and select a number you like. Click Continue.

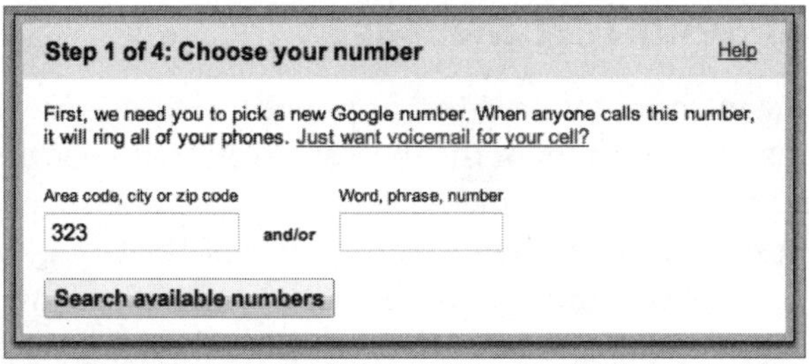

Step 1 of 4: Choose your number   Help

First, we need you to pick a new Google number. When anyone calls this number,
it will ring all of your phones. Just want voicemail for your cell?

Area code, city or zip code   Word, phrase, number

323   and/or

Search available numbers

Figure 9-14: Choose your preferred area code and search
for available numbers.

2. Create the four-digit PIN you'll use to access your Google voicemail
   from phones that aren't associated with your Google Voice account.
   Accept the terms of service and click Continue.

3. Add one of the phones you want to ring when someone calls your
   Google Voice number. At this point, you only add one phone; after
   you finish the setup process, you can add other phones, as detailed
   next. Click Continue.

4. Click the Call Me Now button and Google rings the phone number
   you just entered. When you answer, you'll be prompted to enter the
   verification code you see on your screen.

That's all there is to it. Now when anyone calls your new Google Voice
number (which you can always find at the top-right corner of the Google
Voice homepage), the phone you just set up rings.

The first time you sign into Voice, you see a transcribed voicemail in
the main panel welcoming you to Google Voice. Click the Play button to
listen to it.

NOTE Google's transcription of its own welcome voicemail is spot-on;
don't expect the service's transcriptions of your friends' and family's
voicemail to be quite as accurate. It can be handy for short messages,
but you'd want to listen to most messages before making any important
descriptions based on the transcriptions.

This inbox contains voicemail you receive and text messages sent and
received with your Google Voice number and is a lot like your Gmail inbox:
You can click different items in the sidebar to filter messages by Voicemail,
Text, or by Placed, Received, and Missed calls. You can even Archive, Star,
Delete, and report messages as spam.

Place Calls and Send Text Messages

Reply to any message in your inbox via text or phone call by clicking either the Call or Text links at the bottom of the message. Alternatively, you can place calls and send unlimited text messages to any number by clicking either the Call or Text buttons in the top-left corner of the Google Voice webapp. Either enter a phone number or, if you use Google Contacts to manage your contacts, enter the name of the contact and Google autocompletes the number. If you're making a call, select which phone you want to use to complete the call from the drop-down (shown in Figure 9-15) and click Connect.

Figure 9-15: Place phone calls and send text messages from Google Voice's webapp.

When you place a call from inside Google Voice on the Web, your phone rings first, and when you answer it, Google rings your contact.

Add More Phones to Google Voice

You have one phone number set up, but one of Google Voice's major benefits is that it can ring *multiple* numbers, so you can add additional phone numbers to your Google Voice account

1. Click the Preferences cog in the top-right corner of the page.
2. Select Voice Settings.
3. From the Phones tab, click the Add Another Phone link. Associating additional numbers with your account is a similar process to setting up your first phone, detailed previously. As of this writing, you can add a maximum of six numbers to your Google Voice account.

Set Up Ring Schedules

Just beneath the service, Google Voice offers some powerful tools to manage how it rings your phones. Many of these features are beyond the scope of this hack (see, "Other Benefits of Google Voice" next), but you can find the best ones within the Phones tab of the Google Voice settings and following these instructions.

1. Visit `www.google.com/voice/b/0#phones`, and click the Edit button below one of your phones.

2. Now click the Show Advanced Settings link. Go to the Ring Schedule section.

3. Here you have the option to specify when Google Voice won't ring that number. For example, if it's your work phone, you may want to click Never ring on weekends. Alternatively, you could set a custom schedule telling Voice not to ring your number after work hours, from the hours of 6 p.m. to 9 a.m. as shown in Figure 9-16. If you want to plan a regular No-Fly Zone (detailed in Hack 43) during which no one can disturb you, set a custom schedule that won't ring your phone during that hour. You can add multiple time ranges for the same number.

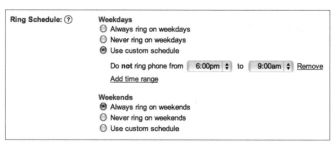

Figure 9-16: Set custom schedules during which Google Voice won't ring your phone.

Set Up Custom Call and Voicemail Behavior by Groups

Similarly, Google Voice can create Groups made up of different contacts to determine which calls are forwarded to which phones, and even which voicemail messages it plays to specific people. Navigate to the Groups tab of the Google Voice Settings (`www.google.com/voice/b/0#groups`) to create different rules for different groups of contacts.

NOTE   To set up different groups in Google Voice, click the Contacts tab in the sidebar. Voice uses any existing groups in your Google Contacts (www.google.com/contacts), so if you already set up contact groups with Google, you have a head start.

If you use your Google Voice number to handle multiple phones, it can field voicemail from both your best friend and your boss. Because your professional self may not always jibe with your personal self, click the Edit button beneath your Coworkers group. On this page, you can edit which phones ring when someone from this group calls you, and you can set or record a new voicemail greeting to play when someone in this group calls you, as shown in Figure 9-17. For example, the voicemail greeting your friends get when they call might be "Hey it's Larry, leave me a message." The greeting everyone else gets could be a more formal "Hello, you've reached Larry Page, Chief Executive Officer of Google, Inc. Please leave a message at the tone and my assistant will get back to you as soon as possible."

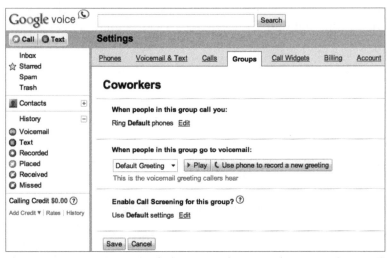

Figure 9-17: Set custom ring behaviors and voicemail greetings for specific contact groups.

Integrate Google Voice with Your Phone

Google Voice is available as a native mobile app for Android, iPhone, and BlackBerry phones at http://m.google.com/voice. The mobile apps offer Google Voice's best functionality — like unlimited text messages — from a native application on your phone.

For more on integrating Google Voice with your Android device, iPhone, or even your "feature" phone (often referred to as dumphones), see `http://lifehacker.com/5775576`.

Other Benefits of Google Voice

Here are even more things you can do and tools you can use with Google Voice:

- **Chrome extension:** The Google Voice Chrome extension enables you to place calls, send text messages, and read and reply to messages in your inbox from the convenience of your Chrome toolbar (`http://tinyurl.com/6hbwvc5`).

- **Number blocking:** If a persistent caller bothers you, click the More link below a message, and select Block Caller. No more nuisance.

- **In-call shortcuts:** Want to record a call? Press 4 on your keyboard during a conversation. (Right now, only the person who has received the call can record it, not the person who initiated the call.) Going over your minutes and want to transfer a call to another phone tied to your number? Press *.

- **Easy conference calling:** To set up a quick conference call with up to four participants, have them all call your Voice number. Answer each call, and press 5 to conference them together.

- **Cheap international calls:** Google Voice's international calling rates are cheaper than most telephone provider's rates (`www.google.com/voice/b/0/rates`).

- **Free calling from Gmail:** When you sign into your Gmail account, you can place calls using your Google Voice number and talk to contacts from your computer.

Hack 82: Augment Reality with Your Phone

Level . . . . **Easy**

Platform . . . . **Android and iOS**

Cost . . . . **Free**

In the not-so-distant future, technology may fuse so tightly with the way you naturally experience the world that you'll learn all about something simply by looking at it. You won't have to find a computer, open up a web browser, and type your search into Google or Wikipedia for information.

Instead, that information may display on top of your vision, perhaps as a heads-up display (HUD) overlaid on your glasses or even specialized contacts. It sounds like the stuff of science fiction or video games, but that sort of convenience is already possible with your smartphone.

The phone you carry in your pocket is, in many ways, considerably smarter than your PC and laptop ever were. It knows where you are, which direction you're pointing it, and it can even see the same things you see. Using that information with its always-on access to the Internet, your phone can give you all sorts of useful information about anything you point it at. This hack highlights several methods to augment your knowledge using your phone.

Learn About Where You Are

Free augmented reality app Layar (www.layar.com/download) uses a combination of your phone's camera, your location, and the direction you point the phone to display information about your surroundings live on your screen. Types of information range from Wikipedia to crime maps and restaurants to apartment listings.

Launch the app, and choose a layer with information you're interested in. Figure 9-18 shows the Wikipedia layer in action. With it enabled, as you point your phone in different directions, you see points of interest as icons — and sometimes images — on the screen with a live image, just like the aforementioned HUD. Tapping on an icon displays information about that point of interest, including links to map directions to its location and a button to take you to the full Wikipedia article.

Anyone can create and submit a layer to Layar, so the kind of information you find is flexible. Some of Layar's layers are more interesting than others; most are free. Some of the best ones include:

- **streetARt:** Displays interesting street art in your area
- **Wikipedia:** The wealth of the online encyclopedia informing what you see
- **FlickAR Photos:** Displays recent images taken nearby and uploaded to the popular photo-sharing web site, Flickr

Browse through the Popular section of the Layers dialog to find some of the more interesting options. If you're looking for something specific, use the Search dialog.

Figure 9-18: Layar overlays nearby points of interest on a map to give you more information about your surroundings.

Learn About What You See with Google Goggles

Google Goggles (`www.google.com/mobile/goggles`) is a visual search application that uses your smartphone's camera to search the Internet. Snap a picture of something you want to identify, catalog, or learn more about, and Google Goggles uploads the image to Google's supercomputers to analyze and identify what's in the image. Click the result Google turns up to search the web for more information on it.

NOTE On iOS, Goggles is a part of the Google Search app available from the iTunes App Store.

What Google Goggles Is Good At

Goggles is surprisingly smart and especially capable of recognizing objects and text. You may want to try using Goggles for the following:

- **Scanning business cards:** When you scan a picture of a business card with Goggles, it recognizes the text and identifies contact information. You can even create a new contact using the scanned information, as shown in Figure 9-19.

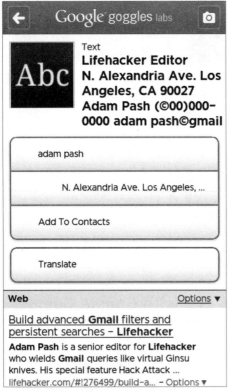

Figure 9-19: Turn business cards into contacts with Google Goggles' smart text recognition features.

- **Translating text:** Next time a language barrier gets between you and a restaurant's menu, snap a picture of the text with Goggles, and it can translate the text from one of more than 50 languages.

- **Learning about things:** When you snap a picture of a landmark or a famous painting, Goggles can identify the object in your picture, give you a little top-level information (for example, a painting's title and artist), and provide Google search results for it.

- **Researching purchases:** Scan a book or DVD cover, the label of a bottle of wine you're interested in, or even a barcode. Goggles can return product search results.

Goggles is clever, and its ability to identify things can only improve in time, but it's not perfect. As of this writing, Goggles has trouble identifying less concrete objects, such as food, plants, animals, cars, or articles of clothing. Tap the stars at the bottom of Goggles' initial result screen to rate search results and fine-tune the app's results.

NOTE You can choose to keep pictures you take with Google Goggles in your Goggles history or discard them entirely after the search is done.

Get Your Money's Worth

Next time you're about to make an impulse buy without comparison shopping first, pull out your smart phone and do a quick price check. Product search apps enable you to comparison shop without leaving the store. These apps use your phone's camera to quickly identify items by scanning barcodes or even by taking pictures. Following are some better options you can download for free and use next time you shop:

- **Amazon (Android/iOS):** Searches the popular online retailer by scanning barcodes or taking a photo. When Amazon recognizes an item (which it does more often than not), it's added to your Amazon Remembers list, as shown in Figure 9-20. Tap on any item to see how much it costs on Amazon, read reviews, add it to your wish list, or go ahead and buy it.

- **Google Shopper (Android):** Scan a barcode or take a picture and Shopper identifies the item and provides an overview, price comparisons for buying either online or at a local store, and product reviews. Google Goggles scans barcodes and returns product search results, but Shopper offers far more comprehensive product search and price comparison tools.

- **Red Laser (iOS):** Scan any barcode and get a quick price comparison from across the Internet and from local stores. (This one doesn't identify products from photographs.)

Figure 9-20: Amazon's mobile app searches prices by barcode or picture.

Hack 83: Remember Where You've Been Using Location Awareness

Level . . . . **Easy**

Platform . . . . **Android and iOS**

Cost . . . . **Free**

You may remember where you had the best meal of your life, but what about that breakfast place you ate at a year ago on your business trip? Or where you stood when you watched (and took pictures of) that beautiful sunset with that special someone?

You may remember vaguely where you were and when, but your smart phone's memory is considerably better. It can remember locations down to your latitude and longitude, and it can remember events to the second.

The next time you try to recall that great Mediterranean place you ate at two years ago when you were visiting family out of state, your phone can do the heavy lifting.

This hack explains how to use your smartphone with free services to remember specific details about the places you've been and things you've done.

NOTE Although many of the tricks discussed here aren't limited to Android and iOS, this hack focuses on those mobile operating systems.

Check In to See Where You've Been

The free, location-based service foursquare (http://foursquare.com) lets you "check in" to your location using your smartphone. Each time you check in, foursquare logs the name of your location (like a restaurant, park, or office) and the time you check in. The service is filled with fun diversions, enabling you to follow friends and earn badges and mayorships by checking in often to your regular haunts, but you don't have to be a fan of social networks or virtual emblems to take advantage of what foursquare has to offer.

Visit foursquare at http://foursquare.com/ and follow the link to download and install its mobile app for your device. Launch foursquare on your smartphone and register for a free account. Now you're ready to check in:

1. Tap the Places tab. Using your location, foursquare can find places of interest nearby. Tap the one you want to check in at, or add a new place if you don't see your location listed. To add a new place on Android, press the Menu button and select Add Place. On iOS, search for the place, and if you still don't find it, tap on Add This Place.

2. Tap the "Check In Here" button. You can optionally add a note or photo to your check in, and you can share the check in with your foursquare friends or via Twitter or Facebook.

3. Tap the "Check In Here" button a second time and your check in is complete.

It may seem like a tedious process, but after you get in the habit, checking in somewhere it takes only a few seconds. Once you've built up a history of check-ins, you'll have a personal log of places you've been. Now you can put that check-in data to good use.

Place Your Check-Ins on a Map

In the olden days, people would hang paper maps on their walls and use thumbtacks to show off where they'd traveled. If you use foursquare, you can do that digitally. Here's how:

1. On your computer, navigate to foursquare's feeds page at http://foursquare.com/feeds. Right-click the KML feed and copy the link address. (KML is a markup language that associates geographic information with data.)

2. Open Google Maps at http://maps.google.com. Paste the link to your KML feed in the search box and click Search Maps.

Google Maps can translate the data from your KML feed into pushpins on a map. Zoom in and click on any pin to see the name of the place you checked in, as shown in Figure 9-21.

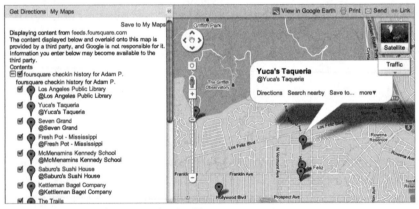

Figure 9-21: See where you checked in on a map.

NOTE The foursquare feeds platform is still in development, and as of this writing, the KML feed contains a few quirks, including a problem with links. For example, in Google Maps, a link to Yuca's Taqueria (the best taco stand in Los Angeles) points to http://maps.google.com/venue/41234 **instead of** http://foursquare.com/venue/41234. **You can manually tweak the URL if you want to see any venue's page on foursquare.**

For an alternate view of your check-in history, Where Do You Go (www.wheredoyougo.net) uses your foursquare check-in frequency to create heat maps that correlate color intensity with check-in frequency.

Place Your Check-Ins on a Calendar

A map of your check-ins can help you find the name of a place when all you can remember is roughly where it is, but if you know *when* you were somewhere, you can use the ICS (calendar format that contains event information) calendar feed instead. Here's how to use it with Google Calendar:

1. Again, navigate to http://foursquare.com/feeds on your computer; this time, copy the link address for your check-in history in ICS.

2. Open Google Calendar at www.google.com/calendar (requires a free Google account, which you can learn how to obtain in Hack 8, "Consolidate Multiple Email Addresses with Gmail").

3. In the sidebar, click the Add link under Other Calendars and select Add by URL.

4. Paste the ICS link you copied in Step 1, and click Add Calendar.

You'll see a new calendar in Google Calendar called foursquare check-ins. This calendar logs all your foursquare check-ins to the minute you checked in.

Put Your Photos on a Map

When you take pictures using your location-aware phone, your phone can embed location into the digital photograph's EXIF metadata. This location data is part of the image file, so when you upload it to a service like the popular photo-sharing site Flickr (www.flickr.com), the service uses that data to place your photos on a map. Flickr does this automatically, so when you view an individual photo on Flickr, you see a map along with the rest of the photo's metadata in the right sidebar. To see all your photos on one big map follow these steps:

1. Visit www.flickr.com/map in your desktop web browser.

2. At the bottom of the page, click Search the Map.

3. Select Your Photostream from the drop-down menu. You can optionally enter tags or title text to filter your photos further, or just click Go to see all your geotagged photos.

4. Depending on how many geotagged photos you upload, you should now see a lot of pink dots on your map. Zoom in and click any dot to see the associated photo, as shown in Figure 9-22.

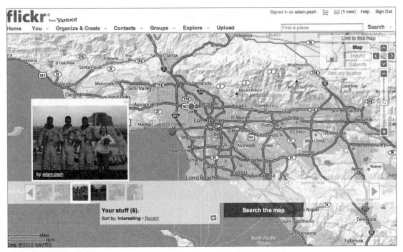

Figure 9-22: See all the geotagged photos you've taken on a map.

Use Google Maps to Find Anything

If you try to recall a place you've been but you don't have a foursquare check-in or geotagged photo to help you find it, as long as you have a vague recollection of where it is, you can turn to Google Maps on your smartphone. Google's full-featured map tool can help you find nearly any point of interest, even if you have no idea what it is called. Here's how:

1. Launch Google Maps, zoom in, and center the map in the general vicinity of what you're looking for.

2. Conduct a search using only Google's wildcard operator, * (asterisk), as your query.

Instead of looking for restaurants or coffee shops, Google returns results for everything in the area. If you know enough about the place you're looking for to refine the search with relevant terms, by all means, use them. If you don't, the asterisk trick works wonders.

Hack 84: Command Your Phone with Your Voice

Level . . . . **Easy**

Platform . . . . **Android**

Cost . . . . **Free**

Who hasn't dreamed of verbally telling a computer what to do and having it actually listen — like we're living in the future promised in *2001: A Space Odyssey* (excluding the whole AI-gone-bad aspect)? Unfortunately, for a variety of reasons, that reality never quite materialized on traditional desktop and laptop computers. It's a different story on smart phones however.

Because of their small screens and limited keyboards, several mobile operating systems have some built-in support for simple voice commands such as "Call Grandpa" or "Play Bob Dylan." Google's Android operating system, however, puts the rest to shame with the voice-to-text transcription available via its software keyboard and the Voice Search application, available in the Android Market at `https://market.android.com/details?id=com.google.android.voicesearch`.

This hack explains how to take advantage of these tools to work faster and better on your phone.

TIP **Press and hold the home button for two seconds on an iOS device to activate its limited Voice Control feature. It includes commands for calling people in your address book ("Call Whitson") and controlling music playback ("Pause music"), but it's not nearly as capable as Android's voice command options. (See a full Voice Control cheat sheet at** `http://atmac.org/iphone-voice-commands-cheat-sheet`.**) Additionally, the Google Search app, available in the iTunes App Store (**`http://itunes.apple.com/us/app/google-search/id284815942?mt=8`**), allows you to search Google by voice, but it only works within the Google Search app.**

Use Your Voice to Type Anywhere

Hack 77, "Speed Up Your Touchscreen Typing," discusses finding a software keyboard to match your typing style, but no matter how good you are at typing on your Android keyboard of choice, you'll never type as easily as you speak. Android has a built-in voice-to-text feature enabled in every text input across the entire operating system, no matter what application you use, and most keyboards support it. To use voice-to-text, follow these steps:

1. Tap the Microphone button on your keyboard when you're focused on a text input.

2. Speak what you want to type into your device and wait for Google to analyze the audio and translate it to text. This normally won't take more than a second or two, depending on the length of your message.

Android's voice-to-text feature isn't perfect. It requires a data connection (which shouldn't be a problem most of the time, as long as your phone has a signal), it doesn't do well with names, and if the recording picks up a lot of ambient noise, it may not translate anything usable. However, for dashing off quick messages — or for a quick starting point that you can edit after the voice-to-text translation has done the heavy lifting — it can be a major timesaver.

Search and Command Your Phone

If your Android device didn't come with Voice Search installed, download and install it from `https://market.android.com/details?id=com`
`.google.android.voicesearch`. To activate Voice Search, press and hold your phone's dedicated search button, or if you have the Google Search widget on your homescreen, tap the microphone button next to the Google search box. Google prompts you to Speak Now.

To perform a simple Google search, just say what you're looking for: for example, "Android shortcuts on Lifehacker." Your voice query uploads to Google's servers where it's analyzed. If Google's sure of what you said, it automatically performs your query. If it's not, it prompts you to confirm what you said, as shown in Figure 9-23.

Figure 9-23: Voice Search gives you options
if it's not sure what you said.

Search is a nice start, but Voice Search also enables you to perform advanced actions by saying things such as, "Send text to Gina, let's get coffee and talk about the book." Here's a list of all the commands — called Voice Actions — built into Voice Search:

VOICE ACTION	SAY
Send a text message	"send text to <recipient> <message>" Message is optional. You can start a text this way and continue composing it either from the keyboard or with voice recognition.
Call a contact	"call <contact name> <phone type>" Phone type, like "mobile" or "work," is optional.
Get turn-by-turn directions	"navigate to <address/city/business name>"
View a map	"map of <address/city>"
Write a note	"note to self <message>"
Listen to music	"listen to <artist/song/album>"
Call a business	"call <business name> <location>" Location is optional. In Figure 9-24, all I had to say was "Call Lucifers." Lucifers isn't even in the contacts; my location informs the search.
Send an email	"send email to <contact> <subject> <body>" Subject and body are optional.
Visit a website	"go to <website name>"

Figure 9-24: Voice Search can automatically perform advanced actions, like calling a business by name.

Voice Search may add more Actions to its arsenal over time; you can visit www.google.com/mobile/voice-actions/ to see all the Voice Actions available.

Hack 85: Use Your Camera Phone as a Scanner

Level . . . . **Easy**

Platform . . . . **Android and iOS**

Cost . . . . **Free**

You're looking at a whiteboard full of notes or a paper document you want to copy quickly. Instead of manually transcribing the text, you can "scan" the information using the digital camera built into your cell phone. Mobile application CamScanner turns digital photos that contain text into PDF files for you automatically. Here's how.

Download CamScanner for your device. You can find it in both the Android Market (https://market.android.com/details?id=com.intsig.camscanner) and iTunes App Store (http://itunes.apple.com/us/app/camscanner-free/id388627783). CamScanner is available for free and with a price. As of this writing, the free version on Android limits the number of documents and pages you can scan, whereas the free iOS app is ad-supported. You can upgrade the free app for $5 to remove limitations or ads and to remove the watermarks the free app places on your images.

> **NOTE** CamScanner works virtually the same whether you use Android or iOS, but the screenshots in this hack are from the Android version.

After you install CamScanner, you're ready to start scanning documents. You can create a new scan by either taking a new photo with your camera or by selecting an image already in your phone's photo library.

1. In the lower-left corner, tap the Add Document button with a camera on the icon, as shown in Figure 9-25. (On iOS, tap the Add Document button with the + sign in the bottom-left corner; then choose to Take Photo.)

2. When you scan something with CamScanner, make sure you have ample light and get in close enough on the text so that you have little wasted space in the photo. Tap the Shutter button on your phone to take the picture.

Figure 9-25: Scan a new document by tapping the Add Document button.

3. Now CamScanner automatically scans the image, identifies, and sets up crop marks if it can, as shown in Figure 9-26. During this step, you can rotate the image to the proper orientation by tapping the 90-degree rotation buttons and adjust the crop by dragging the corners of the Crop tool to the corners of your document. Don't worry if the crop looks askew; when you tap the Checkmark button, CamScanner trims a skewed image and enhances the text so that it's easily readable in PDF format. If you like the results, tap the Checkmark button a second time. If not, tap the on-screen Back button and adjust your settings.

4. Continue adding pages to your current document by snapping more pictures, or go back to the CamScanner home screen to create a new document.

Figure 9-26: CamScanner automatically identifies the borders of your scanned documents.

NOTE CamScanner does not perform Optical Character Recognition (OCR) on text documents. The PDF it produces is legible, but it is an image, not text. If OCR is what you're looking for, see Hack 88, "Develop Your (Digital) Photographic Memory."

Working with CamScanner Scans

After you add document images to CamScanner, you can see them all in a list on the CamScanner home screen. Tap a document to open the Document view. From the menu, you can adjust the page orientation, adjust the page size, tag your document (default tags are Books, Clothes, Building, and Food), and edit the document name.

Sharing Scanned PDFs

At this point, you scanned a document and CamScanner has processed it into a nice, readable PDF, but it's still on your phone. You have several ways to export your scanned PDFs from CamScanner to your computer. When you open a document, tap the Share button on the bottom of the screen. From here, you can email the PDF, share it via Bluetooth, or Upload it to Google Docs, Dropbox (see Hack 67, "Access Your Most Important Files Anywhere with Dropbox"), or file sharing website `http://box.net`.

Hack 86: Make Your "Dumbphone" Smarter via Text Message

Level . . . . **Medium**

Platform . . . . **A mobile phone with text messaging**

Cost . . . . **Dependent on your mobile phone plan**

You're out and about town and you need movie times at theaters nearby, a reminder to feed the parking meter in 60 minutes, and the weather forecast. Contrary to popular belief, you don't need a laptop or even a tricked-out smartphone with an Internet connection to complete all these tasks: you can do it directly from any phone that can send text messages.

Here's how it works: You send a text message that contains a short code — such as `w 90210` or `m 11215`, to check the weather or get movie times. Then, you receive a message response back on your mobile phone within a minute. Take a look at how to do this with a few SMS-enabled tools.

Search the Web via Text Message

Web search engine Google offers SMS search results to your cell phone via text message on the spot. All you have to do is text your query to **466453** — which, if you notice on your phone's keypad, are the corresponding numbers for GOOGLE. The following table provides a list of common tasks, the queries to send, and example replies.

TASK	MESSAGE	REPLY
Find a Wi-Fi hotspot	wifi 11215	Local Listings: Tea Lounge 837 Union Street New York
Find a local business	taxi Marietta, OH	Ohio Valley Cab & Delivery 311 Lancaster Street Marietta, 45750-2738 1 (740) 374-8294
	pizza 11215	Local Listings: Two Boots of Brooklyn Inc 514 2nd Street New York

(continued)

(continued)

TASK	MESSAGE	REPLY
Check flight status for Virgin America flight 409	VX409	17 Mar 2011 VX 409 JFK Depart: 11:45 AM On Time Gate: T4 LAX Arrive: 2:50 PM On Time Gate: T3
Sports scores and stock prices	Yankees mlb	Baseball: New York Yankees (95-67) Next game: vs. Detroit Tigers, Mar 31 1:05pm ET
	yhoo	Did you mean 'YAHOO'? Stock: YHOO (Yahoo! Inc.) 16.84 (+0.16/0.96%) Apr 1 4:00pm ET
Dictionary definitions	d philomath	Glossary: * philomath: a lover of learning
Weather	w los feliz	Weather: Los Feliz, Los Angeles, CA 60F, Clear Wind: N 0 mph Hum: 75% Wed: 52F-68F, Mostly Cloudy Thu: 51F-67F, Mostly Cloudy Fri: 48F-66F, Sunny
Movie times	m 90027	Movies: Los Angeles, CA 90027 1 Battle: Los Angeles 2 Rango 3 Red Riding Hood Send 1 to 3 for showtimes, or NEXT for more movies
	source code 92101	Movies: Source Code 1hr 34min Rated PG-13 Suspense/Thriller/Action/ Adventure 3.8/5 Reading Cinemas Gaslamp 15 1:35 2:50 3:50 5:05 6:05 7:20 8:20 9:35
Translations	translate beautiful in italian	Translation: 'beautiful' in English means 'bello' in Italian
Comparison shopping	price battlestar galactica season 1 dvd	Products: * Battlestar Galactica: Season One [5 Discs] [DVD], $4 - $69, Best Buy (91)

TASK	MESSAGE	REPLY
Driving directions	san francisco ca to santa barbara ca	(See text following table.)
Currency conversion	5 usd in euro	5 U.S. dollars = 3.5945363 Euros

Driving directions messages are long and may come in multiple message installments. Here's the reply to the example message:

```
(1/5)Directions: Distance: 381 mi (about 6 hours 26 mins) 12 steps.
1. Head northeast on Market St toward S Van Ness Ave (0.0)
2. Turn right at S Van Ness Ave

(2/5) 3. Merge onto US-101 S via the ramp to I-80 E/Oakland/San
Jose (0.6)
4. Take exit 433 on the left to merge onto I-80 E toward Bay
Bridge/Oakland
```

TIP Add GOOGLE to your phone's address book for quicker message addressing.

Get Help

No one expects you to remember all the search codes listed in the preceding table. Luckily, Google provides a help command that returns a listing of all the possible commands it supports. Text the word `help` to GOOGLE to get a command reference texted back to you. Save the message to your phone so that you can refer to it any time you want to conduct an SMS search.

Test-Drive SMS Search on the Web

Google offers a web-based demonstration of SMS search via phone. Test-drive a text message search at www.google.com/intl/en_us/mobile/sms/search/.

Access Your Google Calendar via Text Message

Not only can Google Calendar text-message you event notifications (as detailed in Hack 33, "Send Reminders to Your Future Self"), but you can also retrieve and add to your Google Calendar by text-messaging the short code GVENT (**48368**). First, register your phone number in Google Calendar. Then use the following text-message commands to view and add events to your calendar:

- Send the word `next` to GVENT to get a notification regarding your next scheduled event.

- Send `day` to get a notification containing all your scheduled events for the present day.

- Send `nday` to get a notification containing all your events for the following day.

- To add an event, send GVENT the details; for example, `Lunch at Josie's 2PM Saturday`.

Get a full rundown of Google Calendar's text message support and setup at `www.google.com/intl/en_us/mobile/sms/calendar/`.

Track Your Gas Mileage with Fuelly

Another useful personal tracking tool with SMS support is webapp Fuelly (`http://www.fuelly.com`), a gas purchase/mileage tracker that calculates your vehicle's MPG. To use Fuelly's SMS interface perform the following:

1. Sign up for a free account at `www.fuelly.com/login/join.gas`, log in, and add a car to your Fuelly profile. Set whether you prefer tracking miles by your odometer reading or trip miles.

2. Visit the Profile page (`www.fuelly.com/add/profile.gas`), add your phone number to your account, and click the Update Profile button.

3. To track you mileage next time you fill up, send a text message to 503-512-9929 in the format `[miles] [price] [gallons]` (think MPG). Miles should be in the format you chose when you added your car. For example, after you fill your tank with gas, from the station you could send this text message to Fuelly:

```
15476 15.34 4.26
```

which means the odometer read 15,476 when you filled up with 15.34 gallons at $4.26/gallon. Back at the Fuelly website, you can generate charts and reports of gas prices and mileage, calculate your fuel economy over time and distance traveled, and compare your mileage to other Fuelly users.

Command Twitter "Bots" via Text Message

Micro-blogging service Twitter (http://twitter.com) enables users to post short status updates and send messages to other Twitter users via SMS (and via the Web and different Twitter clients). What most Twitter users don't know is that you can also send messages to various "bots" that perform different tasks for you, such as send timed reminders or interact with your to-do list. To use any Twitter bot, you need to register for a free account at Twitter and enable your mobile phone number for direct messages from Twitter.

NOTE   You need to have text message notifications turned on in your Twitter settings for this to work. You can do so at https://twitter .com/devices.

Get Instant Reminders from the @timer Twitter Bot

Schedule a "wake-up call," such as a timed text message to remind yourself to feed the parking meter or put the laundry in the dryer. Follow the Twitter user named @timer (http://twitter.com/timer) and direct-message the Twitter timer user reminder details. A Twitter message that reads d timer 45 pay parking meter triggers an SMS back to your cell phone in the specified number of minutes (in this case, 45) with your reminder message.

Manage Your To-Do List with the @rtm Twitter Bot

Additionally, the rtm Twitter bot acts as a middleman between Twitter and the Remember the Milk task manager (described in Hack 35, "Organize Your Life with Remember the Milk"). Follow the @rtm Twitter user (https://twitter.com/rtm), and direct-message it to add, update, and retrieve your Remember the Milk to-do list via SMS commands. Here are some examples:

- Add to-do's to your list with task and optional time, such as:

```
d rtm pick up the milk
d rtm call jimmy at 5pm tomorrow
d rtm return library books in 2 weeks
```

- Get today's to-do list with d rtm !today.
- Retrieve all tasks for a specific context with d rtm !getlist shopping.

Get more details about Remember the Milk's full-featured Twitter bot at www.rememberthemilk.com/services/twitter/.

Log Financial Transactions with the @buxfer Twitter bot

The key to sticking to a budget is writing down exactly what you spend on what. If you use a web-based money manager, such as Buxfer (http://buxfer.com), you can email expenditure details to your account from your phone on the go so that you don't forget you just dropped 18 bucks on toiletries or that your roommate owes you a portion of the rent. Buxfer's email commands get quite detailed; you can use them to add tags, amounts, and people who are in on a given transaction. For example,

```
toiletries 18.00 tags: household acct:chase
```

adds an $18 expenditure from the account named Chase tagged household. If your phone doesn't have email but does have SMS, you can use Buxfer's Twitter bot. Follow buxfer on Twitter and direct-message it like this:

```
d buxfer starbucks 12.00 tags:coffee
```

to add a 12-buck coffee purchase at Starbucks. More details on SMS interaction with Buxfer are available at www.buxfer.com/help.php?topic=Mobile:Twitter.

Hack 87: Connect Your Computer to the Internet via Mobile Phone by "Tethering"

Level . . . . **Medium**

Platform . . . . **Android and jailbroken iOS**

Cost . . . . **Varies**

Your smartphone's greatest strength may be its constant connection to the Internet. Even when you're not in range of a Wi-Fi network, you can still check your email, browse the web, and access any of your online data as long as you're in range of your provider's towers — and, over time, more and more of the globe will be blanketed with those sweet, sweet wireless signals.

That said, some things are just better done on a larger screen with a mouse and keyboard. This hack explains how to use your cell phone's Internet connection to enable Internet on your computer. The process, often called "tethering," enables you to use the data connection you're already paying for from the comfort of your laptop.

WARNING Some carriers charge an extra monthly fee for the convenience of tethering. The tethering method described here assumes that you're willing to take the risk that your carrier could cut off your data plan or charge you for "unofficial" tethering. Proceed at your own risk!

What You Need

To start using your phone's Internet connection from your computer, you'll need:

- **A data plan:** If you have Internet access on your phone, you're already paying some kind of monthly fee for a data plan.
- **A USB cable:** The syncing or charging cable that came with your phone should work.
- **PdaNet for your phone:** The app is available for Android, iPhone, and BlackBerry devices, with details at www.junefabrics.com/. (This hack only covers Android and iPhone.) PdaNet is available as a free trial; the full version currently costs $15.95.

WARNING iPhone users need to jailbreak their device to install PdaNet through the Cydia store. Jailbreaking is a non-Apple supported way to install third-party applications on your iPhone that aren't available through the App Store. The jailbreaking process changes with nearly every new iOS update. To get step-by-step instructions on the most current method, check Lifehacker's definitive jailbreaking guide at http://lifehacker .com/5771943.

- **PdaNet for your desktop:** The PdaNet desktop client, available for Windows and Mac, should be installed and running on the computer you want to tether your connection with. Download it from www.junefabrics.com/android/download.php for Android and www.junefabrics.com/desktop for iPhone.

How to Tether

After you install all the necessary software, you can tether.

1. Launch PdaNet on your device.
2. On Android, click the Enable USB Tether button (shown in Figure 9-27); on an iPhone, turn USB Tether to ON.

3. Connect your phone to your computer using your USB cable.

4. Click the PdaNet icon (it's in the system tray on Windows, as shown in Figure 9-28, and in the menu bar on Mac OS X); click Connect.

Figure 9-27: Turn on PdaNet with Android.

Figure 9-28: Connect your computer to your phone's data connection with the PdaNet desktop client.

That's all there is to it. PdaNet can set up a connection between your computer and your phone, and you can now browse the Internet using your phone's data connection.

NOTE The most recent version of PdaNet for iPhone is also capable of turning your phone into a Wi-Fi hotspot. To use it, launch PdaNet, turn on the Wi-Fi HotSpot switch, and connect your laptop to your iPhone as you would any Wi-Fi hotspot. It's more convenient, but slightly less reliable than the wired USB connection, and because tethering can quickly drain your iPhone's battery, you need to plug it in anyway.

Hack 88: Develop Your (Digital) Photographic Memory

Level.......**Easy**

Platform....**Web-enabled camera phone**

Cost........**Free for Evernote limited account, $45/year premium subscription**

The miniscule size and large memory capacity of modern digital cameras and camera phones can turn anyone into a constant, impromptu photographer. Documenting your world and the information in it has never been easier and faster than it is now. A ubiquitous capture device can change the way you remember (and forget) things for good. With a photo-capture service such as Evernote (www.evernote.com), you can capture and file your digital photographic memory in the Internet cloud from wherever you are and sync those photos between your desktop, your phone, and the web.

Evernote performs Optical Character Recognition (OCR) on images with text, so in addition to other handy organizational features such as tagging, Evernote's OCR functionality also makes the text *within* the photo searchable, as shown in Figure 9-29. Evernote also uses your phone's geolocation data, so it can map out anywhere you've taken a photo.

NOTE For more on Evernote, see Hack 37, "Set Up a Ubiquitous Note-Taking Inbox Across Devices," which explains how to use Evernote as a universal capture device to organize notes, images, web pages, and other media.

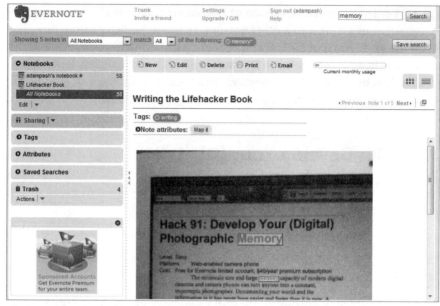

Figure 9-29: Search for text inside images with Evernote.

Upload Photos to Evernote from Your Camera Phone

You can add photos to Evernote via email, through Evernote's desktop clients, and using Evernote's web-based interface, but this hack focuses on using Evernote's mobile applications, available for Android, iOS, BlackBerry, webOS, and Windows Phone 7.

1. Register for an Evernote account at www.evernote.com and download the app from your phone's app market.

2. Launch Evernote on your smartphone and create a new note with a snapshot. Point it at what you want to remember and take your picture. Evernote creates a new note with your photo. You can now assign tags, a title, or a description to your photo. (You can even add more photos to the note if you'd like.)

3. When you're done, tap the Save button; Evernote automatically uploads your photo from your phone to the website, and syncs it with any other devices on which you use the Evernote application.

Create a Photo Reference Database with Evernote

Having mastered on-the-fly snapping and tagging, check out some more creative uses for a personal photo database made with your camera phone on the go:

- **Business cards.** Instead of letting that stack of business cards you collected at the conference gather dust in your desk drawer, snap a picture of each and upload them all to Evernote with tags (people's names and conference name) and descriptions of who they were, where and when you met, and whether you want to follow up about something.

TIP Alternatively, Google's visual search tool Google Goggles, detailed in Hack 82, "Augment Reality with Your Phone," can translate a picture of a business card into contact information for your phone.

- **Photo recipe box.** Eat something at a restaurant or a friend's house you'd like to try to make at home? Take a picture, add some details about the ingredients, and tag it `cooking`. Keep track of all your favorite meals with snapshots that make answering "What should we have for dinner tonight?" as simple as browsing your `meals` tag. You can even tag ingredients such as `chicken`, `vegan`, or `spicy` so that you have some ideas when your vegan brother-in-law comes over for dinner.

- **Wish list.** When you're out and about shopping, take a photo of the items you want to get or to price-compare. Possible tags include `wishlist` and `to research`.

- **Wine labels.** When your sweetheart remarks how much she loves the bottle of wine you got out at dinner, snap a photo of the label so that you can surprise her with a bottle at home. Start your personal wine database with photographs of labels to keep track of what you liked and didn't like.

- **Text or URLs.** You know the signs at a famous landmark that describe its history? Or the website address on the billboard you'll never remember? Take a pic and send to Evernote tagged `reference` or `to visit`.

- **Store hours of places you frequent.** Next time you're at the local post office or bank, snap a photo of the business hours so that you've got a quick reference for what's open when.

- **Home inventory.** A fantastic way to keep track of your home inventory is to snap pictures of serial numbers and include prices of your valuables. They'll come in handy in case your laptop gets swiped or there's a fire or flood in your home.

Hack 89: Send and Receive Money on Your Mobile Phone with PayPal

Level . . . . **Easy**

Platform . . . . **Smart phone or mobile phone with text messaging**

Cost . . . . **Free**

The popular online payment service PayPal (http://paypal.com) offers a quick and easy way to send money to friends and co-workers — to cover your share of the dinner bill, pitch in on a shared gift, or send a payment for work done. PayPal's smartphone apps and SMS service enables you to send and receive money directly from your cell phone when you're out and about.

Mobile-to-mobile payments can come in handy in lieu of cold, hard cash when purchasing something from someone you don't know (say, from Craigslist, http://craigslist.org) or when you can't find an ATM and your buddy's covering you. This hack explains how to initiate cash transactions via PayPal on your cell phone.

PayPal Mobile

You need a free PayPal account to start. To add money to your PayPal account, link your checking account or credit card to it. To enable cell phone payments, you can either:

- Download the PayPal app for Android, iOS, or BlackBerry (http://tinyurl.com/2g8fd47) and login to your account. The native apps are the easiest way to interact with PayPal on the go.

- Send money from any phone using text messages by activating your mobile phone number within your PayPal account.

Send Money Using the PayPal Mobile App

To send a friend $20 for covering your movie tickets, follow these steps:

1. Launch the app and select your friend from your phone's contacts or enter her phone number or email address. Then enter the amount and review your transaction, as shown in Figure 9-30.

2. You can optionally enter a note (such as, "Had a great time!"), and then tap Send.

3. Your friend then receives a notification from PayPal about the payment, either via text message or email.

Figure 9-30: Send money to anyone with a phone number or email address.

Alternatively, if you and your friend both have PayPal Mobile installed on your phones and you're still together, you can both exchange money using the following method:

1. Launch PayPal on both phones and tap the Tools button on the bottom right of the screen.

2. Select the option to Bump Phones.

3. Then, as the name implies, fist-bump your phones together. Using your location, PayPal connects your account with your friend's (shown in Figure 9-31) and allows you to send or request money without typing out email addresses or phone numbers. (As of this writing, Bump works on Android and iOS.)

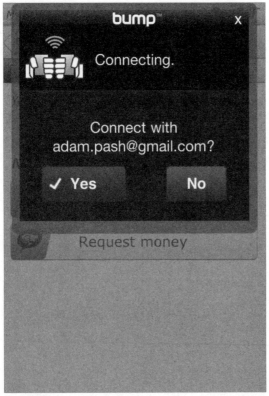

Figure 9-31: Bump two phones running PayPal together to send money between the owners.

TIP The Tools menu in PayPal Mobile has a few handy tricks up its sleeve, including a Split Bill tool that helps you calculate the tip and what each person owes, integrating it all with the mobile payment system.

Send Money via Text Message

You don't need a smartphone to send money via PayPal. You can do so via text message by following these steps.

1. Associate your cell phone with PayPal by entering your cell phone number on the PayPal website in the mobile area (www.paypal.com/ us/cgi-bin/?cmd=_mobile-activate-outside) and set up a mobile PIN (separate from your PayPal password). PayPal calls your phone on the spot and asks you to verify the PIN. When the PIN is matched, your phone is PayPal-enabled.

2. To send someone else's phone $5.50, text-message PAYPAL (or 729725) the following message:

   ```
   send 5.50 to 7185551212
   ```

   with the recipient's phone number in this example being (718) 555-1212.

3. The recipient's phone receives a text message with instructions for picking up the money. In short, the recipient has to go to the website and link her mobile phone number to her PayPal account to claim the payment.

The following table provides examples of all the PayPal Mobile SMS commands.

COMMAND	DESCRIPTION
send 10.99 to 2125551981	Send $10.99 to (212) 555-1981 phone number.
send 5 to name@example.com	Send $5.00 to name@example.com.
s 10.99 t 2125551981	Use the shortcuts s and t for send and to.
s 10.99 t 4150001234 note thx 4 dinn	Add a *thx 4 dinn* note with your payment.
send 5.43 EUR to 3105551212	Send your payment in Euros (CAD for Canadian dollars, GBP for British pounds, AUD for Australian dollars, or JPY for Yen also work).
send 10.99 to 4150001234 share address	Share your address with the recipient to have him ship you an item.

(continued)

(continued)

COMMAND	DESCRIPTION
`send 10.99 to 3105551212 share phone`	Share your phone number with the recipient.
`send 5 to 2125551981 share info note send asap`	Share your phone and address and send a note *send asap* to recipient.
`Bal`	Check your current PayPal balance.
`Cancel`	Cancel a pending payment.

NOTE PayPal takes a standard cut of 2.9% from each payment transaction. For a slightly cheaper, simpler option, you can order a *Square*, a free credit card reader that connects directly to your iPhone, iPad, or Android device. Just sign up at `https://squareup.com` and link it with your bank account. Square ships you a device for free, and takes a smaller 2.75% out of each transaction. Next time you're out to dinner with a group and no one has cash, put the check on your card. Connect your Square to your smartphone, and physically swipe your friends' cards. You'll get the money and the credit card reward points!

Master the Web

Never before have humans been able to instantly access such a vast repository of information in their households as we do today with the World Wide Web. That storehouse of information (and misinformation) grows by leaps and bounds every day. With the proliferation of publishing tools such as blogs, Facebook, and Twitter, as well as capture devices such as smartphones and digital cameras, anyone can publish online, and millions do.

But that kind of information access is useless unless you can hone your searching, filtering, and researching skills. Mastering your web browser, quickly navigating engines and indices, and judging the quality and authority of sources are all skills everyone who uses the Web to their advantage needs. In effect, on the Web, you are your own personal research librarian.

Memorizing facts is less important than the capability to look them up quickly. The Web acts as the outboard memory of millions of people that you both depend on to have the information you need and contribute to when you have information to share. But how do you fashion a query that quickly and accurately extracts those facts from the endless virtual shelves of information, and how do you produce information that successfully answers one?

This chapter's hacks provide tips, tricks, and shortcuts for searching and navigating the Web, customizing your web browser for an optimal experience, and sharing and publishing information about yourself and your area of expertise most effectively.

TIP Read this chapter near a computer with Internet access because it's full of website URLs and services you'll want to try right away.

Hack 90: Google Like a Pro

Level . . . . **Easy**

Platform . . . . **Web**

Cost . . . . **Free**

When you search the Web using Google (`http://google.com`), you're likely to get tens of thousands of web page results that contain your search terms. But who has time to go through them all? Instead, make the engine narrow down its answers for you. Google's single, one-line input box conceals a host of functionality that can decrease web search results down to the most relevant pages. Clicking through thousands of links is time-consuming and unnecessary. Get fewer, more relevant search results with Google's advanced search operators.

You have two ways to issue queries with Google's advanced methods:

∎ Use the Advanced Search form by clicking the small, blue Advanced Search link on the right of the Google search box.

∎ Use Google's advanced search operators inside the single Google search box.

A page full of input boxes (the Advanced Search form) is the easier way to use Google's advanced operators, but it isn't the most efficient. The slightly more complicated but more efficient way to search Google is with Google's operators, which usually appear in the form `operator:criteria`, and special characters, such as quotation marks, plus and minus signs, and the tilde (~). These advanced techniques enable you to easily fine-tune your query from the single search box.

This hack covers only a few of the most useful Google search query formats; refer to Google's Help Center (`http://google.com/intl/en/help/basics.html`) for a Search Guide that details all the options.

Exact Phrase with Quotations

To find web pages that contain an exact phrase, enclose the phrase in quotation marks. This functionality comes in handy when you want to see only the pages that contain a specific sequence of words — especially common words.

For example, searching for `the course has been set` may return any number of odd results. The words are all quite common.

A search for `"the course has been set"` returns pages containing that exact phrase. Adding a second phrase, for example:

```
"the course has been set" "summon your courage"
```

can zero in on exactly the result you're looking for — in this case, that swashbuckling box office disaster *Cutthroat Island*.

The following are some other examples of effective searching by phrase:

- Computer error messages:

    ```
    "cannot delete file"
    "filename too long"
    ```

- Quotes:

    ```
    "I cannot tell a lie"
    ```

- Song lyrics:

    ```
    "in a pear tree"
    ```

- Names:

    ```
    "John Smith, PhD"
    "Anne Rice"
    ```

Include and Exclude Words Using + and −

Force your search results to contain or omit words using + and − signs. This is especially useful for getting more specific about context. The following are two examples:

- Search for information on the Java programming language:

    ```
    java -coffee
    ```

- Find pages that contain the words *computer* and *virus*:

    ```
    computer + virus
    ```

By default, Google disregards common words from queries such as *I*, *the*, *where*, *how*, and other words, letters, or numbers that don't generally improve the accuracy of results. If you want to ensure that a common word is included in your query, use the + operator like so:

```
Star Wars Episode +I
```

Search Within a Site

If the website you're on doesn't have a built-in search feature or have one that works well, Google can search the contents of a single site with the `site:example.com` operator. Specify an entire domain name or just the suffix. Consider these examples:

- Search the Microsoft website for information on Windows security:

  ```
  site:microsoft.com windows security
  ```

- Search the Lifehacker website for keyboard shortcuts:

  ```
  site:lifehacker.com keyboard shortcuts
  ```

- Search only Irish websites that mention the BBC:

  ```
  site:ir BBC
  ```

- Search only government websites for tax forms:

  ```
  site:gov tax forms
  ```

Search Certain Types of Files

Google doesn't just search web pages; it also indexes PDF files, Microsoft Office documents, and other file types. To search for a specific file type, use the `filetype:ext operator`. Here are a couple of examples:

- Find Excel-based budget templates:

  ```
  filetype:xls checkbook
  ```

- Find PDF search-engine cheat sheets:

  ```
  filetype:pdf search cheat sheet
  ```

Calculations

Google search can also perform mathematical equations, currency conversions, and more. The following are some examples:

▪ Find out how many teaspoons are in a quarter cup:

```
quarter cup in teaspoons
```

▪ Multiply 16,758 with 921:

```
16,758 * 921
```

▪ See how many seconds there are in a year:

```
seconds in a year
```

▪ Convert dollars to yen:

```
$5 in yen
```

▪ Not sure of the international currency? This also works:

```
25 Australian money in Italian money
```

▪ Compare gas prices by doing a double currency and measurement conversion:

```
$2.85 per gallon in British money per liter
```

▪ Convert kb to gigabytes:

```
13233434 kb in gigabytes
```

Synonyms

Search for synonyms using the tilde (~) next to keywords. This comes in handy when you search for a concept rather than for a specific word or sequence. Here are a few examples:

▪ "~nutrition ~information muffins" returns exact matches for those words and matches on pages that contain muffins' food facts and muffins' vitamin information.

▪ ~car turns up information on trucks and vehicles.

▪ ~pen yields pencils, graphite, and sketch.

Combine Criteria and Operators

You can combine all the preceding techniques into one query, as in these examples:

- Search for information about privacy and Google that appears on sites not including google.com:

  ```
  google + privacy -site:google.com
  ```

- View any contributions by a specific person on a site:

  ```
  site:digitaljournalist.org "P.F. Bentley"
  ```

- Find pages with the title of a film and the words *movie* and *review*:

  ```
  "Tron" + review + movie
  ```

- Find pages with the word *lifehacker* in them that are not on lifehacker.com:

  ```
  lifehacker -site.lifehacker.com
  ```

- Find Creative Commons–licensed Excel spreadsheets on Lifehacker.com (see Hack 96, "Find Reusable Media Online," for more information about Creative Commons):

  ```
  site:lifehacker.com filetype:xls "Creative Commons"
  ```

- Get pages that display directory listings of .wma or .mp3 music files by the Kleptones:[1]

  ```
  -inurl:(htm|html|php) intitle:"index of" + "last modified" +
  "parent directory"
  + description + size + (wma|mp3) "Girl Talk"
  ```

TIP Print the Google Search Cheat Sheet, available at http://google .com/intl/en/help/cheatsheet.html and place it near your desk to help you incorporate advanced search techniques into your everyday web searching. A complete list of Google's Advanced Search operators is available at http://googleguide.com/advanced_operators.html.

Hack 91: Subscribe to Websites with RSS

Level....... **Medium**

Platform.... **All**

Cost........ **Free**

Information from websites such as newspaper sites or weblogs updates frequently throughout the day, week, or month. You could waste time visiting each site you like, looking for new content, much as you'd go to the newsstand to check for the newest issue of your favorite magazine. But checking all the sites you like every day is tedious and unnecessary. As with a magazine subscription that automatically brings each new issue to your door, you can subscribe to website feeds that push information to your online door.

Website feeds are special XML files that contain all the latest updates to a website or to a section of it. Place the address of any number of these feeds into feedreader software (also called a newsreader or news aggregator) and you can see, all in one place, when new items have appeared on your favorite sites.

This hack explains how to subscribe to feeds and lists the different types of information they can provide you.

How to Subscribe to Website Feeds

To start building your website subscription list, you first need a *feedreader*, either in the form of desktop software or a web-based application. A feedreader lists the newest content available on the sites you choose all in one place. This hack uses Google Reader (`http://google.com/reader`) — an excellent, web-based feedreader. (See the following "Other Popular Feedreaders" section for more options.)

If you use Gmail or Google Calendar, your existing Google account information works for Google Reader. If not, you'll have to sign up for a Google account. After you sign into Google Reader (or set up your desktop or other web-based feedreader), you're ready to build your subscription list.

To subscribe to *The New York Times* Sunday Book Review, for example, go to `http://nytimes.com` and click the RSS link (in the page footer). Doing so opens an entire page listing all the available feeds, as shown in Figure 10-1. You can also go directly to that RSS feeds page at `www.nytimes.com/services/xml/rss/index.html`.

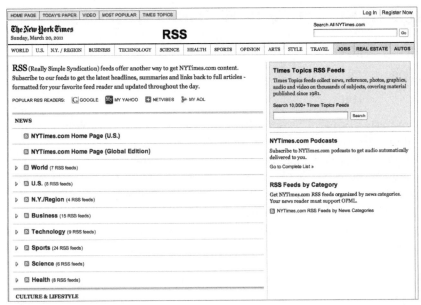

Figure 10-1: *The New York Times* feeds.

You can also subscribe to one specific part of the website.

1. To subscribe to the Book Review, expand the Arts section, and then right-click the Sunday Book Review link.

2. Select Copy Link Address/Location. If you click the feed link as if it were a regular web page, you can view either the raw XML or your browser's default style for RSS feeds; these feeds are meant to be read by a news aggregator, not a human, so these pages aren't that useful on their own.

3. After you copy the feed location to your Clipboard, switch to Google Reader or your desktop feedreader. Go to the area to add a new feed (in Google Reader, click the Add a Subscription link), paste the feed URL into the input box, and then click the Add button.

From there, you can place your subscription into a folder if you'd like. Repeat the process for any other feeds you're interested in. Many websites display the orange RSS icon somewhere on the page.

NOTE In favor of minimalism, Google Chrome and Firefox 4 don't include an RSS icon in the address bar. Google's RSS Subscription Extension brings this functionality back to Chrome (http://tinyurl.com/yjbshqs), and the RSS Icon extension brings this button back to Firefox (https://addons.mozilla.org/en-us/firefox/addon/rss-icon/).

After you subscribe to one or more websites, Google Reader's left panel lists the number of unread items in each site subscription displayed next to its title (see Figure 10-2), much like your email inbox displays unread messages.

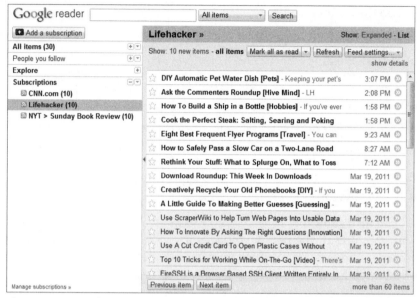

Figure 10-2: Tracking three website feeds on one page using Google Reader.

Click a subscription to display the latest content from that feed in the right panel. Now you can stay abreast of new information from hundreds of websites — an impossible feat if you had to visit each one individually.

Other Popular Feedreaders

If you already use a portal such as My Yahoo!, My AOL, or iGoogle to read news, you don't have to set up a separate feedreader. They all can display website feed updates as well.

The following are some of the more popular desktop feedreaders:

- **NetNewsWire:** (Mac OS X only; free) `http://netnewswireapp.com`
- **Mozilla Thunderbird:** (Mac/Windows/Linux; free) `http://mozilla .org/products/thunderbird`
- **Microsoft Outlook:** (Windows/Mac; $149.99 — with Microsoft Office) `http://office.microsoft.com/en-us/outlook;` `www.microsoft .com/mac/buy`
- **FeedDemon:** (Windows only; free) `www.feeddemon.com`

Search and Track Dynamic Information with Feeds

Website feeds don't just contain headlines from news and blogs. Some feeds can track ever-changing information such as weather, library books, your Netflix queue, and more. Some dynamic feeds you may want to subscribe to include the following:

- Weather: www.accuweather.com/rss-center.asp
- Craigslist listings: http://craigslist.org
- Library book availability: http://libraryelf.com
- Sports and news: http://sports.espn.go.com/espn/rss/index
- Deals: http://slickdeals.net
- Horoscopes: www.astrosage.com/rssfeeds/feed.asp
- Vehicle traffic updates: www.traffic.com
- News keyword searches: http://news.google.com

You can also subscribe to feeds for search-term results — for example, you can monitor all the new web pages in Google search results where your name, company, or product appears. For more, see Hack 65, "Make Google Search Results Automatically Come to You."

Hack 92: Quickly Search Within Specific Websites from the Address Bar

Level....... **Medium**

Platform.... **Web (Firefox/Chrome)**

Cost........ **Free**

Most web browsers have a built-in search box next to or integrated with the address bar for quick access to search engines. By default, this search box is a front door to major engines like Google or Bing. However, sometimes you know what site you want to search within, like Wikipedia or Amazon, but you want to skip the part where you go to Google or Bing results first, and instead just search the site directly using your browser's built-in search feature. Keyword searches are customizable, keyword-based searches that let you do just that: execute a search from your Firefox or Chrome address bar. Using these special searches significantly speeds up queries on your nondefault searches at sites such as IMDB.com or YouTube.

Keyword searches work like this:

1. Enter a short keyword in the address bar that indicates what site you want to search.

2. Press the spacebar.

3. Type your search query.

For example, if you want to search Wikipedia to read up on *Firefly*, type `w firefly` into your browser's address bar and press Enter. If you set up a keyword search that associated 'w' with Wikipedia, your browser automatically looks up 'firefly' using Wikipedia's search engine.

You can set up the same quick-access searches for your favorite online dictionary, thesaurus, image search, encyclopedia, productivity website, and so on. It may not sound like a lot, but if you regularly search sites like Urban Dictionary.com or Yelp in addition to, say, Google, keyword searches can save you considerable time. Here's how to set up and use keyword searches in Firefox and Chrome.

In Firefox

To create a keyword search for Wikipedia using Firefox:

1. Browse to Wikipedia (`www.wikipedia.org`).

2. Right-click Wikipedia's search box, and select Add a Keyword for this Search, as shown in Figure 10-3.

3. Enter a keyword for this search — something short but memorable, like **w** for Wikipedia, as shown in Figure 10-4. Click Save.

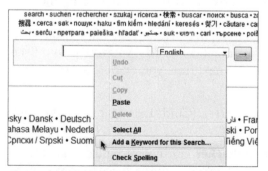

Figure 10-3: Right-click in the search box and select Add A Keyword for this Search.

Figure 10-4: Assign a title and, most important, a keyword to your Quick Search.

Now that you set it up, use it to search Wikipedia for the term Lifehacker:

1. From any page, press Ctrl+L (Cmd+L on Mac) to move your cursor to the address bar, or just do it manually.

2. Type **w lifehacker** into the address bar.

3. Press Enter.

Firefox searches Wikipedia as though you navigated to the Wikipedia home page and entered **lifehacker** directly in Wikipedia's search box — you just cut out the middleman.

You can use the same technique to add any number of quick keyword searches to Firefox.

In Chrome

Chrome's address bar doubles as a search input so there is no separate box; it has built-in search engines for Google, Yahoo!, and Bing, and you can set any of those as your default search engine. But Chrome also has a clever trick up its sleeve: When you visit websites that contain search boxes, Chrome can automatically detect and save new search engines, and then create keyword shortcuts for quickly searching these sites in a few keystrokes.

For example, if you open `http://amazon.com` in Chrome, it detects Amazon's search box and automatically adds Amazon to your list of available search engines. Now, the next time you want to search Amazon, try this out:

1. From any page, press Ctrl+L (Cmd+L on Mac) to move your cursor to the address bar.

2. Type **amazon.com lifehacker**. Chrome recognizes "amazon.com" as a keyword search and, after you enter a space followed by a term, it displays the option to "Search amazon.com," as shown in Figure 10-5 to indicate that you're performing a keyword search.

3. Press Enter. Chrome searches Amazon for this book, and you didn't need to navigate to Amazon first or remember any arcane shortcuts. By default the keyword for new search engines is the site's domain — in this case, Amazon.com.

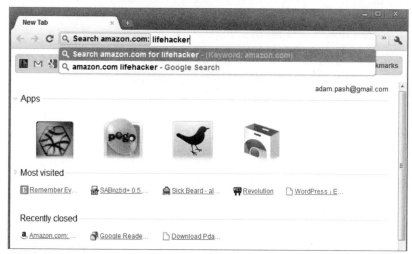

Figure 10-5: Amazon.com keyword search in Chrome.

TIP To see all the search engines Chrome added, click the Wrench button, select Preferences, and then click the Manage Search Engines button.

If you press Ctrl+L and type only **am**, Chrome can guess that you're going to type **amazon.com** and autocompletes the rest of the text for you. You could then visit the site by pressing Enter, but if you want to execute the keyword search for that site, you can press Tab, enter your query, and then press Enter.

NOTE If you prefer to set up even shorter keyword shortcuts in Chrome (like with Firefox), click the Wrench button, select Preferences, and then click Manage Search Engines. From this dialog you can click any of your search engines and change the keyword to something shorter — like "a" instead of "amazon.com." You can also add new search engines from this dialog.

Now you can go through and assign keywords to each search engine you use on a regular basis, or you can download the Lifehacker Bookmark set discussed in the next section.

Download the Bookmark Set

A list of popular keyword searches is available for download on Lifehacker. com for quick installation on Firefox. (As of this writing Chrome doesn't enable you to import keyword searches.) The file includes fifteen popular keywords.

Here's how to install them:

1. Using Firefox, go to the Quick Search bookmarks file at `http://lifehackerbook.com/ch9/quicksearch.html`.

2. Choose File ⇨ Save As and save the file somewhere on your computer.

3. Choose Bookmarks ⇨ Show All Bookmarks.

4. From the Bookmarks Manager, click the Import and Backup button and choose Import HTML, as shown in Figure 10-6. Select From an HTML file, and then browse to and open the `quicksearch.html` file you just saved.

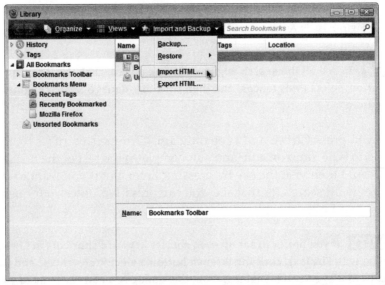

Figure 10-6: Import the Quick Search bookmarks from Firefox's Bookmarks Library.

Now you have a `Lifehacker Quick Searches` folder in your Bookmarks, which includes all sorts of keyword searches, described in the following section.

Lifehacker Quick Searches

What follows is the full list of Quick Searches included in the Lifehacker file:

QUICK SEARCH	TYPE THIS	DESCRIPTION
Acronym Finder	`acronym <acronym>`	Finds an acronym for your word
Amazon.com	`amazon <product name>`	Looks up an item on Amazon.com
Dictionary.com	`dict <word>`	Finds the definition of your word
EBay	`ebay <item>`	Finds the item you want on eBay
Flickr	`flickr <search term>`	Finds all the tags, titles, and descriptions of images at Flickr that match your search term
Google Maps	`map <address>`	Produces a Google map of a street address or location
Google Images	`image <search term>`	Finds images that fit your search term
Lifehacker	`lh <search term>`	Searches the Lifehacker site for information
Thesaurus	`thes <word>`	Finds synonyms for your word
Twitter	`twitter <search term>`	Finds recent tweets which contain your search terms
Urban Dictionary	`slang <expression>`	Defines your slang expression
Wikipedia	`wp <person|place|thing>`	Looks up your search item in the collaboratively- edited encyclopedia Wikipedia
Yahoo! Creative Commons	`cc <word>`	Finds Creative Commons–licensed items available for reuse

(continued)

(continued)

QUICK SEARCH	TYPE THIS	DESCRIPTION
Yelp	`yelp <business>`	Finds a local business listing
YouTube	`youtube <search term>`	Looks for videos posted to YouTube that fit your search

Customize your Quick Searches using the Bookmarks manager (choose Bookmarks ⇨ Organize Bookmarks). Browse to the `Lifehacker Quick Searches` subfolder and click any bookmark to change a keyword shortcut or edit a URL.

Hack 93: Extend Your Web Browser

Level . . . . **Medium**

Platform . . . . **All (Firefox/Chrome)**

Cost . . . . **Free**

The best feature of web browsers such as Firefox and Chrome is their openness: these browsers are built so that anyone can write a feature-adding extension for it. As a result, developers all over the world have made thousands of plugins available to enhance and streamline the way you use your browser.

Several of these Hacks exemplify how browser add-ons can extend the functionality of your browser, including Hack 15, "Securely Track Your Passwords," Hack 39, "Limit Visits to Time-Wasting Websites," Hack 56, "Bypass Free Site Registration with BugMeNot," and Hack 118, "Keep Your Web Browser in Sync Across Computers." This hack discusses in more detail how to find and install some of the best feature-enhancing browser add-ons with Mozilla Firefox and Google Chrome: two free, modern browsers that work on all operating systems with impressive extension support.

How to Install a Firefox Extension

In this example you install the excellent Web of Trust Firefox extension, which helps you identify websites you can trust and sites you shouldn't. Here's what to do:

1. Using Firefox, click the Add to Firefox button on the Web of Trust extension home page at `https://addons.mozilla.org/en-US/firefox/addon/wot-safe-browsing-tool`, and then from the dialog box, click the Install button.

2. Firefox downloads and installs the extension and then prompts you to restart. Click Restart Firefox to complete the installation and enable the new extension.

3. When Firefox starts up again, Web of Trust prompts you to accept its terms of service and then to select your protection setting (Basic, Light, or Parental Control). You'll also notice a new button in your toolbar that displays as red, yellow, or green, depending on the trustworthiness of the site you visit. (Green is good; red is bad.) Click it to display details for that site's trust rating.

NOTE If you're installing an extension from anywhere except Firefox's official add-ons site, Firefox may display a message across the top of the page that reads, Firefox Prevented This Site from Asking You to Install Software on Your Computer. To install extensions hosted on non-official Mozilla sites, click the Allow button for the site address. Keep in mind, however, that Firefox extensions from unverified sites can include malware, so only allow extension installation when you trust the publisher. Mozilla Add-ons verifies and tests all the extensions it hosts before publishing them.

Not all extensions work the same way. When your new extension is installed, it may not be obvious what it does or how it works. If you don't see changes to Firefox's buttons, toolbars, or menus, follow these steps:

1. Choose Tools ⇨ Add-ons to open Firefox's Add-ons Manager dialog, as shown in Figure 10-7.

2. From your list of installed extensions, you can right-click one and choose Visit Homepage to read the extension's instructions and, often, view screenshots of it in action. The Preferences menu item usually enables you to configure the extension as well.

NOTE As with all good software, Firefox is a work in progress, so new versions of it are regularly released, which means extensions have to keep up. At the time of this writing, Firefox 4.0 is the latest release. If you upgrade Firefox soon after the new release comes out, chances are that some of your extensions will be disabled because they haven't yet been updated for the new version. Go to the Add-ons Manager (choose Firefox ⇨ Add-ons) to update your extension versions (click the Cog button and then select Check for Updates).

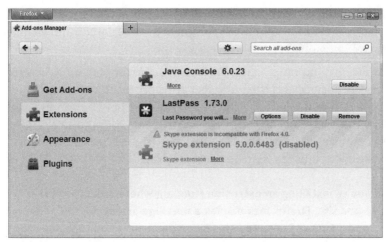

Figure 10-7: Change an extension's preferences and learn more about your installed extensions in the Extensions section of the Add-ons dialog.

How to Install a Chrome Extension

In this example you install the BugMeNot Chrome extension, which enables you to bypass compulsory website registration at free-to-use sites, as discussed in Hack 56, "Bypass Free Site Registration with BugMeNot." Here's what to do:

1. Using Chrome, click the Install button on the BugMeNot extension home page at http://tinyurl.com/28q7val, and then from the dialog box, click Install.

2. Chrome downloads and installs the extension. Unlike Firefox, Chrome doesn't require you to restart the browser to complete the installation.

3. When installed, BugMeNot adds a button to Chrome's address bar that, when clicked, enables BugMeNot to auto-log into a site you're visiting, so you can avoid creating a new account if you're not interested in doing so.

NOTE If you install an extension from anywhere except Google's official add-ons site, Chrome may display a message across the bottom of your browser that reads, Extensions, Apps, and Themes Can Harm Your Computer. Are You Sure You Want to Continue? To install extensions hosted on nonofficial sites, click the Continue button. Keep in mind, however, that extensions from unverified sites can include malware, so only allow extension installation when you trust the publisher.

One Chrome extension works differently from another and if you're not sure what a new extension does or how it works, follow these steps:

1. Click the Wrench menu; then choose Tools ➪ Extensions to open Chrome's Extensions dialog. (You can also type `chrome://extensions` into Chrome's address bar.)

2. From your list of installed extensions, click an extension title to open its home page, read more about it, and view screenshots of it in action. If the extension has configurable options, click the Options link to open its Options dialog. If your extension installs in Chrome's toolbar, you can also access these options by right-clicking its button, as shown in Figure 10-8.

Figure 10-8: Access and change an extension's options.

Recommended Firefox and Chrome Extensions

New versions of Chrome and Firefox are released often, so the types and availability of extensions for the version you run may vary. That said, the following table describes some examples of browser-enhancing extensions (for both Firefox and Chrome, when possible).

EXTENSION	DESCRIPTION
Adblock Plus (Firefox and Chrome): `http://adblockplus.org/en`	Block banner advertisements from all or certain websites with Adblock.
Tab Mix Plus (Firefox): `https://addons.mozilla.org/firefox/1122`	Enhance Firefox's tab behavior with an unread tab style and a Close button on each individual tab.

(continued)

(continued)

EXTENSION	DESCRIPTION

BugMeNot (Firefox and Chrome):
`https://addons.mozilla.org/`
`en-US/firefox/addon/6349` and
`http://tinyurl.com/28q7val`
	Route around free website registration and sign-ins with this community database of auto-filled usernames and passwords. (See Hack 56, "Bypass Free Site Registration with BugMeNot.")

DownThemAll! (Firefox): `http://downthemall.net`	Easily download all the files linked to a web page, pause and resume large file downloads, and increase speed and download performance. (See the following hack, "Supercharge Your Firefox Downloads with DownThemAll!")

URL Shorteners:
Cutyfox (Firefox):
`https://addons.mozilla.org/`
`en-US/firefox/addon/cutyfox-url-`
`shortener-googl-is`
goo.gl URL Shortener (Chrome):
`http://tinyurl.com/ybbhl6f`
	Convert long website addresses into short, more email-friendly URLs. (See Hack 3, "Craft Effective Messages.")

Auto Copy (Firefox and Chrome):
`https://addons.mozilla.org/`
`en-US/firefox/addon/autocopy` and
`http://tinyurl.com/3eb7hge`
	Bypass Ctrl+C and just select text on a web page to automatically add it to the Clipboard. (Great for researchers, bloggers, and writers who quote web pages often.)

Greasemonkey (Firefox):
`https://addons.mozilla`
`.org/en-US/firefox/`
`addon/greasemonkey`
	Customize web pages to your liking with JavaScript that can change the look and functionality of websites. Note: Chrome natively supports user scripts — no extension necessary.

Xmarks (Firefox and Chrome):
`http://download.xmarks.com/`
`download`
	Synchronize your Firefox bookmarks across several computers.

LastPass (Firefox and Chrome):
`https://lastpass.com/misc_`
`download.php`
	Synchronize, manage, and secure passwords across several computers. (See Hack 15, "Securely Track Your Passwords.")

EXTENSION	DESCRIPTION
PriceBlink (Firefox and Chrome): `www.priceblink.com/get-add-on`	Build comparison shopping into your browsers, which notify you when a product you view is available on another site for less.

Be sure to visit the Firefox extension home base at `https://addons.mozilla.org` or the Chrome extensions home page at `https://chrome.google.com/extensions/` to find the most up-to-date extension recommendations and top downloads.

Hack 94: Supercharge Your Firefox Downloads with DownThemAll!

Level . . . . **Advanced**

Platform . . . . **All (with Firefox)**

Cost . . . . **Free**

When it comes to heavy-duty download jobs, your web browser's default downloads manager just doesn't cut it. If you need closer control of multiple, large downloads, you need the DownThemAll! Firefox extension (also known as dTa). This extra-strength download manager can speed up, queue for later, and download sets of files in batches from the Web based on patterns you define in one click.

In this hack, you learn how to finely control and prioritize downloads with DownThemAll and batch-save all the MP3s from a web page in one shot. Before you start, install DownThemAll for free using Firefox at `https://addons.mozilla.org/en-US/firefox/addon/201`.

> **NOTE** Hack 93, "Extend Your Web Browser" covers how to install a Firefox extension such as DownThemAll. As of this writing, DownThemAll is available only for Firefox.

Download Individual Files with DownThemAll!

In DownThemAll's most basic usage, download a particular file from a web page by following these steps:

1. Right-click it and choose Save with DownThemAll from the context menu. Depending on what you select — a video, a link to another web page, an image — this item may read Save Link with DownThemAll as well.

2. Set the destination directory for where dTa should save the files.

3. Click the Start button; dTa opens a window that displays all your downloads, their transfer progress, and several buttons that can pause, resume, cancel, and reorder the priority of your downloads, as shown in Figure 10-9.

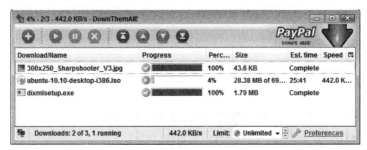

Figure 10-9: Pause, resume, reorder, and cancel downloads in progress with DownThemAll.

One of the greatest benefits of using dTa instead of Firefox's default download managers is that dTa can split large files into several pieces and download each piece individually from the web server. Since many web servers limit the file-transfer bandwidth for each connection, splitting a large download — for example, a bootable Linux CD (see Hack 115, "Recover Files from an Unbootable PC") — into several parts allows you to download the file more quickly. After downloading all the parts, dTa reassembles the original file and you've saved yourself a lot of waiting.

Batch-Download Files with Filters

Say you've stumbled onto a site full of high-resolution images that would be perfect as desktop wallpapers and you want to download the all. Instead of tediously right-clicking each one to start the transfer, DownThemAll! helps you select a large set of files and start their transfer quickly and easily based on certain criteria. It does that by listing all the media available on a web page (such as images and video clips) and all the files to which that page links.

To see these lists, follow these steps:

1. Right-click any web page in Firefox with dTa installed, and choose DownThemAll to open the selection dialog.

2. Use the Links tab and Pictures and Media tab at the top to toggle between lists. From a given list, you can manually select the files

you want, or automatically select a subset using filters — such as the preset Archives (.zip and .rar files), Video (.mpeg, .avi, .wmv) and Images (.gif, .jpg, .png) filters, as shown in Figure 10-10.

3. When you're satisfied with the file selection, click the Start button to begin downloading.

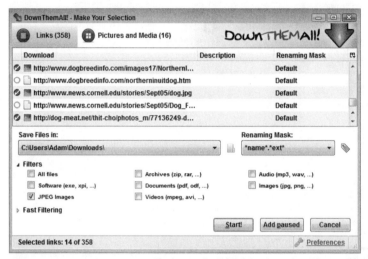

Figure 10-10: Use a preset filter to select files to download in DownThemAll!

Customize a Filter to Download All the MP3s on a Web Page

When you right-click and choose DownThemAll from the context menu on a web page, dTa presents a list of possible downloads from that page — every single link that exists there, whether it's to another web page or a piece of media, such as an image, video or MP3. The power in dTa is the Filters area, where you define a pattern that selects the files you want to download from the often long and crowded list.

If you're visiting a music site that features MP3 downloads (such as www .delicious.com/tag/system:filetype:mp3), you might just want to suck down all the music from the page in one click. Here's how to do so:

1. **Define your filter.** Open DownThemAll's Preferences dialog box by right-clicking any web page, choosing DownThemAll from the context menu, and then clicking the Preferences link at the bottom right of the dialog box. In the Preferences area, go to the Filters tab. There you see several predefined file filters, such as Archives (.zip and .rar files) Videos (.mpeg, .avi, .wmv) and Audio (.mp3, .wav,

.acc, and so on). The Extensions column contains a regular expression that defines the file filter. To create a new filter that downloads only MP3 files, click the Add New Filter button. Set the caption to *.mp3 and set the Filtered Extensions to /\/[^\/\?]+\.mp3$/, as shown in Figure 10-11. Click the OK button to save your new filter.

Figure 10-11: Configure a filter to automatically select all the .mp3 files linked on a web page.

2. **Select all the MP3s with your filter.** On a page that links to music files, such as www.delicious.com/tag/system:filetype:mp3, right-click and choose DownThemAll. Click the MP3 filter check box to select only the music files linked on the page for download — just 9 out of 123, as shown in Figure 10-12. Be sure to select the destination directory on your hard drive as well in the Save Files In: area.

3. **Custom-rename files.** Another useful dTa feature is the capability to set the downloaded filenames using different variables, such as date and time and order number. In the Renaming Mask drop-down list, choose the pattern the downloaded filenames should use. Click the little paper-clip note button to see the Renaming Tags reference table, as shown in Figure 10-13.

4. **Queue or start your download.** Click the Start button to begin down-loading the tracks from the Web. Alternatively, if you don't want to use the bandwidth now, click the Add Paused button (a kind of light download bookmarking tool) to set up the files in dTa for download-ing later on.

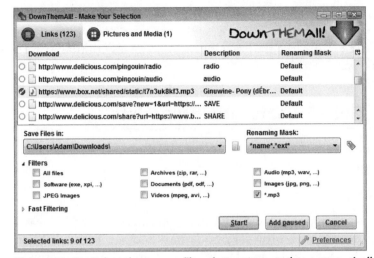

Figure 10-12: Select the *.mp3 filter that you created to automatically select only the MP3 files linked on the current web page for download.

Renaming Tags

name	File name	*qstring*	Query String
ext	Extension	*refer*	Referrer URL
url	Base URL	*num*	Batch number
curl	Full URL	*inum*	Item number
flatcurl	Flat Full URL	*hh*	Hours
subdirs	URL subdirectories	*mm*	Minutes
flatsubdirs	Flat URL subdirectories	*ss*	Seconds
text	Link text	*d*	Day
flattext	Flat link text	*m*	Month
title	Renaming Tags	*y*	Year
flattitle	Title associated with link		

Figure 10-13: Rename downloaded files using custom renaming tags.

One-Click Access to dTa Settings

When you have a list of dTa preferences set up that you want to reuse — say, if you want to periodically download MP3s from several of your favorite music blogs — use dTa OneClick, also available on your right-click context menu. From the Help page:

> *dTa OneClick will start downloading all the links/pictures of the current webpage that will match the filters used in the last dTa session. Downloads will be saved in the last set destination path and will be renamed using the last set renaming mask.*

As can the command-line program wget, detailed in Hack 66, "Automatically Download Music, Movies, and More," dTa easily downloads large sets of files. In contrast to wget, however, you can't schedule regular, recurring downloads with dTa, but most will find DownThemAll's graphical interface and Firefox integration a lot easier to deal with than wget's command-line parameters.

Hack 95: Get 10 Useful Bookmarklets

Level. . . . . . . **Easy**

Platform . . . . **All**

Cost. . . . . **Free**

A *bookmarklet* is a snippet of JavaScript that you can bookmark (or save as a favorite) on your web browser's bookmark toolbar. Bookmarklets can enhance web pages, add special functionality, and make your browsing experience much more efficient by offering one-click access to useful tools.

The following ten bookmarklets can streamline work in your browser. Access them at `http://lifehacker.com/129141`.

- **Acronym lookup:** LOL, RTFM, YMMV, AFAIK! If you stumble upon one of those nutty Internet-speak acronyms online, highlight it, click this bookmarklet, and Acronym Finder automatically looks it up.

- **Translate text:** What do you do when you stumble across a web page that's definitely saying something you want to know, except it's in a language you don't speak? You translate it, of course. This bookmarklet runs a web page through Google's translation service, which automatically detects the language of the page and translates it to English.

NOTE When it comes to translating language, machines never do as clear and correct a job as humans, but automated translations can give you the main idea. Google Chrome already has automatic translation tools built in, so Chrome users can skip this one.

- **Urban Dictionary lookup:** Similar to the acronym lookup, this bookmarklet looks up selected text on a web page in the Urban Dictionary, the collaboratively edited slang dictionary. Cool beans.

- **Wikipedia lookup:** Highlight text on any web page and perform a Wikipedia search.

- **Alexa site profile:** View traffic stats and charts, related sites, and inbound links to any website you're currently viewing using Alexa's profile page.

- **Delicious linkbacks:** See which Delicious users bookmarked a web page and what Delicious tags they assigned to it with one click.

- **View cookies:** *Cookies* are small text files that websites plant on your hard drive to save the state of things, track where you have been on that site, or keep you logged in. Check out all the cookies a site has set for you with this bookmarklet.

- **Toss cookies:** When you see all the cookies a site has set for you, you may want to discard them using this bookmarklet.

WARNING Many sites may not work the way you expect without the cookies they set, and this bookmarklet dumps all the cookies, not selected ones.

- **goo.gl:** Sometimes web page URLs are just too long to easily remember or type. Sometimes you want to email a web page address and it's so lengthy that it wraps around in the message, rendering it unclickable. That's where Google's goo.gl comes in. Go to any web page with an extra long address and hit up this bookmarklet to create a shrunken URL for emailing, IMing, and sharing without the wrap.

- **View passwords:** You know when you're typing a password into a web page form, and it's displayed as *******, and when you try to log in you're told the password is incorrect? Double-check what you've typed with this bookmarklet, which reveals the contents of a password field. This bookmarklet is secure and client-side, so no worries about revealing your password to evildoers. It's just an easy way to verify that you didn't accidentally press that pesky Caps Lock key.

NOTE Several of these bookmarklets are from Jesse's Bookmarklets Site (http://squarefree.com/bookmarklets), a fabulous index of all sorts of bookmarklet fun.

To install a bookmarklet, drag and drop the link that contains the JavaScript to your browser's Bookmarks toolbar.

If this toolbar is not visible in your web browser, enable it: In Firefox, choose View ➪ Toolbars and select Bookmarks. In Chrome, select View ➪ Always Show Bookmarks Bar. In Internet Explorer, choose View ➪ Toolbars, and select Favorites Bar.

To save toolbar real estate, create a `bookmarklets` — or the narrower `bkmrklt` — folder and drag and drop your bookmarklets there.

TIP Technology journalist and screencaster Jon Udell published a short film that demonstrates how bookmarklets work and how to install them. It's available at `http://jonudell.net/udell/gems/bookmarklet/bookmarklet.html`.

Hack 96: Find Reusable Media Online

Level . . . . **Easy**

Platform . . . . **Web**

Cost . . . . **Free**

You're designing a new brochure, PowerPoint presentation, website, or flyer, and you need the right image to use with it fast. Put your hands in the air and step away from the cheesy clip art. Thanks to organizations such as Creative Commons, licenses such as the GNU Free Documentation License, and the public domain, there are tons of photos, songs, movies, and documents freely available for you to download and republish without fear of the copyright police.

What's Reusable Media?

Traditionally photographers, artists, writers, musicians, and other creatives copyright their work to restrict usage by others — and charge fees or royalties to do so. But in recent years, a new "free culture" movement arose on the Web, advocating the benefits of proactively permitting others to republish creative work. A new set of licenses that give explicit permission to reuse and republish media (versus restrict it) was born.

NOTE Lawrence Lessig's Creative Commons–licensed book, *Free Culture*, inspired and fully explores the free-culture movement.

If you're looking for an image to include in your published work — whether it's a movie, brochure, or e-book — you can't use copyrighted material without the permission of the copyright holder. But media licensed for reuse (or that's in the public domain) is now widely available online — allowed for use in your own projects. This hack covers a few places you can find it.

Six Reusable-Media Search Engines and Sources

The following are some of the best reusable-media search engines and sources online:

■ **Creative Commons (CC)** search interface (`http://search.creativecommons.org`)

What you'll find: *Video, music, images, and documents*

Creative Commons' tabbed search interface looks up CC-licensed photos from Flickr and Google Image Search, any file type on Google, audio on Jamendo Music Search, videos on Blip.TV, and mixed media on Wikimedia Commons and SpinXpress in one convenient place. (Before you go republish Creative Commons–licensed work, be sure to check exactly which CC license that perfect photo carries — whether it can be modified, used for commercial purposes, or should include attribution.)

■ Wikimedia (`http://commons.wikimedia.org`)

What you'll find: *Video, music, images, documents*

User-edited Wikimedia Commons contains more than 700,000 pieces of freely available, modifiable (even for commercial purposes) media that's categorized and tagged by users. Need a photo of the moon for your blog? Type `Category:Moon` into the Wikimedia search box.

■ SoundCloud (`http://soundcloud.com/creativecommons`) and CCMixter (`http://ccmixter.org`)

What you'll find: *Music*

Find podcastable, remixable, put-your-iMovie-to-it music at the SoundCloud and CCMixter listings of Creative Commons–licensed songs.

■ EveryStockPhoto (`http://everystockphoto.com`)

What you'll find: *Images*

There are dozens of stock photo sites out there, but EveryStockPhoto (ESP) aggregates photos licensed for reuse from several sources.

■ Google (`http://google.com`)

What you'll find: *Images, documents*

Although Google has an Advanced Search option to find reusable content (as does Yahoo!), some advanced Google search techniques work as well.

For instance, to find Creative Commons–licensed Excel documents with the words *time map* in them, try

```
filetype:xls time map "this work is licensed under a Creative
Commons"
```

Similarly, to find PDFs licensed under the GNU FDL, try

```
filetype:pdf "published under the GNU Free Documentation
License"
```

See Hack 90, "Google Like a Pro," for more on advanced search operators.

■ Public Domain Torrents (www.publicdomaintorrents.com)

What you'll find: *Video*

This collection of public-domain A and B movies is available for download via BitTorrent. Use it to spice up your indie film with a clip of *Dr. Jekyll and Mr. Hyde* or *Tom and Jerry*.

Hack 97: Get Your Data on a Map

Level . . . . **Easy**

Platform . . . . **Web**

Cost. . . . . **Free**

The launch of Google Maps (http://maps.google.com), the search engine's online geographical mapping application, ushered in a revolution in visualizing location-based data. Not only do Google Maps' built-in features help you find establishments, addresses, and driving directions, but Google opened its maps interface to third-party developers for their own use. The result is a host of Google Maps mashups, which plot sets of data onto web-based maps.

These map mashups are an incredible way to see geographical information in a new manner. This hack points you to several of the best mashups that can help you adjust your commute home from work for traffic, decide where to live, help you find a nearby used car for sale, and figure out how far your jog across the bridge this morning really was.

■ Flippity (www.flippity.com): In this eBay maps mashup, browse items on eBay for sale near you.

- **gCensus** (www.gcensus.com): View census data associated with the area you're viewing on a map.

- **MapMyRun** (http://mapmyrun.com): Plot running routes and calculate the distance and your speed based on time.

- **Trulia Home Price Maps** (www.trulia.com/home_prices): See how much homes sold for near a specified address or within a certain ZIP Code.

- **Fast food restaurants** (http://fastfoodmaps.com): View all the locations of popular fast-food chains by area.

- **Full Screen Weather** (www.wunderground.com/auto/wxmap): See the weather for a particular place on the map, as shown in Figure 10-14.

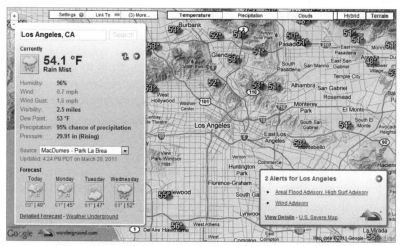

Figure 10-14: The weather for Los Angeles, CA, displayed on the Weather Underground's Full Screen Weather map.

- **Boxoh Universal Package Tracking** (http://boxoh.com): View the progress of your DHL, UPS, USPS, or FedEx package as it travels to your doorstep. This tracker also generates a feed you can subscribe to for updates.

- **Dealmap** (www.thedealmap.com): Find deals and coupons based on your location.

NOTE New map mashups appear every day. Two good sources to use for keeping up with the latest and greatest map developments are the Google Maps Mania weblog (http://googlemapsmania.blogspot.com) and Lifehacker.com's maps tag (http://lifehacker.com /maps).

In addition to plotting various sets of data, Google Maps' open API enables a new breed of user-generated maps to flourish. Several of those applications enable users — or groups of users — to create annotated maps with photos and video. For example, a knitting group may publish a map of all the best yarn stores across the country. Or someone who just moved to Seattle may want to share a map with photos and videos of new favorite spots. These things are all possible with this new breed of web application. For more clever ways to put your life on a map, see Hack 83, "Remember Where You've Been Using Location Awareness."

Hack 98: Set Multiple Sites as Your Home Page

Level . . . . **Easy**

Platform . . . . **All (with Firefox, Chrome, or Internet Explorer 7+)**

Cost . . . . **Free**

The advent of tabbed browsing enables web surfers to work with sets of pages rather than individual websites. You can set several web pages as your home page in tabbed browsers (such as Firefox and Internet Explorer 7) and bookmark and open sets of tabs.

Multitab Homepage

Say, for example, that when you launch your web browser, you look at three sites first thing: your Google Reader subscriptions, your Gmail account, and CNN. To make your three regular morning reads open automatically when you launch Firefox or IE7, set them as your home page.

Firefox

To set multiple home pages in Firefox, follow these steps:

1. Choose Firefox ➪ Options ➪ General.
2. In the Location(s) field of the Home Page section, enter the addresses of the sites separated by a pipe (|), as shown in Figure 10-15.
3. Alternatively, you can open all the web pages in tabs and then click the Use Current Pages button below the Location(s) field, also shown in Figure 10-15.

Figure 10-15: Separate multiple URLs with a pipe (|).

Chrome

To do the same thing in Chrome, perform the following:

1. Click the Wrench button ➪ Options (Preferences on OS X).

2. In the On startup section, select Open the Following Pages, and click the Add button to add as many sites as you like, as shown in Figure 10-16.

3. As with Firefox, you can also open all the pages you want in tabs and click the Use Current Pages button, also shown in Figure 10-16.

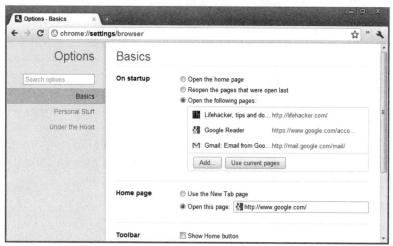

Figure 10-16: Add startup pages to Chrome by clicking the Add button.

Internet Explorer 7+

Internet Explorer 7 and above also support multiple tabbed home pages. To set them, do the following:

1. Choose Tools ⇨ Internet Options.
2. In the General tab, enter the URL of each page on its own line (not separated by a | as in Firefox).
3. Alternatively, you can open the pages in tabs and click the Use Current button.

Bookmark Sets of Tabs

You can also save and open sets of tabs. For example, say you're working on a research project for the next few months. The project involves a company Intranet web page, an external client login page, and a weblog that you and your teammates use to keep each other updated. You can save this set of pages and easily launch them with a click when it's time to work on the report.

To bookmark a set of tabs in Firefox, Chrome, and Internet Explorer, open and bookmark each page in a separate tab and save them all into a dedicated bookmarks folder. The process varies slightly by browser, but most have agreed on using a Star button to signify bookmarks and favorites.

1. In Chrome and Firefox, click the Star button in the address bar; then click the Folder drop-down and select Choose. In Internet Explorer, click the Star button ⇨ Add to Favorites.
2. Now click the New Folder button. Name your folder; then save the rest of your bookmarks to that folder.

Open a Set of Tabs

After you save your set of tabs, you can launch all those pages with one click in Firefox, Chrome, and Internet Explorer 9.

In Firefox and Internet Explorer, click the bookmark folder you want to open and select Open All in Tabs (Firefox) or Open in Tabs (Internet Explorer 9).

Alternatively, in all three browsers, right-click the folder, and select Open All, as shown in Figure 10-17. If you have a mouse with a scroll wheel button, you can also click the folder with your scroll wheel button.

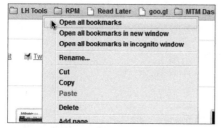

Figure 10-17: Open a folder of bookmarks all at one time in Chrome.

Hack 99: Access Unavailable Websites via Google

Level . . . . **Easy**

Platform . . . . **Web**

Cost. . . . . **Free**

Websites go offline. They move, occasionally suffer from temporary unavailability or errors, or become slow to respond because of technical difficulties or a period of high user demand. Some websites may not be reachable from your particular Internet connection or network. In those cases, when you need the information right away, you need a mirror of that website's content.

Unless a site explicitly denies it, Google creates a full copy of a site's pages on its servers. When you do a Google search, you can notice that there are light blue links on the bottom right of each result. One of these — the Cached link — is the doorway to Google's copy of a site.

For example, if Lifehacker.com is down (although that never happens!) but you need the article published there about creating a DVD photo slideshow for Mom's birthday tomorrow, you can execute a Google search to find that article (`site:lifehacker.com DVD photo slideshow`). The results will look something like Figure 10-18; click the Cached link to see the article that you need, courtesy of Google.

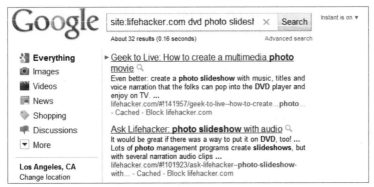

Figure 10-18: Search results with Cached links to view Google's copy of those web pages.

Alternatively, you can simply view Google's copy of a site's front page by using the `cache:` operator. That is, simply search for `cache:lifehacker.com`.

Hack 100: Have a Say in What Google Says About You

Level . . . . **Medium**

Platform . . . . **Web**

Cost . . . . **Starting at $10 a month**

Someone out there's trying to find information about you right now, whether it's a potential employer, a date, or a long-lost friend. What happens when she Googles you?

More than half the time, she'll get information about someone else with the same name or a website that you don't control. This hack provides the ins and outs of setting up a nameplate website that makes you "Googleable" with a web page whose content *you* control.

But I Already Have a Website

You may already have a personal blog with photos of your kids on it or a page dedicated to your monstrous LEGO collection that comes up when your name is searched. But is that the first point of contact you want a Google cold-caller to have? Consider your nameplate site your Internet business card, where you publish contact and professional info in a context-insensitive way that can help Googlers get a bird's-eye view of who you are and what you do — beyond the LEGO collection.

Get Your Domain

Do what you can to register a `yourname.com` (or `.org`) domain. This costs a small yearly fee, starting around $10, depending on the top-level domain you choose (`.com`, `.net`, `.org`, `.tv`, and so on). There was a time you may have thought one domain to one individual person was egotistical and unnecessary, but that time is over. You will change jobs, move, go freelance, and switch email addresses more in your lifetime than any other past generation did. Personal findability is more important than ever. Investing in a `yourname.com` domain is worth it. If you can't get `yourname.com` or `.org`, try `.net`, or even `.me`.

A NOTE ABOUT NAMES

Many people in the world probably have the same name as you, and there will be more and more coming online each year. Do what you can to brand yourself uniquely online, either by including your middle name, initial, or using your full first name (James instead of Jim or Deborah instead of Deb). Of course, you want to use the name people will most likely use to search for you, but if you decide to go with a more formal (read: unique) form of your name, be sure to also use it as your email name (`james@jamesdoe.com`) and on your resume and other paperwork.

You lucky people with unique names? Your domain name is waiting — its availability is payback for all the years of misspellings and mispronunciation.

You don't absolutely have to get `yourname.com` to set up your nameplate site, but it's a better option than a page on a free host with a predetermined URL, as at a university because someday that service might change its address or go away. If you own `yourname.com`, you control it forever, and you can point it anywhere you like — blog, static page, whatever — for as long as you pay for it.

NOTE Lifehacker.com readers recommend domain registrars at `http://lifehacker.com/5683682`.

Author Your Nameplate

Now's the time to decide what to put on your "web business card." Your profession, location, and email address is a good start, maybe with links to your kids' pictures and your LEGO-collection site. Needless to say, do not give away your physical address, Social Security number, or phone number here — this is general info so that others can identify you (as in, "Oh, yes, John Smith the architect in Santa Cruz"). Figure 10-19 shows an example of a simple, well-done site.

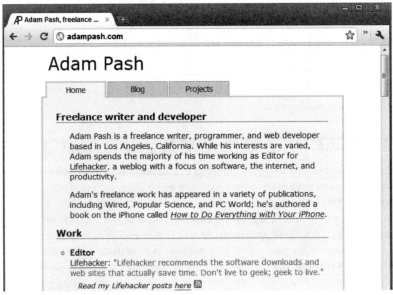

Figure 10-19: A Google-friendly nameplate site includes information you want to advertise about yourself.

An HTML tutorial this hack is not, but do make sure that your full name is prominent within a header tag (`<h1>`) at the top of the page, and within the title (`<title>`) of the document. Ensure that all the content of the page you want Google to know about is in text (not in images or Flash). Finally, be sure to mask your email address to keep it from spammers. (Google "email address obfuscator" for websites that can help you mask your email address from spammers online.)

Customize a Nameplate Template

If you're not a skilled designer, you may prefer to customize an existing nameplate template. Lifehacker writer Adam Dachis designed and released a template called Lifehacker.me, available for download at `http://lifehacker .com/5636983`, that makes it easy to start with your own attractive, custom nameplate site, like the one shown in Figure 10-20.

To use Lifehacker.me, your web host must support the PHP scripting language. Most do, but check with your host if you have trouble.

Figure 10-20: Lifehacker.me is an attractive, customizable template for nameplate sites.

Find a Web Host

The next thing to do is find a web host, which can entail a monthly fee. If your nameplate site is only one page (and it doesn't have to be more), this cost will be minimal. (See Lifehacker.com readers' recommendation for web hosting providers at http://lifehacker.com/5545568.) A nice benefit to having your own domain and host is having a memorable email address, such as joe@joesmith.com, which you can use as a future-proofed email address (see Hack 7, "Future-Proof Your Email Address," for more). Upload your new nameplate and associate it with your new domain name according to your hosting provider's instructions.

Dedicated do-it-yourselfers with always-on broadband can host their nameplate website at home, but go this route only if your site is very low on bandwidth, your computer is always on, and you're not concerned about site responsiveness, which will be slow for typical cable and DSL connections, especially if many visitors go to your site at one time.

Link Up Your Nameplate Site

Just because you build it doesn't mean that Google will come. Search engines will find your nameplate site and associate it with your name only if it is linked to your name on other, indexed pages. For example, if you're a member of an online community such as Twitter, MetaFilter, or Slashdot and you want Google to find your nameplate site, just add it to your profile pages in those communities. You can also send a request to the webmaster of other sites that mention you to link your name to your new site.

Get a Nameplate Site Without the Hassle

If manually creating and finding a place to host your nameplate site is more work than you've signed up for, you can also get your name out there — and have a say in what search results turn up for you — using one of several services made specifically for this purpose:

- **Google Profiles** (https://profiles.google.com): A service launched by Google specifically to make it easier for someone to find you via Google. Even if you've made your own nameplate site, you should consider setting up a Google Profile and adding a link to your site from it, since it helps Google know what sites to associate with you.

- **About.me** (https://about.me): A nameplate service with built-in analytics for tracking how many people view your site, where they're coming from, and what they're looking at when they're there.

- **Flavors.me** (http://flavors.me): Another attractive and customizable nameplate site for aggregating your online identity in one place.

None of these tools give you the flexibility of creating and hosting your own nameplate site, but they are easy and effective.

Hack 101: Clear Your Web Browsing Tracks

Level . . . . **Easy**

Platform . . . . **All (with Internet Explorer, Chrome, or Firefox)**

Cost . . . . **Free**

Your web browser saves a lot of information about where you go and what you do online while you're surfing the Web. The sites you visit, copies of the images and text you view, cookies, and information you type into form fields (such as username and password or your mailing address and credit card number) are all saved to your computer's hard drive and web browser cache for the sake of convenience so that those pages can load faster or your browser can suggest auto-filling the address of a site you visited before.

However, if you use a shared or public computer, you may not want the web browser to remember your website logins, history, or even your usernames. Maybe you don't want your spouse to discover you ordered flowers for her at FTD.com when she types *f* into the address bar. Maybe you don't want your roommate to know that you searched for "apartments for rent" on Google last night.

This hack explains how to sweep away your browsing tracks after you finish surfing the Web using history clearing tools and built-in private browsing features.

Go Private or Incognito

The newest releases of Chrome, Firefox, and Internet Explorer all have built-in private browsing features that automatically clear your history, cookies, temporary files, and other potentially sensitive data as soon as you end your browsing session. Here's how they work:

Internet Explorer 8+

In Internet Explorer 8 and above, you can enable private browsing mode — called InPrivate — by selecting Tools ⇨ InPrivate Browsing. A new window opens with this message:

> InPrivate Browsing *helps prevent Internet Explorer from storing data about your browsing session. This includes cookies, temporary Internet files, history, and other data.*

You can browse privately with your InPrivate session, and when you finish, simply close the window. To end InPrivate browsing, close the InPrivate window.

Chrome

Chrome's private browsing mode is called Incognito. To start an Incognito browsing session, select File ⇨ New Incognito Window. A new window launches with a different colored window theme and an anonymous character with a fedora and sunglasses in the top right of the window, as shown in Figure 10-21, to indicate that this window is an Incognito window.

TIP Incognito mode isn't just good for covering your browsing tracks. Because it sandboxes session cookies to a separate window, it's also a good way, for example, to log into your Gmail account on a friend's computer without logging out of your friend's current Google session.

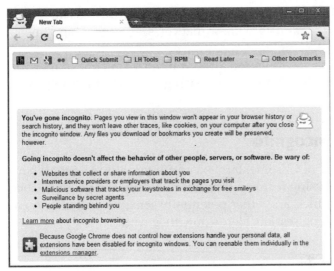

Figure 10-21: Chrome's window theme changes colors to indicate that you're in Incognito mode.

Firefox

To start Private Browsing in Firefox, select Tools ➪ Start Private Browsing. Firefox closes your current browsing session and opens a new window in Private Browsing mode, as indicated by a Venetian mask, shown in Figure 10-22.

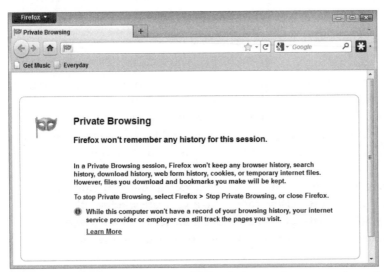

Figure 10-22: In Private Browsing Mode, Firefox won't save your browsing history.

Clear Data After a Browsing Session

For most purposes, your browser's built-in private browsing mode works well — provided you remembered to turn it on before you start browsing. For those times you forget to go incognito before you start a sensitive browsing session, you can still clear your browsing data after the fact.

Internet Explorer 7+

In Internet Explorer 7 and above, follow these steps to clear your browsing history after the fact.

1. Choose Tools ⇨ Internet Options, and under Browsing History on the General tab, click the Delete button.

2. In the Delete Browsing History dialog box, you can remove all your browsing-session information by clicking the Delete All button at the bottom. (In Internet Explorer 8, you can access this dialog more quickly by selecting Tools ⇨ Delete Browsing History.)

You erased your web tracks in one fell swoop.

Chrome

Delete your browsing history in Chrome like this:

1. Click the Wrench button ⇨ Options (or Preferences on Mac), and then select the Under the Hood tab in the sidebar.

2. Click the Clear Browsing Data button and check the items you want to delete — Browsing and Download history, Cache, Cookies, Saved Passwords, and Autofill form data.

3. From the drop-down menu, select to clear your browsing data from the past hour, day, week, four weeks, or "the beginning of time."

You can also use the Ctrl+Shift+Delete (or Cmd+Shift+Delete on Mac) to automatically open this menu.

Firefox

To delete your browsing tracks in Firefox, follow these steps:

1. Choose Tools ⇨ Clear Recent History.

2. Check the items you want to delete — Browsing and Download History, Form and Search History, Cookies, Cache, and Active Logins — and click the Clear Now button.

If you regularly use a shared computer with Firefox, configure the Clear Recent History tool to delete your tracks automatically at the end of every browsing session. To do so:

1. Choose Tools ➪ Options, and on the Privacy tab, click the Settings button next to the Clear Private Data tool information.

2. Select the Clear Private Data When Closing Firefox box in the Settings area.

You can also use the Ctrl+Shift+Del keyboard shortcut (Cmd+Shift+Del for Mac users) to clear your private data in Firefox without navigating any menus or dialog boxes.

Go Nuclear

The private browsing and data clearing methods previously detailed can sufficiently mask your browsing history when you don't want, say, your significant other to stumble onto what you've been browsing while he's using your computer. They won't, however, remove some harder to get at information that an extremely determined snoop might look for.

If you want to *really* browse without leaving a trace, you'll want to clear the more advanced and hard-to-find traces you left behind, like cached DNS entries and Flash cookies. See how to do just that at `http://lifehacker .com/5395267`.

Reference

1. Search recipe courtesy of The Google Tutor & Advisor article, "Voyeur Heaven" (`http://googletutor.com/2005/04/15/voyeur-heaven`).

CHAPTER 11

Hone Your Computer Survival Skills

In an age of always-on PCs connected to the open Internet at high speed, rogue software tries to install itself on your computer at every turn. Viruses sent via email with inviting subject lines such as "Christina Hendricks pics ;)" and "I love you" threaten home computers and entire office networks. Pushy programs put themselves in your computer's startup process and slow down overall performance. Toolbars install themselves in your web browser and redirect you to advertising websites. Your nine-year-old downloads and installs malicious software that looks a lot like Tetris on your PC. Your toddler gets hold of the mouse and deletes a critical folder in one click.

Computer disasters happen, but when they do, you don't have to pay the local computer repair shop hundreds of dollars to recover from them. Plenty of free, easy, do-it-yourself fix-it options are available to help you get back to a speedy, secure, and stable system.

This chapter's hacks include: simple methods to protect your computer from malicious software; getting the most out of the disks that house your important data; reverting your broken PC to a past, working state; freeing much-needed disk space; and restoring accidentally deleted files. Some of the hacks cover ways to proactively insure your computer against possible system failures or infections, such as creating a mirror image of your computer in a known, working state (Hacks 113 and 114) or firewalling it against unwanted network connections (Hacks 108 and 109.) Others describe reactive fixes for already problematic PCs, such as cleaning a spyware-laden system (Hack 102) or recovering data from an unbootable hard drive (Hack 115.) Still others can help you speed up your system (Hacks 104 and 110) and free space on your hard drive (Hacks 107 and 111). Although this chapter has far more Windows-related than Mac-related hacks, Mac users can find tips in Hacks 106, 109, 111, and 114.

Several utilities are built right into modern operating systems to perform these tasks, but not all of them are the best ones available. These hacks contain information your operating-system vendor won't tell you about, and they use some of the best (and usually free) software tools out there to keep your computer in tip-top shape.

Hack 102: Rescue Your PC from Malware

Level....... **Medium**

Platform.... **Windows**

Cost........ **Free**

The scourge of personal computing is malware: malicious software that installs itself without your consent and undermines your computer's operation for various nefarious purposes, ranging from identity theft to aggressive advertising to common vandalism.

There are several different types of malware, but none of them is desirable:

- **Spyware** tracks what you do on your computer and sends information about that back to its originating service, which then uses that information to target ads to you, or worse, steal your credit card or identity.

- **Adware** pops up constant, unwanted advertising on your computer even when you're not browsing the Web, interrupting your work.

- **Browser hijackers** take over your web browser's site requests and redirect them to unintended websites, usually advertisements.

- **Viruses** are a different animal than spyware, but just as destructive and usually spread via email (but not always). They can also wreak havoc on your PC's files and operation, and replicate by emailing themselves to all the addresses in your contacts list.

Symptoms

Some unexpected behaviors you may see on a malware-infected system include the following:

- Constant advertising pop-ups

- Unfamiliar or unknown programs running in the taskbar (that may or may not log your activity on the computer)

- Unknown web browser toolbars, or plug-ins that cause web pages to redirect to unintended websites automatically

- An overall system slowdown, or processes running in the background that were not started with your consent

You can remove all these types of malware from your PC and protect it from future infection with a set of free software tools available for download.

Malware-Removal and -Prevention Tools

Anti-spyware software cleans existing spyware, prevents new malware installations, or both. Here are some of the tools:

- **Microsoft Security Essentials** (protection and removal tool; free; `www.microsoft.com/security_essentials/`): Microsoft Security Essentials is a real-time tool that runs in the background and protects against and removes malicious software.

- **Spybot Search and Destroy** (removal; free; `www.safer-networking .org/en/spybotsd/index.html`): Spybot Search and Destroy scans your system for existing spyware and removes it.

- **avast! Free Antivirus** (protection and removal; free; `www.avast.com/ free-antivirus-download`): Protects your system from malware and removes malware it finds.

Each of these malware tools has two components: the scanning engine and the malicious-software definitions. Because new types of malware are released every day, scanning software must have the latest list of known offending software to clean it up. Each of these tools has an Update feature that downloads the latest malware definitions for the engine to use.

How to Clean an Infected System

A system that displays the symptoms listed previously is most likely infected with malware. To clean it, download Microsoft Security Essentials and Spybot Search and Destroy (to start). When the cleaners are installed, launch each and select Update to get the latest definitions.

> **NOTE** If your web browser is hijacked, you may be unable to use the infected machine to download the software. Alternatively, download the software on a clean machine and burn it to CD or save it to a USB drive. If no other machine is available, try downloading it using a non-Internet Explorer–based web browser, such as Mozilla Firefox (http://mozilla .org/firefox) or Google Chrome (www.google.com/chrome/), which is less likely to be hijacked.

Before you scan your computer, unload any spyware processes that are already up and running on your machine. To unload spyware processes and scan your computer, follow these steps:

1. Disconnect your PC from the Internet connection and shut it down.

2. Start the computer again, and press the F8 key while it is booting up (before you get to the blue-toned Windows welcome screens).

3. Choose to start the computer in Safe Mode, which runs only the bare-essential processes and drives to make a system work.

4. When the computer is up and running in Safe Mode, open Microsoft Security Essentials. Set your Scan Options to Full; then click the Scan Now button. The scanning process can take a while to run, but as it's scanning it displays a list of possibly malicious objects it found on your system, as shown in Figure 11-1.

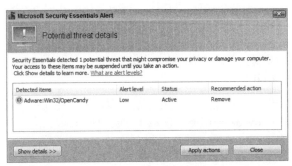

Figure 11-1: Microsoft Security Essentials notifies you of threats and recommends a course of action.

5. Select any item, and click Show Details to read about the potential threat. You can choose to Remove, Quarantine, or Allow any item in this list; normally you simply stick with the Recommended Action. Click the Apply Actions button to take the action set for each item in the list.

6. Quit Microsoft Security Essentials and launch Spybot Search and Destroy. Choose Check for Problems. This scan might also take some time. Remove anything Spybot finds.

7. While you're still in Safe Mode, go to Add/Remove Programs in Control Panel and comb through your installed software list. Uninstall anything you don't recognize or need. Any piece of software whose title contains the words *bargain, tracker, snoop,* or *monitor* should be removed immediately (and their authors roasted for long, painful hours over a hot fire).

8. Reestablish your Internet connection and reboot your computer normally (not in Safe Mode).

9. When you're back in Windows, visit Windows Update (`http://update.microsoft.com`) or open the Start menu and search for and launch Windows Update to make sure your copy of Windows has all the latest security patches and updates — at least all the critical updates, if not all recommended upgrades. This process can take a long time, depending on the speed and age of your computer, and it may require rebooting your PC (sometimes more than once).

10. In the Windows Update sidebar, click Change Settings to turn Automatic Updates on, as shown in Figure 11-2.

11. Finally, weed out any unnecessary programs that start up with your computer. (Hack 104, "Clean Up Your Start Up" provides more on how to do that.)

Figure 11-2: Microsoft Windows Automatic Updates keep your PC's system patched and secure.

Web-Browser Hijacking

The best indicator that your PC is host to malicious software is unexpected web-browser behavior. If an unfamiliar toolbar has suddenly appeared, if your home page has mysteriously changed, if the built-in search functionality uses "Joe's Super-Duper Marketing-Enhanced SearchIt!" instead of your usual search engine, chances are, your web browser has been hijacked.

If scanning with Security Essentials and Spybot Search and Destroy doesn't resolve your web browser's erratic behavior, a free diagnosis tool called HijackThis is available at `http://spychecker.com/program/hijackthis.html`.

The HijackThis freeware does not identify browser-hijacking programs but only lists all the add-ons, buttons, and startup items associated with your browser. Using it, you can disable whichever items you choose, but the trick is identifying the unwanted items. The list includes every browser startup object, including the benign ones, so using HijackThis requires research or expert review of your log before you decide what to remove. A free tool that can analyze your HijackThis log and point out known malicious browser add-ons listed there is available at `http://hijackthis.de/en`.

Typically, malicious browser-hijacking programs target the Microsoft Internet Explorer web browser. A good way to avoid future infection is to switch your system's default web browser to Firefox (`http://mozilla.org/firefox`) or Chrome (`www.google.com/chrome`), both of which are available as free downloads. (Fear not: Firefox and Chrome can easily import your current Internet Explorer bookmarks.)

Hack 103: Protect Your PC from Malware

Level . . . . **Medium**

Platform . . . . **Windows**

Cost . . . . **Free**

The previous hack detailed how to rescue your PC from malicious software, but prevention can save you a lot of headache in the future. After all, the worst time to start thinking about protecting your PC from malware is *after* you've fallen victim to a virus, adware, or spyware. Most PCs ship with a preinstalled antivirus tool — one that usually starts nagging you to pay for a subscription after the 3-month trial is over. Pay-for antivirus solutions do a fine job, but you can set up strong Windows security without a price tag.

Preventative Malware Protection

A popular, free anti-malware tool is Microsoft Security Essentials, previously discussed and available as a free download at www.microsoft.com/security_essentials.

Microsoft Security Essentials integrates with Windows and provides real-time protection from viruses, spyware, and other malware. Download and launch Microsoft Security Essentials and click Update to ensure it has the latest virus definitions. Select the type of scan you prefer — Quick, Custom, or Full — and click the Scan Now button to perform an initial system scan.

Unlike many free antivirus solutions, MSE doesn't require you to manually scan your system every time you want to check for malware. By default, MSE provides real-time protection, meaning that once it's installed, enabled, and running in your system tray, it alerts you when any detected malware attempts to install or run on your PC without waiting for you to run a scan. From the Settings tab, you can set MSE to scan your downloads, monitor incoming and outgoing file traffic on your computer, scan USB drives, scan file archives (like ZIP), schedule fuller automatic system scans (a good idea whether or not you enabled real-time protection), and set rules for how it should handle potential threats.

Scan a Suspicious File with 30 Antivirus Tools at Once

Antivirus applications certainly have the best of intentions, but sometimes they can make mistakes. When you run into a file or program that's been flagged as a virus but you suspect it might be a false positive, upload the file to Virus Total (www.virustotal.com), a free web-based service that scans files with more than 30 different popular antivirus applications and returns the results of each scan (see Figure 11-3). If a file isn't flagged as a virus by the most of the scanners, and it's a legitimate download (for example, something from a trusted source), then most often you can feel safe assuming that the file is clean.

TIP Virus Total's advanced tools (available at www.virustotal.com/advanced.html) make uploading to and scanning files with Virus Total a breeze. On Windows, install the VT Uploader to add VirusTotal to the Send To context menu in Windows Explorer.

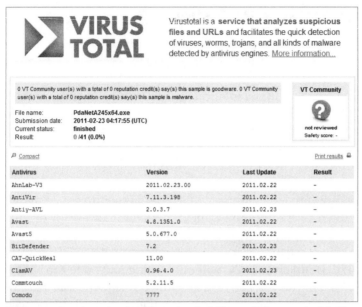

Figure 11-3: Virus Total scans uploaded files to help you decide if a questionable file contains a virus.

Hack 104: Clean Up Your Startup

Level . . . . **Easy to Advanced**

Platform . . . . **Windows**

Cost . . . . **Free**

Does your computer seem a lot slower starting up now than it did the day you took it out of the box? When it comes to computer slowdowns that get worse over time, one of the biggest culprits is software installations that plant themselves in your PC's login sequence and start up automatically with your computer. These programs — which you may or may not use during your session — are unnecessarily taking up memory and CPU cycles.

Say you install a media player such as Apple's popular QuickTime player. QuickTime wants to be your media player of choice, and it wants to start up fast whenever you need it. To that end, QuickTime places a link to start itself up in the background *whenever you start your computer*, whether or not you need to run QuickTime, so that it can detect when you come across a QuickTime playable file and run. When several different pieces of software also do this, the result is a much longer lag between the time you log into your PC and the time it's ready to get to work for you.

A few methods and utilities of varying levels of difficulty (easy to advanced) are available to prune those unneeded programs from your computer's Startup directory and speed it up again.

Start Menu (Easy)

A special folder in your PC's Start ⇨ Programs menu contains shortcuts to programs that start automatically when you log in. This folder is called, appropriately, Startup (see Figure 11-4).

Figure 11-4: The Startup group contains shortcuts to programs that automatically start with your computer.

To edit these auto-starting programs, follow these steps:

1. Navigate to the Startup folder in the Start menu.

2. Right-click any item you want to remove from your Startup and choose Delete.

Audit the programs listed there, deleting anything you don't use on a regular basis. Deleting a program from your Startup folder removes only the shortcut for that application, preventing it from starting with Windows; it does not delete or uninstall the application from your system.

System Configuration Utility (Medium)

Not every auto-starting program is listed in the `Startup` folder. View additional startup items using the built-in Windows System Configuration. To get to it, following these steps:

1. Choose Start, type **MSCONFIG**, and press Enter.
2. In the Startup tab of the System Configuration Utility (see Figure 11-5), deselect anything you don't need to load automatically on boot.

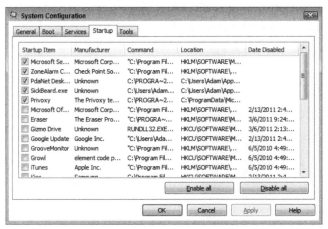

Figure 11-5: View the items that start up automatically using the System Configuration Utility.

3. Because many of these programs have opaque names that give little hint as to what they do or whether you actually need them, you may want to expand the width of the Command column and view the entire path. If `qttask` is in the `Program Files/QuickTime` folder, chances are it starts QuickTime. If you don't want QuickTime to start automatically (there's little reason you would; it works without this helper utility) deselect that task.

Using the System Configuration Utility is a bit of a hit-or-miss proposition. Many of the programs listed there are unidentifiable on sight. If the file path doesn't help, Google the process name for more information. When in doubt, keep it checked.

TIP It's a great idea to create a system restore point first — before you make any system changes — just in case you have to roll back to the original state. Hack 105, "Undo System Configuration Changes," provides more information on that.

Autoruns (Advanced)

A third-party freeware utility called Autoruns can also help you weed out any unneeded tasks from starting automatically. Download the free Autoruns from `http://technet.microsoft.com/en-us/sysinternals/bb963902`. When Autoruns is installed and running, view items that automatically start up with your computer in several different categories, including services, drivers, Internet Explorer add-ons, Start menu items, scheduled tasks, and more, as shown in Figure 11-6.

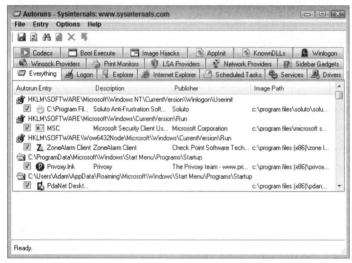

Figure 11-6: Autoruns provides a detailed list of items set to automatically start with your computer.

One of the more convenient features of Autoruns is a built-in Google search for an entry. To use it, select an entry for which you'd like more information and choose Entry ⮕ Search Online to go directly to Google search results for it.

Diagnose and Banish Programs That Are Slowing Down Your System

All the previous methods can help you remove unneeded applications from your system startup, but none of them can tell you which auto-starting applications are the biggest culprits for slowing down your system. The free application Soluto (available at `www.soluto.com`), which bills itself as an antifrustration software, monitors your PC's startup, measures which applications are causing the biggest slowdowns, and helps you disable or delay their startup. Follow these steps to get started:

1. After installing Soluto, you are prompted to reboot your PC. Reboot, and you will see Soluto running in the bottom left of your screen, monitoring the bootup process.

2. When your PC's boot is completed, launch Soluto. It looks up your startup applications in its database (what it calls the PC Genome), and then presents you with your boot analysis. Applications are categorized into three categories:

   ■ No-brainers, which are programs Soluto recommends removing from your boot

   ■ Potentially Removable apps

   ■ Cannot Be Removed with Soluto

The Boot Analysis also displays how much time each program took to launch, so you can see the biggest slowdowns.

3. You can remove an item from boot with Soluto in two ways:

   ■ **Pause:** Pausing a program completely stops it from launching automatically (as discussed in the previous methods).

   ■ **Delay:** Delaying a program waits until your PC is idle before running the application so that your system is less bogged down at startup.

Hover over an item in the Boot Analysis to read Soluto's recommendation for each application (Figure 11-7).

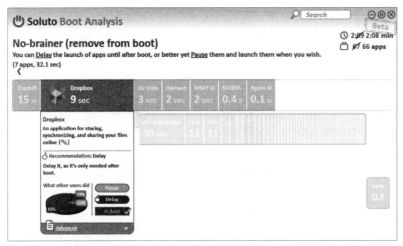

Figure 11-7: Soluto recommends whether you should keep a program launching at boot, remove it, or delay it.

Hack 105: Undo System Configuration Changes

Level....... **Medium**

Platform.... **Windows**

Cost........ **Free**

You install buggy software or change a setting on your PC, and things get ugly — now nothing works. But all is not lost. Luckily, you can save your PC from that bad decision with a powerful tool that's built into Windows. It's called System Restore.

You know how it goes: You edit your Registry, you install beta — okay, alpha — software, you throw caution to the wind and test unstable applications and drivers all willy-nilly. But one false move can render your machine unusable — or make it start popping up 30 missing .dll alerts every time you log in.

System Restore takes snapshots of your computer's configuration over time. In the event of a disastrous installation or configuration change that didn't go your way, System Restore can roll back a current Windows state to a working version without affecting any of your data.

By default, System Restore in Windows is turned on for all your computer's hard drives if you had more than 300MB of disk space available after Windows was installed (and most likely, you did). To see whether System Restore is enabled, do the following:

1. Open the Start menu, right-click Computer, and select Properties.

2. In the left sidebar, click the System Protection link.

3. Under Protection Settings, select the drive you want to enable, click Configure, and select Restore System Settings and Previous Versions of Files. This enables System Restore for that drive (if it's not already enabled).

Make sure that your computer's drive — at least the one that contains your system and program files (usually the c: drive) — Protection status is listed as On, as shown in Figure 11-8.

NOTE If your hard drive doesn't have enough space to enable System Restore, see Hack 111, "Free Up Hard-Drive Space."

System Restore tracks changes in the Windows Registry, user profiles, .dlls, and other internal Windows files over time. If you have multiple drives or partitions on your computer, but only one runs Windows, it makes sense to set System Restore to monitor just the drive on which your operating system and applications reside.

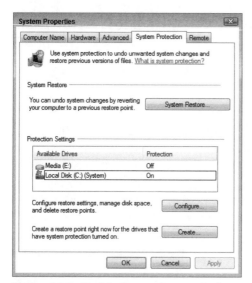

Figure 11-8: Enable System Restore in the System Properties dialog box.

Create or Restore a Saved Point with System Restore

To manually create a restore point, follow these steps:

1. Open the same System Properties window. (Right-click Computer in the Start menu, select Properties, and click the System Protection link.)

2. Click the Create button under System Protection and name your restore point — for example, `Prestartup cleanup`.

To restore your computer to a previous state, follow these steps:

1. Run System Restore. (Choose Start ⇨ Programs ⇨ Accessories ⇨ System Tools ⇨ System Restore.)

2. From there, choose your restore point. The Recommended Restore reverts to your most recent restore point, but you can choose any restore point still available by selecting Choose a Different Restore Point. If you restore your computer to a previous state, current documents, files, and email are *not* affected.

3. Choose your previous state from the list, as shown in Figure 11-9. Click Next and then click Finish to restore.

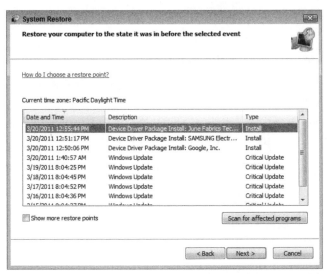

Figure 11-9: Return your system to a past working state with System Restore.

A restoration can also be undone. To reverse your restoration, start System Restore, choose Undo System Restore, and click Next.

WARNING System Restore is not a replacement for file backup; it takes snapshots of your computer's configuration and program files, not your personal data and information. (See Hack 60, "Set Up an Automated, Bulletproof File Back Up Solution," for more on backing up your personal data.)

When System Restore Takes Snapshots

System Restore takes system snapshots every day the computer is on during idle time, and *before* system changes such as Windows Automatic Updates, driver installations, software installations, and system restorations take place. The Microsoft website lists specific times and instances in which System Restore snapshots are taken at `http://windows.microsoft.com/ en-US/windows7/System-Restore-frequently-asked-questions`.

Limit System Restore's Disk Usage

One of the gripes about System Restore is that its snapshots can take up a significant bit of hard-drive space. By default, System Restore is given between 3 and 5 percent of disk space in Windows 7. To reduce that amount, follow these steps:

1. Open the Start menu, right-click Computer, and choose Properties.

2. Click the System Protection link, select the disk you want to adjust, and click Configure.

3. From the System Protection dialog, adjust the Max Usage slider in the Disk Space Usage area, as shown in Figure 11-10.

Figure 11-10: Adjust the amount of disk space allocated to System Restore points.

New snapshots overwrite old ones, so the more disk space you can allocate to System Restore, the more restore points you have available if a system misconfiguration occurs.

Hack 106: Truly Delete Data from Your Hard Drive

Level . . . . **Medium**

Platform . . . . **Windows, Mac OS X**

Cost. . . . . **Free**

You're about to sell, donate, or give away your old computer. Did you know that file-undelete software can easily resurrect those files you just emptied out of the Recycle Bin? Even though it *looks* as though you erased the files, in reality your computer has only marked the space they took up on disk as available — the 1s and 0s that make up those deleted files still exist.

The only sure way to securely and permanently delete sensitive files — such as a customer database, secret company documents, or personal photos you don't want the guy who buys your hard drive on eBay to see — is to overwrite them several times with new data. Utilities to do this are available for both Mac and Windows systems.

WARNING According to a 2011 study by engineers at the University of California, current secure delete methods aren't always reliable on newer, faster solid-state drives (SSDs), so you may want to think twice about selling a used SSD for now.[1]

Windows

Free, open-source Windows software Eraser (http://eraser.heidi.ie) permanently deletes files from disk using your choice of methods, including a Department of Defense standard (DoD 5220.22-M). Eraser can do both on-demand and scheduled scrub-downs of unused disk space on your entire hard drive; either way, it permanently deletes files.

If you're passing a computer on to a co-worker or family member or selling it, delete your data as usual, and then use Eraser to permanently remove any trace of that data from the free space on your disks. To do so, follow these steps:

1. Open Eraser, and in the drop-down next to Erase Schedule, choose New Task.

2. Name the task (for example, `Tin Foil Delete`); then click the Add Data button.

3. Choose the drive, folder, or file you want to permanently delete, and click OK twice. The location is added to Eraser's task list, as shown in Figure 11-11.

4. To go ahead with the delete action, right-click your new task and select Run Now.

5. Eraser is also integrated with Windows Explorer. With Eraser installed, right-click any file, choose Erase from the context menu, and confirm deletion.

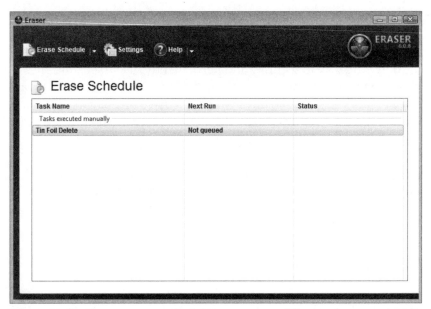

Figure 11-11: Eraser permanently deletes any trace of files on the unused portions of a disk.

WARNING When you erase a file with Eraser, it does not go into the Recycle Bin, nor can it be recovered using undelete software. It is permanently deleted, so use it sparingly and with caution.

Mac OS X

No third-party software is required to permanently delete sensitive data in the Trash on a Mac (OS X 10.4 and higher). Simply choose Finder ⇨ Secure Empty Trash. (That menu option is enabled only if the Trash bin contains any files.) In Mac OS 10.5 and above, you can set your Mac to always securely empty the Trash. To do so, choose Finder ⇨ Preferences, and select Empty Trash Securely in the Advanced tab.

To white out all the current free space on your Mac, launch Disk Utility, and choose your Mac's hard drive. On the Erase tab, click the Erase Free Space button to choose your erasing method, as shown in Figure 11-12; then click the Erase Free Space button to finish the process.

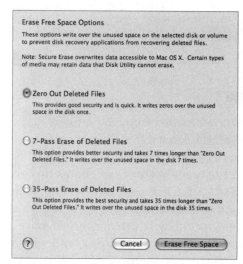

Erase Free Space Options

These options write over the unused space on the selected disk or volume
to prevent disk recovery applications from recovering deleted files.

Note: Secure Erase overwrites data accessible to Mac OS X. Certain types
of media may retain data that Disk Utility cannot erase.

⊙ Zero Out Deleted Files

This provides good security and is quick. It writes zeros over the unused
space in the disk once.

○ 7-Pass Erase of Deleted Files

This option provides better security and takes 7 times longer than "Zero Out
Deleted Files." It writes over the unused space in the disk 7 times.

○ 35-Pass Erase of Deleted Files

This option provides the best security and takes 35 times longer than "Zero
Out Deleted Files." It writes over the unused space in the disk 35 times.

(?)   (Cancel) (Erase Free Space)

Figure 11-12: The built-in Mac OS X erase
feature scrubs deleted file fragments from
unused disk space.

Hack 107: Compare and Merge Files and Folders with WinMerge

Level . . . . **Medium**

Platform . . . . **Windows**

Cost . . . . **Free**

When several people work on the same set of files — making changes and
copies — multiple versions can blossom out of control. Figuring out what's
been updated on which version and merging it all back together can be a
gargantuan task, but it doesn't have to be. If your kids download images
from the digital camera repeatedly to different locations on the computer,
or you and your co-worker lost track of who made the latest changes to
that PowerPoint presentation, you need the free, open-source Windows
utility WinMerge. WinMerge can compare and merge documents and
folders on your computer.

Download WinMerge (available at `http://winmerge.org`) and install it
on your PC. During installation, select the Windows Explorer integration
option, which comes in handy later.

At first glance, WinMerge is a little intimidating — especially to users who haven't worked with file diff utilities before — but it's quite helpful after you make it your friend.

Compare and Merge Folders

You have two directories of photos downloaded from the camera. Some were cropped and had the red-eye removed, some weren't; new photos were taken and old ones redownloaded. Here's how WinMerge can help.

First, in Windows Explorer, select the two directories of photos (in this example, C:\photos\ and C:\pics\) by Ctrl+Clicking each directory, then choose WinMerge from the right-click context menu. You get a file listing that displays all the files in both folders, including which ones are identical, which are different, the last time each version was modified, and which exist on the "left" or "right" folder, as shown in Figure 11-13.

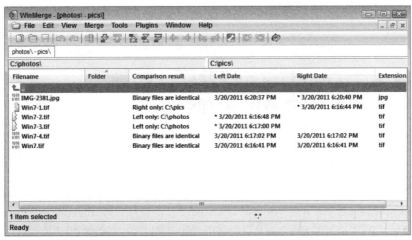

Figure 11-13: WinMerge lists all the files in both selected folders.

From the file listing, right-click any entry to open it (or its other version) to view the differences and determine which you want to keep and which are duplicates you don't need. Toss the ones you don't need in the Recycle Bin. Alternatively, you can copy files that exist on one side to the other using the Copy Left and Copy Right buttons in the toolbar (or key combinations Alt+Left Arrow and Alt+Right Arrow) and then trash the remaining side.

Diff and Merge Text Files

WinMerge can not only detail differences in file listings but can also visually identify differences within files it understands, such as text files. Figure 11-14 shows the differences between two text files containing Lifehacker brainstorming notes.

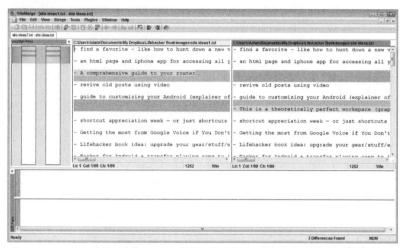

Figure 11-14: WinMerge can compare the contents of text files, line by line.

In this text-file comparison three-pane interface, the leftmost pane displays a map of the file differences:

- The dark yellow areas on your screen (gray here) indicate lines that differ.
- When a yellow area is selected, the difference is highlighted in red.
- The gray areas on your screen show lines that exist in one file but not the other.
- The white areas on your screen show identical lines in the file.

Click any one of those areas to skip directly to that section of the two files, which are shown in the two right panes. Using the toolbar buttons, you can merge all or selected changes from the left to the right file.

Compare and Merge Office Documents

Most people don't work exclusively in text files, but WinMerge can also compare proprietary file formats, such as Microsoft Office files. WinMerge comes with Word and Excel support out-of-the- box. If you have difficulty getting that to work, or you want broader support, download and install the `xdocdiff` WinMerge plugin (available at `http://freemind.s57 .xrea.com/xdocdiffPlugin/en/index.html`). The `xdocdiff` plugin can compare Word, Excel, PowerPoint, PDF, Outlook Email, RTF documents, OpenOffice, and Lotus 1-2-3 files. The plugin installation isn't a one-click process; be sure to extract the `.zip` file and copy the appropriate files into the WinMerge program folder according to the instructions on the plugin page.

Figure 11-15 shows what a comparison of two Word documents (drafts of this chapter in progress) looks like in WinMerge.

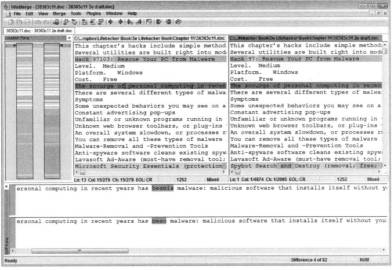

Figure 11-15: WinMerge compares the text contents of Office documents, such as Microsoft Word and more.

The downside is that WinMerge doesn't display the document formatting, just the contents of the file in a straight textual display. But all the same text-comparison features listed in the previous section, "Diff and Merge Text Files," apply. Move all or selected changes left or right, and navigate the differences using the leftmost pane. Then you can save your changes to a new document.

These three examples cover only basic usage of WinMerge. Be sure to check out the WinMerge online manual to roll up your sleeves and get down and dirty with this useful utility. It's available at `http://manual .winmerge.org/`.

NOTE If you're using Mac OS X or Linux, the open source software KDiff3 (`http://kdiff3.sourceforge.net/`) is a cross-platform alternative for comparing and merging files.

Hack 108: Firewall Your Windows PC

Level . . . . **Medium**

Platform . . . . **Windows**

Cost . . . . **Free**

A home PC connected directly to the Internet — especially with an always-on broadband connection such as cable or DSL — is a prime target for malicious software attacks. Predatory software constantly scans public networks (such as your ISP's network) looking for insecure computers to attack, take over, and use for its own purposes. A criminal hacker can use an unsecured home PC to send out spam email, steal credit card or other identity information, or simply delete data or crash the machine for the fun of it.

A firewall can protect your computer against these types of attacks. Without a firewall, a PC connected directly to a cable modem is exposed to the wilds of the Internet — which runs rampant with infected PCs just waiting to spread their viruses and key-log your credit card numbers.

Does Your Computer Need a Firewall?

If you're on a secure network — like at the office — or if your home computer is connected to a wireless router with a built-in firewall, it may already be protected. If not, running a software firewall can greatly reduce the chances of an outsider's gaining access to your PC without your knowledge or consent.

Open ports on your computer represent possible entry points and vulnerabilities on your machine. Test out how secure your PC is by using a free online port scan application at `www.t1shopper.com/tools/port-scanner/`. If your machine has open ports, run a firewall to explicitly allow and disallow traffic from the Internet in and out of your computer.

NOTE If you run a home server as described in Hacks 71 and 72, you have purposefully opened ports on your machine. Make sure those servers are secured with difficult-to-guess passwords. When you're not using the servers, shut them down to close their open ports.

If you can, get a hardware firewall to protect your home desktop computers. (Most modern wireless network routers come with a firewall built in.) A hardware firewall is ideal because it frees up CPU cycles (because your computer doesn't have to run the firewall itself) and is often more effective than a software firewall. However, software firewalls are sometimes necessary, especially for roaming laptops that connect to open wireless networks such as at the local coffee shop or airport.

ZoneAlarm Software Firewall

Several commercial firewall applications are available for home use. Zone Labs offers a free version of its feature-full ZoneAlarm firewall for download at `www.zonealarm.com/security/en-us/zonealarm-pc-security-free-firewall.htm`

When ZoneAlarm is installed, it monitors and asks you to confirm or deny incoming and outgoing Internet traffic from your computer. Also, for troubleshooting purposes (and a great sense of satisfaction), ZoneAlarm reports the details and total of how many possible intrusions it blocked — attempts from other computers to connect to yours, as shown in Figure 11-16.

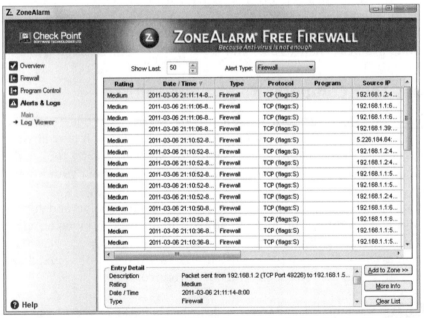

Figure 11-16: The ZoneAlarm firewall's main console displays blocked intrusions and secure programs.

NOTE As of this writing, ZoneAlarm automatically installs a browser toolbar and sets your default search and home page to Bing during its installation. If you'd rather not let it do that, click the Customize Your Installation check box during installation and uncheck those options.

Control What Programs Can Connect to the Internet

After ZoneAlarm is installed and you begin using your computer as usual, you notice that it interrupts you every time a program tries to connect to the Internet. (These days, most software applications do — mostly for legitimate purposes, such as checking to see whether you use the most updated version.) Allow or deny Internet access to those programs using ZoneAlarm's (somewhat annoying) pop-ups, such as the one shown in Figure 11-17, which appears when you click a link in a Microsoft Word document.

Figure 11-17: ZoneAlarm asks you to authorize or deny individual programs' access to the Internet.

To avoid constant ZoneAlarm interruptions, you can edit the program whitelist and blacklist all at one time. In ZoneAlarm's Program Control section, choose the Programs tab. There, click each program and choose Allow, Block, or Ask, as shown in Figure 11-18.

With ZoneAlarm running, you can rest easy, knowing that no one can connect to your computer without your explicit permission.

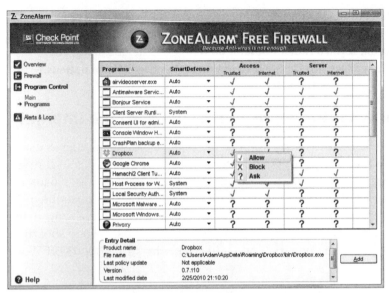

Figure 11-18: Update the Access control setting for each program on your computer within ZoneAlarm.

NOTE Windows now ships with a built-in firewall available in the Control Panel System and Security Center. The Windows Firewall offers similar protection to ZoneAlarm, but it's not as informative or configurable. Get more information about the Windows Firewall and the benefits of firewalls in general at http://microsoft.com/athome/security/protect/firewall.mspx.

Hack 109: Firewall Your Mac

Level . . . . **Easy**

Platform . . . . **Mac OS X**

Cost . . . . **Free**

Surprisingly, a new Mac doesn't ship with its firewall turned on by default. That's not a problem if your Mac accesses the Internet through another device that has a firewall on, such as a wireless router. But if you connect your Mac to the Internet at public wireless hotspots, or plug it directly into your broadband Internet connection, you should enable the firewall because when it's turned off, any computer on the same network as your Mac could make incoming connections to it and "see" that your Mac exists on the network.

NOTE Macs are advertised as and generally known as being more secure than PCs. Instances of malware, such as viruses and Trojan horses, are extremely rare in Mac OS X — but they do exist. Because Mac OS X includes several services that help you share files and connect to other computers, the security-minded user should turn on the Mac's built-in firewall.

To turn on Mac OS X's firewall, follow these steps:

1. In System Preferences, choose Security.

2. On the Firewall tab, click the Start button, as shown in Figure 11-19, to turn the firewall on. (You may have to click the padlock in the lower left corner of the Preferences dialog and enter your password first.)

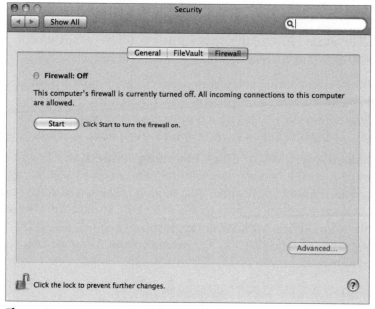

Figure 11-19: Turn on Mac OS X's firewall.

Choose Your Firewall Setting

Now that you've turned your firewall on, you can pick and choose specific settings for how your firewall handles connections. Click the Advanced button for more granular options, shown in Figure 11-20.

☐ Block all incoming connections
  Blocks all incoming connections except those required for basic Internet services,
  such as DHCP, Bonjour, and IPSec.

Remote Apple Events	⊝ Allow incoming connections
Remote Login (SSH)	⊝ Allow incoming connections
Screen Sharing	⊝ Allow incoming connections
🗃 Dropbox	⊝ Allow incoming connections ⇕
🐾 GrowlHelperApp	⊝ Allow incoming connections ⇕
🎵 iTunes	⊝ Allow incoming connections ⇕

[+] [–]

☑ Automatically allow signed software to receive incoming connections
  Allows software signed by a valid certificate authority to provide services accessed
  from the network.

☐ Enable stealth mode
  Don't respond to or acknowledge attempts to access this computer from the network
  by test applications using ICMP, such as Ping.

(?)   (Cancel) (OK)

Figure 11-20: The advanced firewall settings dialog box.

The Advanced Firewall dialog box gives you several advanced options
for handling connections:

- **Block all incoming connections**: Selecting this option disables access
  to the Internet for all applications except for those "required for basic
  Internet services." This option provides the strongest security, which
  makes it a good choice when you're on a public wireless hotspot.

- **Selectively allow or block incoming connections:** If you're not
  blocking all incoming connections, you need to adjust incoming
  connections by application. To add an application to your whitelist,
  click the + button, browse to and select the application you want to
  allow, and click Add. When applications request access but aren't
  yet on your whitelist, OS X prompts you to Allow or Deny access,
  as shown in Figure 11-21.

Figure 11-21: Allow or deny requests from
applications to access incoming connections.

Services that aren't application-specific — such as file or screen-sharing settings that you enable in the Sharing section of the System Preferences — automatically appear as allowed in your whitelist, as shown previously in Figure 11-20.

- **Automatically allow signed software to receive incoming connections:** If an application is signed by a valid security certificate, enabling this option will allow that app to automatically receive incoming connections.

- **Enable stealth mode:** Computers running rogue software usually scan open networks for potential victims — all the computers that exist on them. Even with your firewall on, your Mac is still visible to this type of software. For added security, you can turn on Stealth mode — which is essentially an invisibility cloak for your Mac — other computers on the network can't detect that your machine is there at all, meaning that uninvited connections won't receive any response or acknowledgment.

Hack 110: Speed Up Windows with a Thumb Drive

Level........**Easy**

Platform....**Windows**

Cost........**Free**

One of the best ways to make a computer run faster is to add more system memory, or RAM. But not all computers have expansion slots available for additional memory, and installing internal memory sticks can be an intimidating undertaking for those who've never opened their computer and faced its silicon innards. That's why Microsoft introduced a feature into Windows called ReadyBoost (available in Vista and Windows 7), which enables you to add memory to your PC with a regular USB flash drive. If you have a spare USB drive with unused space on it and you'd like your Vista PC to be more responsive, ReadyBoost is for you. Here's how to set it up.

Enable ReadyBoost for a Flash Drive

When you plug a USB drive into your Windows PC, the AutoPlay dialog box comes up by default, asking what you'd like to do with the drive. This dialog box contains a Speed Up My System option.

Click Speed Up My System to enable ReadyBoost for the flash drive. ReadyBoost isn't compatible with *all* flash drives, but only with drives that meet a certain speed requirement. If it's a relatively new and roomy flash drive, ReadyBoost should work.

Allocate How Much Space ReadyBoost Uses

You can use the same flash drive for both ReadyBoost *and* file storage. To allocate a certain amount of space on your flash drive for ReadyBoost, follow these steps:

1. In My Computer, right-click the USB drive and select Properties.

2. In its Properties dialog box, choose the ReadyBoost tab, shown in Figure 11-22. (This dialog box is also opened when you click the Speed Up My System option in the AutoPlay dialog.)

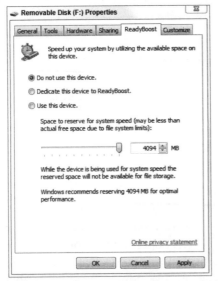

Figure 11-22: Adjust ReadyBoost settings for a USB drive.

3. Select Use this Device and then adjust the slider to set how much space Windows should reserve on the stick to use for ReadyBoost. If you change your mind about ReadyBoost, here you can also disable it by selecting the Do Not Use This Device option.

Read more about ReadyBoost in Windows 7 at `http://windows.microsoft`
`.com/en-US/windows7/products/features/readyboost`.

Hack 111: Free Up Hard-Drive Space

Level. . . . . . . **Easy**

Platform . . . . **Windows, Mac OS X**

Cost. . . . . **Free**

When you bought your computer two years ago, you thought it had a much bigger hard drive than you'd ever need. However, as your computer aged, all that space got eaten up by who knows what. Hard-drive space is cheap and plentiful, but you don't have to run out to buy a whole new drive the minute you start pushing your current disk's space limits. There are easy ways to inventory what's hogging your hard drive, and then you can offload some of it to external disks or simply delete it.

Visualize Disk Hogs

Two utilities — WinDirStat and GrandPerspective — analyze your hard drive and map its usage statistics. They're discussed in the following sections.

WinDirStat (Windows)

The free, open-source utility WinDirStat (`http://windirstat.sourceforge`
`.net`, Windows only) displays your disk usage in a color-coded map that shows what file types and folders take up the most space on your hard drive.

Using WinDirStat, you can easily identify the biggest space hogs on your disk. The utility provides a three-paned view: tree view, list view, and treemap view (see Figure 11-23).

The treemap represents each file as a colored rectangle, the area of which is proportional to the file's size. The rectangles are arranged so that directories make up rectangles that contain all their files and subdirectories. You can select files by folder name, file type, or colored rectangle, and delete or move them from within WinDirStat.

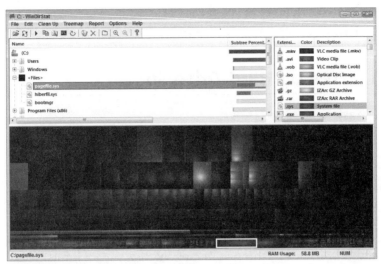

Figure 11-23: WinDirStat graphs disk usage based on a color-coded map.

GrandPerspective (Mac)

Free, open-source application GrandPerspective (http://grandperspectiv .sourceforge.net/, Mac only) provides graphical disk-usage statistics as WinDirStat does, but for Mac OS X. GrandPerspective uses the same treemap style of color-coded rectangles, as shown in Figure 11-24, to hunt down your biggest space hogs.

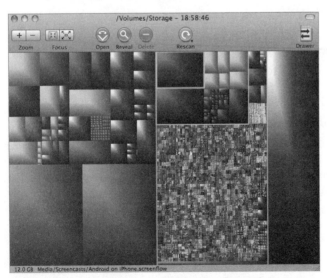

Figure 11-24: GrandPerspective for Mac charts disk usage to identify hard-drive space hogs.

Clean Your Entire System with CCleaner

Another free utility for Windows, CCleaner (which stands for Crap Cleaner), identifies system files — such as Internet browsing history, temporary setup files, and logs — that can be deleted to free up space on your hard drive. CCleaner includes an interface for uninstalling programs (also available in the Control Panel Add/Remove Programs area), fixing broken shortcuts, and removing unused Registry items and outdated software. Download it from `www.piriform.com/ccleaner`.

Hack 112: Resurrect Deleted Files

Level. . . . . . . **Medium**

Platform . . . . **Windows**

Cost. . . . . **Free**

When you delete files from your computer's hard drive, the data is not actually erased. In reality, the space it occupies is marked as available for your operating system to overwrite with new data.

As a result, special file-recovery undelete programs can often resurrect deleted files from the space on your disk marked as free (which still holds fragments of the old file). Although sometimes you don't ever want your deleted files to see the light of day again, in the case of accidental deletion, an undelete process can retrieve what you thought was permanently lost data.

The moment you realize you've accidentally deleted files you want back, stop. Those files may still be on disk, but any computer activity that writes to disk may overwrite whatever's left of them and render them unrecoverable. Don't restart your computer (boot up writes temp files to disk) and don't do any other work on the machine; instead, get straight to the recovery process.

Download the portable version of Recuva, a free undelete utility, from `www.piriform.com/recuva/download/portable` and unzip it, preferably using a computer other than the one where your deleted files live. If that's not possible, save and unzip the file to an external drive (such as a USB drive). Recuva can restore deleted files on your Windows PC's hard drive or on external disks such as a digital camera memory card and USB stick. To recover files with Recuva, follow these steps:

1. Launch Recuva and walk through the wizard, choosing the file type — Pictures, Music, Documents, Video, Compressed, Emails, and all files — as shown in Figure 11-25. Click Next.

TIP Recuva is an excellent addition to a PC helper's USB drive, along with spyware- and virus-cleaning utilities. (See Hack 103, "Protect Your PC from Malware," and Hack 69, "Carry Your Life on a Flash Drive.")

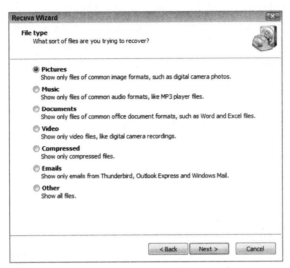

Figure 11-25: Select the type of file you want to recover in the Recuva Wizard.

2. If you know where the file was, point Recuva to the directory In a Specific Location. You can also select: I'm Not Sure; On My Media Card or iPod; In My Documents; or In the Recycle Bin.

3. During the last step of the Recuva Wizard, you have the option to Enable Deep Scan — a feature that takes much longer but can also recover more files.

4. Click Start. Recuva lists all the deleted files that match your file type.

5. To get a deleted file back, select it, click the Recover button, and choose a location for the restored copy.

TIP If you accidentally deleted photos from your digital camera, connect it to your PC. Many modern digital-camera memory cards appear as an external hard drive in My Computer. Use Recuva to scan your camera as an external disk and recover deleted pictures.

Restoring deleted files is a hit-or-miss operation that can miss often, especially in the case of large files such as video or music that Windows might overwrite quickly.

This type of file restoration is no replacement for not having a solid backup system.

Hack 113: Hot Image Your PC for Instant Restoration

Level.......**Medium**

Platform....**Windows**

Cost........**Free**

Over time and with heavy usage, your PC can become slow and unstable, bogged down with programs you don't use and victim of system changes that make it behave in ways you never intended. If you've ever encountered the "blue screen of death" — that is, had your Windows PC crash entirely — you may know what a tedious job rebuilding your computer can be. Reinstalling the operating system and applications and restoring your documents can take time you don't have.

However, if you saved a mirror image of your PC in a known, working state first, you could restore it from a crash or slowdown quickly and easily. Commercial software such as Norton Ghost and Acronis True Image take complete snapshots of your PC for insurance in case of a crash. Although these programs retail for between $50 and $70 each, a free program called DriveImage XML also acts as a virtual copy machine for your PC. DriveImage XML takes a snapshot of your entire computer's hard drive; that is, Windows itself, its configuration, and your software and documents. You can use this snapshot to copy back individual files that have since been overwritten or deleted, or restore your entire computer to its past state. Here's how.

NOTE Hack 105, "Undo System Configuration Changes," describes how to use a built-in Windows utility to roll back changes you make to your computer over time. DriveImage XML is a more comprehensive hard-drive imaging program that you can use as both a file backup and a system-restore utility.

Create a New System Image

Download DriveImage XML for free from www.runtime.org/driveimage-xml .htm and install it as usual. DriveImage XML requires Administrator privileges, so when you launch it, right-click the program and select Run as Administrator.

You can store your system image anywhere you'd like, but the best place to save it is on a disk *other than* the one you're imaging. So if you plan to image your c: drive, purchase an external hard drive to store c:'s image; or, right after you create the image, burn the files to a CD or DVD. This way, if your c: drive fails or breaks, you still have your image available on a separate physical disk.

When you launch DriveImage XML (DiX), click the Backup button on the lower left of the screen. It will scan your PC and list all the hard drives connected to your system. To image your c: drive (most likely your system's primary, active disk), select it and click the Next button to launch DriveImage XML's backup wizard. Click Next again to set where DiX should save your image, and a few additional options, as shown in Figure 11-26.

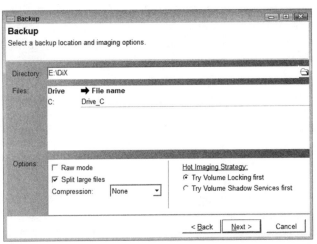

Figure 11-26: Set various options, such as where DriveImage XML should save your image, in the Backup Wizard.

These settings affect how large your image file is and how it can be restored. Here's a rundown of what each setting does.

Raw Mode

In raw mode, DriveImage XML makes a sector-by-sector copy of your drive, including unused space. This means your image file will be the same exact size of the drive, and it can be restored only to a drive of that same exact size. For most home-use situations, leave this box unselected. (No sense backing up blank disk space.)

Split Large Files

If you plan to burn your disk image to CDs or DVDs, select Split Large Files, which breaks your image file down into smaller chunks so that you can easily save them to smaller-sized disks later. If you don't select Split Large Files, you get one giant image file, either as large as the disk itself or as large as the used space on the disk (depending on whether Raw Mode is enabled).

Compressed

If space on your destination drive is at a premium, select the Compressed option to make your image file up to 40 percent smaller than when compression is disabled. Compression slows down the imaging process, but it helps save on disk space.

Hot Imaging Strategy

The best feature of DriveImage XML is that it can image your drive while you work — but that means that files you're using while it does its thing have to be locked to be copied correctly. DiX will try two strategies: locking the drive entirely (if you're not using the computer and saving files) or using the Windows built-in Volume Shadow Services to get the last saved state of the drive. Leaving this at the default (Try Volume Locking First) is fine for home use.

Click the Next button to start creating the drive image file. Depending on the speed of your computer, the size of your hard drive, and the amount of used space, this process can take a significant amount of time. Consider starting it before you leave your computer for the evening, or during your lunch break. DriveImage XML keeps a running counter of how much time it has been copying the disk and how much time is left until it completes, as shown in Figure 11-27.

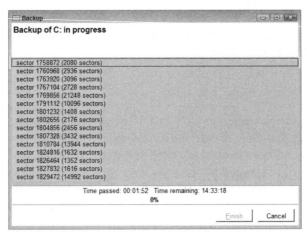

Figure 11-27: Monitor how long the process of creating your drive's image will take.

DiX isn't fast, especially if you have a lot of data to image. When the imaging process is complete, you have two types of files stored on the destination:

- **A single XML file (hence DriveImage XML's name):** The `.xml` file is a list of all the files in the image.

- **Either one or several DAT files:** This depends on whether you selected Split Large Files. The `.dat` file(s) contain the actual image data. Figure 11-28 displays the file listing on the external drive after the image was complete.

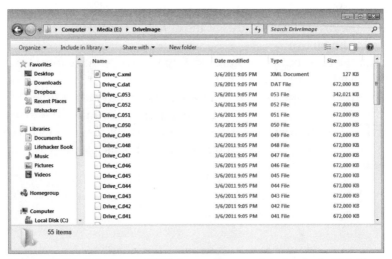

Figure 11-28: DriveImage XML's image files consist of a single XML file and DAT file(s).

Restore Your System Image

After you save a system image, you can use it to:

- Restore individual files from their saved state.
- Restore your PC to the exact state it was when you saved the image.
- Make an exact copy of the drive to another partition or hard drive.

Browse and Restore Individual Files

To view and copy files contained within an image to your PC:

1. Click the Browse button on the lower left of the DriveImage XML window and click Load Image.
2. Select the .xml file for the image you saved. (Remember, every image has exactly one XML file associated with it.) DiX can read the XML listing and display all the files contained within the image.
3. Navigate the folder tree as usual.
4. Right-click any file to view it, launch it using its associated application, or extract it (that is, restore it to your current PC setup).

You can also right-click an entire folder — such as My Documents — and choose Extract (or press Ctrl+S) to copy it to your current PC setup.

Perform a Complete System Restore (Advanced)

If your computer's hard drive crashes entirely, you can restore it to its past state using the DiX image you created. Restoring an image to a target disk deletes everything on the disk and copies the contents of the image to it. That means you *cannot* restore an image to a drive you're already using (because you can't delete the contents of a disk already in use). So if you booted up your computer on your c: drive, you can't restore an image to your c: drive. You need access to the target drive as a secondary disk. There are a few ways to do this. You can install the target drive in a PC in addition to its primary boot drive, or you can buy a hard-drive enclosure and connect the target as an external drive.

Either way, to restore a disk image to a drive you intend to boot from, you need the following:

- A PC running DriveImage XML

- The saved disk image files, whether they're on CD, DVD, the host PC, or an external drive
- A target drive with a partition at least the size of the drive image files

To start the restore process, in DriveImage XML, click the Restore button and then click the Next button, which will launch the drive restore wizard.

From there, select the .xml file associated with the image and choose the target drive. (Remember, the target drive must be an existing partition that's the same size or larger than the image, and it must not be the active system drive.) *All files will be deleted from the target drive on restore*, so be sure nothing is there that you need to save. As with the image-creation process, DiX will display a progress bar and estimated time left as it restores the image to the drive.

NOTE You can format and repartition the target drive using the Windows built-in Disk Management console or any partitioning software of your choice. To use the built-in disk manager, from the Start menu, choose **Run, type** windows disk management, **and press Enter. In the console tree, choose Disk Management. Read more on how to create and edit partitions with the Disk Management console at** http://windows .microsoft.com/en-US/windows-vista/Create-and-format-a-hard-disk-partition.

After the image has been copied and restored to the target drive, make that drive the active, boot partition for your PC to start using it. Either install the disk back into your PC or use the Disk Management console to set the target partition as Active and reboot your PC.

TIP See a video tutorial on using DriveImage XML on YouTube at http://youtube.com/watch?v=PTEnKA7tOXM.

Hack 114: Hot Image Your Mac for Instant Restoration

Level.......**Medium**

Platform....**Windows**

Cost........**Free**

If your Mac's system drive were to fail, reinstalling OS X and restoring the operating system to its previous state — including all your must-have apps and preferences — is an incredibly time-consuming process. Even if you back up your computer's files regularly using Time Machine (Hack 60), rebuilding a system is a daunting task.

The previous Hack detailed how to clone your Windows PC for a quick restore using DriveImage XML. For Mac users, freeware application Carbon Copy Cloner (www.bombich.com) creates a bootable backup of your entire system that you can restore to a new hard drive if something goes wrong with your system. Here's how to use it.

Create a New System Image

To create a new, cloned system image, follow these steps:

1. Download and install Carbon Copy Cloner (CCC) and run the application.

2. On CCC's left pane, choose your Source Disk — the hard drive containing the operating system you want to clone.

3. Choose New Disk Image from the Select a Target drop-down, then navigate to where you want to save the cloned image of your system drive (ideally you'll save the new disk image to a separate drive — either a separate data disk or an external drive), give that disk image a name, and set any additional disk image options. This example uses the default setting: Create a Read-Only Disk Image.

NOTE If you have a spare hard drive, you can clone your current drive to that disk as a bootable drive. It's more convenient when it's time to restore, but you won't use that disk for storage.

4. From the Cloning Options drop-down, select Backup Everything, and then click Clone, as shown in Figure 11-29. CCC begins cloning your system drive to a new disk image. This process may take a while, depending on the size of your drive. When it completes, you have a large disk image on a separate drive — in this case, it's called os.dmg — that contains a complete clone of your operating system, files, applications, and settings.

NOTE If you didn't clone your source disk to a target image on a separate drive, you should burn the image to a DVD or copy it to an external drive as soon as you can. After all, your clone won't do you a lot of good on the same failed hard drive as your operating system.

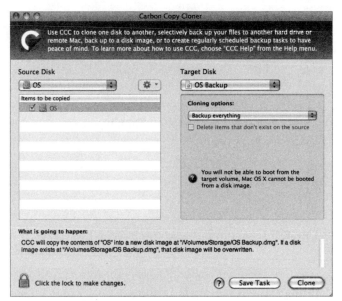

Figure 11-29: Select your source and target disks, and then click Clone.

Restore Your System Image

Now that you saved a system image, you can use it to restore your Mac to the exact state it was when you saved the image — if, for example, your computer's hard drive crashes. Restoring an image to a target disk deletes everything on the disk and copies the contents of the image to it, so you *cannot* restore an image to a drive you're already using. You need access to the target drive as a secondary disk, which you can do by booting from your target disk (if you cloned to an entire drive), or by buying a hard-drive enclosure and connecting the target as an external drive.

> **TIP** To boot from an external target disk in OS X, open System Preferences ⇨ Startup Disk. Select the disk you want to boot from and click Restart.

Either way, to restore a disk image to a drive you intend to boot from, you need the following:

- A Mac running Carbon Copy Cloner
- A saved disk image, whether it's on CD, DVD, the host PC, or an external drive
- A target drive with a partition at least the size of the drive image files

The restore process in CCC is essentially the same as the clone process, only your source is the cloned disk image. Follow these steps:

1. Select Restore from Disk Image in the Select a Source drop-down, and choose the cloned disk image.

2. Select your new replacement hard drive as the target, set Cloning Method to Backup Everything, and select Delete Items That Don't Exist on the Source (required to make the drive bootable).

3. Click Clone. *All files will be deleted from the target drive on restore*, so be doubly sure nothing is there that you need to save. As with the image-creation process, CCC displays a progress bar and estimated time left as it restores the image to the drive.

Advanced CCC

Cloning and restoring a Mac OS X installation with CCC is just the beginning. Like DriveImage XML, CCC's advanced feature set supports the following:

- **Incremental Backups:** Copy only files that have changed since your last backup.

- **Scheduled Tasks:** Set backups to run hourly, daily, weekly, or monthly.

- **Network Backup:** Clone your drive to another Mac on your home network.

For the full feature set, see www.bombich.com/ccc_features.html.

Hack 115: Recover Files from an Unbootable PC

Level. . . . . . . **Advanced**

Platform . . . . **Windows**

Cost. . . . . **Free**

Few moments in computing are as heartbreaking as when you turn on your trusty PC only to receive that bone-chilling message:

```
Boot sector corrupt. Config.sys missing. Disk cannot be read.
```

In other words, you're dead in the water.

Or are you? Just because your computer can't boot up Windows from your hard drive doesn't mean you can't boot it up with another operating system on another disk just long enough to rescue your important files. This hack uses the completely free KNOPPIX Linux Live boot disk (`http://knopper.net/knoppix/index-en.html`) to safely move your files from a failing hard drive to a healthy USB drive — no Windows required.

NOTE There are lots of flavors of bootable CDs and DVDs that you can use to get your computer running long enough to grab your files. Some of them require your original Windows installation disk to build, though. KNOPPIX is for users who have lost or no longer have access to their original Windows disks, don't want to build a boot disk, and who aren't afraid of a different-looking operating system.

What You Need

For the latest version (as of this writing, 6.44) of KNOPPIX to run, you need the following:

- Intel/AMD-compatible CPU (i486 and up)
- At least 120MB for graphic mode (which is what you want)
- A bootable CD-ROM/DVD drive (IDE/ATAPI/SATA, Firewire, USB) or USB flash disk
- A standard SVGA-compatible graphics card
- A standard PS/2 or USB Mouse

Ready to turn your machine into a Linux-CD-booted powerhouse?

Prepare Your KNOPPIX Disk

You have two options for getting the Knoppix bootable disk: download and burn one yourself, or order one by mail.

Do-it-yourselfers in a hurry can use another computer to download an `.iso` file (`http://knopper.net/knoppix-mirrors/index-en.html`) and burn it to their own CD or DVD. (This, naturally, requires a CD or DVD burner and burning software.) If you opt to go this route, make sure you choose the most recent `.iso` file available (currently `KNOPPIX_V6.4.4DVD-2011-01-30-EN.iso`). The DVD files are available from the DVD folder on the download server.

Set Your Computer to Boot from the DVD Drive

Here, things get as tricky as they're going to get. When your computer starts up, it boots itself on disks in a particular order (usually the floppy A: drive and then the C: drive) as set in the computer's base configuration (called the BIOS). To boot from a CD or DVD, you have to edit the disk order to make your computer go to the CD or DVD *first*. How you do so will differ from machine to machine. For example, when my Dell first starts up, it has a message saying `Press F2 to enter setup`. That's what you want.

So here's what to do:

1. Insert the KNOPPIX CD into your CD/DVD drive.

2. Shut down your computer.

3. Disconnect any peripherals you don't need to grab your files (printer, Wi-Fi adapter, remote-control IR device — anything unnecessary).

4. Connect the drive to which you want to move your files — such as a USB drive or external hard drive.

5. Start up your computer and watch carefully for the message on how to enter your BIOS settings (such as the F2 message) and then press the correct key.

6. When you're in the BIOS settings, find the Boot Sequence option. Go into it and select the CD drive as the first bootable option.

NOTE One false move inside your BIOS can seriously affect your computer's operation. Be careful, and edit only the boot-sequence settings.

7. When your PC is set to boot from CD first, save and quit the BIOS.

Start KNOPPIX

The CD is in the drive and your computer is set to boot from it — you're golden. When you restart, you hear the KNOPPIX CD or DVD spinning right away. Your computer will bypass your crippled hard drive and begin booting up Linux. The first things you see are the Linux Penguin and a boot prompt. It seems like you're supposed to do something at this prompt, but don't; wait a few seconds, and KNOPPIX begins booting up. It can take some time to detect your devices, but eventually you get to the full-on KNOPPIX desktop.

Rescue Your Data

If you have no Linux experience, KNOPPIX may look odd and scary, but it isn't. See the KNOPPIX folder on the desktop? Click it to open the KNOPPIX File Manager, which is a lot like Windows Explorer. In the sidebar, you see your Windows hard drive(s).

To copy your important documents, just open your USB drive (open another File Manager window and click its icon in the sidebar) and simply drag and drop files from your Windows drive to your USB drive.

When you attempt the copy, you may receive a message saying, "You cannot drop any items in a directory in which you do not have write permission." If you receive this message, change the permissions by right-clicking the USB drive or folder and choosing Properties. Click the Permissions tab, as shown in Figure 11-30, and set the Access Control to Read and Write.

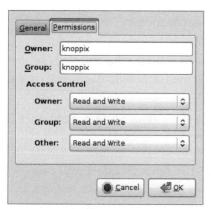

Figure 11-30: Change the permissions to write to your external drive in KNOPPIX.

When you're finished, you can shut down, reset your boot order to where it should be, and rebuild or repair your PC, knowing that your data is safe and sound.

A Linux boot CD or DVD such as KNOPPIX is also a low-overhead way for the curious to try Linux without having to install it. Just pop in the CD, reset your boot order, and go.

TIP Another popular bootable Linux distribution, Damn Small Linux (http://damnsmalllinux.org), can run within Windows from a USB drive or can boot from CD or DVD.

Reference

1. John E. Dunn, "SSD drives difficult to wipe securely, researchers find," Techworld, (`http://news.techworld.com/storage/3262210/ssd-drives-difficult-to-wipe-securely-researchers-find`)

CHAPTER 12

Manage Multiple Computers

You use more computers on a regular basis than any previous generation did. You have your computer at work, your PC at home, your spouse's laptop, and the family Mac to take care of, so getting simple tasks done between them all can be tedious. If you tend to work between several computers, you should know about several utilities already built into your operating system or available for free that can make sharing information and resources easy.

Using multiple computers enables you to get online and work on files from lots of different locations, but with that capability comes complications — such as your work getting out of sync. If you bookmark a website at the office, it won't be there when you get to your home computer. If you bring work home from the office and you forget your updated files there, you're up a creek. If your spouse downloads photos from the digital camera onto her laptop, you don't get to see them — unless you have the right setup.

Personal computers once amounted to giant, stand-alone calculators until someone came up with the idea of connecting them to exchange information. All the computers in your life are connected in some way, whether on your home network or over the Internet, and that means you can do a lot more with them, such as share disks and devices and even automatically sync files between them. This chapter covers several techniques for synchronizing files and bookmarks between computers over the Internet and on the same network.

If you have several computers on your home network — such as your teenager's laptop and your spouse's PC — see Hack 116, "Share Windows Files," and Hack 117, "Share Mac Files," to find out how to set up shared folders for you all to open and save files to a single place, whether you work in Windows or Mac OS X. If you have many computers but just one printer, see Hack 119, "Share a Single Printer Between Computers," for how to share that printer so that any computer can print documents to it. If you have dual monitors or a laptop hooked up to an external monitor, see Hack 120, "Optimize Your Dual Monitors," to find out how to get the most out of the extended screen real estate. Finally, if you have two computers at one desk, you can control them both with a single mouse and keyboard; Hack 121, "Control Multiple Computers with a Single Keyboard and Mouse," covers how.

Operating multiple computers can complicate the way information moves from one to the other, but there are ways to simplify the relationships between the computers you use most often. Whether you share information between local computers, between operating systems, or over the Internet, this chapter shows you how to get all the computers in your life under control and sharing common resources.

Hack 116: Share Windows Files

Level........**Medium**

Platform....**Windows and Mac OS X**

Cost.........**Free**

If you have several computers at home, you want to easily transfer files between them without manually copying them to a disk and walking it across the room (so-called "sneaker net"). All versions of Windows come with built-in support for sharing folders and opening and saving files to them from other computers on the network. This hack shows you how to share a Windows folder of family photos to all the other computers in the house (PCs and Macs alike).

Share a Folder

Here's how to share a folder of photos from a central PC to other computers in the house:

1. Browse to that folder in Windows Explorer, right-click it, and choose Properties.

2. On the Sharing tab, click the Advanced Sharing button, click Share this folder, and set the shared folder name, as shown in Figure 12-1. The name you set here is what other computers will see. This name can be different from the folder name itself. If you try to use a name more than twelve characters long, Windows warns you about a possible incompatibility with some operating systems. Figure 12-1 shows the My Pictures folder shared as Lifehacker Pics.

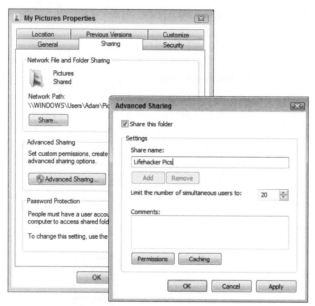

Figure 12-1: Share a folder in the folder's Properties dialog box under the Sharing tab.

3. Next make the folder writable from other computers by clicking the Permissions button and ticking the Full Control check box.

NOTE By default, Windows security still allows you to access only shared folders from another computer if you enter a valid username and password for the shared computer. It's not a bad security setting to leave turned on, but if you'd prefer the folders were public to everyone on your network without requiring a password, open the Start menu, type **Advanced sharing settings,** and press Enter. Find the section labeled Password Protected Sharing and turn it off.

4. Now, right-click your shared folder, select Properties, and click on the Security tab. Click the Edit button; then click Add. Type guest into the large text area, click Check Names, and then click OK.

5. Select the Guest user in the Group or usernames section and set permissions to full control. This gives any user on your local network full read-and-write access to this shared folder.

Determine Your Computer Name

For other computers to connect to your shared folder, it's helpful to know your PC's network name. Most likely, you chose your computer's name when you first set it up (or maybe its manufacturer or previous owner did) and you've since forgotten it. To determine your PC's name, open the Windows Start menu, right-click Computer, and click Properties. Find the Computer name, domain, and workgroup settings section and write down the name listed next to Full Computer Name, as shown in Figure 12-2.

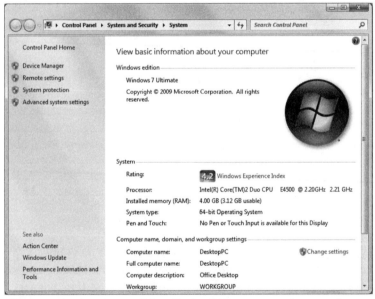

Figure 12-2: The System dialog displays your computer's network name.

In Figure 12-2, the PC is simply called DesktopPC. Take note of your computer's name, which is what other computers on the network will see and access. (If you want to change your PC's name, click the Change

Settings link; then click the Change button. To save the new name, you
need to restart your computer.)

Access the Shared Folder from Another PC

Now that your shared folder is all set up, you're ready to access it from
another PC. This is the fun part: from any other Windows PC on the
same network as the computer with the shared folder, you should now
see your computer's name below Network in the sidebar. Click the shared
computer, and you can see all the shared items available on the host PC.
In Figure 12-3, you see the `Lifehacker Pics` shared folder, along with a
few other shared media folders. Alternatively, from the Start menu, type
two backslashes and the computer's name that you just wrote down. For
this example, type **Windows** into the Run box to browse the PC named
Windows in Explorer.

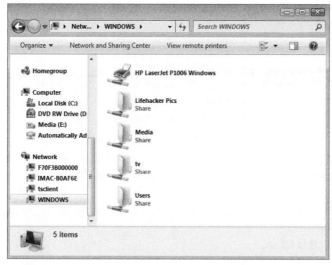

Figure 12-3: Browse to the computer with shared files or printers
by clicking on the host computer in the Windows Explorer sidebar.

TIP You can access shared folders between PCs on a local network only
unless you run a virtual private network (VPN) as described in Hack 70,
"Create a Virtual Private Network (VPN) with Hamachi." Using a VPN,
you can access shared folders from your PC over the Internet — your
home PC from the office, for example.

Access the Shared Folder from a Mac

After you set up a shared folder on your PC, a Mac on the same local network can view, open, and save files there as well. Under the Shared header in the Finder's sidebar, you see the PC sharing files listed automatically. From there, you can browse its available shared folders, as shown in Figure 12-4. Just remember that unless you add Guest access as detailed in the previous "Share a Folder" section, you need to click Connect As and enter your Windows username and password to browse the shared folders.

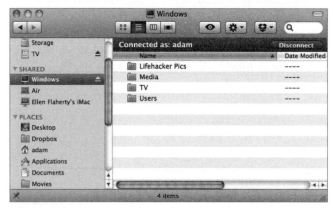

Figure 12-4: Browse to the PC hosting a shared folder by using the Shared header in the Finder's sidebar.

TIP You can add a shared folder to the Finder's sidebar for quick access. To do so, select the shared folder, and from the Finder's File menu, choose Add to Sidebar.

Troubleshooting Tips

If you have difficulty connecting to your PC's shared folder, ensure the following:

■ **The computers are on the same local network.** If the computers connect to the same wireless router, for example, they're on the same local network, which means they have similar IP addresses. To check whether the computers can communicate with one another, you can try pinging one from the other. From the command line on the host PC, type `ipconfig` to determine the computer's local IP address. Then, from the command line of the computer that's trying to connect, type **`ping 123.56.7.8`** (where 123.56.7.8 is the host PC's IP address). If the ping program gets a response from the host PC, the two machines can talk to one another.

▪ **The PC's firewall must allow file sharing.** Make sure the firewall running on the host PC allows for incoming connections to its shared folders. If you use the Windows built-in firewall and you enable sharing, file sharing is automatically added to the firewall's Exceptions list. However, you may have to manually let file-sharing connections through on third-party firewalls.

Hack 117: Share Mac Files

Level . . . . **Medium**
Platform . . . . **Mac OS X and Windows**
Cost. . . . . **Free**

Just as you can share folders from Windows, Mac OS X also has a built-in sharing feature that works with other Macs and PCs. Here's how to share a folder from your Mac and access it from other computers in your home or on any local network.

Share a Folder

To make a folder available to other computers on the network, go to your Mac's System Preferences' Sharing pane. Here you see a list of all the ways other computers can access your Mac. Select File Sharing, and then click the + button under the Shared Folders column to add the folder you want to share, as shown in Figure 12-5.

In this area, you can see which users and groups have what access permissions to those folders. Add and remove folders in the list by clicking the + and – buttons below the Shared Folders list. For a given folder, you can use Apple Filing Protocol (AFP) to share the folder with other Macs, Server Message Block (SMB) to share the folder with PCs, and FTP to access the folder from any device that has an FTP client (see Figure 12-6). You can turn on all or any subset of those options for a given folder.

If you choose SMB sharing, select the user account with whom you want to share and, when prompted, enter your password.

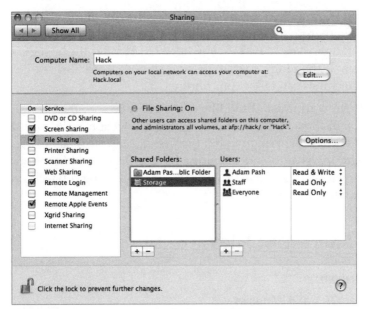

Figure 12-5: Manage your Mac's shared folders list and set access permissions for each shared folder.

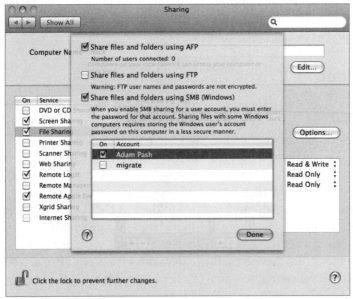

Figure 12-6: Click the Options button to select which protocols your Mac should use to share the selected folders.

WARNING Sharing with Windows PCs will not work if no user account is set to On.

Access the Shared Folder from Another Mac

After you've shared a Mac's folder using AFP, all the other Macs on the network can see and connect to the share immediately. Macs running OS X 10.5 and higher will list the other Mac's name under the Shared heading in the Finder's sidebar. For example, if the Mac sharing a folder is named `Air`, on other Macs it will appear in the Finder as shown in Figure 12-7.

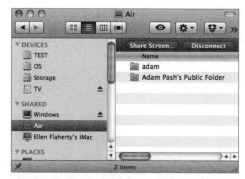

Figure 12-7: Networked Macs that are sharing files automatically show up under Shared in the Finder's sidebar.

Click the Mac's name to browse its list of shared folders. If you can't see the shared folder that you know is there, it's probably not shared with everyone. Click the Connect As button on the top right (under the Finder's search box) and type in the username and password that has share access rights. After you connect as an authorized user, you can open and save files there (depending on your access permissions).

Access the Shared Folder from a PC

When you turn on SMB (or Windows sharing) for a folder, Mac OS X gives you a message that reads something like:

```
Windows users can access your computer at smb://computername
```

where computername is your Mac's name, which you can set at the top of the Sharing preference pane. Either way, from your PC's Start menu search box, type in your Mac's name prefixed by two backslashes, as shown in Figure 12-8.

Figure 12-8: Search for the Mac's shared folders in Windows Explorer.

In this example the Mac's name is Hack so typing **Hack** into the search box (or any Explorer address bar) launches a Windows Explorer window that browses the Mac's shared folders. (Depending on the permissions you set in the Sharing preferences, you may need to enter the username and password from your Mac.) From that window, you can open, copy, edit, and save files from the shared folder over the network from your PC.

Hack 118: Keep Your Web Browser in Sync Across Computers

Level . . . . **Medium**

Platform . . . . **All operating systems**

Cost . . . . **Free**

You've worked hard to perfect your browser bookmark list, generate secure passwords for your logins, and cull together the best combination of browser-boosting extensions and settings. Now that you've built the greatest possible browser to fit your needs, you want those same bookmarks, passwords, extensions, and preferences available to you at work, at home, and on your laptop. Instead of manually adding the same bookmark, installing the same extension, or tweaking the same settings on every one of your computers — only to let them get out of sync again when you edit them on another computer — you can automatically sync your browser data. Here's how.

Enable Your Browser's Default Syncing Tool

As of this writing, both Google Chrome and Mozilla Firefox have syncing tools built directly into their browsers, and both make it simple to set up basic browser syncing. The syncable features vary slightly by browser.

Firefox Sync (`www.mozilla.com/en-US/mobile/sync/`) can sync the following:

- Bookmarks
- Passwords
- Preferences
- History
- Tabs

In contrast, Chrome's built-in tool syncs the following:

- Apps
- Autofill data
- Bookmarks
- Extensions
- Passwords
- Preferences
- Themes

Both browsers tools can selectively sync any of the options, and both sync bookmarks, passwords, and preferences — arguably the most important data you want synced. As of this writing, Chrome's leg up on Firefox is that it also syncs extensions, which is convenient if you're extending your browser with extensions, as detailed in Hack 93 "Extend Your Web Browser."

Here's how to enable browser sync.

On Firefox

If you use Firefox 4 or later, Firefox Sync (`www.mozilla.com/en-US/mobile/sync`) is built into the browser; if you use an earlier version of Firefox, you need to install Firefox Sync as a browser extension from `https://addons.mozilla.org/en-US/firefox/addon/firefox-sync/`. To enable it, select Tools ➪

Set Up Sync to walk through the Setup Wizard. If it's your first sync, you need to create a new sync account, save your unique sync key, and then click the Options button to select the data you'd prefer to sync. You can also change what's syncing at any time by opening the Firefox Options dialog and clicking the Sync tab, as shown in Figure 12-9.

Figure 12-9: Adjust what data Firefox syncs from the Sync tab.

On Chrome

To enable browser syncing in Chrome, click the wrench button and then Preferences. Select Personal Stuff in the Preferences sidebar, and click the Setup Sync button. You need to sign in with a free Google Account to sync your Chrome data; then choose what you want to sync, as shown in Figure 12-10, click OK, and you're all set up.

Figure 12-10: Choose what you want Chrome to sync between your browsers.

Beef Up Syncing with Extensions

Chrome and Firefox's built-in syncing tools are convenient, but they're not always the best option for syncing your bookmarks and passwords. For example, if you don't — or can't — use the same browser at work that you do at home, you may still want to sync passwords and bookmarks, but the built-in syncing tools don't sync with different browsers.

Set Up Cross-Browser Bookmark Sync with Xmarks

For cross-browser bookmark sync, there's Xmarks (www.xmarks.com). The Xmarks add-on syncs browser bookmarks seamlessly with Internet Explorer, Firefox, Safari, and Chrome. To use Xmarks, just download the add-on for your browser and walk through the simple Setup Wizard.

As an added bonus, for those times when you need to get to your bookmarks from a computer that doesn't have Xmarks installed — such as at an Internet café or from your in-laws' computer over the holidays — you can get your bookmarks list on Xmarks' website at https://my.xmarks.com/. Log in with your Xmarks username and password to view your bookmarks list on a web page, as shown in Figure 12-11. You can search, preview, edit, and rearrange your bookmarks while you're logged into My Xmarks on the web as well.

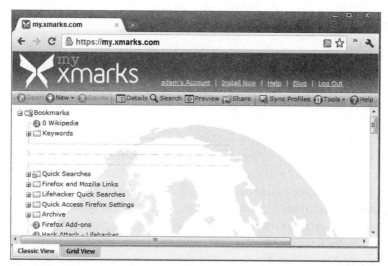

Figure 12-11: Access your synced bookmarks from any web browser at Xmarks.

Get Better Password Management with LastPass

Although Firefox and Chrome can both sync your passwords using their default syncing tools, you should still consider using the browser add-on LastPass (`http://lastpass.com`) instead. As detailed in Hack 15, "Securely Track Your Passwords," LastPass is a robust browser extension with advanced security features, time-saving form-filling tools, a secure password generator, and more. It also works with every popular browser, so if you use Internet Explorer at work and Google Chrome at home, you can still keep your passwords in sync.

LastPass is also available on every popular mobile operating system, so you don't have to type in complex passwords on your tiny screen. To use LastPass on a mobile device, subscribe to LastPass Premium for $1 per month.

Hack 119: Share a Single Printer Between Computers

Level....... **Medium**

Platform.... **Windows and Mac**

Cost........ **Free**

You're typing a letter on the laptop in the living room and you want to print it — except that the printer's in the bedroom. Sharing a printer connected to a PC on your home network and printing to it from any other computer, even over a wireless connection, is a breeze. Whether you want to print from a Mac or another PC, here's how to share a single printer for use by any computer on your home network.

> **NOTE** If every computer on your network runs Windows 7, you can use the HomeGroup feature to share your printers without all the hassle. Just open the HomeGroup dialog in the Control Panel, create a new HomeGroup if you haven't already, and make sure Printers is checked. After the new HomeGroup is created, use the automatically generated password to join your HomeGroup from other computers. The HomeGroup feature makes sharing files, printers, and media between Windows 7 PCs simple, but if you need to share your printer with other, non-Windows 7 PCs, you need to follow these instructions.

Share the Printer

First, you have to make the printer connected to the computer available for other computers to use. Here's how:

1. On the PC where the printer is connected, powered on, and working correctly, open the Control Panel and navigate to the Network and Sharing Center. In the sidebar, click Change Advanced Sharing Settings and ensure that File and Printer Sharing is turned on. If it's not, turn it on; then click the Save button.

2. Next, in the Devices and Printers dialog of the Control Panel, right-click on the printer you want to share and select Printer Properties. On the Sharing tab, click the Share this Printer check box. Some older versions of Windows and other operating systems (such as Mac OS X) can have trouble detecting printer names with spaces in them, so name your shared printer something that's all one word, such as EPSON_SHARE, as shown in Figure 12-12.

Figure 12-12: Name your shared printer.

Now your printer is ready for other computers on the same network to use it.

Connect to the Shared Printer from Windows

To print to a shared printer, your client PC (that is, the PC without the printer connected directly to it) must be a member of the same Windows workgroup that the server is. If it isn't a member already, open the Advanced System Settings dialog to set the computer name and workgroup name (in this example, WORKGROUP.) You may have to restart your client PC to save those settings.

NOTE You don't have to enable file and printer sharing on the client as you did on the printer server.

Then, follow these steps:

1. After the client is in the same workgroup as the shared printer, in Printers, click Add Printer to start the wizard, and select the network printer option.

2. In the next screen of the Add Printer Wizard, browse the network's shared printers (see Figure 12-13), and click Next to connect.

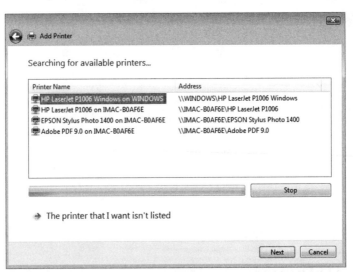

Figure 12-13: Browse for networked printers in the Add Printer dialog.

You're done! Your PC's shared printer is available for use from the other PC on your home network.

Connect to the Shared Printer from a Mac

You can print documents to your shared Windows printer from a Mac as well. To set it up in OS X, first you must set the Windows workgroup that the printer lives in. Follow these steps to do so:

1. In System Preferences, go to Network. In the leftmost column, select the connection to the network where your PC lives (for example, AirPort) and click the Advanced button. On the WINS tab, enter your workgroup name and click OK. Then click Apply to save your setting.

2. Now, while still in System Preferences, choose Print & Fax. Click the + button to add a new printer, and choose Windows on the toolbar. In the leftmost column, select the Windows workgroup where the printer is located and select the printer.

3. From the Print Using drop-down list, choose Select a Driver to Use and type in your printer name, which, if all goes well, will appear on the available driver list, as shown in Figure 12-14.

4. Click the Add button to put the shared printer on your printer list. Now, from any application on your Mac, you can print to the shared printer on the PC.

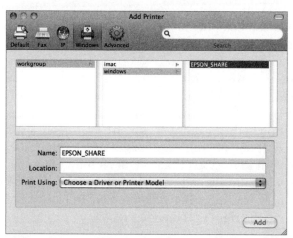

Figure 12-14: Browse the Windows workgroup to find the shared printer in the Mac OS X Add Printer box.

NOTE If your printer driver isn't listed, try installing the Mac driver from the disk that came with your printer or search the printer manufacturer's homepage for drivers.

Hack 120: Optimize Your Dual Monitors

Level . . . . **Advanced**

Platform . . . . **Windows**

Cost . . . . **Free**

Studies show that the extra screen real estate afforded by multiple monitors can increase computer users' productivity.[1] If you've added another monitor to your computer setup, you've got double the screen real estate to get things done — but are you putting all that space to good use? Whether you want to stretch your desktop wallpaper or taskbar across two screens or perfectly snap all your windows into place every time, a few utilities are available that can help you make the most of every last pixel of your dual monitors. Read on to take a look.

The Basics

If you haven't taken the plunge into doubling up on monitors and your computer doesn't currently support two video outputs, you have a few options. You can install a second video card inside your computer or replace your current video card with one that supports two monitors. Alternatively (and most easily), you can just plug an external display into your laptop and use your laptop's flip-up screen as your second monitor.

When you have your dual screens hooked up, go to your system's display settings to configure their arrangement. (Right-click your desktop and select Screen resolution.) One of the screens will be your primary monitor (numbered 1) and the other will be the secondary (numbered 2). Click the Identify button to throw numbers up on each screen, letting you know which is which. If one of your monitors is smaller than the other, drag and drop it to align to the top or bottom of its comrade in the same way the screens are physically aligned on your desk, to ensure the smoothest window and mouse movement between the two. In Figure 12-15, the primary monitor sits to the right of the widescreen.

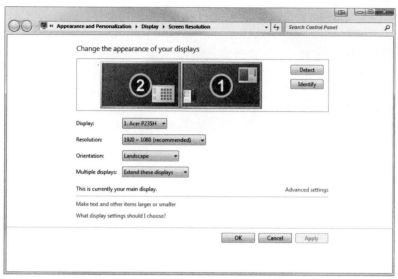

Figure 12-15: Identify and arrange your dual monitors in the Windows Screen Resolution dialog box.

Get Your Dual-Monitor Wallpaper On

Mac OS X handles dual monitors better than Windows: you can set screen-specific wallpaper images by default without any extra software. Just choose Set Desktop Background, and a panel appears on each screen to configure them separately.

Windows can't set different wallpaper images on a per-screen basis by default; when you choose your wallpaper, it appears on both screens. That wouldn't be so bad except for Windows' inability to deal with different-sized monitors. If you choose the "stretch" option and you have two monitors of different sizes, Windows has problems stretching the image properly to fill in each screen. If you've installed a dual-monitor video card, its drivers may give you the capability to configure each screen individually, but that leaves the laptop-with-second-monitor types out of luck — without the right software, that is.

One free utility, DisplayFusion, sets per-monitor wallpaper *or* stretches one panoramic image across two screens, as shown in Figure 12-16. Download DisplayFusion from `http://binaryfortress.com/displayfusion`.

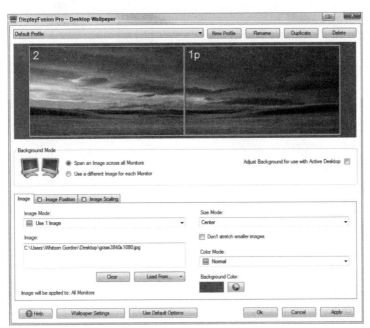

Figure 12-16: Stretch panoramic wallpaper across two monitors using DisplayFusion.

The Pro version of DisplayFusion ($25) offers a nice perk: the capability to search the popular photo-sharing site Flickr.com for wallpaper images built right in. DisplayFusion requires the free .NET runtime program.

Extend Your Taskbar Across Monitors

It's easy to move your taskbar from one monitor to the other in Windows without any special software. Make sure it's not locked (right-click and deselect Lock the Taskbar) and then just click and drag it to any side of either monitor to make it stick. The problem is that you don't want to have to scoot your mouse over to the screen where the taskbar lives every time you need it (especially now that your mouse has all that way to travel). Instead, DisplayFusion can extend the taskbar across both your screens, as shown in Figure 12-17.

If you're willing to plunk down some cash for superior multiple monitor management — with extended taskbars, per-monitor taskbar settings and screensavers, and lots more dual-monitor control — you need to upgrade to DisplayFusion Pro. A single license will only set you back $25 and includes all the multimonitor features you want in one package. You can compare the features available to the free and pro versions at www.displayfusion .com/Compare/.

Figure 12-17: Multimonitor manager DisplayFusion Pro stretches the taskbar across your second monitor and shows on each taskbar only the programs that appear on each taskbar's screen.

Managing Windows

Now that you have your wallpaper and taskbar sussed out, it's time to start taking advantage of all that screen real estate with the apps you're actually using all day. The biggest benefit of multiple monitors is having fewer overlapping windows. You can have several documents and programs open and visible without obscuring the others — which means you can multitask without having to switch between windows by clicking your taskbar or pressing Alt+Tab.

As of Windows 7, you have shortcuts galore for managing windows from your keyboard. We discussed some of the most important Windows shortcuts in Hack 50, "Command Your Windows PC from the Keyboard," but the following are especially useful for window management:

SHORTCUT	RESULT
Win+Home	Clear all but the active window.
Win+Space	All windows become transparent, so you can see through to the desktop.
Win+⇧	Maximize the active window.
Shift+Win+⇧	Maximize the active window vertically.
Win+⇩	Minimize the window/Restore the window if it's maximized.
Win+⇦ or Win+⇨	Dock the window to each side of the monitor; additional presses push the active window to the next monitor edge, then center, and then opposite edge across all available monitors.
Shift+Win+⇦ or Shift+Win+⇨	Move the window to the monitor on the left or right.

Desktop Pinups and Overlays

Of course, you don't have to fill your entire desktop with active windows. Multiple monitors are also a nice way to keep "ambient" information in your visual field without it being right in your face all day. A second monitor off to the side can be used for secondary applications (such as IM, email, a music player), but it also comes in handy for to-do lists, system-monitoring graphs, and even a calendar. Some favorite desktop overlay utilities are Rainmeter for Windows (`http://rainmeter.net/RainCMS`) and GeekTool for Mac (`http://projects.tynsoe.org/en/geektool`). Both can embed your to-do list and calendar on your desktop, plus they can embed images such as website traffic graphs. You can also embed a Microsoft Outlook calendar on your secondary monitor and even use Windows Active Desktop to embed your Google Calendar.

Hack 121: Control Multiple Computers with a Single Keyboard and Mouse

Level . . . . **Advanced**

Platform . . . . **All platforms**

Cost . . . . **Free**

If you have two or more computers at one desk, you don't want two or more sets of keyboards and mice cluttering up the tabletop, too. You can buy a hardware gadget that enables you to share a single keyboard and mouse with several computers (which involves a mess of tangled wires), or you could use a free software solution called Synergy. The Synergy application runs on all the computers you use — the one that has the keyboard and mouse connected and the one(s) that do not — and enables you to control all of them from that keyboard and mouse. That means you can move your mouse off one computer's screen and it will appear on the other, where you can type and work as well. Synergy also lets you share Clipboard contents between computers. If you copy information to the Clipboard on one computer and move your mouse to the other, you can paste it there, even though they're two different systems. Sound too good to be true? It's not!

Synergy works between any number of PC, Mac, and Linux desktops. For simplicity's sake, this hack sets up two PCs to share a single keyboard and mouse using Synergy; sharing your keyboard and mouse between Windows and Mac follows a similar process using SynergyKM on Mac OS X (http://sourceforge .net/projects/synergykm).

Before you start, you need to know two terms — *server PC* and *client PC*. When you set up Synergy, you'll have one "server:" This is the computer that has the keyboard and mouse physically connected to it. The rest of the computers will be "clients." First, set up the server.

NOTE If you're sharing a keyboard and mouse between two Macs, consider Teleport (www.abyssoft.com/software/teleport), a free, Mac-only tool that works much like Synergy but is a little easier to set up with Macs.

Set Up the Synergy Server

Download Synergy for Windows free from http://synergy-foss.org and install it on your PC. As of this writing, the most current version is Synergy 1.4.2. Install and run Synergy; then select Server (Share This Computer's Mouse and Keyboard), as shown in Figure 12-18.

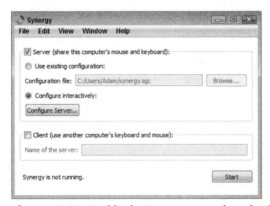

Figure 12-18: Enable the Synergy server by selecting the Server option.

Then click the Configure Server button to open a Server Configuration dialog, where you'll add all the computers that will be controlled by the server's keyboard and mouse and their position in relation to each other.

Configure Multiple Synergy Screens

In the Screens and Links tab, you should already see your host computer in the graphical layout screen. In the following examples the server computer name is `Windows`, so that's what the first Synergy screen name is.

Now, to add the other computer to Synergy, you need to know its name as well (`Hack`). Once you know the name, follow these steps:

1. Drag and drop the monitor icon from the top right of the Screens and Links dialog onto the layout; drop it next to your server in the same layout as your monitors are on your desk.

2. Double-click the Unnamed screen you just added; then enter the other client's screen name, as shown in Figure 12-19.

3. When you're done, you should see two computers on the Screens and Links grid that mirror the monitor setup on your workspace. For example, my Mac (called Hack) is to the left of my PC (called DesktopPC), as shown in Figure 12-20.

Figure 12-19: Add the server's name to Synergy's list of controlled screens.

If you have a particularly wild screen position (a checkerboard of flat-screens, perhaps?), you can even set up screens on top of and below each other here.

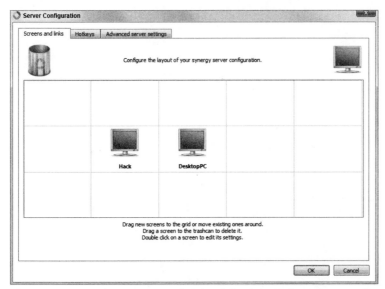

Figure 12-20: In the Screens and Links dialog box, define where each screen is positioned in relation to the other.

Set Up the Synergy Client

Download and install Synergy on the client computer (the one without the keyboard and mouse connected) exactly the same way as you did on the server, except choose Client (Use Another Computer's Keyboard and Mouse). Enter the name of the server computer. To try the connection, click the Start button: first on the server and then on the client PC. Try moving the mouse off the server screen. If all goes well, it will land on the client screen safely.

When you're satisfied with the results, close the Synergy window. Synergy continues running in your system tray, from which you can start or stop the application as needed. Now you're sharing the mouse and keyboard between two computers simultaneously.

Reference

1. Ivan Berger, "The Virtues of a Second Screen," *The New York Times*, April 20, 2006 (http://nytimes.com/2006/04/20/technology/20basics.html).

Index

SYMBOLS

-
  Gmail search operator, 22
  include/exclude words and, 351
  Spotlight search operator, 49, 50
  Windows Search search operator, 47, 48
*: (Windows Search search operator), 47
+ include/exclude words and, 351
" "
  exact phrase with, 351
  Gmail search operator, 22
  Spotlight search operator, 49, 50
  Windows Search search operator, 47, 48
0Boxer, 111–112

A

A4/A5 D*I*Y Planners, 85
About.me, 388
Acrobat, Adobe, 85
Acronis TrueImage, 427. See also DriveImage XML
Acronym lookup bookmarklet, 374
Actions, 309
ActiveX, 252
AdBlock, 206
AdBlock Plus, 206, 367
add-ons, RTM, 130–131. See also extensions
Adobe Acrobat, 85
ADT (Attention Deficit Trait), 147–148
Advanced Encryption Standard (AES), 73, 75, 78
Advanced Search form, Google search, 350
adware, 394
Aero Glass, 287
Aerofoil, 287
AES (Advanced Encryption Standard), 73, 75, 78
AFP (Apple Filing Protocol), 447, 449
after: search operator, 22
AIM, 127, 256

albums
  music, Quicksilver and, 186
  password-protected Picasa albums, 66
  Picasa, 65
  Picasa Web Albums, 67
alerts, 109, 234–235. See also timers
Alexa site profile bookmarklet, 375
Allen, David, 51, 86, 89, 93, 115, 117
Alt+Enter, 176
alternative keyboards, Android, 297–299
Alt+Spacebar, 181, 182
Alt+Tab, 179, 461
Amazon, 19–20, 321, 322
AND search operator, 235
Android, 292
  alternative keyboards, 297–299
  Amazon app, 321, 322
  augment reality with, 317–322
  autocorrect features, 293
  Bump, 346
  CamScanner, 330–333
  Chrome to Phone, 300, 302–304
  computer to, 302–304
  Dropbox, 135, 247
  Evernote, 141, 342–344
  Google Authenticator app, 80, 81, 82
  Google Search widget, 328
  Google Shopper, 321
  Google Voice, 316–317
  GroceryIQ, 168
  Instapaper, 144
  JiWire, 290
  location awareness, 322–326
  mNote, 137
  PayPal app, 344
  PocketCloud, 304–307
  punctuation shortcuts, 296–297
  remote control applications, 307
  remote control your computer, 304–307
  RTM, 130
  Simplenote, 137
  Square credit card reader, 348
  Tasker, 308–311

tethering, 338–341
todo.txt Touch, 135
touch screen typing, 292–299
voice command, 326–330
Voice Search, 327, 328–330
voice-to-text feature, 327
Android Market, 297, 298, 304, 327, 330
Apache HTTP server, 265–270
apology, automated email, 2
App Store, iTunes, 196, 304, 319, 327, 330
Apple computers. See Macs
Apple Filing Protocol (AFP), 447, 449
applications, portable, 256–257
appointments, post-work, 109
apps, RTM, 130–131
Archive folder, 4, 5, 20, 42–43
archive/purge, filing cabinet, 52
Assistant mode, 89
At Delimiter, 193
attachments, email, 12, 14
Attention Deficit Trait (ADT), 147–148
attention firewall, 147–170. See also firewalls
  clearing desktops, 162–164
  communication quiet hours, 160–162
  data/information death row folder, 168–169
  email interruptions, 153–155
  home usability, 165–168
  multiple desktops, 155–158
  no-fly zone, 158–160
  pink noise, 169–170
  time-wasting web sites, 148–153
augment reality, with smartphones, 317–322
Auto Copy, 368
auto fill profiles, LastPass, 197–199
auto-accept invitations feature, GCal's, 212
autocorrect features, Android/iOS, 293
AutoCorrect snippet, 194
auto-forwarding email, to Gmail, 28
automatic backups. See backups
automation of tasks, 215–239
  download files, 236–239
  email apology, 2

Google search results, 234–235
launch software/documents, 233
Mac clean up, 229–231
PC clean up, 226–229
reboot computer, 231–233
scripted repetitive email responses, 30–33
Tasker, 308–311
web-browsing session, 233–234
Autoruns, 403
avast!, 395
awareness, location, 322–326

B

BackBlaze, 222
backup folder. *See* bak folder
backups
    automatic, 216–226
    Dropbox, 243–245
    laptop, 289
    media folder and, 43
bacn, 34–36
bak (backup) folder, 42
bandwidth hogs, block/disable, 206
bankruptcy, email, 2
base passwords, 54
batch resizing photos, 200–202
battery life, laptop, 287
Beagle search, 45
before: search operator, 23
Belvedere, 227–229
Bit.Ly, 12
BitTorrent, 206, 229, 378
Black Belt, scheduling. *See* Google Calendar
BlackBerry devices
    Dropbox, 247
    Evernote, 141, 342
    Google Authenticator app, 80, 81, 82
    Google Voice, 316
    PayPal app, 344
    PdaNet, 339
    Site to Phone, 300
blocked web sites, 149–153
Bloglines, 19
blue highlighting, email, 17–18
blue screen of death, 427
Bluetooth, 287, 290, 309, 333
bookmarklets, 203, 374–376
bookmarks, 59–62, 382
Boss mode, 89
bots, Twitter, 337–338
Botsko's Notepad Generator, 122–123
Boxoh Universal Package Tracking, 379
brain, 104, 116
breaking down tasks, 110, 111
brevity, email, 2, 12
bribe yourself, 110–111
Brother P-Touch Home and Hobby Label Maker, 51
browsers. *See* web browsers
BugMeNot, 202–203, 366–367, 368
bullet points, email, 13
bundles, Texter, 189–190
business cards, 320, 343, 384, 385
busywork, 216. *See also* automation of tasks
@buxfer Twitter bot, 338

C

cached DNS, 392
calculations, Google search, 353
calendars. *See also* Google Calendar
    iCal, 95, 109, 130, 212
    WebCalendar, 271
camera phones, 330–333, 341–344
CamScanner, 330–332

Canned Responses feature, 31
captions, Picasa, 65
capture, ubiquitous, 135, 136, 138, 341
Carbon Copy Cloner (CCC), 432–435
Carbonite, 222
CC: (Windows Search search operator), 48
CCC. *See* Carbon Copy Cloner
CCed messages, filtering, 35–36
CCleaner (Crap Cleaner), 425
CCMixter, 377
centers, task-based, 167
chains, Seinfeld's, 105–107
Cheat Sheet, Google Search, 354
checking, email, 7, 9, 93, 154, 155
Chicken of the VNC, 282
Chore Wars, 111
Chromapaper extension, 144
Chrome
    AdBlock, 206
    browser hijacking and, 398
    BugMeNot extension, 203, 366–367
    built-in search box, 175, 176–177
    Chromapaper extension, 144
    clearing tracks, 391
    download, 234
    extensions, 366–369
    Google Voice Chrome extension, 317
    Incognito browsing session, 389–390
    keyword searches in, 360–361
    openness, 364
    Portable, 256
    RSS Subscription Extension, 356
    StayFocusd extension, 149–151
    syncing tool, 451, 452
Chrome to Phone, 300, 302–304
chunks, task, 110, 111
Cirillo, Francesco, 104
Classic D*I*Y Planner, 85
clean up
    Macs, 229–231
    PCs, 226–229
    startup, 400–404
clearing
    desktops, 162–164
    of mind, 115–145
    web browsing tracks, 388–392
cloning. *See* Carbon Copy Cloner; DriveImage XML
cloud applications, 79, 242. *See also* Google Docs; webapps
Cmd+`, 183
Cmd+, 185
Cmd+B, 184
Cmd+C, 139, 183
Cmd+Ctrl+V, 139
Cmd+I, 184
Cmd+K, 175
Cmd+L, 360
Cmd+Q, 183
Cmd+S, 183
Cmd+Shift+Delete, 391, 392
Cmd+Shift+Z, 184
Cmd+Space, 183
Cmd+Tab, 183
Cmd+U, 184
Cmd+V, 183
Cmd+X, 183
Cmd+Z, 184
collaboration, 110, 167–168. *See also* sharing; web-based office suites
Command + F, 48
Command + Option + Space, 48
Command + Space, 48
command line management, of text files, 134
communication quiet hours, 160–162
competition, tasks and, 110

computers. *See also* Macs; PCs
    to Android, 302–304
    to iOS, 300–301
    multiple, 441–465
    remote control of, 279–283, 304–307
    sale example, Quicktext and, 31–33
    startup cleanup, 400–404
    survival skills, 393–439
    tasks, streamlining, 173–214
    voice command and, 327
    web address for, 283–286
conditional formatting rule, highlighting messages and, 17–18
Conference Room B calendar, 212
constraints, time, 104
Contexts, 308–309
controlling email. *See* email
cookies, 375, 392
coolness/heat, laptops and, 288
Cornell Method PDF Generator, 122
Cornell note-taking method, 122
corral folders, 67–68
Covey, Stephen, 85
Craigslist, 344, 358
Crap Cleaner (CCleaner), 425
CrashPlan, 216–222
Create Event, 117, 119, 214
Creative Commons, 354, 377, 378
creativity, 104, 148
credit cards, LastPass and, 198
Ctrl+_, 176
Ctrl+Alt+Delete, 267
Ctrl+Alt+L, 100
Ctrl+B, 179
Ctrl+C, 139, 179
Ctrl+Esc, 179
Ctrl+I, 179, 180
Ctrl+K, 175, 176
Ctrl+L, 176, 360, 361
Ctrl+S, 179
Ctrl+Shift+/, 127
Ctrl+Shift+Delete, 391, 392
Ctrl+Shift+H, 191
Ctrl+Shift+M, 174, 191
Ctrl+U, 179, 180
Ctrl+V, 179
Ctrl+X, 179
Ctrl+Y, 179
Ctrl+Z, 179
Cue column, 122
custom note paper, 122–123
Cutyfox, 368
Cydia store, 339
Cygwin Unix emulator, 134

D

daily agenda email feature, 212. *See also* Google Calendar
Damn Small Linux, 438
dashes. *See also* tasks
    Emergent Task Timer, 97–98
    morning, 93–95
        automatic setup, 233
        important tasks first, 107–108
        timer for, 102–104
data. *See also* data to go; files; restore files
    death row folder, 168–169
    encryption, 72–79, 222
    on flash drives, 258
    overload, 39–41
    storage/retrieval, 40–41
data organization
    bookmark tags, 60–61
    filing cabinet overhaul, 50–52
    password-protected disks, 71–77
    photos, 63–67
    planners, 84–86

data storage. *See* storage, data
data to go. *See also* Dropbox; flash
    drives; laptops; virtual private
    network; web servers; webapps;
    web-based office suites
    flash drives, 255–260
    Hamachi VPN, 242, 260–264
    home web servers, 264–270
    laptop optimization, 286–290
    personal Wikipedia, 276–279
    remote control of computers, 279–
       283, 304–307
    web address for computer, 283–286
Davidson, Mike, 2
deafness, tone-, 16
Dealmap, 379
Deals (web feed), 358
death row folder, 168–169
deleted files
    completely from hard drives,
       409–411
    cookies, bookmarklet for, 375
    recovery of, 425–427
Delicious, 59–62, 375
delimiter, text expansion, 193–194
desktop office software, web-based
    office suites *v.*, 250–251
desktop pinups, multiple monitors
    and, 462
desktop software, webapps *v.*, 247–251
desktops, 156–158, 162–164
Dexpot, 156–157
dictionary
    Merriam-Webster, 176
    Quicksilver and, 186
    TidBITS AutoCorrect Dictionary, 194
    Urban Dictionary Lifehacker Quick
       Search, 363
    Urban Dictionary lookup
       bookmarklet, 374
    Urban Dictionary.com, 359
Disk Utility, password-protected disk,
    75–77
DisplayFusion, 459–461
disposable email addresses, 19–20
DiX. *See* DriveImage XML
D*I*Y Planner system, 84–86
DLLs, 256, 405
DMZ email folder, 7
doable to-do lists, 88–93
docs folder, 42
docs-archive folder, 42–43
Documents folder, 41–44
Documents library, 67
Dodgit, 19
domain names
    custom, DynDNS and, 286
    people's names and, 385
    web address for home computers,
       283–286
    web-based email and, 25–26
Don't Break the Chain website, 105, 106
dotProject, 271
downloading files, automation of,
    236–239
Downloads folder, 227–230
DownThemAll! (dTa), 368, 369–374
    download
       batch files with filters, 370–371
       individual files, 369–370
       MP3s, 371–373
    dTaOneClick, 373–374
dreaded tasks, 110
DriveImage XML (DiX), 427–432
Dropbox, 222, 242–247, 254, 255
Dropbox Folder Sync, 246–247
dTa. *See* DownThemAll!
dTaOneClick, 373–374

dual monitors. *See* multiple monitors
due: search operator, 128
dueWithin: search operator, 128
DynDNS, 265, 284–285

E

editing tools, Picasa, 66
Eggers, Dave, 162
electronic mail. *See* email
email, 1–38. *See also* Gmail; inbox;
    instant messenger programs;
    Outlook; Thunderbird
    bankruptcy, 2
    brevity, 2, 12
    bullet points, 13
    checking, 7, 9, 93, 154, 155
    composition, 10–14, 16
    email-enabled smartphones, 8
    email-free day, 2
    filters, 18, 35–36
    folders
       Archive, 4, 5, 20
       DMZ, 7
       Follow Up, 5
       Hold, 6
    GCal daily agenda email feature, 212
    highlighting, 17–18
    hosting services, recommendations,
       26
    HTML, 12
    important to-me-only, 17–18
    Instapaper and, 143
    interruptions, reduction of, 8–9,
       153–155
    line breaks, 13
    multiple recipients, 13
    overload, 2–3
    phone calling *v.*, 9, 16
    privacy, 16
    processing, 6, 8–9
    purpose, 11
    push email notifications, 154
    reference library, 5
    reminders, 120
    replying to, 2, 14–16
    responsiveness, 8–10
       inline responses, 14, 15
       one-minute rule, 9
       real time responding, 15
       scripted repetitive responses,
         30–33
       task requests, 9–10, 14–15
    searches, 20–24, 48, 50
    shut down, 153–154, 159
    subject-only, 12
    tasks added to RTM via, 129–130
    tone of, 16
    volume, 2
    web-based, 25–26. *See also* Gmail
    weight reduction, 12–13
    Yahoo! Mail, 26, 209
email addresses
    disposable, 19–20
    future-proofing, 24–26
    multi-domain, 19–20
    shortening, 12
    web-based public, 19
Emergent Task Timer, 97–98
encryption, data, 72–79, 222
End of Message (EOM), 12
Ephron, Nora, 162
Epic Win, 111
Erase Free Space options, 410–411
Eraser, 409–410
event invitations, GCal, 213
Evernote, 138–142, 341–344
EveryStockPhoto.com search
    plugin, 377

Excel
    Creative Commons-licensed Excel
       documents, 351, 378
    Spotlight's index and, 48
    time map, 95–96
    web-based office suites *v.*, 251
    Windows Search index and, 46
    WinMerge and, 414
    xdocdiff plugin, 414
exclude/include words, with +, -,
    351–352
export
    bookmarks, from Delicious, 61–62
    web-based office files, onto desktop,
       251–252
extensions, 364–369. *See also*
    DownThemAll!; *specific extensions*
    BugMeNot, 203, 366–367
    Chrome, 366–369
    Firefox, 367–369
    Web of Trust, 364–366

F

Fast food restaurants map, 379
favorites. *See* bookmarks
FeedDemon, 357
feedreaders, 19, 144, 355–357, 380
feeds, web site, 355–358
filename: search operator, 22
filer, piler *v.*, 45. *See also* searches
files. *See also* data; media files; restore
    files
    automatic processing
       Belvedere and, 227–229
       Hazel and, 229–231
    compare/merge, WinMerge and, 413
    hosts, 152, 153
    recovery of deleted files, 425–427
    reminder, 116–120
    restoring
       with CrashPlan, 221–222
       with Time Machine, 225–226
    sharing, on multiple computers
       Mac, 447–450
       Windows, 442–447
    text, 131–135
    tickler, 117
filing cabinet, 50–52
filters, email, 18, 35–36
Firefox
    Adblock Plus, 206, 367
    browser hijacking and, 398
    BugMeNot extension, 203
    built-in search box, 175–176
    clearing tracks, 391–392
    download, 234
    DownThemAll!, 368, 369–374
    extensions, 367–369
    FoxToPhone extension, 302
    keyword searches in, 359–360
    LeechBlock, 149
    master password, 207–210
    multiple tabbed homepages, 380–381
    openness, 364
    Portable, 256
    Private Browsing, 390
    RSS Icon extension, 356
    Sync, 451–452
    Web of Trust extension, 364–366
firewalls. *See also* attention firewall
    home web server access and, 265
    Mac, 418–421
    MediaWiki and, 276
    PC, 415–418
    software, 289, 416–418
    Windows Firewall, 261, 265, 266,
       272, 418
    ZoneAlarm, 416–418

Flash cookies, 392
flash drives, 255–260
  data encryption, 75
  Dropbox v., 255
  LastPass on, 257
  portable applications, 256–257
  ReadyBoost, 421–423
  reasons for using, 255
  securing, 258–260
  spyware and, 260
  TrueCrypt on, 257
  useful data on, 258
  using, 260
  viruses and, 260
Flavors.me, 388
FlickAR Photos, 318
Flickr, 318, 325, 363, 377, 460
Flippity, 378
flow, 148
FM3 Buddha Machine Wall, 169–170
Focus Booster, 104–105
folder: (Windows Search search
    operator), 48
Folder Sync, Dropbox, 246–247
folders
  Archive, 5, 42–43
    Gmail, 4
    searching in, 5, 20
  bookmark tags v., 60–61
  compare/merge, WinMerge and, 412
  corral, 67–68
  death row, 168–169
  DMZ, 7
  Documents, 41–43
  Downloads
    Belvedere and, 227–228
    Hazel and, 229–230
  Follow Up, 5
  Hold, 6
  one filing folder per hanging
    folder, 51
  Public, 245–246
  saved search, 23–24
    Outlook, 24
    Thunderbird, 24
  shared
    Dropbox, 246
    Mac, 447–450
    Windows, 442–447
  Smart, 71
  three-folder system, 4–7
  Windows 7 libraries and, 67–68
Follow Up folder, 5
Forgotten Attachment Detector
    plugin, 14
forms, automatically fill, 196–200
forwarding messages automatically,
    to Gmail, 28
foursquare, 323–325, 326
Foxit, 85
FoxToPhone extension, 302
Franklin, Benjamin, 107
Free Culture (Lessig), 376
free culture movement, 376
free up hard-drive space, 423–425
freedom from email, 2
Freedom utility, 162
From: addresses, added to Gmail, 28–30
from: search operator, 21, 48, 50
Fuelly, 336
Full Screen Weather, 379
future-proofing email addresses, 24–26
FYI prefix, 11

G

Gallery, 271
game play, tasks as, 109–111. *See also*
    tasks

garbage in, garbage out (GIGO), 10
Gates, Bill, 156
GCal. *See* Google Calendar
gCensus, 379
Gears, Google, 250
GeekTool, 462
genius grants, MacArthur, 148
geo-location, 64
Getting Things Done (Allen), 51, 86, 89,
    93, 117. *See also* to-do lists
GIGO (garbage in, garbage out), 10
Gmail, 26
  archive folder, 4
  Canned Responses feature, 31
  forgotten attachments, 14
  From: addresses added to, 28–30
  highlighting email, 18
  Mail Fetcher, 27–28
  mail-fetch frequency, 28
  multiple email addresses
    auto-forwarding to Gmail, 28
  Priority Inbox feature, 36–37
  RTM for, 130
  search operators, 20–23
Gmail Labs, 16, 23, 31
GNU Free Documentation, 376
Godin, Seth, 162
Goggles
  Google Goggles, 319–321, 343
  Mail Goggles, 16
goo.gl, 12, 368, 375
Google. *See also* Android; Chrome;
    Gmail; Google Calendar
  account, 2-step verification, 79–84
  Alerts, 234–235
  Apps, 26, 80
  GOOGLE and numbers, 333, 335
  Instant, 177–178
  nameplate websites for, 384–388
    authoring, 385–386
    custom template, 386–387
    getting a domain, 385
    linking up, 387
    services for, 388
    web hosting providers, 387
  reusable media searches, 377–378
  searches
    Advanced Search form, 350
    advanced search operators,
      350–354
    calculations, 353
    Chrome and, 175
    combining criteria/operators, 354
    contents of site, 352
    exact phrase with quotations, 351
    Google Goggles, 319–321, 343
    Google Search Cheat Sheet, 354
    include/exclude words, with +, -,
      351–352
    keyboard shortcuts and, 174
    Launchy and, 182
    received automatically, 234–235
    reusable media, 377–378
    specific file types, 352
    synonyms, 353
    via SMS, 333–335
    widget, 328
  unavailable/offline websites via,
    383–384
Google Authenticator apps, 80, 81, 82
Google Calendar (GCal), 210–214
  advanced features, 210–214
  auto-accept invitations feature, 212
  Create Event, 117, 119, 214
  daily agenda email feature, 212
  event invitations, 213
  ICS calendar feed, 325
  keyboard shortcuts, 214
  Launchy and, 182

  Quick Add feature, 119, 210–211, 214
  reminder system, 116–120
  shared calendars, 211–212
  SMS and, 213
  time zone, 118
  weather forecast, 213
Google Cloud Connect, 254
Google Desktop Search, 23
Google Docs, 79, 248. *See also* web-
    based office suites
  desktop office software v., 250–251
  offline work and, 250
  Word v., 248
  Zoho v., 248, 250–251
Google Gears, 250
Google Goggles, 319–321, 343
Google Maps, 308, 324, 326
  Mania weblog, 379
  open API, 380
  using, 326
Google Profiles, 388
Google Reader, 144, 355–357, 380
Google Search Cheat Sheet, 354
Google Shopper, 321
Google Talk, 127, 256
Google Voice, 312–317
  benefits, 317
  place calls, 314
  send SMS, 314
  set up, 312–313
GPS, 309
GrandPerspective, 424
Greasemonkey, 368
grep command, 134
GroceryIQ, 168
guests, GCal and, 118
GVENT, 213, 336

H

habits, new, 105–106
Haller, John, 257
Hallowell, Edward, 147
Hamachi VPN, 242, 260–264
hard drives. *See also* flash drives
  delete data completely from
    Eraser, 409–410
    Mac OS X erase feature, 410–411
  password-protected
    Mac, 75–77
    PC, 71–75
  space
    freeing up, 423–425
    System Restore and, 405–408
has:attachment search operator, 22
Hazel, 229–231
heat/coolness, laptops and, 288
highlighting, email, 17–18
  Gmail, 18
  other email programs, 18
  Outlook, 17–18
hijackers, browser, 394, 398
HijackThis, 398
Hipster PDA index cards, 85
Hold folder, 6
home directory, 43–44, 217–218
home networks. *See* networks, home
home usability, 165–168
home web servers. *See* web servers
HomeGroup feature, 454
horoscopes (web feed), 358
hosts file, 152, 153
hot images. *See* Carbon Copy Cloner;
    DriveImage XML
hotspots, 290, 333
hotstrings, Texter, 187–189
household tasks, 111, 167–168
.htaccess file, 269
HTML Code Snippet file, 194

HTML email, 12
HTML5, 250
httpd.conf file, 238, 267
Hurst, Mark, 7
Hyatt, Michael, 8

I

iCal, 95, 109, 130, 212
iCal Share, 212
ICQ, 127
ICS calendar feed, 325
If Found, Please Return file, 258, 260
iGoogle, 106, 130, 357
image creation/restoration. *See* Carbon
    Copy Cloner; DriveImage XML
Image Resizer, 200–201
IMDb (Internet Movie Database), 176,
    203, 359
import
    bookmarks, into Delicious, 61–62
    photos, into Picasa, 62–63
    web-based office files, onto desktop,
        251–252
IMPORTANT prefix, 11
important to-me-only email, 17–18
inaccessibility, interruptions and,
    159–160
inbox
    empty, 3–8, 10
        0Boxer and, 111–112
        three-folder system, 4–7
    physical, 167
    ubiquitous note-taking, across
        devices, 135–142
Inbox Zero series, 8
"The Inbox Makeover," 8
include/exclude words, with +, -,
    351–352
Incognito browsing session, 389–390
incoming items, house usability and,
    165–166
incremental backups, 224
indexes
    Spotlight, 48–50
    Windows Search, 45–48
information. *See* data
inline responses, to email, 14, 15
InPrivate Browsing, 389
InstaFetch, 144
Instant, Google, 177–178
instant messenger programs
    AIM, 127, 256
    Google Talk, 127, 256
    MSN Messenger, 127, 256
    Portable Pidgin, 256
    RTM reminders, 126–127
    shut down, 159
    Skype, 127, 161, 265, 266
    Yahoo !Messenger, 127, 256
Instapaper, 142–144
Internet connection, speed up, 204–207
Internet Explorer 7
    browser hijacking and, 398
    clearing tracks, 391
    multiple tabbed homepages, 382
Internet Explorer 8, 389, 391
Internet Movie Database (IMDb), 176,
    203, 359
interruptions. *See also* attention
    firewall
    email, reduction of, 8–9, 153–155
    inaccessibility and, 159–160
    no-fly zone, 158–160
invitations, GCal
    auto-accept invitations feature, 212
    event invitations, 213
iOS, 292. *See also* iPhones
    Amazon app, 321, 322

augment reality with, 317–322
autocorrect features, 293
Bump, 346
CamScanner, 330–333
computer to, 300–302
Dropbox, 247
Epic Win, 111
Evernote, 342–344
FM3 Buddha Machine Wall, 170
Google Authenticator app, 80, 81, 82
Google Voice, 316–317
GroceryIQ, 168
Instapaper, 142, 144
JiWire, 290
location awareness, 322–326
mNote, 137
PayPal app, 344
PocketCloud, 304–307
punctuation shortcuts, 296–297
Red Laser, 321
remote control applications, 307
remote control your computer,
    304–307
RTM, 130
Simplenote, 137
snippets in, 196
Square credit card reader, 348
tethering, 338–341
TextExpander, 196, 297
todo.txt Touch, 135
touch screen typing, 292–299
voice command, 327
IP addresses
    DynDNS and, 284–286
    WhatIsMyIP, 269, 282
iPad, 130, 141, 142, 144, 196, 206, 292,
    297, 348
ipconfig, 447
iPhones. *See also* iOS; iTunes
    Evernote, 141
    Google Authenticator app, 80,
        81, 82
    Google Voice, 316, 317
    Instapaper, 142, 144
    jailbreaking, 339
    JiWire, 290
    PdaNet, 339–341
    RTM, 130
    Square credit card reader, 348
    tethering, 339–341
    TextExpander, 196, 297
    touch screen typing, 292, 294
iPod touch, 130, 142, 144, 196, 292, 297
iPods, 75, 110, 142, 144, 148, 426
Issac, Brad, 107
iStumbler, 290
iTunes. *See also* iPhones; iPods
    App Store, 196, 304, 319, 327, 330
    bandwidth hogs and, 206
    Belvedere and, 228
    Hamachi VPN and, 261, 264
    Hazel and, 231
    Quicksilver and, 186
    Smart Playlists, 50, 71
    Spaces and, 157

J

Jabber, 127
jailbreaking process, 339
Jerry Seinfeld's chains, 105–107
Jesse's Bookmarklets Site, 375
JiWire, 290
Johnson, Clay, 156
Jon Peddie Research, 156
junk email. *See* spam
junkdrawer (temp) folder, 43
"just do it," 102

K

KDiff3, 415
keyboard shortcuts. *See also specific*
    shortcuts
    creation, OS X and, 184
    Evernote, 139
    GCal, 214
    Google Instant and, 177–178
    Mac, 182–187
    reason for using, 174
    RTM, 130
    search Web and, 174–178
    Windows, 178–182
    windows management (multiple
        monitors) and, 461
keyboards
    alternative, Android, 297–299
    laptop, 287–288
Keynote, web-based office applications
    v., 251
keyword searches, 177, 358–364
Kim, Amy Jo, 111
kind: (Windows Search search
    operator), 48
Kindle, Instapaper on, 144
kitchen timer, 103, 104
KML feed, 324
Knoppix Linux Live boot disk,
    435–439

L

label maker, 51
labeling/organizing photos, 63–65
laptops. *See also* smartphones; Wi-Fi
    backup, 289
    battery life, 287
    CrashPlan and, 221
    flash drive v., 242, 255
    Hamachi and, 261
    helpful extras, 290
    hotspots, 290, 333
    keyboard protection, 287–288
    MacBook Pro, 288
    as monitors, 458, 459
    optimization, 286–290
    resume partial downloads, 237–238
    sale example, Quicktext and, 31–33
    screen protection, 287–288
    security, 289
    smartphones v., 291, 318, 327
    software firewalls, 416
    stolen, 258
    tethering and, 339–341
    turning off, 162
    VNC and, 280
LastPass, 55–59, 196–200
    automatically fill repetitive web
        forms, 196–200
    extension, 368
    find and use passwords, 58–59
    on flash drives, 257
    master password, 55–57, 196, 198
    security, 196, 198
    set up and store passwords, 55–57
    syncing passwords, 454
launching software/documents
    automatic, 233
    Quicksilver, 184–187
    from Start menu, 180–181
Launchy, 177, 181–182
Layar, 318–319
LeechBlock, 149
left brain/right brain activity, 104
Leopard. *See* Mac OS X
Lessig, Lawrence, 2, 376
letter size D*I*Y Planner, 85
level-o-meter, 110

libraries
  book availability (web feed), 358
  email reference library, 5
  Windows 7, 67–68
lifehackerbook.com, 3, 187, 236, 362
lifehacker.com
  map developments, 379
  Quick Searches, 362–364
line breaks, email, 13
Linux
  Beagle search, 45
  Damn Small Linux, 438
  Hamachi and, 261
  KDiff3, 415
  Knoppix Linux Live boot disk,
    435–439
location
  awareness, 322–326
  Picasa photos and, 64
LockNote, 258
LogMeIn website, 260, 263, 279. *See also*
  Hamachi VPN
logs. *See* work logs
Lotus 1-2-3
  web-based office suites *v.*, 251
  xdocdiff plugin, 414
low-priority email filters, 33–38
  CCed messages, 35–36
  Priority Inbox feature, 36–37
  Thunderbird, 34–35

M

Mac OS X
  clearing desktops, 164
  erase feature, 410–411
  Hazel, 229–231
  KDiff3, 415
  keyboard shortcut creation, 184
  redirect home directory, 44
  saved search folders, 71
  Screen Sharing, 281
  Spaces virtual desktop, 157–158
  Spotlight search, 48–50
  Terminal, 134
  Time Machine, 223–226
MacArthur genius grants, 148
MacBook Pro, 288
MacDropAny, 246–247
Macs
  CCC and, 432–435
  cleaning up, 229–231
  firewalls, 418–421
  keyboard command of, 182–187
  password-protected disk, 75–77
  sharing files on multiple computers,
    447–450
Macworld Magazine, 8, 93
mail. *See* email
Mail Fetcher, 27–28
Mail Goggles, 16
Mailinator, 19
malware, 394–400. *See also* viruses
  browser hijackers, 394, 398
  cleaning, 395–397
  prevention, 398–400
  removal/prevention tools, 395
  symptoms, 395
  types, 394
MAMP, 271
Mann, Merlin, 7, 8, 93
MapMyRun, 379
mapping time. *See* time maps
maps, 378–380. *See also* Google Maps;
  specific maps
  lifehacker.com, 379
  mind maps, 86
  photos on, 325–326
  time, 95–97

actual *v.* ideal, 97
submaps, 96–97
template, 96
Market, Android, 297, 298, 304, 327,
  330. *See also* Android
mashups. *See* maps
master message search, 20–24
master password
  Firefox, 207–210
  LastPass, 55–57, 196, 198
  TrueCrypt, 73, 79
mastery, Web, 349–392
media, reusable, 376–378
media files
  on flash drives, 258
  moving
    Belvedere, 228
    Hazel, 231
  Spotlight's index and, 49
  Windows Search's index and, 46
media folder, 43
MediaWiki, 271, 272
  setup, 276–277
  User Guide, 279
  video demo, 278
Merriam-Webster dictionary, 176
Michael Botsko's Notepad Generator,
  122–123
micromovements, 90
Microsoft Office. *See also* Excel;
  Outlook; PowerPoint; web-based
  office suites; Word
  Google Cloud Connect and, 254
  Office Web Apps *v.*, 250–251, 253
  SkyDrive and, 254
  WinMerge and, 413–414
Microsoft Security Essentials,
  395–399
Microsoft's naming conventions, 254
MilkSync for Outlook, 130
mind, clearing your, 115–145
mind maps, 86
mirror image. *See* Carbon Copy
  Cloner; DriveImage XML
mirroring web sites, with wget, 237
mNote for Android, 137
mobile phones. *See also* smartphones
  push email notifications, 154
monitors. *See* multiple monitors
Morgenstern, Julie, 93, 94, 95, 110
morning dash, 93–95
  automatic setup, 233
  important tasks first, 107–108
Mozilla Firefox. *See* Firefox
Mozilla Thunderbird. *See* Thunderbird
Mozy, 222
MP3s
  Belvedere and, 228
  DownThemAll! and, 371–373
MSCONFIG, 402
MSN Messenger, 127, 256
multi-domain email addresses, 19–20
multimedia files. *See* media files
multimedia notes. *See* Evernote
multiple computers, 441–465
  sharing on
    Mac files, 447–450
    single printer, 454–457
    Windows files, 442–447
  single keyboard/mouse and,
    462–465
  synchronization across, 450–454
multiple desktops, 155–158. *See also*
  virtual desktops
multiple monitors, 155–156
  laptops and, 458, 459
  optimization of, 458–462
multiple recipients, email, 13

multiple tabbed homepages, 380–382
music downloads, with wget, 238–239
Music library, 67
My Documents folder. *See* Documents
  folder
MySQL
  credentials, 274, 275
  PHP/MySQL/Apache, 271, 272, 276

N

nameplate web sites, 384–388
naming conventions, Microsoft's, 254
Nature Sounds for Me, 170
NetNewsWire, 357
NetStumbler, 290
Netvibes, 130
Network Tools, 284
networks, home
  computer name, 444–445
  shared folder, Mac, 447–450
  shared folder, Windows, 442–447
  shared printer, 454–457
Never Check Email in the Morning
  (Morgenstern), 93
new habits, 105–106
news aggregators, 355, 356. *See also*
  feedreaders
news keyword searches (web feed), 358
no-fly zone, 158–160
noise
  FM3 Buddha Machine Wall, 169–170
  inaccessibility and, 159–160
  Nature Sounds for Me, 170
  pink, 169–170
  white, 169
Norton Ghost, 427. *See also* DriveImage
  XML
Notational Velocity for Mac, 137
note capturing, Evernote and, 139–141
note paper, custom, 122–123
Notepad++, 132, 133, 134, 273
Notepad Generator, 122–123
Notepad .LOG file, 98–99
Notepad text editor, 132
Notepaper Generator, 122
Notes
  archive folder, Gmail, 4
  avoiding web sign-ups, 20
  bacn, 34
  bak/backup folder, 42
  BugMeNot and paid subscriptions,
    203
  Canned Responses feature, 31
  chains, 107
  CrashPlan, 222
  At Delimiter, 193
  Dropbox as mobile application, 247
  Evernote pay version, 141
  Firefox master password, 210
  FM3 Buddha Machine Wall, 170
  Free Culture, 376
  Gmail mail fetch frequency, 28
  Google Calendar time zone, 118
  Google Desktop Search, 23
  Instapaper, 143
  Issac, 107
  Jesse's Bookmarklets Site, 375
  lifehackerbook.com, 3
  Mann, 8
  password-generator bookmarklet, 54
  Picasa caption system, 65
  push email notifications, 154
  "Putting the Fun into Functional,"
    111
  Quick Links feature, 23
  Quicksilver plugins, 187
  Remember the Milk, 123
  RescueTime, 102

RTM, 120, 127
Simplenote tags, 137
subject-only email, 12
three-folder system, 7
to-do lists, 93
Web Clipper, 138
wget manual, 237
note-taking
Evernote, 138–142
leave writing material
everywhere, 167
methods, 120–123
Simplenote, 135–138
ubiquitous note-taking inbox across
devices, 135–142
not-to-me filter, 18

O

O'Brien, Danny, 132
OCR (Optical Character Recognition),
332, 341
office noise. See noise
office suites. See Microsoft Office; web-
based office suites
Office Web Apps, 250–251, 253
offline
Thunderbird, 207, 288
webapps, 250
work, with laptops, 288
working, 206–207
offsite backups, CrashPlan+ and,
218, 221
one phone number. See Google Voice
one-minute rule, email
responsiveness, 9
online backups, 217
online office suites. See web-based
office suites
open loops, 115
openness, Firefox/Chrome, 364
OpenOffice.org, 237, 238, 251, 256, 414
operating systems. See Android; iOS;
Linux; Mac OS X; Windows;
Windows Phone 7
Optical Character Recognition (OCR),
332, 341
Option+Spacebar, 184, 185
OR search operator, 21, 47, 235
Orman, Suze, 148
outboard brain, 116
Outlook
check messages hourly, 154, 155
feedreader, 357
Forgotten Attachment Detector
plugin, 14
highlighting email, 17–18
saved search folders, 24
overhaul, file cabinet, 50–52
overheating, laptop, 288
overlays, multiple monitors and, 462
overload. See also data organization
data, 39–41
email, 2–3

P

partial downloads, wget and, 237–238
password-protected disks
Mac, 75–77
PC, 71–75
passwords, 52–59. See also LastPass
7-Zip software and, 259, 276
base, 54
Disk Utility, 76
home web servers, 268–270
master
Firefox, 207–210
LastPass, 55–57, 196, 198
TrueCrypt, 73, 79

password-generator bookmarklet,
54
password-protected albums,
Picasa, 66
rules-based, 52–54
same, for everything, 53
7-Zip software and, 259, 276
syncing, 454
tracking, 54–59
TrueCrypt, 73, 79
2-step verification and, 79–84
view passwords bookmarklet, 375
PayPal Mobile, 344–348
PCs (personal computers)
cleaning up, 226–229
firewalls, 415–418
keyboard command of, 178–182
password-protected disk, 71–75
ReadyBoost and, 421–423
sharing files on multiple computers,
442–447
PdaNet, 339–341
People panel, 63–64
People recognition feature, 63
permanently blocked web sites,
151–153
personal computers. See PCs
personal Wikipedia, 276–279
personalpedia, 276
phone calls. See also mobile phones;
smartphones
email v., 9, 16, 153
Google Voice and, 314
Internet, 238
Skype, 127, 161, 265, 266
photos. See also camera phones;
Evernote; Flickr; Picasa
batch resizing, 200–202
on map, 325–326
Recuva and, 426
PHP scripting language, 386
phpBB, 271
PHP/MySQL/Apache, 271, 272, 276.
See also WampServer
Picasa, 62–67, 201–202
Pictures library, 67
PID (Process ID), 267
piler, filer v., 45. See also searches
ping, 284, 447
pink noise, 169–170
planners, 84–86, 129
plugins. See extensions; specific plugins
PocketCloud, 304–307
PocketCloud Pro, 304
Pomodoro Technique, 104
pomodoros, 104
POP (Post Office Protocol), 27–28
port
80, 265, 266, 267, 270, 282, 304
portable applications, 256–257
email, 256
instant messenger, 256
office suite, 256
Portable Apps site, 257
remote login, 257
Texter, 187–191
virus scanner, 257
web browser, 256
Portable Apps site, 257
Portable Chrome, 256
Portable ClamWin, 257
Portable Firefox, 256
Portable OpenOffice.org, 256
Portable Pidgin, 256
portable remote login, 257
Portable Thunderbird, 256
Post Office Protocol. See POP
post-work appointments, 109

PowerPoint
reusable media and, 376
Spotlight's index and, 48
web-based office suites v., 248, 251
Windows Search index and, 46
xdocdiff plugin, 414
prefixes, subject line and, 11
Pressfield, Steven, 88
PriceBlink, 369
printer, shared with multiple
computers, 454–457
priority: search operator, 128
Priority Inbox feature, 36–37
priority matrix, 85
privacy, email, 16
Private Browsing, 390
Process ID (PID), 267
processing email, 6, 8–9
procrastination, 87–88, 90, 102
product search apps, smartphones
and, 321–322
Professional, 88
Profiles, 308
projects, 90, 91. See also to-do lists
public domain, 376
Public Domain Torrents, 378
Public folder, 245–246
publishing, web-based office suites
and, 253
pull technology, 117
punctuation shortcuts, Android/iOS,
296–297
purge/archive, filing cabinet, 52
push email notifications, 154
push technology, 117
"Putting the Fun into Functional," 111

Q

QUESTION prefix, 11
Quick Add feature, 119, 210–211, 214.
See also Google Calendar
Quick Links feature, 23
Quick Logger VB script, 99–101
Quick Searches, 362–364
Quick-Log your workday, 97–103, 108
Quicksilver, 177, 184–187
Quicktext Thunderbird extension,
30–33
quiet hours, communication, 160–162
Quiet Hours application, 161, 162

R

Rainmeter, 462
RAM, short-term memory v., 115–116
RDP (Remote Desktop Protocol), 305
reading later, Instapaper and, 142–144
ReadyBoost, 421–423
real time responses, to email, 15
RealVNC Free Edition Viewer, 257, 283
reboot computer, automation of,
231–233
recipients, multiple email, 13
recovery, of deleted files, 425–427
Recuva, 425–427
Recycle Bin, 228, 410. See also Trash bin
Red Laser, 321
redirect home directory/Documents
folder, 43–44
reference database, photo, 343–344
reference library, email, 5. See also
Archive folder
registrations, web site, 19–20, 202–203
Registry, Windows, 256, 405, 425
Remember the Milk (RTM), 123–131
add-ons, 130–131
for Android, 130
apps, 130–131
for Gmail, 130

instant messenger reminders, 126–127
for iOS, 130
keyboard shortcuts, for navigation, 130
Launchy and, 182
managing lists/tags, 125–126
managing tasks, 124–125
reminders, SMS/email, 120, 126–127
@rtm Twitter bot, 337–338
search operators, 128
searching tasks, 127–129
Smart Lists, 128–129
task reminders, 126–127
tasks added via email, 129–130
time zone, 127
to-do lists, 125–126
weekly planner, 129
reminders
email, 120
GCal, 116–120
SMS, 118, 120, 126–127
tasks, RTM, 126–127
remote control, of computers
Android, 304–307
VNC, 279–283
remote control applications, 307. See also PocketCloud
Remote Desktop Protocol (RDP), 305
remote login, portable, 257
repetitive tasks. See automation of tasks
repetitive typing
scripted email responses, 30–33
Texter, 187–191
TextExpander, 192–196
repetitive web forms, automatically fill, 196–200
replying to email, 14–16. See also responsiveness, email
brevity policy, 2
inline responses, 14, 15
REQUEST prefix, 11
RescueTime, 102
Resistance, 88
resizing photos, in batches, 200–202
ResophNotes for Windows, 137
responsiveness, email, 8–10
inline responses, 14, 15
real time responding, 15
scripted repetitive responses, 30–33
task requests, 9–10, 14–15
restore files
CCC and, 434–435
with CrashPlan, 221–222
DiX and, 431–432
System Restore and, 405–408
with Time Machine, 225–226
resuming partial downloads, 237–238
retrieval, data, 40–41. See also data organization
Spotlight search and, 48–50
Windows Search and, 45–48
Return if Lost file, 258, 260
reusable media, 376–378
rewards, for tasks, 110
right brain/left brain activity, 104
ring schedules, Google Voice, 315
RSS. See also feeds; website
Dodgit and, 19
Google Alerts via, 235
Icon extension, 356
Subscription Extension, 356
RTM. See Remember the Milk
@rtm Twitter bot, 337–338
rules-based passwords, 52–54

S
Sabo, Itzy, 17
same passwords, 53
SARK, 90
saved search folders, 23–24, 69–71
creating, 69–71
Mac OS X, 71
Windows 7, 69–70
defined, 69
Outlook, 24
Thunderbird, 24
schedules. See time maps
scheduling Black Belt. See Google Calendar
screen protection, laptop, 287–288
Screen Sharing, 281
scripted repetitive email responses, 30–33
scripts folder, 43
Seah, Dave, 97, 98
search box, browser
Chrome, 175, 176–177
Firefox, 175–176
search operators. See also specific search operators
advanced, Google, 350–354
Gmail, 20–23
RTM, 128
Spotlight, 49–50
Windows Search, 47–48
searches. See also Google
Archive folder, 5, 20
Beagle, 45
email, 20–24, 48
Evernote, 141
Google Desktop Search, 23
Google Instant, 177–178
Google web searches, 234–235
photos, in Picasa, 65–66
Quicksilver, 177
Spotlight, 48–50
Start menu, 180–181
tasks, in RTM, 127–129
Web, three-keystroke, 174–178
Windows Search, 45–48
Secure Empty Trash, 410
security
flash drives, 258–260
laptop, 289
LastPass, 55, 196, 198
VNC, 279, 283
Seinfeld, Jerry, 105, 106, 107
Seinfeld's chains, 105–107
Server Message Block. See SMB
server stack, 270, 271
servers. See web servers
sets of tabs, 382–383
7-Zip, 259, 276
sharing. See also web-based office suites
calendars, GCal and, 211–212
with Dropbox, 245–246
household tasks, 167–168
on multiple computers
Mac files, 447–450
single printer, 454–457
Windows files, 442–447
web-based office suites and, 252
Sheet, Zoho, 251
Shift+Cmd+Q, 183
Shift+Enter, 178
Shift+Spacebar, 185
Shift+Win+_, 180, 461
Shopper, Google, 321
Short Message Service. See SMS
shortcuts. See keyboard shortcuts
shorteners, URL, 368

shortening email addresses, 12
short-term memory, RAM *v.*, 115–116
Show, Zoho, 251
shut down email programs, 153–154, 159
Sierra, Kathy, 104
silencing smartphones, 309–311
Simplenote, 135–138. See also Evernote
simpson.net, Notepad Generator, 122
single password-generation rule, 52–54
SingleClick UltraVNC server, 283
Site to Phone, 300–302
six-folder structure, Documents, 41–42
sizing photos, in batches, 200–202
SkyDrive, 250, 253, 254
Skype, 127, 161, 265, 266
SlideIt, 299
SlideRocket, 251
slideshows, Picasa photos, 66
Smart Folders, 71. See also saved search folders
Smart Lists, 128–129
Smart Playlists, 50, 71
smartphones. See also Android; BlackBerry devices; iOS; iPhones; mobile phones
augment reality with, 317–322
email-enabled, 8
foursquare, 323–325, 326
Google Authenticator apps, 80, 81, 82
Google Voice, 312–317
limitations, 291
location awareness, 322–326
Nature Sounds for Me, 170
PayPal Mobile and, 344–348
product search apps, 321–322
push email notifications, 154
silencing, 309–311
Site to Phone, 300–302
SMS and, 333–338
tethering, 204, 333–341
touchscreen typing, 292–299
voice command, 326–330
Wikipedia and, 317, 318
Windows Phone 7, 300, 342
SMB (Server Message Block), 447, 449
SmileOnMyMac, 194
SMS (Short Message Service)
Fuelly and, 336
GCal and, 213, 335–336
Google searches via, 333–335
Google Voice, 314
PayPal Mobile and, 344–348
reminders, 118, 120, 126–127
smartphones and, 333–338
Twitter and, 337–338
snippets
Quicktext Thunderbird extension, 30–33
TextExpander, 192–196, 297
Social Security numbers, LastPass and, 198
software firewalls, 289, 416–418
software-based timers, 104–105
Soluto, 403–404
sorting items, 133
SoundCloud, 377
spaces
virtual desktop manager, 157–158
zoned-off, 160
spaciousness, filing cabinet, 51
spam, 2, 19, 20, 34
speed, creativity and, 104
speed up slow Internet connection, 204–207
split page into quadrants, 121

sports scores and news (web feed), 358
Spotlight search, 48–50. *See also specific search operators*
Spybot Search and Destroy, 395, 396, 397, 398
spyware, 216, 255, 260, 394, 426
Square credit card reader, 348
SSL secure connection, 25, 28
stack, server, 270, 271
STAR!, 101
stars, for Picasa photos, 65
Start menu, 180–181, 401
startup cleanup, 400–404
static tasks, 102–103
Statistics button, TextExpander's, 196
StayFocusd extension, 149–151
storage, data. *See also* data organization; flash drives; Hamachi VPN; webapps
  flash drives and, 242
  organization and, 40–41
  SkyDrive, 250, 253, 254
  TrueCrypt, 74–75
  webapps and, 242
stow away items, 166
strategically place items, 166
streamlining computer tasks, 173–214
streetARt, 318
subdomains, 284, 285, 286
subfolders, in docs folder, 42
subject: search operator, 22, 48, 50
subject line, email, 11–12
subject-only email, 12
submaps, 96–97. *See also* time maps
sub-subdomains, 286
survival skills, computer, 393–439
SwiftKey, 299
Swype, 299
synchronization
  Chrome syncing tool, 451, 452
  Dropbox, 243–245, 254
  Dropbox Folder Sync, 246–247
  Firefox Sync, 451–452
  LastPass, 454
  MacDropAny, 246–247
  across multiple computers, 450–454
  snippets, 195
  Xmarks, 368, 453
Synergy application, 462–465
synonyms, Google search, 353
system buckets, 86
System Configuration Utility, 402
System Restore, 405–408

T

Tab Mix Plus, 367
tabbed browsing, 142–144, 206, 380–382, 383
tags
  bookmark, 60–61
  defined, 59
  Evernote, 141
  RTM, 126
  Simplenote, 137
Task Scheduler, 232, 239
taskbar across monitors, 460–461
tasks. *See also* automation of tasks; to-do lists
  added to RTM, via email, 129–130
  breaking down, 110, 111
  chunks, 110, 111
  collaboration and, 110
  competition and, 110
  completable, 89
  computer, streamlining, 173–214
  dreaded, 110

Emergent Task Timer, 97–98
  as game play, 109–111
  household, 111, 167–168
  keep moving, 92
  logs for completed, 93
  morning dash, 93–95
    automatic setup, 233
    important tasks first, 107–108
  next sequential action, 90–91
  prioritize, 92
  purge/update, 92
  reminders, RTM, 126–127
  requests, 90
    projects *v.*, 90
    responding to, 9–10, 14–15
  rewards for, 110
  searching, in RTM, 127–129
  specific active verbs, 91
  specific details, 91
  static, 102–103
  symbols for, 121
  task-based centers, 167
  tiny, 89–90, 111
  20 items, 91–92
  work day, controlling of, 107–109
temp folder. *See* junkdrawer folder
templates, 84–86, 96
Terminal, Mac OS X, 134
tethering, 204, 338–341
text editors, 132, 133, 134, 273
text expansion delimiter, 193–194
text files, 131–135
text messaging. *See* SMS
TextEdit, 132
Texter, 187–191, 257
TextExpander, 192–196, 297
TextWrangler, 132, 133, 134
ThinkFree, 250
three-folder system, 4–7
three-keystroke Web searches, 174–178
thumb drives. *See* flash drives
ThumbsUp, 201
Thunderbird
  feedreader, 357
  low-priority email filters, 34–35
  offline work, 207, 288
  Portable, 256
  Quicktext extension, 30–33
  saved search folders, 24
tickler file, 117
TidBITS AutoCorrect Dictionary, 194
TightVNC, 281–282
time constraints, 104
Time Machine, 223–226
Time Management from the Inside Out (Morgenstern), 95
time maps, 95–97
time pressure, creativity and, 104
time sinks, 108
time zones, 118, 127
time-based tasks, 111
timeEstimate: search operators, 128
TimeMachineEditor, 226
timers, 97–98, 102–105
@timer Twitter bot, 337
TimeSheet, 101–102
time-wasting web sites, 148–153
tiny tasks, 89–90, 111
TinyURL, 12
Tips
  Alt+Enter, 176
  Gmail, not-to-me filter, 18
  Google Apps, 26
  GroceryIQ, 168
  guests and GCal, 118
  keyboard shortcut creation and OS X, 184

LeechBlock, 149
Mail Goggles, 16
work log accomplishments, 101
to: search operator, 21, 48, 50
to-do lists, 5, 6, 87–111. *See also* tasks
  doable, 88–93
  Epic Win and, 111
  Follow Up folder, 5
  Mann and, 93
  RTM, 125–126
  tasks on
    completable, 89
    keep moving, 92
    logging for completed, 93
    morning dash, 93–95
    next sequential action, 90–91
    prioritize, 92
    purge/update, 92
    specific active verbs, 91
    specific details, 91
    tiny, 89–90
    20 items, 91–92
todo.sh, 134–135
todo.txt, 131–135
todo.txt Touch, 134, 135
tone, of email, 16
Touch Pointer tool, 307
touchscreen typing, 292–299
tracking passwords, 54–59
tracking tasks, 123–131
tracks, browsing, 388–392
Translate text bookmarklet, 374
Trash bin, 230–231, 410–411. *See also* Recycle Bin
Trillian, 265
Trojan horses, 419
TrueCrypt, 72–75, 77–79, 257, 276
Trulia Home Price Maps, 379
Twitter, 235
Twitter bots, 337–338
2-step verification, Google account, 79–84
20 item to-do list, 91–92
280 Slides, 251
typing, repetitive, 187–196
  scripted email responses, 30–33
  Texter, 187–191
  TextExpander, 192–196

U

ubiquitous capture, 135, 136, 138, 341. *See also* Evernote; Simplenote
ubiquitous note-taking inbox across devices, 135–142
Udell, Jon, 376
UltraVNC server, SingleClick, 283
unavailable web sites, via Google, 383–384
undo system configuration changes. *See* System Restore
unique passwords, 53
upload photos to Evernote, 342
Urban Dictionary Lifehacker Quick Search, 363
Urban Dictionary lookup bookmarklet, 374
Urban Dictionary.com, 359
URLs
  navigating Delicious by, 61
  shorteners, 368
  TinyURL, 12

V

vehicle traffic updates (web feed), 358
videos library, Windows 7, 67

view passwords bookmarklet, 375
virtual desktops, 156–158
Virtual Network Computing. *See* VNC
virtual private network (VPN)
  Hamachi, 242, 260–264
  home web server and, 268
  VNC and, 283
Virus Total, 399–400
viruses, 255, 257, 260, 394. *See also* malware
VNC (Virtual Network Computing), 279–283
  LogMeIn *v.*, 260, 263, 279
  PocketCloud and, 304–307
  port 5900, 282, 304
  RealVNC Free Edition Viewer, 257, 283
  Screen Sharing, 281
  Single Click UltraVNC server, 283
  TightVNC, 281–282
  VPN and, 283
voice command, 326–330
Voice Search, 327, 328–330
voicemail, Google Voice, 315–316
voice-to-text feature, Android, 327
volume, email, 2
VPN. *See* virtual private network

W

wallpaper, multiple monitor, 459–460
WampServer, 270–273
The War of Art (Pressfield), 88
weather, 213, 358, 379
Web (World Wide Web)
  mastery, 349–392
  searches, three-keystroke, 174–178
web address, for home computers, 283–286
web applications. *See* webapps
web browsers. *See also* Chrome; Firefox; Internet Explorer 7; tabbed browsing
  automatic session, 233–234
  clearing tracks, 388–392
  extending, 364–369
  hijackers, 394, 398
  portable, 256
  speed up slow connection on, 204–207
Web Clipper, 138
web forms, automatically fill, 196–200
Web of Trust Firefox extension, 364–366
web servers
  defined, 264
  home, 264–270
    Apache HTTP server, 265–270
    firewall, 265
    password protection, 268–270
    webapps on, 270–275
  stack, 270, 271
  VNC, 281–282
web sites
  addresses, TinyURL and, 13

blocked, 149–153
Don't Break the Chain, 105, 106
nameplate, 384–388
registrations, 19–20, 202–203
time-wasting, 148–153
webapps (web applications)
  cloud applications, 79, 242
  desktop software *v.*, 247–251
  on home web server, 270–275
  offline, 250
  Simplenote, 135–138
web-based email, 25–26
web-based office suites, 247–254. *See also* Google Docs
  desktop office software *v.*, 250–251
  features, 251–253
  import/export files onto desktop, 251–252
  limitations of, 249
  reasons for using, 248–249
  ThinkFree, 250
  Zoho, 248, 250–251
web-based public email addresses, 19
WebCalendar, 271
WebOs, 141, 300, 342
weekly planner, RTM, 129
weight reduction, email, 12–13
wget, 236–239
What You See Is What You Get (WYSIWYG), 249
WhatIsMyIP, 269, 282
white noise, 169
widget, Google Search, 328
Wi-Fi. *See also* laptops; smartphones
  antenna, 162
  directory, JiWire and, 290
  disable, 287, 437
  hotspots, 290, 333
  networks, 55, 58
  PdaNet and, 341
  smartphones and, 291, 338
  Tasker and, 309
Wikimedia, 377
Wikipedia
  Layar and, 318
  lookup, bookmarklet for, 374
  MediaWiki, 276–279
  personal, 276–279
  smartphone and, 317, 318
wikis, 276–279
Wikitext primer, 278–279
Win+_, 180, 461
Win+A, 139
WinDirStat, 423–424
Windows
  clearing desktops, 163
  encryption of operating system, 77–79
  ReadyBoost and, 421–423
  7
    libraries, 67–68
    redirect home directory, 43–44
    saved search folders, 69–70
    shared folders, 442–447

  Task Scheduler, 232, 239
  XP
    saved search folders and, 69
    Windows Search and, 46
Windows Firewall, 261, 265, 266, 272, 418
Windows keyboard shortcuts, 178–182
Windows Live SkyDrive, 250, 253, 254
windows management, multiple monitors and, 461
Windows Phone 7, 300, 342
Windows Registry, 256, 405, 425
Windows Search, 45–48. *See also* specific search operators
Windows+D, 179
Windows+F, 45
Windows+L, 179
Windows+R, 179
Win+Home, 180, 461
WinMerge, 411–415
Win+Space, 180, 461
Win+Tab, 179
Word
  Google Docs *v.*, 248
  Spotlight's index and, 48
  web-based office suites *v.*, 249, 250
  Windows Search index and, 46
  WinMerge and, 414
WordPerfect, 250
WordPress, 271–275
work logs, 97–103
workday, 97–103, 107–109
working offline, 206–207
World Wide Web. *See* Web
wrap-up alerts, 109
wrap-up timers, 109
Writer, Zoho, 250
WYSIWYG (What You See Is What You Get), 249

X

xdocdiff plugin, 414
Xmarks, 368, 453

Y

Yahoo!. *See also* Delicious
  advanced search option, 377
  Creative Commons (Quick Search), 363
  Delicious and, 59
  Mail, 26, 209
  Messenger, 127, 256
YouTube
  DriveImage XML tutorial, 432
  Quick Search, 364

Z

0Boxer, 111–112
Zip archives, 222, 259, 276
Zoho, 248, 250–251
Zone Labs, 416
ZoneAlarm firewall, 416–418
zoned-off spaces, 160
the zone, 148, 158–160